P9-CJH-883

Canadian
Industrial Organization

Stylianos Perrakis

Faculty of Administration and Department of Economics

University of Ottawa

Prentice-Hall Canada Inc., Scarborough, Ontario

Canadian Cataloguing in Publication Data

Perrakis, Stylianos, 1938—
  Canadian industrial organization

Bibliography: p.
Includes index.
ISBN 0-13-116096-6

1. Industrial organization (Economic theory).
2. Industrial organization—Canada.   3. Industry
and state.   4. Industry and state—Canada.
I. Title.

HD2326.P47 1989   338.6   C89-094129-7

Prentice-Hall, Inc., Englewood Cliffs, New Jersey
Prentice-Hall International, Inc., London
Prentice-Hall of Australia, Pty., Ltd., Sydney
Prentice-Hall of India Pvt., Ltd., New Delhi
Prentice-Hall of Japan, Inc., Tokyo
Prentice-Hall of Southeast Asia (Pte.) Ltd., Singapore
Editora Prentice-Hall do Brasil Ltda., Rio de Janeiro
Prentice-Hall Hispanoamericana, S.A., Mexico

ISBN 0-13-116096-6

Production Editor: Ted Emerson
Production Coordinator: Sandra Paige
Cover Art: Sandra Calderaro
Cover Design: Anita Macklin
Typesetting: Q Composition Inc.

1 2 3 4 5 THB 93 92 91 90
Printed and bound in Canada by T.H. Best Printing Company

To my parents Evangelos and Maria who first taught me the meanings of fairness and efficiency, and to my sons Evan-Evangelos and Daniel-Dimitrios who make me forget both on occasion.

Contents

CHAPTER 3

The Theory of Monopoly / 72

CHAPTER 4

The Theory of Oligopoly I: Static Analysis / 107

CHAPTER 5

The Theory of Oligopoly II: Long Run Analysis / 142

CHAPTER 6

Other Topics in Monopolies and Oligopolies / 178

CHAPTER 7

Performance Standards / 202

CHAPTER 8

Public Policy I: The Control of Structure / 245

CHAPTER 9

Public Policy II: Policing Conduct / 269

CHAPTER 10

Economic Regulation / 298

Preface

This text is intended for students who are taking a first course in industrial organization within an economics or business school program. Its aim is to provide a simple yet rigorous survey of one of the largest and fastest-growing fields of economics. The analysis is primarily diagrammatic and uses a minimum of calculus, which is relegated to appendices. Thus, the prerequisite to the text is an intermediate course in microeconomics, or even a good course in principles of microeconomics. On the other hand, the advanced material in the appendices makes the text also suitable for students with a good knowledge of calculus and microeconomic theory. It can therefore be used for a more advanced treatment of the subject matter.

An important and challenging application of such theory is in the formulation of public policy. In this respect, the field of industrial organization allows the student to relate the abstract constructs of theory to the practical concerns of policy-makers. The contents and structure of the text have been planned with this relation in mind.

The dominant position held by economists in the field of industrial organization is relatively recent. Lawyers and public administrators played a major role in earlier years and, to some extent, continue to do so today. Traditionally, the focus of economic theory has centred on the polar cases of perfect competition and monopoly, which are the exception rather than the rule in most economies. In addition, the analysis was primarily static, and the highly abstract constructs bore little resemblance to the real world. These constructs were built on such unrealistic assumptions as:

- markets always clear, in both the short and long runs
- economic agents have perfect information, and their behaviour conforms rigidly to postulated axioms
- products are homogeneous with respect to quality, location, or any other characteristics
- the legal and political environment plays little, if any, role in the decision-making by business firms

For these reasons, economic theory has very often tended to be ignored by those entrusted with the enactment of laws and the formulation of public policy.

In the last twenty to thirty years, economists have incorporated greater realism into their models, and as a result have made valuable contributions to industrial organization. These contributions extend to problems where traditional microeconomic theory offers little or no help. For example:

—markets do not clear in the short run because of economic uncertainty or public policy
—economic agents possess asymmetrical information
—one or more "large" firms undertake investments for the purpose of keeping out potential competitors
—policies which ostensibly are designed to protect the consumer are transformed into shelters for corporate inefficiency, whose cost is then passed on to the consumer

Ideally, a course in industrial organization should present to the student models of the situations that are most frequently met in practice. The course should incorporate new theoretical material into the traditional microeconomic constructs. It should also assess the degree to which this material agrees or disagrees with prevailing policies and regulations.

These considerations have been used as guidelines in the design of the present text. The purpose is to construct a successful blend of economic theory and public policy. The former is examined in Chapters 2 through 7 and the latter in Chapters 8 through 11. Nonetheless, there are constant references to policy questions in the theory chapters, and vice-versa. Further, the theory is enriched with numerous references to real-world situations and cases.

The text is developed around the structure-conduct-performance paradigm, which underlies most of modern industrial organization. Some attention is also devoted to the alternative reverse structure-performance model that has emerged as a powerful challenger in recent years. The economic theory of monopoly and oligopoly underlies the first half of the book, while the second half is structured around the three main policy areas of mergers, control of conduct, and regulation.

The perfectly competitive model, which appears on the surface to be missing from the list of topics covered in the text, is used as a standard of comparison in most chapters. A short summary of its main predictions is contained in an appendix to Chapter 1. (The only reason for this comparative lack of attention is the empirical observation through classroom experience that most students are familiar with it through their microeconomics principles course. The material in Chapter 1 is intended only as a brief reminder. It should be supplemented with refresher readings on the theory of the firm from a microeconomics textbook if there is any suspicion that students have trouble remembering the relevant concepts.)

There are extensive references to perfect competition in the chapters on the determinants of industry structure and on performance standards. The predictive importance of the competitive model is emphasized clearly in Chapter 2, where it is stated that large parts (and perhaps most) of the Canadian economy are structured competitively. The relevance of perfect competition as a standard of performance is a major part of the corresponding Chapter 7. The competitive standard also makes an important appearance in the discussion of both short- and long-run conduct in oligopolies, as well as in all policy chapters.

In part, the omission of perfect competition from the text is related to the objectives of the subject matter. Most economists believe that a competitive sector should be left alone by public policy makers, with the exception of laws to control externalities or fraudulent behaviour. On the other hand, industrial organization is structured around public policies and the need to formulate economic models to explain or predict their consequences. Hence, it has to place greater emphasis on situations where public intervention may be justified. These almost always exclude the competitive markets.

As in every first course on any subject, the choice of topics to be included was motivated by their relative importance, as well as by methodological considerations concerning the students' preparation. Thus, I believe that most economists would agree on the need for full-chapter treatment of the topics covered in Chapters 2, 3, 4, 5, 7, 8, 9 and 10, without necessarily endorsing the material contained in each one of these chapters. Similarly, they would agree on the general approach followed in the book, which focusses on the simplest possible cases of single-product firms in homogeneous markets.

Unfortunately, this leaves aside many interesting recent theoretical developments, some of which have already had an impact on public policy. Here, by necessity, an arbitrary choice was made of the material to be included in the appendices and the supplementary Chapters 6 and 11. As already noted, this choice was based on my subjective evaluation of the importance of each topic, as well as on the availability of analytical tools that would not hopelessly confuse the students. Several colleagues would disagree with my choices, both inclusions and omissions. Here is a brief justification for my decisions.

The importance of multiproduct firms was recognized extensively in Chapters 2 and 3, primarily in the appendices. This material was included in spite of the difficulty of the subject matter, both because it has policy applications and because it proved possible to explain it, at least in part, with only elementary tools. The appendix to Chapter 2 contains a geometric derivation of multiproduct cost functions and of the optimal industry structure in the multiproduct case. The important applications of this theory to the determination of the regulatory frontier were included in Chapter 3. However, the appendix material is intended only for third- or fourth-year students, who have already had a solid course in intermediate microeconomics, as well as some knowledge of calculus. As for the main body of the chapters, I believe that Chapter 2 is easily accessible to every student in the course, while Chapter

3 is rather more difficult. This last chapter includes the troublesome issues of relative pricing in multiproduct regulated firms, as well as of the application of contestability theory to regulated industries. The policy relevance of these topics justifies an effort to give at least an idea of the ongoing debate to every student.

By contrast, the text does not do justice to the large and growing theoretical literature on oligopoly and product differentiation. So far the topic has had little impact on the policy front. I also found it too difficult to explain the concepts of horizontal and vertical differentiation and of competition in quality space using geometry or even simple calculus. Nonetheless, there are extensive references to differentiated markets in Chapters 5 and 6, respectively, in the context of entry-deterrence and advertising.

The topic of monopsony or market power on the buyer side has been omitted, even though it would have been easy to include it. I believe that it is neither prevalent nor an important part of public policy. Needless to say, not everyone would agree with this assessment. However, I can think of only one Canadian public policy case where market power on the buyer side was involved. This was the acquisition of control by Bell Canada over its major equipment supplier, Northern Telecom. For this reason there are brief mentions of monopsony in the section on vertical mergers, where it may become relevant to public policy.

The related topics of vertical integration and, more generally, vertical relationships between a firm and its suppliers, are also treated briefly in the context of vertical mergers. They make a more extensive appearance in Chapter 9, which deals with policies to control firm conduct. Some may again find this extent of coverage inadequate, although it is difficult to see how it can be improved without lengthening the text or sacrificing other valuable material.

Last, not everybody would feel comfortable with the inclusion of a section on the control of externalities in Chapter 10. This subject lies outside the main body of the course, and has little in common with the rest of the material in Chapter 10 except for the name "regulation." On the other hand, it is difficult to justify the omission of restrictions related to environmental protection and occupational health and safety from a chapter dealing with economic regulation. I chose to include this section mainly for the benefit of students who are not economics majors and who may not have another chance to see material related to these highly important topics.

The selection of chapters to be covered in a course would depend very much on the course's length and prerequisites. For a one-semester course with only a principles prerequisite I would omit all appendices, as well as all of Chapter 6 and parts of Chapters 3, 4 and 5. At the other extreme, the entire text may be easily covered in a full-year course with both calculus and intermediate microeconomics prerequisites. Between these two extremes many combinations are feasible.

For instance, in a one-semester course with both calculus and micro prerequisites I usually start with Chapter 2 (without the appendices), and then proceed to the oligopoly Chapters 4 and 5 including the appendices, parts of which students have already seen. I continue with the performance Chapter 7, including appendix B only, and then to Chapters 8 and 9, the second one without the appendix. Chapters 3 and 10 on monopoly and regulation are discussed next in an abbreviated form, while Chapters 6 and 11 are used as sources of term paper subjects, or for class discussion of issues of topical interest.

Another possibility is to group the theory of oligopoly with the corresponding policy chapters 8 and 9. This requires that Chapter 7 be done first, immediately after Chapter 2. The monopoly Chapters 3 and 10 can come next, followed by a selection from Chapters 6 and 11. Overall, there is enough flexibility in the structure of the text to accommodate many different approaches, depending on time and points of view.

Acknowledgments

The impetus for this book was provided by the writing of a training manual for bank executives, developed under contract for the Institute of Canadian Bankers (ICB). That manual, entitled *Economic and Industrial Analysis*, was co-authored by Professor Lorne Switzer of Concordia University and myself. It contains elements of macro- and microeconomics, as well as case studies, and its primary focus is the use of economic theory for the evaluation of commercial loan applications. In the division of labour Lorne Switzer was primarily responsible for the macro part, while I wrote all industrial organization-related chapters, with the exception of the one devoted to technological change.

Although the present text contains extensive quotes from the ICB manual in Chapters 2, 4, 5, 10 and 11, the bulk of the material is new. Nonetheless, there is little doubt in my mind that the experience gained in developing the banking text and teaching from it was invaluable in writing this book. Accordingly, I wish to thank Dr. Rosaire Couturier, the ICB's Executive Director, and his assistants Mark Webb and Serge Bourassa, for giving me the opportunity to learn the essentials of commercial banking, and for providing advice all along the way.

Many of the ideas presented in this book were developed in the course of my joint research with a number of collaborators over the past fifteen years. It was the late John Zerbinis, who died from cancer ten years ago at the age of thirty-three, who first introduced me to the usefulness of the total surplus tool in evaluating public policy changes. This was in 1973, three years before the publication of Robert Willig's classic article in the *American Economic Review*. Similarly, several of my views on regulation owe much to George Warskett, Alain de Fontenay, and Julio Silva Echenique. My colleague Jean-Emile Denis provided helpful comments on the sections dealing with foreign trade.

It is, however, to Lorne Switzer that I am most indebted. During the last several years that we spent together writing the ICB text and teaching from it we had the chance to learn much from each other and modify our ideas on many crucial points. This is particularly true, as far as this book is concerned, for some of the material in Chapter 11. The sections on foreign trade and the Canada-U.S. free trade agreement have used much of his research. The section on technological change, on which he is probably Canada's leading economic expert, relies heavily on his insights. Needless to say, all responsibility for errors or omissions rests solely on my shoulders.

Last, I would like to acknowledge the assistance of several reviewers who read and commented extensively on every single chapter of this book. They include Douglas West, University of British Columbia; D.L. McLachlan, University of Calgary; and John Henderson, Lambton College. The help that they provided was always appreciated, both for improving the text and for providing me with information concerning the range of opinions prevailing in the economics profession.

Stylianos Perrakis
Ottawa, December 1988

Sources

Special thanks are extended to the authors and publishers who have allowed material to be reproduced from the following sources.

Economic Council of Canada, from *Making Technology Work: Innovation and Jobs in Canada* (Ottawa, Ont.: Minister of Supply and Services Canada, 1987), "Industry ranking by technological status" (p. 9). Reprinted with permission of the Minister of Supply and Services Canada, 1989.

Fuss, M. and V.K. Gupta, from "A Cost Function Approach to the Estimation of Minimum Efficient Scale, Returns to Scale and Suboptimal Scale," *European Economic Review* (15:2, 1981), Tables 1 and 2. Reprinted with permission of the *European Economic Review* and M. Fuss.

Masson, R.T., P.D. Qualls, Keeler and Gaskins, from *Essays on Industrial Organization in Honor of Joe S. Bain*, copyright © 1975 by Ballinger Publishing Company, pp. 128-131. Used by permission of Ballinger Division, Harper and Row, Publishers, Inc.

Scherer, F.M., A. Beckenstein, E. Kaufer, and R.D. Murphy, from *The Economics of Multi-Plant Operations: an International Comparisons Study* (Cambridge, Mass.: Harvard University Press, 1975), pp. 80-94. Reprinted by permission.

Statistics Canada, from *Industrial Organization and Concentration in the Manufacturing, Mining, and Logging Industries*. Catalogues 31-402 (1983) and 31-402P (1985) (Ottawa, Ont.: Minister of Supply and Services). Reproduced with permission of the Minister of Supply and Services, 1989.

Statistics Canada, from Industrial Research and Development Statistics, Catalogue 88-202 (Ottawa, Ont.: Minister of Supply and Services, 1987). Reproduced with permission of the Minister of Supply and Services Canada, 1989.

List of Frequently Used Symbols and Notation

Q	Output
P	Price
MC	Marginal cost
AC	Average cost
AVC	Average variable cost
DD′	Demand curve
SS′	Supply curve
SAC	Short-run average cost
LAC	Long-run average cost
MES	Minimum efficient scale
X_1, X_2	Production inputs
$F(X_1, X_2)$	Production function
$C(Q)$	Cost function
SIC	Standard industrial classification
CR_n	Concentration ratio, n largest firms
H	Herfindahl index
AIC	Average incremental cost
π	Profit
w	Wage rate
r	Cost of capital
K	Capital stock
L	Labour input
s	Maximum allowed rate of return

ϵ	Price elasticity of demand
Q(P)	Demand function
D(Q)	Inverse demand function
R(Q)	Revenue function
MR	Marginal revenue
ΔP	Change in price
ΔQ	Change in quantity
W	Welfare loss due to monopoly
U^i	Utility function of the ith consumer
F_1, F_2	Marginal products
m	Consumer income

CHAPTER 1

The Scope and Method

··

# of Industrial Organization

··

The purpose of this book is to apply the tools of microeconomic theory to the analysis of real-life cases of
industries, firms, and markets. To achieve this objective the text must also
enrich this theory, by incorporating features that were left out of introductory
courses. Such features deal mainly with the interactions between firms, and
with the impact of public policies on these interactions.

Any student who has taken a course in the theory of the firm must
have noticed the contrast between the elegant, stylized models of firms and
industries studied in the course, and their complex, multidimensional, real-
world counterparts. Such a contrast is commonly encountered in many fields
of study. After all, the purpose of model building is to simplify the object of
study in order to focus on the phenomena of one's interest. Nonetheless, a
transition back to reality is necessary at some point. This transition is particularly important in economics, in which there are high stakes that hinge on the
conclusions derived from the stylized models, and it forms the main objective
of this text.

The fundamental concepts of microeconomic theory are the building
blocks that we'll use throughout this book. Demand and costs, profit maximization, and price formation will retain the importance they had in earlier
courses. What will concern us more, though, are the particular forms and

methods of their application in concrete cases. In that sense, therefore, industrial organization can be described as applied microeconomics (or applied price theory).

Yet such a description misses some important dimensions of the topic. For one thing, industrial organization is a field in which economists are by no means the only professionals with claims to being experts. Lawyers, political scientists, and civil servants have had at times at least as much influence on the subject. Any treatment, therefore, that focuses only on the narrow economic perspective would present a misleading view of the outstanding issues.

The issues in this book are varied and multidimensional, and not always recognizable as economic problems. They occupy a significant share of the time and attention of our politicians, civil servants, and legal scholars. These are after all the people who define the policies, rules, and institutions that govern the operation of our economic system. They are, in other words, the people that set the rules of the game, under which firms interact with the consumers and with each other. These rules of the game are highly relevant to the predictions of our economic models, as we'll become aware time and again in this course.

The political climate under which public policies are formulated must also form part of our concerns. Economic agents such as business firms, industry associations, labour unions, consumers, and other such groups are not passive actors in the stage of policy formulation. They have their own concerns, and they are keenly aware of the impacts of the various public policies on their narrow economic interests. These interests are not always coincident with those of the general public. For this reason their spokesmen will at times present a biased and distorted view of reality. Such a view may become embodied in the laws and public policies, depending on the government of the day. As we shall see, there are many instances in which public policies have been adopted in spite of the quasi-unanimous opposition from the economics profession.

For all these reasons the study of the field of industrial organization does not always follow the same track within the various university-level courses devoted to it. Even within an economics curriculum there are varying degrees of emphasis that one may devote to each aspect of the topic. Some treatments tend to stress policies and institutions, with economic theory used as an adjunct element, mostly in the context of case studies. Others use a historical and ideological approach, focussing on the major currents of political and economic thinking that have at times caused intense debate within Canada.

Although these different approaches are certainly valid and useful, they do not necessarily represent the current mainstream of economic thinking. As a field of study, industrial organization has become very popular in recent years. It claims a major share of student interest, as shown by surveys and enrollment data.[1] Its predictions and conclusions have increasingly been reflected in new policies and laws on both sides of the Canada-U.S. border.[2] In all these contributions it is microeconomic theory that occupies the centre of the stage, with other disciplines and currents of thought serving as auxiliaries. This is also the path that will be followed here.

In this chapter, after defining in some detail the subject matter of this book, we'll describe the basic conceptual model that underlies the course. Other alternative approaches, as well as the general methodology that will be followed in each subtopic, will be examined next. We conclude with a brief historical review of the development of the entire field of industrial organization as it appears in this treatment, and a short description of the following chapters.

Definition of Industrial Organization

As you may have already seen in a principles course, much of the analysis of economic activity hinges around the interaction of buyers and sellers in particular markets. In addition to bringing into contact economic interests who wish to exchange goods and money, these markets are also contact points for business units engaged in similar activities. Such units are collectively known as an *industry*, and they are defined in terms of the product(s) that they produce. Hence, an industry represents the seller part of a given market.

The operation of a given market depends to a large extent on the way that industry is organized. The main type of organization studied in introductory courses, the *perfectly competitive* industry or market, corresponds to a certain type of firm behaviour; its main features are summarized in an appendix to this chapter. Other types of markets, such as monopolies and oligopolies, behave differently. In this course we study the interaction between the way sellers are organized and the way markets behave.

At first glance this description looks very much like a more detailed study of price theory. Yet, as noted earlier, there is much material that is not to be found in theory courses. To begin with, the description of the competitive industry given in theory courses does not correspond to any recognizable real-life industry. On the other hand, a large number of such real-life industries behave as if they were competitive. Our theory courses gave us little help in recognizing a real-life competitive industry, as distinct from the models of such industries that were studied. Here, by contrast, it is the real world that is the focus of our study, with the models used as the tools of analysis.

Once we admit to this change in emphasis we must also recognize that there are now a whole host of real features of industries or markets that may become relevant to their analysis. The ideal markets of microeconomic theory were quick to adjust to an equilibrium in which there were no shortages and no accumulation of unwanted stocks; both are of course commonly found in real markets. Business firms in our theory models were presumed to be equally efficient and well-informed in their profit-seeking objectives, but this is difficult to reconcile with the fact that in any given industry many firms fail while others prosper. Similarly, one would be hard-pressed to find in theory texts key features of business firms such as advertising, investment planning, and research or innovation. The alert student can easily supply many other examples of simplifying assumptions that clearly differ from objective reality. The relaxation of these assumptions and the subsequent impact on theoretical predictions has formed the subject matter of many industrial organization studies.

Last, the realism of the models is enhanced by incorporating public policy features that are relevant to the operation of industries and markets. Examples of such features are regulation, antitrust, patent and contract law, trade barriers, and public ownership. Their role is pivotal, especially in those industries that are furthest from the competitive model.

The introduction of all these new and complex features into our microeconomic models of business firm behaviour will hopelessly complicate their predictions, unless we have some way of organizing the new material. Fortunately, a conceptual way of structuring this material has been developed over the last several years, and has proved invaluable. This is known as the *Structure-Conduct-Performance* (SCP) model, and it forms the cornerstone of the industrial organization field.

The Structure-Conduct-Performance Model

The main constituent elements of the SCP model are relatively simple to grasp. They form a chain of causality that starts from the notion of *market* or *industry structure*, which is loosely defined as the number and relative size of firms in an industry. This structure determines the various dimensions of firm *conduct*, such as pricing, advertising, product selection, entry, and so forth. *Performance*, on the other hand, covers items of interest to public policy, such as efficiency, fairness, and growth; it is an outcome of firm conduct.

These elements must be extended in several directions. To begin with, industry structure is itself determined by a number of *basic conditions* that have been incorporated into the SCP model. These conditions are product demand, technology and costs, and public policies. Second, public policies also affect firm conduct independently of structure. Last, the objectives of a business form part of both conduct and performance. In the latter case, they frequently clash with the fairness and efficiency dimensions of performance.

These extensions of the model weaken somewhat the chain of causality of the SCP model. The schematic diagram in Figure 1.1 shows this modified form of the model, which also represents the spirit of the approach taken in this book.

FIGURE 1.1
The structure–conduct–performance model

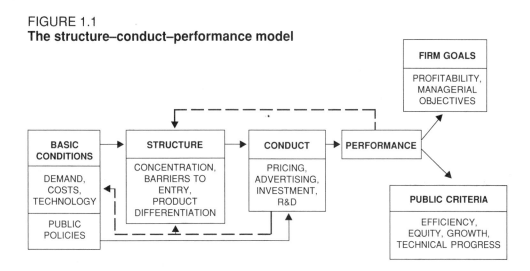

The causality aspect of SCP is its most controversial feature, chiefly because of its public policy implications. The solid lines in the above diagram show the conventional form of the SCP model, with basic conditions defining structure, from which result conduct and performance. Nonetheless, important additional causal flows, running in the reverse directions from those of the conventional SCP, have been identified in more recent years. They are shown in Figure 1.1 by the broken lines. Although most economists accept that such reverse effects exist, their extent and importance within the overall SCP model are highly controversial. Only a few examples of such controversies are given here.

Firm conduct can influence industry structure in a number of ways. Innovations induced by research and development (R&D) activity can affect basic conditions through changes in product demand or costs; the latter have a direct effect on structure. Advertising campaigns can change directly the market share of firms in a given industry, thus bringing changes in structure. Similarly, predatory conduct, whose purpose is to prevent potential competitors from entering the industry, can be adopted with respect to pricing, investment, advertising, or other dimensions of conduct; this also changes structure.

But it is the possible causal impact of *performance on structure* that has caused by far the highest degree of controversy among economists and policy-makers working in the industrial organization field. This causal effect is sometimes known as the reverse SCP model. It claims that performance affects structure, because the more efficient firms are also the ones that grow faster than their competitors. This differential growth results in a less competitive industry structure. The policy implications, therefore, are that public policy has no reason to be concerned about non-competitive industry structures, since such structures reflect the superior efficiency of leading firms.[3] The reverse SCP model therefore makes a strong pitch for more laissez-faire public policy attitudes towards industry structures, for instance with respect to mergers and acquisitions.

The difference therefore between the traditional SCP model and its reverse form lies in the importance that one attaches to the direction of causality. This makes it difficult to solve the controversy over which model is more appropriate for the economy as a whole. Most empirical tests cannot distinguish causality. More carefully designed econometric work has appeared in recent years, but its results have been contradictory. We shall encounter such work all through this book, especially in Chapter 7, which focusses on performance.

The debate over the two differing views of the links between industry structure and performance is heavily coloured by ideologically biased views of the appropriate role of the state in regulating economic activity. For instance, extreme laissez-faire positions would go as far as denying all importance of firm conduct in affecting performance in the long run. This implies that there is little justification even for public policies regulating firm conduct, let alone for those affecting structure. Needless to say, such views have been embraced with enthusiasm by representatives of the business sector.

These extreme positions need not concern us here. It is safe at this point to state that the mainstream of the economics profession follows at least a diluted version of the SCP model, one that recognizes the existence of the reverse causal flows of Figure 1.1. Perhaps the best justification, though, for adopting the traditional SCP view as a framework for analysis is the emphasis it places on the study of industries and markets.[4] By contrast, in the reverse SCP model it is individual firms that become the focus of study. Most economists work with published data, which is almost always aggregated by industry; hence they are likely to find the traditional SCP more helpful than its reverse form. Also, as it stands now, the reverse model has not been formulated in its entirety, leaving a number of questions unanswered.

For all these reasons the overall plan of the book follows the logical structure of the traditional SCP model. Alternative approaches that include but are not limited to the reverse model are mentioned extensively in several places, especially where they have significantly affected mainstream thinking. In all chapters the core of the arguments is anchored in the microeconomic theory of the firm, which forms the basis of our analysis.

A Brief Historical Overview

For all its current popularity, industrial organization is a relatively recent addition to the fields of economic studies. It was created almost exclusively by U.S. economists, a fact that reflects our southern neighbours' preoccupation with competitive market behaviour. This preoccupation was embodied in what was, until very recently, the world's only effective legislation designed to promote competition throughout the economy.

The development of the SCP model is generally linked to a group of economists associated with Harvard University, in particular E. S. Mason, whose work appeared mainly in the 1930s and 40s. For this reason this mainstream view of industrial organization is sometimes referred to as the Harvard School. Its immediate intellectual antecedents are to be found in Edward H. Chamberlin's work on monopolistic competition, originally published in 1933.

Mason's work was extended in the 1950s and 60s by Joe S. Bain, whose 1956 book *Barriers to New Competition* is a major contribution to the topic. Bain also provided empirical evidence documenting the links between oligopolistic markets and non-competitive pricing.[5] By that time several of the concepts developed in the context of the SCP model, such as barriers to entry and product differentiation, had become part of mainstream microeconomic theory. Nonetheless, the Harvard School has kept more or less the same fundamental approach throughout this time, enriched by new advances in theory and econometric methods. In the 1960s and 70s the SCP model had become a standard tool for antitrust analysis in the U.S., and provided the rationale for many important court decisions.

The three key features of the Harvard School's SCP approach are the link between structure and conduct; the emphasis on the industry as the unit of analysis; and the causal link between structure, conduct, and economic performance. The first aspect uses the profit maximization hypothesis of the microeconomic theory of the firm, whose form depends on whether we have competitive, oligopolistic, or monopolistic market structure. The third key feature is based on the presumption that there is a direct link between structure and profitability: a small number of firms in an industry induces tacit or overt collusion among them which in turn yields high profits.

As already noted, several economists have criticized one or more of these crucial features of SCP, particularly with respect to their policy implications. Many of these criticisms have become known as the Chicago School's view of industrial organization, even though Harold Demsetz, one of the most articulate proponents of this view, is not at the University of Chicago. Chicago-based economists have opposed the SCP model from the outset, starting from Edward Chamberlin's ideas in the 1930s.[6] Their criticisms include but are not limited to the reverse SCP model mentioned in the previous section.

Briefly speaking, the Chicago School's view is that perfect competition provides an adequate paradigm for evaluating industries and firms.[7] The key to observed profitability differentials in the real world is the superior efficiency of some firms. These efficiency advantages are the main cause of non-competitive market structures, since the more profitable firms are also those that grow bigger over time. Nonetheless, in the long run profitable firms and industries are bound to earn only the "normal" rate of profit, unless they manage to keep ahead of everybody else through successful innovation. The reason for this is that their success is bound to attract competition under the form of new entry, which will eventually erode their dominant position. For all these reasons the rationale for public policy interventions is rather weak, although most of the Chicago School's adherents accept the need to prohibit price collusion.

Several of the Chicago views have been accepted as part of the mainstream view and incorporated into the SCP model. In particular, most economists would agree that the more efficient firms are able to translate their superiority into dominance in their industry. Similarly, the Chicago writers' ideas on vertical integration also form part of the majority economic thinking. Other Chicago opinions, though, have been rejected by recent theoretical advances. For instance, a cornerstone of the Chicago approach is the infeasibility or unprofitability of strategic or predatory behaviour on the part of dominant firms in order to maintain their position. In fact, several theoretical and empirical studies have shown that such behaviour is profitable and documented it in a few case studies.

We close this brief review by mentioning two very recent developments. The first one is an outgrowth of the Harvard School's traditional SCP approach, which created a new discipline known as *strategic management*. This was developed by M. Porter and his associates at Harvard,[8] and it is currently very popular in business schools. As the name implies, it is a normative discipline that describes the dominant firms' policies aimed at maintaining and enhancing their position under various types of environment.

The second important recent work is the so-called *contestable markets* approach, pioneered by W. Baumol and his associates (1982). Its main contributions have been in the deregulation movement of the late 1970s and early 1980s. Several of its postulates have been incorporated into standard theory, while others remain controversial. As with the Chicago view, we shall refrain from examining this approach in detail until later chapters.

Plan of the Book

The remaining chapters of this book are divided into two parts. Chapters 2 to 7 focus mainly on theory, while Chapters 8 to 12 deal primarily with policy. Nonetheless there are many references to policy in the theory chapters, and all policy issues are firmly tied to theoretical models.

Chapter 2 presents the determination of industry structure, starting from an industry's cost and demand functions. It also defines the various existing measures of industry structure, and reviews the empirical evidence as presented in several recent Canadian studies. This chapter contains a number of basic concepts related to the application of the SCP model to the Canadian economy, which are used throughout the book.

Chapters 3, 4 and 5 review the theory of firm conduct in non-competitive market structures, i.e. monopoly and oligopoly, and link it to the key policy issues concerning these structures. Chapter 3 deals with monopoly and its regulation under the various forms that it appears in the Canadian context. Some recent theoretical developments arising out of the deregulation movement of the late 1970s and early 1980s are also presented here.

Chapters 4 and 5 examine oligopolies in both the short and long runs. The first chapter discusses the various theoretical models of interaction of existing firms in a given market, in which participants are aware of their interdependence. Special attention is paid to the issue of coordinated action and the mechanisms by which it takes place in practice. Chapter 5, on the other hand, continues the study of firm conduct by examining potential entry by new firms in a monopolistic or oligopolistic market. A key feature of this chapter is an examination of the strategic conduct undertaken by incumbent firms attempting to keep out potential entrants.

Chapter 6 presents various other aspects of non-competitive firm conduct that do not form part of traditional microeconomic theory. These are issues related to price discrimination, advertising, and product differentiation, especially as they pertain to policy problems.

Chapter 7 closes the theoretical part of the book by focussing on the key relationships between structure, conduct, and performance. It contains a discussion of the behavioural objectives of the firm, and the limits that they impose on the profit-maximization assumption. A brief review of welfare-theoretical issues is also included in this chapter, together with the justification of the use of the consumer surplus as a policy evaluation instrument. The chapter concludes with a review of the empirical evidence linking structure to performance, and the use of the SCP model for policy formulation. This chapter sets the stage for the policy chapters that follow.

Chapters 8 and 9 examine Canadian public policy as it pertains to industry structure and conduct respectively. The focus in Chapter 8 is on mergers. Canadian merger laws are examined for their economic implications, mainly through case studies. In Chapter 9, on the other hand, laws and cases dealing with pricing in oligopolies are studied. These include price collusion, predatory pricing, resale price maintenance, and other types of vertical restraints.

Chapter 10 is the counterpart of Chapter 3 in the theory section. It is focussed on economic regulation and the control of natural monopolies. It also includes many other topics that fall under the term of regulation even though they have little to do with monopolies, such as environmental pollution, occupational health and safety, and the allocation of scarce public resources.

Finally, the last two chapters include a number of topics that are very important for Canadian public policy, but do not fall readily within the SCP model. Chief among them are foreign trade and foreign investment, the policies dealing with patents and innovations, and the role of public enterprises; these form the subject of Chapter 11. In Chapter 12 there is a global overview of Canadian economic policy as it relates to the SCP model, and some discussion of the lessons to be learned from the U.S. experience.

Appendix 1A   THE THEORY OF PERFECT COMPETITION

The perfectly competitive model of firm conduct and industry or market equilibrium is based on the following basic assumptions:

 (i) The number of buyers and sellers in the market is sufficiently large, and their size so small, that no single one of them can influence price or quantity.
 (ii) The product is homogeneous and cannot be distinguished according to the seller.
(iii) Entry and exit of new firms are free in the long run, and there is perfect mobility of resources across industries.
(iv) Buyers and sellers are fully informed about conditions such as prices, quantities, costs, and demand that prevail in the market.

The lack of realism of these assumptions does not preclude the validity of the predictions of the perfectly competitive model in many (and some would say most) real-life markets. Further, the model can also serve as a useful yardstick against which one may measure the performance of other market structures.

Given that each individual firm cannot influence market price, its profit-maximizing quantity choice Q_1 can be easily shown to be the quantity that equates this market price P_M to marginal cost. The output that maximizes profits is the quantity for which the incremental revenue of the last unit produced just equals its cost of production. The former equals the output price, while the latter is by definition the firm's marginal cost. In the short run this output decision will create profits or losses, depending on whether the price exceeds the corresponding average cost SAC_1 at the chosen output level. The firm will stop producing if the price falls below the average variable cost. Figure 1A.1(a) shows the resulting firm behaviour.

The cross-hatched lines of Figure 1A.1(a) (along the vertical axis and the SMC curve) show the individual firm's short-run output supply curve. For

FIGURE 1A.1
Firm short-run supply curve (a); and short-run industry equilibrium (b)

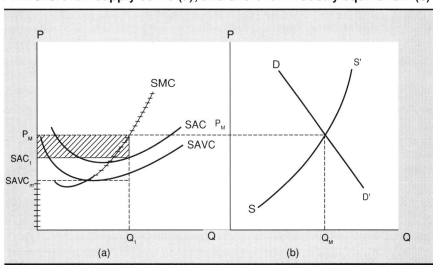

(a)   (b)

every price level in the vertical axis the curve yields the output supplied, which is measured along the horizontal axis. This output is positive as long as the market price exceeds the minimum short-run average variable cost, $SAVC_m$.

The short-run market equilibrium is shown in Figure 1A.1(b). The market supply curve SS' is found by the horizontal aggregation of the supply curves of all firms in the market. The intersection of this market supply with the market demand curve DD' determines the price P_M prevailing in the market, as well as the total quantity Q_M produced and sold by all firms.

At the price level shown in Figure 1A.1(a), each individual firm in the market realizes positive economic profits, denoted in Figure 1A.1(a) by the cross-hatched area. Such profits exist as long as the market price P_M exceeds the average cost at the chosen output level. These profits imply that the firm covers all its materials and labour costs, and receives an "excessive" remuneration for the capital invested in the business. In other words, capital in this industry earns more than its opportunity cost elsewhere in the economy, on a risk-adjusted basis.

Our assumptions about free entry and perfect information imply that the economic profits realized in any given market are observable by outsiders. Since capital earns more in that market than elsewhere in the economy, there is an incentive to establish new firms in that particular industry. Such entry is possible in the long run.

Figure 1A.2 shows the effects that successive entry of new firms has upon market equilibrium. Figure 1A.2(a) shows the long-run average cost and marginal cost curves of an individual firm (AC and MC).* As with the short run, the firm's supply curve coincides with its marginal cost curve. This time, though, the firm will stop producing in the long run when price falls below average cost. The sum of all existing firms' supply curves is again denoted by SS'; this, however, does not represent the industry long-run supply curve since it ignores new entry. Each new entrant's supply curve must be added to the SS' curve. This shifts the curve to the right, as in SS", increasing total output supplied at all price levels. The result is that equilibrium price P_1 decreases to P_1' and total industry output increases from Q_M to Q_M'.

How long will this entry process go on? Clearly, there will be an incentive for new firms to enter as long as existing firms realize profits in that industry. From Figure 1A.2 one can easily see that profits exist when equilibrium price exceeds average cost. For profits to be eliminated, therefore, firms must enter until price declines to the level P_0 at which average and marginal costs are equal. At that level profits are equal to zero and average cost is at a minimum. In the long run, therefore, the industry supply curve is horizontal, at a level equal to the minimum average cost.

FIGURE 1A.2
Firm long-run supply curve (a); and long-run industry equilibrium (b)

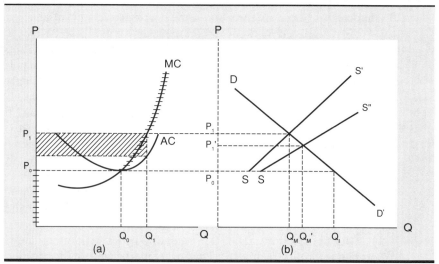

* In this text, long-run average cost and marginal cost will be denoted simply as AC and MC, while short-run average and marginal cost will be denoted by SAC and SMC.

The individual firm's output at this long-run equilibrium price level is equal to Q_0. The *industry* output level, on the other hand, is given by the market demand curve evaluated at P_0; it is denoted by Q_I in Figure 1A.2(b). If, as normally assumed, all firms in the industry are of equal size, then the total number of firms in the industry when it is in long-run equilibrium is given by the ratio Q_I/Q_0. This ratio plays an important role in determining the structure of the industry.

We close this brief survey of the theory of the competitive firm with Figure 1A.3, which shows the relationship of short- and long-run average cost curves, SAC and AC. Both are generally assumed U-shaped, as in part (a), although the long-run curve is sometimes represented by a horizontal line, as in part (b). Each short-run curve is characterized by the size of the fixed factor of production, which remains constant as one moves along the SAC curve. This factor is normally represented by the output level at which the two average cost curves are tangent to each other, called the capacity output. Q_1 is an example of such a capacity output for the fixed factor of production represented by the curve SAC_1. It should be noted that in Figure 1A.3(a), and with the exception of the output level Q_0, at which the AC curve attains its minimum, the capacity output does not correspond to the lowest average cost level in the short run. Each SAC curve attains its minimum to the right (left) of the capacity output if the latter is smaller (larger) than Q_0. This is a consequence of the U-shaped AC curve.

FIGURE 1A.3
AC and SAC curves

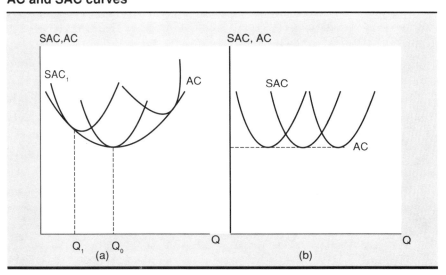

The industry equilibrium shown in Figure 1A.2 has some obviously desirable characteristics. It achieves the lowest possible product price that is consistent with the firms covering their costs of production. It also guarantees that the firm size that will prevail in the long run is the one represented by the output Q_0 in Figure 1A.2(a) and 1A.3, which is the one that minimizes long-run average cost. This is the cheapest way of producing the total industry output. As we shall see in subsequent chapters, these highly attractive properties of perfectly competitive equilibrium are not replicated in other industry structures. Much of the remainder of this book is concerned with identifying the characteristics that bring a given industry close to the perfectly competitive model.

Endnotes

1. See Siegfried and Wilkinson (1982), and Colander and Klamer (1987).

2. For some recent examples see Nelson (1987).

3. This opinion seems to have first been articulated by Harold Demsetz (1973). An excellent discussion and testing of the various contrasting views is by Richard Schmalensee (1985). See also Green (1987) for a Canadian perspective.

4. This emphasis has received some important empirical support in a recent study by Schmalensee (1985), in which it is shown that a firm's industrial specialization is by far the most important factor determining its profitability.

5. See Bain (1951).

6. For these early controversies see Chamberlin's essay on the Chicago School (1957).

7. For an example of these arguments see Posner (1979).

8. See, for instance, Porter (1976, 1980).

References

Bain, J.S. "Relation of Profit Rates to Industry Concentration: American Manufacturing 1936-40," *Quarterly Journal of Economics*, 65 (August 1951), pp. 293-324.

————. *Barriers to New Competition*. Cambridge, Mass.: Harvard University Press, 1956.

Baumol, W.J., J.C. Panzar, and R.D. Willig. *Contestable Markets and the Theory of Industry Structure*. New York, N.Y.: Harcourt Brace, Jovanovich, 1982.

Chamberlin, E.H. *The Theory of Monopolistic Competition*. Cambridge, Mass.: Harvard University Press, 1933.

————. "The Chicago School," essay #15 in *Towards a More General Theory of Value*. New York, N.Y.: Oxford University Press, 1957, pp. 296-306.

Colander, D.C. and A. Klamer. "The Making of an Economist," *Journal of Economic Perspectives*, 1 (Fall 1987), pp. 95-111.

Demsetz, H. "Industry Structure, Market Rivalry and Public Policy," *Journal of Law and Economics*, 16 (April 1973), pp. 1-9.

Green, C. "Industrial Organization Paradigms, Empirical Evidence, and the Economic Case for Competition Policy," *Canadian Journal of Economics*, 20:3 (August 1987), pp. 482-505.

Mason, E.S. "Price and Production Policies of Large-Scale Enterprise," *American Economic Review*, 29 (suppl. 1939), pp. 61-74.

————. *Economic Concentration and the Monopoly Problem*. Cambridge Mass.: Harvard University Press, 1957.

Nelson, R.H. "The Economics Profession and the Making of Public Policy," *Journal of Economic Literature*, 25 (March 1987), pp. 45-91.

Porter, M.E. *Interbrand Choice, Strategy and Bilateral Market Power*. Cambridge, Mass.: Harvard University Press, 1976.

————. *Competitive Strategy*. New York, N.Y.: Free Press, 1980.

Posner, R. "The Chicago School of Antitrust Analysis," *University of Pennsylvania Law Review*, 127 (April 1979), pp. 925-48.

Schmalensee, R. "Do Markets Differ Much?" *American Economic Review*, 75:3 (June 1985), pp. 341-351.

Siegfried, J.J. and J.T. Wilkinson. "The Economics Curriculum in the United States: 1980," *American Economic Review Papers and Proceedings*, 72 (May 1982), pp. 125-138.

CHAPTER 2

The Determinants

···

# of Industry Structure

···

In the previous chapter, we defined industry structure within the context of the structure-conduct-performance (SCP) model as the number and relative size of firms in a given industry. This rather loose definition implies that it is these two particular characteristics that define the behaviour of firms in the industry, as well as industry performance. The reality, of course, is considerably more complex. Even if one accepts the SCP model in its entirety, those dimensions of an industry that influence firm conduct are considerably more complex and varied than can be revealed by a simple count and comparison of firms in the industry.

Microeconomic theory defines the two polar opposite cases of structure, perfect competition and monopoly, as situations in which there are, respectively, infinitely many firms or only a single firm in a certain industry. Oligopolistic structures are situated between these extremes. Yet it should not be forgotten that even within the formal, stylized models of microeconomics there are a number of additional assumptions that must be satisfied for these structures to be properly defined: for example, new firm entry must be free and information must be perfect in competition, while entry must be completely blocked and the product must not have any close substitutes in a monopoly. Few if any of these assumptions are satisfied in the real world. Since the subject matter of industrial organization is concerned precisely with the real world, the question that arises is how crucial the unfulfilled assumptions are to the predictions of the formal models of microeconomics. Alternatively, one must determine how these predictions need to be modified given the violations of some of the underlying assumptions.

In this chapter we start off by examining the basic conditions determining industry structure. In the first section we look at the building blocks of industry equilibrium in microeconomic theory, namely demand and cost conditions. While these building blocks are useful in defining industry structure in a static sense, they are not sufficient to describe the evolution of this structure over time. Dynamic factors affecting industry structure include entry, mergers, tariffs and imports, random effects, and public policies, which are examined in the second section. All of these can be at least as important as the static elements in determining industry structure at any given time.

The third section presents the various summary measures that have been developed in order to characterize industry structure. We conclude in the last section with a brief survey of the empirical studies of industry structure in Canada. Since all the theory presented in this chapter refers to the (unrealistic) case of an industry producing a single homogeneous commodity, Appendix 2A discusses the extension of the theory to multiproduct firms. Much of Appendix 2A is devoted to a brief presentation of the theory of cost functions for multiproduct firms, which was developed recently by Baumol *et al.* (1982).

Market Size and Economies of Scale

The basic determinant of industry structure is the size of the market in comparison to the size of the firms. Each firm must be large enough to operate at as low a unit cost as possible. This means in practice that the firm must be able to exhaust all possible *economies of scale*. The smallest such firm size is known as the *minimum efficient scale* (MES).

The definition of economies (diseconomies) of scale or increasing (decreasing) returns to scale is usually given from the production function side. Let $Q = F(X_1, X_2)$ denote a two-input production function, where X_1, X_2 and Q respectively denote the input and output quantities. Then economies (diseconomies) of scale exist if a proportional expansion of both inputs results in a larger (smaller) expansion of output. In other words, if $\theta > 1$ is the proportionality factor, we have economies of scale if $F(\theta X_1, \theta X_2) > \theta Q$, and diseconomies of scale if $F(\theta X_1, \theta X_2) < \theta Q$.

More useful for our purposes though is an equivalent definition that uses the *long-run* average cost (AC) of the firm.* According to this definition, economies (diseconomies) of scale exist whenever AC decreases (increases) as Q expands; a horizontal portion of the AC curve corresponds to constant

* Long-run average cost is denoted as simply "AC" throughout the text.

returns to scale. In Appendix 2B it is shown that the two definitions are equivalent. Hence, economies (diseconomies) of scale imply that the slope of the AC curve is negative (positive) and vice-versa.

Figure 2.1 illustrates the relationship between the two definitions. Part (a) shows the production function-based definition of economies of scale. At the point A with coordinates (X_1', X_2') a proportional expansion of both inputs to point B yields an output Q_2 that exceeds θQ_1, where Q_1 is the output of the isoquant passing through A. In part (b), on the other hand, we have the average cost function $AC(Q) = \dfrac{C(Q)}{Q}$, where $C(Q)$ is the cost function derived from input prices W_1 and W_2 such that isocost and isoquant are tangent at (X_1', X_2'). As shown in Appendix 2B, the definition of economies of scale in part (a) is strictly equivalent to the negativity of the slope of the AC curve at Q_1 in (b). The latter is in turn strictly equivalent to AC exceeding the marginal cost MC.

Average Cost and MES

In Figure 2.1(b) the average cost curve is initially decreasing until the output Q_0 where it reaches its minimum; it turns into an increasing function thereafter. This reflects an assumption that is adopted very frequently in industrial organization (and, indeed, in much of microeconomics). According to this

FIGURE 2.1
Economies of scale, production and cost sides

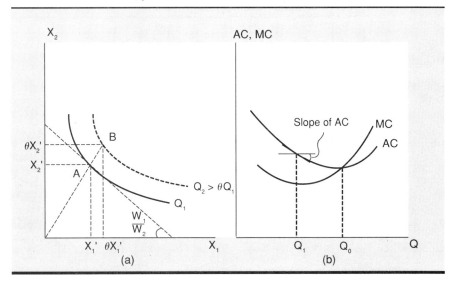

assumption, economies of scale exist for low values of production because of a variety of reasons, some of which were given as early as Adam Smith: increased productivity due to the specialization of labour, the indivisibility of certain inputs, etc. These increasing returns to scale disappear once the MES is reached. Beyond MES diseconomies of scale eventually set in, again for well-known reasons: the difficulties of managerial control, scarcity and the increasing cost of several inputs, etc. All these reasons will be reviewed in more detail further on in this section. Figure 2.2 shows two possible shapes of the AC curve consistent with these properties. Q_0 denotes the MES, which is found analytically by setting the slope of the AC curve equal to zero if the cost function is known mathematically. In both (a) and (b) economies of scale exist in the interval $[0, Q_0]$.

The shape of these figures reflects the presumptions that were stated above with respect to the onset and eventual disappearance of economies of scale. As the rate of production increases to the level of Q_0 units per period, the total cost per unit declines to the level of AC_m. Hence, any rate of production below Q_0 is inefficiently small, and the producing firm is vulnerable to competition from larger units. Beyond Q_0, on the other hand, the economies of scale disappear, and it is no longer possible to reduce unit costs by expanding the rate of production. In Figure 2.2(a), diseconomies of scale set in almost immediately as soon as the rate Q_0 is exceeded. In Figure 2.2(b), on the other hand, the firm may operate at minimum cost for any rate of production

FIGURE 2.2
AC curves and MES

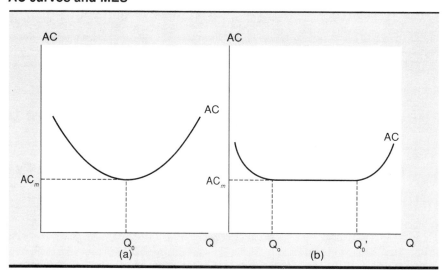

between Q_0 and Q_0'. Within that range there are constant returns to scale, implying that the factors that tend to decrease or increase the unit costs of production tend roughly to balance. Beyond Q_0', on the other hand, the adverse factors predominate, and diseconomies of scale set in.

The main difference between the two types of firms represented in Figures 2.2(a) and 2.2(b) is in the implied predictions with respect to observed production rates in real world firms. If the industry's technology conforms to the shape presented in Figure 2.2(a) then we expect that firms in the industry produce in the long run at more or less similar rates. Figure 2.2(b), on the other hand, predicts that firms of varying sizes can coexist in an industry with the corresponding cost structure. In other words, the dispersion of observed production rates is much greater in an industry represented by Figure 2.2(b) than by Figure 2.2(a).

In practice, it is rather difficult to distinguish between the two cases by simply looking at the distribution of firm sizes in a given industry. At any particular time this distribution would reflect transient factors such as over-expansion due to inadequate forecasting, or firms below MES that exist solely because the industry price has been kept too high. The latter effect, which will be discussed extensively in the last section of this chapter, is particularly prevalent in Canadian industries.

Nonetheless, certain conclusions can be drawn by observing the industry over a long time period. Suppose for instance that we observe an increasing concentration of the industry's output in the largest firms. Then we suspect that firms in the industry have been operating below MES, so that growth allows them to realize economies of scale. The industry's technology is close to the one represented in Figure 2.2(a). Beer brewing is an example of such an industry and it will be discussed in more detail further on. By contrast, an industry such as pharmaceuticals and medicines has been remarkably stable with respect to the position of the four largest firms in the industry:[1] their share has fluctuated between 25.6 percent and 29.6 percent for the entire period of 1965-1982. Here, large firms have grown at the same pace as the entire industry, and the dispersion in observed production rates has not decreased over time. Hence, this industry conforms to the case presented in Figure 2.2(b).

As already noted, the production rate Q_0, the smallest rate at which economies of scale are fully realized, is variously known as the *minimum efficient scale, minimum efficient size,* or *minimum optimal scale.* This rate is a very important parameter characterizing the industry at any one time. The factors that determine it, as well as the role that it plays in defining the industry structure, will be discussed in detail in the following sections. For the moment, it suffices to note that the MES is obviously dependent on the technology of production, as well as on economic factors pertaining to the markets where the firm purchases its production inputs.[2] Consequently it is affected by the appearance of new technology, but also by economic or institutional changes that affect the markets where the firm purchases its labour, capital, or raw materials. These effects should be kept in mind in examining the role played by MES in defining the industry structure.

Examples of technological changes or institutional or economic developments in the input markets that brought major changes in the industry MES abound in recent years. New technology has revolutionized the computer industry, bringing about a much smaller MES and a much more competitive industry structure in the small computer market. The deregulation of passenger air transport has brought similar changes to the travel services industry. On the other hand, there are current indications that the MES may rise in the automobile industry due to the increasing automation of assembly plants.

Types and Sources of Economies of Scale

Economies of scale are sometimes classified as *real* or *pecuniary*. Further, depending on where their sources lie, economies of scale are distinguished as *plant-level* or *firm-level*, with a corresponding MES. Last, there are also *product-specific* economies of scale, which refer, strictly speaking, to multiproduct firms. Nonetheless, the concept has existed before the recent rigorous formulation of the theory of multiproduct firms.

Real economies of scale correspond to real resource savings per unit output as production expands. By contrast, pecuniary economies of scale occur when a large firm uses the same resources per unit output, but manages to acquire them at a lower cost because of its superior bargaining power. They correspond to discriminatory pricing by the suppliers of the resources, with larger firms being entitled to lower prices without any corresponding savings for the suppliers.

A frequently-cited source of pecuniary economies of scale is in the supply of capital:[3] there is little doubt that small firms pay higher rates for both equity and debt funds than their larger competitors. This has been frequently attributed to discriminatory pricing in favour of the large units. Banks, however, as well as other capital suppliers have always disputed this pecuniary explanation of the differential rates. They claim, with some justification, that large firms are *ceteris paribus* less risky than small ones, and that higher rates are meant to compensate for increased risk. Therefore these economies of scale would be real rather than pecuniary. The exact truth is difficult to ascertain, but it is probable that some pecuniary elements remain even after all differences in risk have been accounted for.

Although the existence of pecuniary economies of scale in obtaining capital is controversial, there is little doubt that such pecuniary economies are present in the purchase of raw materials, supplies, or other inputs. Many quantity discounts offered to large purchasers are very clearly far greater than the amounts justified by the ease of processing large orders. Electric utilities offer preferential tariffs to large industrial consumers. Some financial institutions pay higher interest rates to investment instruments that are available only in large denominations. Since these discounts and preferential tariffs or interest rates are available only to large firms, these firms are the beneficiaries of pecuniary economies of scale.

Diseconomies of scale can also be real or pecuniary. For instance, real diseconomies of scale appear eventually when firms expand their required financing beyond a certain volume: internally-generated funds are insufficient, and new equity shares may have to be sold, at a higher cost. On the other hand, there may be pecuniary diseconomies of scale in the purchase of the labour input: large firms are more vulnerable to successful unionization drives, which put upward pressure on the wage rate. They may then become vulnerable to competition from smaller, lower-cost competitors. Several major U.S. airlines became painfully aware of the disadvantages of large scale after the deregulation movement of the late 1970s.

Pecuniary economies or diseconomies of scale are essentially discriminatory pricing and as such are almost always controversial. They are an advantage to large size that is not considered as contributing to overall economic efficiency, and for this reason they are not encouraged by public policy. Their effects on firms' costs, though, are indistinguishable from those of real economies of scale.[4] Since they are not as a rule considered to be very important, they will be either ignored from now on, or else they will be lumped together with the real economies.

Most traditional discussions of economies of scale classify them into plant level or firm level economies, the latter are also called *multiplant* scale economies. These discussions use as typical starting points situations that are normally encountered in the manufacturing and process industries; they also include the product-specific economies of scale. In such situations there is a basic physical production unit, the plant, which groups both general-purpose and specialized machinery and workers, and which produces an array of products. These products share most but not all of the production facilities and machinery, and they are broadly similar in their physical characteristics and end-uses. Plant-level economies of scale exist when there is a cost reduction per unit of output as the size of the plant increases. Product-specific economies, on the other hand, arise when the volume of a particular product produced at a given plant expands. This would normally mean that fewer products would also be produced at that plant. Finally, firm-level economies of scale are created when many similar plants are grouped under a single organization, with attendant unit cost reductions for the end product(s).

Although this classification of economies of scale implies that more than one different product is produced in the same plant, the conceptual approach to their definition and measurement has been developed within the framework of a single-product firm. The technological circumstances of production are often similar enough for the entire range of product lines, so that a meaningful aggregation of the quantities of different products is possible.[5] Alternatively, the technology requires that all products must be produced in fixed proportions as in the chemical process industries. In such a case, the knowledge of the quantity of one product would automatically determine the other product quantities, and an average cost (as in Figures 2.1 and 2.2) can be defined in a meaningful way. In other multiproduct industries such as telecommunications, however, there is no meaningful aggregation of the various products, and the product-mix differs widely from one firm to another. These industries require a somewhat different analytical approach based on the theory of multiproduct firms, which is presented in Appendix 2A.

The economies of scale resulting from the increasing specialization of tasks and the learning effect can be classified as either plant-specific or product-specific. More narrowly product-specific are the economies that result from the longer production runs that follow when fewer types of products are produced at a given plant. Not only is there less specialized equipment to be amortized during a given period, but the time lost in setup operations decreases dramatically. On the other hand, more narrowly plant-specific economies of scale arise from the expansion of the size of individual processing units. As the capacity of these units increases, their cost also increases, but at a slower rate than capacity. Finally, an additional advantage in unit costs of a larger plant size comes from what is known as "the economies of massed reserves." These are savings in equipment and supplies that are kept on reserve for the cases of malfunctions or breakdowns. The proportion of such reserves over the total equipment and supplies decreases, for a given degree of reliability, as the size of the plant increases.

The last source of economies of scale occurs at the level of the firm when it operates more than one plant. Such a multiplant firm can centralize the accounting, marketing, finance, personnel and R&D functions for all its plants and products. In this way it gains both from the increased productivity of these functions, due to specialization, and from the fact that their costs are now spread over a larger number of units.

It is clear that each source of economies of scale may increase or decline in importance as technology or input prices change. For instance, new technology in the capital goods industry can change capacity expansion costs. Similarly, setup costs are affected by the cost of labour as well as by technological change. An example of such a change, which brought dramatic reductions in setup costs, was the introduction of numerically-controlled machine tools in heavy engineering.

Minimum Efficient Scale and Industry Structure

For the purposes of determining industry structure, the relevant MES is the smallest firm size at which all economies of scale, real and pecuniary, are exhausted. Once this MES is known the key question is how many of such efficiently-sized firms can be accommodated by the market. This brings us to the determination of the appropriate market size for our firm.

Markets can be local or regional, national, or international, depending on the type of product, the product price, the transportation costs, and the public policies concerning trade. The determination of the market in which a given firm operates is usually the first question to answer when studying a firm's behaviour. In general the market must be defined not only geographically, but also with respect to the appropriate range of products that are considered close substitutes to those produced by our firm. In theory this requires knowledge of the cross-elasticities of substitution, as well as all prices of related products.

In practice, though, such detailed information is seldom available. Most empirical studies use customary ways of defining industries based on the Standard Industrial Classification (SIC) system, through which most data is collected. Similarly, most industries are treated as if they have national markets, at least in manufacturing (where most studies were conducted). Nonetheless, there are several manufacturing sectors with regional markets, and similarly many sectors in which imports and exports play a major role. Until later in the chapter, we shall defer the question of the precise market size definition. Here we shall examine how it interacts with the MES to define the industry structure. Hence, we shall assume that the market demand curve is known.

Figure 2.3 shows the average cost curve of a firm in an industry, together with the market demand curve D for the industry's product. The output Q_0, the minimum efficient scale, must be compared to the total market demand Q_I, the quantity that would be demanded if the market price were set equal to the minimum average cost, denoted by AC_m. The ratio Q_I/Q_0 shows the approximate maximum number of efficient firms that are able to produce the entire market demand if price is set equal to minimum average cost, which is also equal to marginal cost. If this number is large, then the resulting industry performance, assuming such a structure and conduct can be achieved, has highly desirable welfare properties: prices are as low as possible, consistent with covering firms' costs, and the cost of producing the total industry output is as low as possible, since all economies of scale are exhausted.

Needless to say, few industries achieve in practice this ideal state. Nonetheless, it is thought that such a state is approached in the long run if a number of conditions are fulfilled. These conditions are those characterizing a competitive industry, and will be reviewed in some detail in Chapter 7. At any rate, the

FIGURE 2.3
MES and industry size

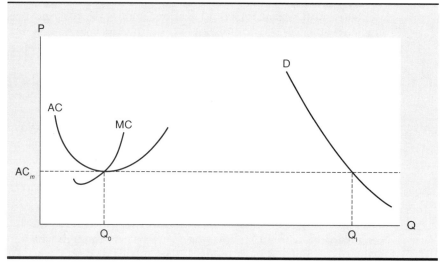

situation depicted in Figure 2.3, in which price is set equal to average and marginal costs and all economies of scale are exhausted, can serve as a benchmark in judging industry performance and designing public policies.

Figure 2.4 illustrates the polar opposite of the perfectly competitive industry structure, the case of a *natural monopoly* in a single-product firm. The main characteristic of this structure is that the MES is large in comparison to the size of the market. Hence, the total industry output is produced at minimum cost when all production is concentrated in a single firm, which forms the entire industry. This firm is then subjected to public regulation in order to insure that the consumers benefit from this minimum cost production. The regulated price must be set at or slightly above the level AC_m for demand to be completely satisfied and for the monopoly firm to cover its costs without realizing any economic profit.

In practice monopoly regulation is considerably more complicated than the simple model shown in Figure 2.4. In most regulated industries the firms are multiproduct, and an important question that has to be addressed by the regulators concerns the relative pricing of the various products and services. The firm's costs are not known in advance by the regulators, and some evidence has surfaced that regulated firms tend to engage in cost-padding[6] or at least do not strive hard enough to improve the firm's cost performance. Nevertheless, the situation depicted in Figure 2.4 still remains the basis of the regulatory

FIGURE 2.4
Natural monopoly with MES exceeding the industry size

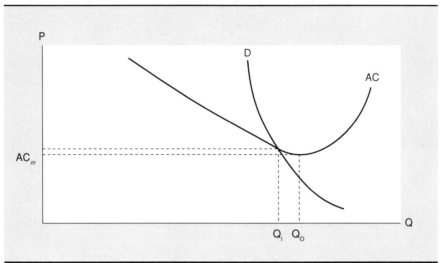

scheme currently in place in most of such industries. We shall return to these issues in the next chapter.

The precise definition of a natural monopoly is actually somewhat more complicated than the situation shown in Figure 2.4. The MES level of Q_0 need not exceed or be equal to Q_I for a natural monopoly to exist. It is possible for a situation to exist in which a firm's MES is below Q_I but it is still cheaper to concentrate all production in a single firm. Figure 2.5 shows one such hypothetical situation.

Here, although $Q_I > Q_0$, and the corresponding unit cost AC_I is also greater than AC_m, it is not possible to find a non-monopoly industry structure that manages simultaneously to satisfy all demand, cover all costs without any profit, and produce the total output at a lower total cost. For instance, if Q_I is partitioned into two equal portions, each one to be produced by a single firm in a duopoly market, the unit cost will become $AC_I' > AC_I$. The general condition for the existence of a natural monopoly is known as *cost subadditivity*. It is formally expressed as follows: any partition of the total industry output Q_I into $m > 1$ segments $Q_1, \ldots, Q_m$, such that $\sum_{j=1}^{m} Q_j = Q_I$ must produce a total cost of production $\sum_{j=1}^{m} C(Q_j) > C(Q_I)$ for a natural monopoly to exist,

FIGURE 2.5
Natural monopoly when MES is less than the industry size

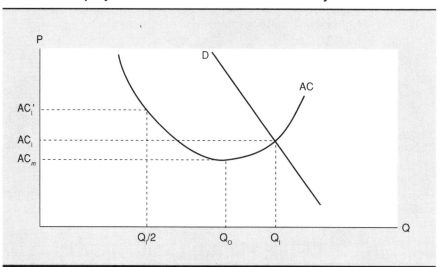

where $C(Q)$ is the cost function for firms in the industry. It can be shown that
the subadditivity property holds whenever $Q_0 \geq Q_1$, but not vice-versa. In other
words, we have a natural monopoly if the MES exceeds the market size,
but a natural monopoly can also exist, as in Figure 2.5, when Q_1 is somewhat
above Q_0.

Returning now to Figure 2.3, we examine the ratio Q_1/Q_0, the maximum
number of efficient firms that can be accommodated by the market. If this
number is large then the industry has the potential of becoming competitive
and approaching the optimal equilibrium state depicted in Figure 2.3, with
prices equal to AC_m and industry output at Q_1. To achieve this result, we must
have free and quick entry of new firms into the industry, unimpeded by
economic or public policy obstacles. The large number of efficient firms that
would be established in the industry in this way would preclude their cooperation in fixing the product price. For such industries, therefore, the costs and
prices can converge to the desired equilibrium without any need for public
policy intervention.

In spite of the small size of the domestic market, many (and perhaps
most) Canadian industries are thought to conform to this desirable structure.
For some of these industries, such as sawmills, textiles, apparel, and furniture,
the size of the MES is very small in relation to the domestic market. In other
industries the MES is large, but their market is international, and they operate

under competitive conditions in that market. Iron and steel and pulp and paper are prime examples of such industries.

The situation is different when the ratio Q_t/Q_0 is small, i.e. when only a few efficient firms can operate in the industry. In such a case these firms can jointly determine the product price and realize economic profits. They can also at times establish policies that will deter entry by new competitors. Such industries do not achieve the socially optimal equilibrium state shown in Figure 2.3 without substantial public policy intervention. These oligopolistic industry structures include some of the most important Canadian industries: beer brewing, the motor vehicle industry, major electrical appliance firms, financial institutions, major food retailers, and so on. Their conduct and performance will be reviewed in detail in Chapters 4 and 5.

Although market size and MES appear on the basis of the above analysis as the principal if not the sole determinants of market structure, their importance should not be exaggerated. To begin with, the ratio of market size to MES represents the maximum number of efficiently-sized firms that can be accommodated by the market. It is possible, if the firms' cost curves have the shape indicated by Figure 2.2(b), to have an industry structure with a smaller number of firms than the one indicated by such a ratio if some of them have grown above MES. Likewise, there are situations in which there are more firms in the industry than the maximum number of MES firms that it can accommodate. The factors that allow or encourage these differences are sufficiently important by themselves to warrant examination in a separate section.

Dynamic Evolution of Industry Structure

At any given time an industry may contain firms that are below the MES. Such firms may have entered the industry at a time when prices were high. Eventually, competitive downward pressures on those prices will force the firms to either grow to the MES, merge with others, or go out of business. Figure 2.6 shows such a situation, which was thought to characterize many Canadian industries in the recent past.[7] The small internal market, combined with a generous tariff protection against imports, had contributed to keep product prices at the level P_1. This in turn allowed a number of firms to enter profitably below the MES level of Q_0. The removal of tariff protection would increase the market size by shifting the demand curve to D_2, but would also force the price down to P_2. At that price the suboptimal firms can no longer survive.

This existence of suboptimally-sized firms within a given market can be temporary or long-term. The factors that are responsible for the evolution of market structures over time are primarily related to special types of public

FIGURE 2.6
A tariff-protected industry

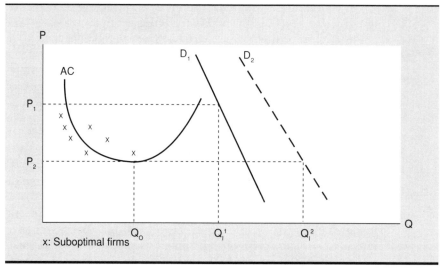

x: Suboptimal firms

policies. These policies are those affecting tariffs and foreign trade, mergers, conditions of entry into particular sectors, and firm conduct in oligopolies. Each one of them will be examined in detail in subsequent chapters. Here we give only a brief overview of the way these policies affect market structure.

Foreign trade is very important for Canada. Imports and exports account for close to 30 percent of total economic activity. More important perhaps is the fact that their distribution is highly uneven across sectors. Table 2.1 presents some data on the importance of foreign trade in the Canadian manufacturing sector for 1966 and 1983. In virtually every instance the shares of both imports and exports have increased between these two dates, reflecting the gradual liberalization of international trade over the last twenty years. Nonetheless, the pattern varies significantly from sector to sector. In some industries, such as textiles, imports play major role, while others are basically exporting industries, such as wood or paper and allied products. In other industries, such as transportation equipment or chemicals, both imports and exports play a major role.

As the table shows, the impact of more liberal policies concerning foreign trade upon industry structure can be major for industries such as leather, rubber and plastics, or transportation equipment. Although the analysis of the determinants of structure presented in the previous section is still valid, the determination of the relevant market size becomes quite difficult, given that such industries are now subjected to significant competition from imports, or

TABLE 2.1
The importance of exports and imports in manufacturing

SIC Codes (2 digit)	Industry	M/(S − E + M)		E/S	
		1966	1983	1966	1983
10	Food and beverages	6.6	8.8	9.6	11.7
15	Tobacco	1.0	2.5	0.5	1.0
16	Rubber and plastics	14.5	22.6	4.1	17.2
17	Leather	14.4	37.5	4.4	8.6
18	Textiles	25.2	25.4	4.8	6.8
23	Knitting mills	11.3	31.6	1.8	1.3
24	Clothing	5.1	16.0	2.2	5.3
25	Wood	8.0	10.2	38.9	52.0
26	Furniture	5.1	11.6	2.1	14.1
27	Paper and allied products	5.5	10.5	49.9	52.8
28	Printing and publishing	12.3	15.6	1.3	5.2
29	Primary metals	23.5	31.9	42.2	49.4
30	Fabricated metals	11.6	15.4	2.7	8.6
31	Machinery	64.2	77.6	33.0	58.7
32	Transportation equipment	39.1	82.9	31.2	84.0
33	Electrical products	21.9	45.2	9.2	27.4
35	Non-metallic minerals	15.3	17.5	5.8	11.0
36	Petroleum and coal	10.8	4.0	1.0	7.9
37	Chemicals	23.0	30.7	14.4	24.9

E = exports
M = imports
S = domestic shipments
Source: McFetridge (1986), p. 9.

are heavily involved in export trade. In such cases the structure of the domestic market, on which most statistics and summary indices are available, is not the only or even the most important determinant of firm conduct. For these reasons all public policies, such as tariffs, quotas, or "voluntary" restraints that promote or hinder the integration of a particular Canadian industry to the world markets, play a crucial role in the ability of market structure to affect firm conduct.

Similarly, public policies concerning *mergers and acquisitions* exert a direct influence on market structure. The guiding principles and manner of application of these policies will be reviewed in detail in Chapter 8. Public policies towards mergers essentially define the "rules of the game", under which a given market structure can become less competitive by the reduction of the number of firms in that particular market.

Economists distinguish three types of mergers: *horizontal, vertical,* and *conglomerate.* Of these, the horizontal mergers, in which the merging firms belong to the same sector, have the most obvious direct effect on market structure. For these reasons they come directly under the scrutiny of antitrust authorities and are the ones usually affected by public policies towards mergers. Vertical mergers, on the other hand, are those in which a firm merges with one of its input suppliers or with one of its customers. They are also respectively known as upstream and downstream vertical integration. Last, in conglomerate mergers the merging firms belong to completely unrelated sectors.

There are circumstances under which a vertical merger can affect the structure of the sector of one of the merging firms. This can happen if the other merging firm possesses market power, which it may at times transfer to the sector of its merging partner. Conglomerate mergers, by contrast, are mostly undertaken for diversification purposes, and are not thought to contribute to market power. For these reasons they have until now escaped the scrutiny of antitrust authorities.

In order to fully understand the effects on industry structure caused by both mergers and related public policies, and the conditions and policies concerning the entry of new firms, we provide a hypothetical example of an industry in which the firms' average cost curve has the shape shown in Figure 2.2(b). Suppose that the MES level of Q_0 is equal to 100 units per year, but that the AC curve stays horizontal and equal to AC_m beyond that level until a production rate of 200 units per year, after which it starts rising again. If the industry demand curve at a price equal to AC_m corresponds to a quantity equal to 1000 units per year, then the industry structure is compatible with anywhere from 5 to 10 firms of optimal size, producing respectively from 200 to 100 units per year, and selling them at minimum cost.

With our previous notation, since $Q_1 = 1000$ and $Q_0 = 100$, the key ratio Q_1/Q_0 is equal to 10. Yet this ratio means very little with respect to the actually prevailing industry structure in the absence of any additional information about the conditions of entry, the public policy attitudes towards mergers, and the vigilance of antitrust authorities towards price-fixing conspiracies. Indeed, suppose that the industry starts initially with 10 MES firms, each one producing 100 units per year. Since these firms realize no profits under such circumstances, they would be tempted to combine and form fewer units; this would allow them to collude, raise prices and restrain output, thus enjoying profits. Whether they are able to do so would depend, as already noted, on public policies towards mergers and price collusion.

The matter, though, does not end here. Suppose that the 10 original firms have merged into 5 units that manage to operate in a perfectly collusive way; they have curtailed output, charge high prices, and realize economic profits. These profits, though, now serve as an attraction to other firms that wish to enter the sector and share in its profits. This entry, occurring at the MES level of 100, may eventually force the industry back to its initial structure. Such an outcome, though, is possible only under certain appropriate entry conditions, as we shall see in detail in later chapters.

This example shows that knowledge of the industry demand curve and the individual firms' average cost function, including the MES level, are not sufficient data to determine industry structure. An economic analyst observing the industry at any given time is likely to find that the number of firms in the industry diverges from the key ratio of market size to MES. The prices charged by these firms would generally lie above their minimum average cost. Nor is there any guarantee that over a long time the industry would converge to a given structure, barring special circumstances. For all these reasons the MES and market size are but one of the determinants of market structure, together with the elements affecting the dynamic evolution of structures such as tariffs and entry conditions.

Table 2.2 provides a comparison of the ratio of MES to market size as estimated in one study, together with the observed market share of the largest firms in each industry at about the same date in the U.S. and Canada. As the data shows, there is little correspondence between the two numbers. In most of the U.S. sectors the largest firms have market shares far in excess of MES. The corresponding Canadian sectors, however, contain many firms of

TABLE 2.2
MES and market share of large firms, selected U.S. industries

Industry	Firm-level MES, % of 1967 market		Average market share (%) of largest firms, 1970	
	U.S.	Canada	U.S. (3 firms)	Canada (4 firms)
Beer brewing	10-14	Over 100	13	23.5
Cigarettes	6-12	Around 100	23	24.2
Fabric weaving	1	20-30	10	n.a.
Paints	1.4	15.9	9	9.9
Petroleum refining	4-6	40-50	8	19.7
Shoes	1	5-10	6	6.2
Glass bottles	4-6	40-50	22	18.4
Cement	2	15.2	7	19.8
Ordinary steel	3	38.5	14	18.8
Bearings	4-7	50-70	14	n.a.
Refrigerators	14-20	Over 100	21	12.5
Storage batteries	2	21.7	18	19.3

Note: n.a. = not available.
Source: Constructed from data in Scherer *et al.* (1975) and Statistics Canada Catalogue 31-402 (1983).

suboptimal scale, for reasons that will be discussed in a later section.

We close this section with a brief mention of an interesting hypothesis concerning market structures, according to which market concentration is the result of pure luck. This hypothesis, which is known under the name of *Gibrat's law*, is based on the observation that under certain conditions a purely random process of firm growth starting from equal firm sizes ends up with a very unequal distribution of industry output. One form of this random process arises when each firm has the same average growth rate, but each year its actual rate is a randomly drawn observation from a normal distribution. Contrary to intuition, this random process creates, after a number of years, very unequal market shares and hence a much more concentrated structure. The reasons for this phenomenon are due to the probabilistic properties of the assumed process and need not concern us here. Although this hypothesis that ascribes market structure to pure luck has many interesting aspects, it is not yet sufficiently powerful to displace more conventional explanations, and will be ignored from now on.[8]

Measurement Problems: Market Size, MES, and Industry Structure

In this section we provide a summary of the principal methods and approaches available to researchers, economic analysts, and policy-makers for the application of the theory outlined in this chapter. Such an application needs summary measures of the various concepts, preferably available from published data. Here we shall examine the measures, as well as the problems associated with their use, for market size, MES, and the industry structure.

The problems associated with the market definition for a given firm's products were discussed earlier. Such a definition is to a large extent dependent on the purpose of the associated study. As already noted, economic researchers primarily use national markets and 3- or 4-digit SIC code industries. This market definition is adequate for their purposes for most sectors, with a few important exceptions. These are, from the geographical point of view, industries whose markets are local or regional, and industries in which imports and/or exports play a major role. Similarly, from the point of view of product definition the 3- or 4-digit SIC category can sometimes be too broad, encompassing very disparate products; two examples are 311 (agricultural implement industry), and 374 (pharmaceuticals and medicine). More rarely, it can be too narrow, when its products compete in some uses with those of another industry; for instance, 2230 (cotton and jute bag industry), and 2733 (paper and plastic bag manufacturers).

Business analysts and antitrust law enforcers, on the other hand, use more narrowly defined industries and markets, relying on specialized studies in order to define more precisely a given firm's competition. This requires a great deal of judgment and can at times be very controversial, especially in court actions when the financial stakes are usually very big. Obviously, the more narrow the market definition the less competitive the market structure would appear to be.

Next we turn to the measurement of industry structure. From the previous discussion we have identified the concept that we wish to measure, namely the extent of competition in the market. This should be inversely related to market power, which is the ability of firms in the industry to influence the price of their product. Market power is directly related to the number and relative size of firms in the industry. The fewer the firms, the more control they have over price. Similarly, the larger firms have more price-fixing power than their smaller competitors.

Unfortunately, no one-to-one correspondence exists between number of firms and relative inequality on the one hand, and market power on the other hand. At the one extreme there may be industries dominated by a single firm, whose market power is very small over a certain range of products. IBM's position in the small computer market is the most obvious example. At the other extreme are industries with many firms that collectively possess a great deal of market power, most often because they have managed to secure the assistance of the public sector. Agricultural marketing boards in eggs, milk, and poultry are the best illustrations of this extreme.

The summary statistics presented in this section are unable to measure market power. What they measure is the relative inequality of firms, or the number and importance of the largest firms in a given market. To the extent that these factors are indicative of market power, the statistics introduced can be used to broadly describe an industry's structure. These measures are collectively known as *measures of industrial concentration*, a term that has been often used, even though somewhat misleadingly, as synonymous with structure. Industrial concentration can be measured in terms of output, value added, employment, or assets. The most commonly used variables (which are the ones that will be used in our illustrations as well) are sales or shipments, measured in terms of dollars.

Of the concentration measures presented here the first three, concentration ratios, the Herfindahl index, and the Lorenz curve with the associated Gini coefficient, are available or can be extracted from published data at the national level and upon request at the local level. For this reason they are the most widely used. The remaining measures are not available for individual industries, given that their computation requires knowledge of the market shares of individual firms. They have been proposed at various times by researchers, but they are rarely used in practice. Hence they will be covered very briefly.

Concentration Ratios

The summary statistic that is the most easily available and widely used is the *concentration ratio*, usually denoted by CR_n, where n is most often equal to 4. This statistic represents the share of total industry sales or shipments accounted for by the n largest firms in the industry. As already noted an industry is typically defined by a 2, 3, or 4 digit SIC code in Canada. Analytically, if P_i represents the market share, the proportion of total industry sales represented by firm $i = 1, 2, \ldots$, with $P_1 \geqslant P_2 \geqslant P_3 \geqslant \ldots$, then the n-firm concentration ratio CR_n is given by:

$$CR_n = \sum_{i=1}^{n} P_i.$$

Clearly, the larger the value of CR_n the more concentrated is the industry.

Concentration ratios are numbers between zero and one, but their particular value needs to be treated with care. It is highly dependent on the total number of firms in the industry. Suppose for instance that there are 10 firms in the industry. Then CR_4 can achieve a minimum value of 0.4 if all 10 firms are of equal size, and a maximum value that is very close to 1 if all production is concentrated in the four largest firms. Within these limits CR_4 gives us an idea of the relative importance of the four largest firms in the industry, but most often it tells us very little about the relation of these four firms to each other. Suppose for instance that we observe $CR_4 = 0.60$. Then we may have four firms of equal size, each accounting for 15 percent of total industry sales, while the remaining firms share the other 40 percent of sales at roughly equal parts. Alternatively, the value $CR_4 = 0.60$ is consistent with one firm producing and selling 41.5 percent of total industry output, while the nine remaining firms have equal shares of 6.5 percent. In the latter case there is a dominant firm in the industry that may play a leadership role if it wishes, while in the former there is no clear-cut leader.

The dependence of concentration ratios on the number of firms in the industry is shown very clearly in Table 2.3. This table shows the CR_4, CR_8, and total number of firms in the industry for selected Canadian industries as published by Statistics Canada. It is easy to see that the concentration ratios tend to decrease as the number of firms in the industry rises, even though the tendency is in the statistical sense and several counterexamples can be observed.

The concentration ratio is sometimes used in inverse form, and known as the *inverse index*. In other words, the inverse index shows the number of firms necessary to attain a certain percentage of total industry sales. This percentage is usually equal to 80 percent in Canada. Hence the inverse index is the smallest number n such that $CR_n \geqslant .80$. It is clear that the inverse index is simply another way of expressing the information given by the concentration ratios[9] and therefore has the same advantages and drawbacks.

TABLE 2.3
**1982 concentration ratios (%), and Herfindahl indices,
selected Canadian industries**

SIC code	Description	CR_4	CF_8	H	# of firms
104	Dairy products	40.4	54.5	0.0538	236
153	Tobacco products	99.5	n.a.	0.3469	10
162	Rubber products	57.4	77.1	0.0993	121
374	Pharmaceuticals and medicines	28.9	44.0	0.0386	114
376	Soap and cleaning compounds	63.5	78.6	0.1548	110
3651	Petroleum refining	61.4	86.4	0.1258	16
3561	Glass	n.a.	100.0	0.3317	5
3562	Glass products	n.a.	79.0	0.1611	102
352	Cement	84.3	n.a.	0.2385	9
355	Ready-mix concrete	44.4	53.3	0.0662	343
295	Smelting and refining	75.7	97.2	0.228	14
311	Agricultural implement industry	57.4	68.5	0.1086	187
334	Household radio and TV	87.9	98.4	0.2128	16
323	Motor vehicles	94.7	98.6	0.345	14
321	Aircraft and aircraft parts	68.4	80.2	0.1555	143

Note: n.a. = not available because of confidentiality
Source: Statistics Canada Catalogue 31-402P (1985).

Herfindahl Index

Another very important measure of industrial concentration is the *Herfindahl index*, which is also known as the Hirschman-Herfindahl index and denoted by H. This index is equal to the sum of the squared shares of sales of all firms in the industry. Specifically, if there is a total of *m* firms in the industry we have

$$H = \sum_{i=1}^{m} P_i^2$$

This index is generally considered superior to the concentration ratios in its theoretical properties, but it does require more data than the ratios, since the shares of all firms in the industry (and not just the largest ones) must be known. It can be shown that H can be decomposed into the product of two components, one of which represents the inequality of shares and the other the number of firms in the industry. Let s_i denote the sales of the ith firm, and

$$\overline{S} \equiv \frac{\sum_{i=1}^{m} s_i}{m}$$

will denote the average volume of sales in the industry. The variance of sales is equal to $\frac{1}{m}\sum_{i=1}^{m} s_i^2 - \overline{S}^2 \equiv \sigma^2$ and it is easy to see[10] that

$$H = \frac{1}{m}[1 + (\sigma/\overline{S})^2]$$

The term $1 + (\sigma/\overline{S})^2$ becomes equal to 1 when all values of s_i are equal. In that case H achieves its lowest possble value of $\frac{1}{m}$ which decreases as m rises. The maximum H, on the other hand, is when the industry is a monopoly and H becomes 1. The inverse of H, equal to $\frac{m}{1 + (\sigma/\overline{S})^2}$ is also known as the *numbers equivalent*; it represents the number of equally-sized firms that yield the same value of the Herfindahl index.

The Herfindahl index takes into account the contributions of all firms to the industry's output, and does not limit itself to the largest ones. Suppose for instance that two relatively small firms (not among the four largest ones) merge. Unless the merged firm becomes one of the four largest the CR_4 will remain the same. The Herfindahl index, on the other hand, will always change. For instance, suppose that $P_1 = .2$, $P_2 = P_3 = P_4 = .15$, implying $CR_4 = 65\%$; if $P_5 = P_6 = .06$, and these two firms merge, the index H will rise by the amount $(.06 + .06)^2 - 2 \times (.06)^2 = .0072$. Generally, if the firms with shares P_i and P_j merge the increase in H will be equal to $(P_i + P_j)^2 - P_i^2 - P_j^2 = 2 P_iP_j$.

Table 2.4 shows a comparison of the concentration ratios and the Herfindahl index for three different hypothetical industry structures. For all industries, $m = 5$.

It is clear that H becomes more sensitive to changes in structure as we move from the less concentrated structure (1) to the more concentrated structure (3). For this reason the use of the Herfindahl index has been increas-

TABLE 2.4
Comparison of CR and H

Firm shares	CR_4	CR_5	H
(1) $P_1 = P_2 = P_3 = P_4 = P_5 = .20$	.80	1.00	.20
(2) $P_1 = .30$ $P_2 = .25$ $P_3 = .15$ $P_4 = .15$ $P_5 = .15$	.85	1.00	.220
(3) $P_1 = .5$ $P_2 = .26$ $P_3 = .10$ $P_4 = .08$ $P_5 = .06$	.94	1.00	.3376

ing,[11] even though it is not as widely available as the concentration ratios.

In Canada, both the concentration ratios (CR_4, CR_8, CR_{12}, CR_{16}, CR_{20} and CR_{50}) and the Herfindahl index have been available every two years since 1968, even though they are published with a significant lag. Table 2.3 above shows the Herfindahl index for the chosen sample of Canadian industries, for which concentration ratios are also given. As the table shows, the two sets of statistics are highly intercorrelated, and the choice of one over the other is not going to affect the results in most likely uses of the data.

Lorenz Curve and Gini Coefficient

The *Gini coefficient* is another type of summary statistic that can be extracted from published data. This coefficient is derived from the *Lorenz curve*, which is a curve relating the cumulative share of company sales to the number of firms in the industry arranged in order of increasing size.[12] This curve, together with its associated coefficient, is well-known in economics because of its applications in the measurement of the inequality of income distribution. Its use in measuring industry structure is less common, although it does contain all information embodied in concentration ratios CR_n for all possible values of n.

Figure 2.7 shows an example of a Lorenz curve. The total number m of firms in the industry, arrayed in increasing order of sales, is in the horizontal

FIGURE 2.7
The Lorenz Curve

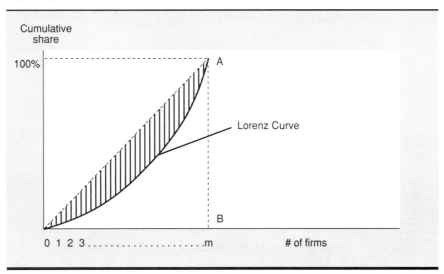

axis, while the ordinates of the curve represent the cumulative share of industry output. If all firms in the industry have equal shares then the Lorenz curve will coincide with the line OA. On the other hand, if all firms but one are infinitesimal in size, the curve would follow the lines OBA. The Gini coefficient is defined as the ratio of the shaded area in the diagram, between the line OA and the Lorenz curve, to the area of the triangle OBA. Its maximum and minimum values are one and zero, representing total inequality and total equality respectively.

As a description of industry structure, the Lorenz curve and the associated Gini coefficient have some serious drawbacks. They measure inequality rather than structure per se, with the result that an industry with two or three firms of equal size would show a coefficient of zero. Another less obvious drawback is the sensitivity of the curve to the inclusion or omission of any firm in the industry. This is especially serious, given the existence of borderline firms in several industries that may or may not belong to the included sectors. On the other hand the Lorenz curve contains all possible concentration ratios CR_n. For instance, the value of CR_4 can be read from Figure 2.7 by subtracting the curve's ordinate at the point $m = 4$ on the horizontal axis from 100 percent. Hence the curve is approximately available for most Canadian industries in manufacturing, mining, and logging, from the source cited in Table 2.3. From that source the Lorenz curve can be traced approximately from the 4-, 8-, 12-, 16-, 20- and 50- firm concentration ratios.

The remaining indices are as already noted very rarely used. The *entropy index* E has its roots in communications theory. It is equal to

$$E = \sum_{i=1}^{m} P_i ln\left(\frac{1}{P_i}\right) = -\sum_{i=1}^{m} P_i ln\, P_i$$

In other words, it weighs the share of each firm by its Neperian logarithm. Its smallest value is 0 under monopoly, and its largest value is equal to $ln\, m$ when $P_i = 1/m$ for all i (all firms have equal shares). In other words, E is inversely correlated with the other concentration measures.

The Rosenbluth index R is given by the expression

$$R = 1 \Big/ \left[\left(2 \sum_{i=1}^{m} iP_i\right) - 1\right]$$

It achieves its highest value of 1 under monopoly, while for $P_i = 1/m$ for all i it is equal to $1/m$. This index, developed by Rosenbluth (1957), attaches higher weights to small firms since firms are ranked in *descending* order of market share.[13]

An interesting generalization of the Herfindahl index was proposed by Davies (1980). This index, termed the U index, is easily derivable from H by the relation $U = H^\gamma m^{\gamma - 1}$, where m is the number of firms in the industry, and the parameter γ is restricted to being between 0 and 1. For $\gamma = 1$ U and H coincide. It can be shown that U retains the attractive properties of H with respect to mergers and firm entry. In addition, it is more sensitive to mergers between large rather than small firms in the sector. The parameter γ can be estimated from the data under the (questionable) assumption that performance is directly related to concentration.

Still another generalization of the Herfindahl index was proposed by Hannah and Kay (1977). Their index, denoted by Q, also depends on an unspecified parameter α, which must be > 0 and $\neq 1$. Then we have

$$Q = \left(\sum_{i=1}^{m} P_i^{\alpha} \right)^{\frac{1}{(1-\alpha)}}$$

which coincides with the inverse of H for $\alpha = 2$. The Hannah-Kay index also maintains the desirable properties of H while being more sensitive to mergers involving large firms. It should also be noted that Q is an inverse concentration measure, decreasing as concentration increases.

More generally, Hannah and Kay (1977) have proposed a set of seven desirable properties that must be satisfied by a useful concentration index. Their index satisfies these properties, as do the H and U indices. Still more indices have been proposed at times by various researchers. It should be noted that most available indices are highly intercorrelated, as shown by Marfels (1972). The interested reader is referred to Curry and George (1983) for a comparison of the properties of the various indices.

The Measurement of MES

We close this section by providing a brief summary of the principal techniques that have been used at times to measure MES. Each one of them has its own advantages and drawbacks, generally involving tradeoffs between effort and accuracy. Further, within each category of techniques there are several variants (depending on the ingenuity of the individual researchers). The empirical results of the application of these techniques to Canadian industries will be reviewed in the last section of this chapter.

One category of techniques is based on *statistical cost analysis*, which uses observed cost data from existing plants. Such data result in the statistical estimation of various relationships between average cost, output, and a variety of other variables that are thought to affect costs, such as capacity utilization, input prices, age of the capital stock, etc. The estimation methods range from very simple linear ad hoc relationships to highly sophisticated econometric models and techniques. These methods, which use historical data, do not necessarily reflect the current situation which is based on the most recent technology, nor the currently prevailing or anticipated input prices.

The *engineering approach* to MES measurement avoids many of these drawbacks. It is based on questionnaires and interviews with design or planning engineers, from whom information is solicited about available technologies, together with associated capacities and costs. This approach is costly and time-consuming but it is thought by some researchers to provide "the best single source of information on the cost-scale question".[14] It is however most suitable for plant-level or product-specific economies of scale, and less so for economies of scale at the level of the entire firm.

A much simpler method is the *survivor test*, originally developed by G. Stigler (1958). The logic of this test is very straightforward: a firm size that survives over a long time and supplies a stable or growing share of industry output is efficient; a size that supplies a declining share of that same output is inefficiently large or small. This test is very simple to apply but it does not always produce logical results. In addition, it does not estimate only the economies of scale, but also a whole host of other effects such as monopoly power or discriminatory legislation. As Scherer notes, the survivor test is thought to be more appropriate as an addendum and cross-check of other estimation methods.[15]

The last technique to be included in our list is a simple practice that estimates MES as the average plant or firm size among the largest plants or firms accounting for 50 percent of industry output. This practice is probably the least accurate of all the methods, but it is one that can be easily applied with published data and does not need a major research effort. For instance in 1980 the industry under SIC code 301 (boiler and plate works) had four enterprises producing 50.4 percent of the total industry sales of approximately 634 million dollars in all of Canada. The average of these four firms therefore corresponded to sales of approximately 79.3 million dollars. According to this technique, this would represent the MES at the level of the firm. Needless to say, this is only a rough approximation of the prevailing industry norms, but it is a computation easy enough to perform by anybody with access to published data, allowing the comparison of any given firm with the largest firms in its sector.

Empirical Evidence: MES and the Structure of Canadian Industry

The studies reviewed in this section fall into two distinct categories. The first group, focussed almost exclusively on the manufacturing sector, has measured the MES for a number of Canadian industries. The purpose of the majority of these studies was to ascertain whether the small size of the Canadian market was an obstacle to the efficient performance of the Canadian economy. This would happen if for instance there are too many firms below MES. Several of these studies will be reviewed again in a different context in other chapters of this book.

By contrast, the second group of studies examines the structure of Canadian industry taken as a whole. Data on concentration is presented for a variety of sectors and at several levels of aggregation. Several of the studies from which these data were extracted were prepared for the MacDonald Royal Commission, investigating the desirability of free trade with the U.S.

MES and Economies of Scale in Canada

All three types of MES estimation methods presented in the previous section have been used at times in Canada. Unfortunately the results of the various studies are seldom consistent, principally because of differing industry definitions. Typically, MES estimates by the engineering method use narrower industry definitions than the other two methods, which are usually based on the four-digit SIC categories.

As a result, the different methods have at times produced vastly differing results. Nonetheless, a certain degree of consensus is emerging in several conclusions. The following section is a brief summary of the principal studies and their results.

The engineering estimates are particularly suited to the evaluation of plant-level MES. Such estimates were carried out for 16 industries in a 1967 study by Eastman and Stykolt, which used data from the late 1950s. The study found that over 50 percent of industry capacity in the industries studied was of inefficient size. In half the industries four MES plants were sufficient to cover 50 percent or more of total industry demand, while in four of these industries the four plants covered 100 percent or more of the demand. Not surprisingly, the observed industry structure turned out to be much less concentrated than warranted by plant-level efficiency considerations. According to the study the widespread existence of plants of suboptimal size was made possible by the high protective tariffs surrounding Canadian manufacturing.

These pessimistic findings have essentially withstood the test of time, albeit in a more qualified version. To begin with, the effective tariff protection has been eroded over the years for a large number of industries and products, with the result that competition from imports has increased. The inevitable result is that some of the inefficient plants must have been retired from production, perhaps by natural attrition or through mergers, acquisitions, or consolidations. Second, there are questions whether the sample of 16 industries is representative of the situation existing in the entire Canadian manufacturing sector. Third, the MES estimates produced by the engineering approach are much larger than those of the other two methods. Last, the increase in average costs caused by suboptimal scale may not be very large for many industries. This last result has been confirmed by statistical methods as well as by the engineering approach.

Figure 2.8 reproduces the basic concepts associated with MES and the rise in unit cost for plants at suboptimal scale. The output Q_0 denotes the MES,

FIGURE 2.8
Cost disadvantage of suboptimal firms

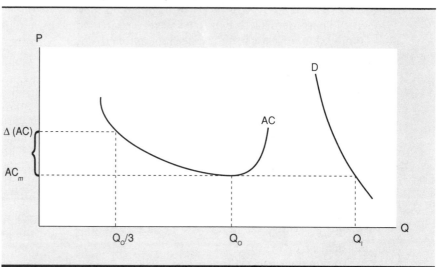

while Q_I is the total industry output. The quantity $\dfrac{\Delta(AC)}{AC_m}$ at a value of Q equal to one-third of the MES is an estimate of the "slope" of the unit cost function AC, the speed at which the unit cost rises as the plant scale decreases below MES. The ratio Q_0/Q_I for the Canadian market is shown in Table 2.5, together with the slope of AC at $Q_0/3$ for a sample of 10 industries. These estimates are taken from a well-known study by Scherer *et al.* (1975), and the industry sample is broadly similar to the one used in Table 2.2.[16] The MES was estimated by the engineering method.

The ratio Q_0/Q_I in Table 2.5 includes only the plant-level MES. In some industries, for example beer brewing, there are also economies of scale that can be realized at the firm level, since the cost of these activities can be spread over a number of plants. This means that the ratio Q_0/Q_I may increase by a factor of two, three, or more, making the firm-level MES in an industry such as brewing larger than the entire Canadian market.

As we noted earlier, though, the engineering estimates are considered to be somewhat exaggerated for at least some industries such as steel.[17] Other methods generate different results. For instance, the survivor method, applied by Gorecki (1976) to a sample of 56 manufacturing industries for the period 1961-1972, produced consistently lower estimates of MES for Canada. As we saw above, this method considers as efficient a plant size category whose share of total industry output has increased over time. In other words, that which

TABLE 2.5
**MES (engineering method) as a percentage of industry size (Q_0/Q_l),
and slope of AC curve, selected Canadian industries, 1967**

SIC code	Industry	Q_0/Q_l (%)	$\frac{\Delta(AC)}{AC_m}$ (%)
1450	Breweries	34.5	5.0
1530	Cigarettes	76.9	2.2
1740	Nonrubber shoes	1.7	1.5
2910	Steel	38.5	11.0
3370	Storage batteries	21.7	4.0
3410	Cement	15.2	26.0
3551	Glass bottles	13.9	11.0
3651	Petroleum refining	16.7	4.8
3750	Paint and varnish	15.9	4.4
3320	Refrigerators and freezers	142.9	6.5

Source: Scherer *et al.* (1975), p. 94

survives and prospers is efficient. Perhaps for this reason, a widely-used proxy for MES in empirical studies is the average observed capacity of the largest plants in the industry. As noted earlier, these are defined as the minimum number of plants necessary to produce 50 percent of industry output. This proxy is easy to measure and it is certainly inspired by the principle embodied in the survivor technique that what is is what ought to be.

Comparable MES estimates by the engineering and survivor methods are available for only seven industries. They are given in Table 2.6. This table is

TABLE 2.6
Comparison of survivor and engineering estimates

SIC Code	Industry	Q_0/Q_l (%)		Observed CR_4 (%)
		Survivor	Engineering	
3651	Petroleum refining	1.1	16.7	78
1740	Non-rubber shoes	1.0	1.7	19
2910	Integrated steel	0.2	38.5	77
3320	Refrigerators & freezers	3.7	142.9	50
3370	Automobile storage batteries	4.3	21.7	79
1072	Bakeries	0.3	2.5	31
3511	Bricks	1.4	3.1	54

Source: Gorecki (1976), p. 62.

drawn from Gorecki (1976), whose sources for the engineering estimates were the Scherer *et al.* (1975) study as well as an earlier study by Pratten (1971). Not only is the difference between the estimates too large, but there does not also seem to be any correlation between the relative MES sizes of the industries in the sample.

The conflict between the survivor and engineering estimates of MES has generally been interpreted as signifying the inadequacy of the survivor method, at least for Canadian industries.[18] The reasons that are generally given for this inadequacy are, briefly speaking, related to the existence of market power in many Canadian sectors, sustained by oligopolistic concentration and high tariff walls. These help to maintain high prices, allowing even inefficiently small firms to survive. Yet these real disadvantages of the survivor method should not obscure the fact that the engineering approach has also produced consistently larger estimates of MES than the third available method, statistical and econometric measurements. Thus, an important econometric study by Fuss and Gupta (1981) attempted to measure the MES by fitting an average cost function to production and cost data for 91 Canadian manufacturing industries. The data covered the years 1965, 1969, and 1970, and was disaggregated by several plant-size categories for each industry.

This study avoided many of the drawbacks of the survivor method. Although it was based on existing plants, it did not assume that any of them were of efficient size. It took specific notice of possible changes in input prices, and contained no elements of subjective judgement such as those inherent in the engineering method. Last, it covered a large sample of industries, thus avoiding the often-repeated claim that engineering estimates are biased in favour of industries with a large MES. In spite of these, it produced estimates of MES that were far smaller than those of the engineering approach. Table 2.7 shows the MES estimates of this study, together with the slope of AC at one-half MES, for the sample of industries whose engineering estimates were given in Table 2.5.

A comparison of Tables 2.5 and 2.7 shows that the cost function estimates of MES are far below those of the engineering approach. The average MES is more than four times larger in Table 2.5 than in Table 2.7. On the other hand, the relative size of MES between the industries in the sample is roughly similar in both approaches.[19] The statistical correlation between the Q_0/Q_I columns in the two tables is on the order of 90 percent. By contrast, engineering and survivor methods produce a corresponding correlation coefficient of 5 percent.

With its lower estimates of MES, the statistical cost analysis approach presented in the Fuss-Gupta (1981) study gives a much more optimistic picture of the Canadian manufacturing sector than the engineering estimates. Table 2.8 shows the distributions of Q_0/Q_I, of the slope of the AC curve at one-half MES, and of the percentage of suboptimal capacity, for their entire sample of 91 industries. Thus for 52 industries the ratio Q_0/Q_I of MES to total market

TABLE 2.7
**Q_0/Q_1 and slope of AC curve, cost function approach,
selected Canadian industries**

SIC Code	Industry	Q_0/Q_1 (%)	$\frac{\Delta(AC)}{AC_m}$ (%)
1450	Breweries	8.85	4.80
1530	Cigarettes	13.13	2.35
1740	Non-rubber shoes	0.07	0.01
2910	Steel	7.34	1.62
3370	Storage batteries	3.32	2.46
3410	Cement	4.19	36.60
3551	Glass bottles	6.84	4.53
3651	Petroleum refining	1.09	1.65
3750	Paint and varnish	1.95	35.04
3320	Refrigerators and freezers	n.a.	n.a.

Note: n.a. = not available.
Source: Fuss and Gupta (1981), Table 2

size was between 0 and 2 percent, while for no industry did this ratio exceed
20.1 percent. Similarly, the last two lines show that inefficiently small firms
were a major problem for only 19 industries, less than a quarter of the total,
and the percentage of suboptimal (below MES) capacity exceeded 50 percent
in those industries. Perhaps most important was the fact that the cost disadvantage incurred by below-MES plants was very small: as the middle two lines

TABLE 2.8

**Distributions of Q_0/Q_1, $\frac{\Delta(AC)}{AC_m}$ and suboptimal capacity in Canadian
manufacturing, Fuss-Gupta study**

Number of industries	52	21	14	4	0
Q_0/Q_1 (%)	0-2	2.1-5	5.1-10	10.1-20	20.1-100
Number of industries	18	26	38	6	3
$\frac{\Delta(AC)}{AC_m}$ at $\frac{1}{2}Q_0$ (%)	0.1-1.0	1.1-2.0	2.1-5.0	5.1-10.0	>10.0
Number of industries	22	25		25	19
% suboptimal capacity	0-10.9	11.0-30.9		31.0-50.9	51-100

Source: Fuss and Gupta (1981), Table 1

show, even plants one-half as large as MES had excess costs of less than 10 percent in all but 3 industries out of the total of 91.

These Fuss-Gupta results have been criticized on methodological grounds as yielding potentially biased estimates of MES.[20] The main criticisms focus on the fact that the estimations were carried out on the variable (rather than the total) cost functions. This can create downward biases on the degree of returns to scale (implying, in turn, a lower estimate of MES) if there are scale economies due to savings in the capital input. Other related biases can arise from the positive association between wage rates and firm size, or from possible systematic variations of capacity utilization as a function of firm size. Although none of these potential biases was convincingly demonstrated, the criticisms have prevented the widespread acceptance of the Fuss-Gupta results.

The optimistic picture emerging from these results was somewhat contradicted by a later study by Baldwin and Gorecki (1986). That study was not directly concerned with MES, but with the performance of Canadian manufacturing relative to its U.S. counterpart. As such, it will be reviewed in more detail in later chapters. Here we only note that the Baldwin-Gorecki study found a significant efficiency lag of Canadian vis-à-vis U.S. firms. Much of this lag was attributable to the smaller size of Canadian firms, which did not allow them to reap all the benefits of economies of scale. Hence, suboptimally-sized firms continue to be a problem in Canadian manufacturing, thus confirming in part the Eastman-Stykolt results of twenty years earlier.

The Structure of Canadian Industry

Given the need for suboptimal firms to grow at least to the MES, there are some crucial public policy dilemmas that must be faced. An important instrument of firm growth is merger with another firm. Such a merger always results in a less competitive structure. The question that arises is whether the tradeoff of improved efficiency versus reduced competition is worth pursuing with "permissive" merger legislation.

This question lies at the core of merger policy, which forms the topic of Chapter 8. Here we provide an overall view of the state of competition in the Canadian economy as it appears in several recent studies. Clearly, more competition means less need to worry about the anticompetitive effects of mergers. Conversely, mergers need to be more carefully screened when there is already substantial market power in the merging firms' sector.

Table 2.9 shows the structure of the various sectors of the Canadian economy as assessed in a recent study by Khemani (1986). It distinguishes (somewhat subjectively) three different types of structure: effectively competitive, oligopolistic, and government-supervised or regulated. These types were assessed from a variety of data and criteria applied over the period 1970-80. The subjective nature of several such criteria implies that the entries in Table

TABLE 2.9
Contribution to GDP by sector and market structure, Canada 1980

Sector	Distribution by type of structure			Total GDP contribution $ millions (%)
	Competitive	Oligopolistic	Regulated	
Agriculture, forestry, fishing & trapping	53	0	47	11,571.2 (4.2)
Mining	7	70	23	18,890.5 (6.9)
Manufacturing	72	28	0	56,170.4 (20.6)
Construction	100	0	0	15,071.8 (5.5)
Transportation, communications & utilities	18	0	82	32,999.4 (12.1)
Trade	54	44	2	29,443.1 (10.8)
Finance, insurance & real estate	34	17	49	35,505.6 (13.0)
Services	42	1	57	52,688.5 (19.3)
Public administration and defence	0	0	100	20,101 (7.4)
Total (all sectors)	44	18	38	272,682.8
Total (excl. public admin. & defence)	47	19	34	252,521.8

Source: Khemani (1986), pp. 140-141.

2.9 must be considered only as rough indicators of the structure of the corresponding sector. Specifically, the competitive type of structure was defined residually by subtracting the other two types from the total. The government-supervised or regulated type was defined by isolating the firms or sectors that are subject to price, output, and/or entry controls. Industries were assigned to the oligopolistic type by using a variety of criteria: stable four-firm concentration ratios that were larger than 50 percent over the decade, imports of less than 20 percent of total industry supply, a history of anticompetitive practices, and other relevant information such as links with multinationals and net changes in the number of enterprises in the sector. An industry was classified as oligopolistic if it satisfied at least two of the above criteria.

As the table shows, approximately two fifths or 44 percent of the total Canadian Gross Domestic Product originates in competitive sectors and about one-fifth in oligopolistic industries, while the rest is from government-supervised or regulated industries. These figures should be contrasted with those of a recent U.S. study by Shepherd (1982), that used a methodology similar to the one underlying Table 2.9. According to Shepherd's study, in 1980 77 percent of U.S. national income was generated by effectively competitive sectors of the economy. Hence the degree of competitiveness in the U.S. is significantly higher than in Canada.

A detailed sector by sector examination of the Canadian and U.S. data as it appears in the Khemani and Shepherd studies tends to confirm the picture that emerges from the aggregate figures. Thus with the exception of construction, and perhaps manufacturing, every sector in Canada has a lower percentage of effective competition than its U.S. counterpart. The share of competition in manufacturing is about three percentage points lower in the U.S. than in Canada, but that difference may not be statistically significant. Nonetheless, it is counterintuitive, and does not conform to popular belief. It is due to the much greater role that imports play in Canada compared to the U.S.

Shepherd's study also shows quite convincingly that the extent of competition in the U.S. has been rising in recent years: the percentage of national income originating in competitive sectors rose from 52 percent in 1939 to 77 percent in 1980. Unfortunately no comparable data for earlier years exists in Canada. Some indication of the changes in the Canadian structure can be obtained from a comparison of the distribution of the four-firm concentration ratios CR_4 within Canadian manufacturing for the years 1970 and 1980. Statistics Canada data shows a small change towards more competition over this ten-year period: in 1980, 21 percent of total value added in Canadian manufacturing originated in sectors with a CR_4 below 25 percent, as distinct from 19.7 percent in 1970.[21] Needless to say, this is only an indication of a change in structure, given the different basis from which Table 2.9 was constructed.

Of particular interest to our purpose is the extent to which the concentration ratios give a misleading picture of the existing state of competition. Table 2.9 indicated that more than 70 percent of manufacturing activity (as measured by its contribution to GDP) was effectively competitive in 1980. By contrast, the Statistics Canada data shows that a substantially smaller proportion (58.7 percent) of the manufacturing sector's total value added had a CR_4 below 50 percent in the same year. This means that several concentrated manufacturing industries were classified as effectively competitive in Table 2.9, a fact that no doubt reflects the influence of imports. On the other hand, the residual definition of effectively competitive industries in the study that underlies Table 2.9 may have tended to overstate competition. Evidence of such an overstatement can be deduced from some additional data presented in that same study, in which concentration ratios CR_4 are given at the level of the individual products, which in Canada corresponds to the five-digit SIC code. Table 2.10 shows the distribution of these ratios by number of products and by percentage of total value of shipments.

As it can be seen from Table 2.10, the levels of concentration at the product level are considerably higher than at the sectoral (three or four-digit) level. It is this product level that is theoretically the most relevant for assessing the state of competition, in conjunction with the associated product market and geographical market definition. The table shows that slightly less than three quarters of the entire value of shipments in 1980 in Canada had concentration ratios of over 50 percent, which is a much higher proportion than the 41.3 percent given in the Statistics Canada data for manufacturing, and higher than the share of noncompetitive industries in total GDP as deduced from Table 2.9 for the manufacturing and primary industries. Again it is the competition from imports, which is not reflected in CR_4, that may turn a highly concentrated product market into an effectively competitive one.

The exclusion of imports from the concentration measures tends to produce a misleading picture of the structure of a particular sector because of two main factors. In the first place, a high concentration ratio CR_4 may in fact correspond to a much lower share of the four leading firms in total demand if imports are significant. Second, the market power of the firms in the sector is not well-represented by the concentration ratios: the ability of domestic firms to affect product price hinges on the exchange rate, and on tariffs,

TABLE 2.10
CR_4 at the five-digit SIC code (product level), Canada 1980

CR_4 Range	Number of Products	% Value of Shipments
10.0 - 19.9	2	0.53
20.0 - 29.9	34	7.13
30.0 - 39.9	58	5.75
40.0 - 49.9	94	11.72
50.0 - 59.9	141	6.53
60.0 - 69.9	176	11.84
70.0 - 79.9	248	7.17
80.0 - 89.9	357	12.32
90.0 - 99.9	697	16.49
100.0	2,324	20.51
Total	4,131	100.00

Source: Khemani (1986), p. 156

quotas, and transportation costs for imports.[22] Only the first factor can be corrected: one must take into account the imports in the total demand and then redefine the concentration ratios as shares of this total demand. This correction was attempted in a 1984 study by Baldwin *et al.* for 140 manufacturing industries, using 1979 data. The results are shown in Table 2.11.

The table shows very clearly the reduction in CR_4 when imports are taken into account. The average concentration decreases by 10 percentage points, and less than a third of the manufacturing industries now have a ratio CR_4 exceeding 50 percent. Further, if a similar adjustment is carried out in the equivalent U.S. industries the resulting decrease in concentration would be much smaller, thus somewhat bridging the gap with Canada. As noted above, the (perhaps more important) curbs in market power implied by imports are not reflected in Table 2.11.

Tables 2.10 and 2.11 demonstrate the large range of variation in industrial concentration that exists within the Canadian manufacturing sector. In Table 2.12 we show the four- and eight-firm concentration ratios for 1980 for several important industries in Canada. These industries are drawn from trade, services, and manufacturing.

The value of such sectoral data is that they allow the quick characterization of a sector as essentially competitive or oligopolistic, provided that it is located at the extremes of the range, it possesses a national market, and it is not subject to regulation if its concentration is low. For instance, it is clear from Table 2.12 that tobacco, department stores, and banks are oligopolistic and/or regulated, while clothing and the area of agriculture that is not subject to marketing boards are essentially competitive. The statistics, though, tell us very little at the intermediate ranges (where most industries are located) because of the influence of imports and the possible geographical limitations on the product market.

As noted earlier, the market for many sectors is regional or local. Hence

TABLE 2.11
CR_4 adjusted for imports for manufacturing industries, 1979

CR_4 Range	Number of Industries			
	Unadjusted	% of total value added	Adjusted for imports	% of total
75 - 100	28	22.4	10	9.0
50 - 75	45	19.74	36	26.5
25 - 49	50	41.8	69	45.1
0 - 25	17	16.1	25	19.3
Total	140	100.0	140	100.0

Source: Baldwin *et al.* (1984), page 28.

TABLE 2.12
CR_4 and CR_8, selected industries, 1980

Industry	CR_4	CR_8
Agriculture	1.3	2.6
Metal mining	48.7	65.3
Mineral fuels	25.8	38.2
Manufacturing		
Food	16.9	23.6
Tobacco	98.2	99.8
Rubber	63.0	83.9
Leather	20.0	34.9
Clothing	9.8	13.7
Paper & allied	32.5	48.9
Primary metals	67.2	79.7
Petroleum & coal	56.1	84.2
Wholesale Trade		
Grain	65.7	93.0
General merchandising	65.3	70.7
Food	26.8	41.0
Retail Trade		
Food stores	54.8	60.5
Department stores	85.2	94.1
Gas & service stations	23.9	26.5
Financial & Services		
Trust companies	51.7	72.2
Banks	74.6	95.5
Mutual funds	61.3	81.2
Advertising	10.0	20.4
Motion picture and theatre	57.4	61.5

Source: Khemani (1986), Table 3-4.

the national statistics give a misleading picture of market power in these sectors. The relevant market coverage is not always easy to assess, given overlaps between adjacent markets and the effect of transportation costs. Evidence on the regionalization of Canadian manufacturing was collected in a 1971 study, using data from 1965. In that study 34 industries (out of a total of 154) were classified as regional. Concentration ratios in those regional markets were computed and compared with the national ratios for 18 of the 34 industries for which complete data was available. These comparisons are shown in Table 2.13, in which the national ratios are set against average regional ratios, weighed by the shares of each region's shipments. As the table shows, most regional ratios are higher than national ratios, and the difference can be more than 100%.

Some idea of the variation in regional ratios within Canada is provided by Table 2.14, in which the highest and lowest regional ratios are provided for a small subsample of the 34 industries. As we can see from this subsample, the national ratios quite often conceal the existence of market power at the regional level. Although the data on which Tables 2.13 and 2.14 are based are quite old, there is evidence that a similar situation also exists today.[23]

The overall picture of the structure of Canadian industry that emerges from these data is therefore quite complex, meaning that there is no way of escaping the policy dilemma in mergers and acquisitions. The data of Table 2.9 show that the majority of Canadian production takes place under non-

TABLE 2.13
National and weighted regional CR_4, selected Canadian manufacturing industries, 1965

SIC Codes	Industry	CR_4	
		National	Weighted Regional Concentration Ratios
1010	Slaughtering & meat processors	58.07	66.78
1030	Poultry processors	24.19	47.45
1110	Fish products industry	37.09	51.10
1120	Fruit & vegetable canners & preservers	39.27	51.02
1290	Bakeries	32.26	38.30
1310	Confectionery manufacturers	46.65	64.73
1392	Miscellaneous food manufacturers	32.79	46.97
1410	Soft drink manufacturers	40.86	48.70
2513	Sawmills & planing mills	16.26	18.71
2541	Sash, door and other millwork plants	9.13	20.85
2560	Wooden box factories	44.70	60.29
2850	Commercial printing, publishing only, publishing and printing	13.21	23.78
2870	Platemaking, typesetting and trade bindery plants	25.53	32.00
3020	Fabricated structural metal industry	46.94	54.93
3475	Concrete products manufacturers, ready-mix concrete manufacturers	21.30	37.88
3530	Stone products manufacturers	21.92	44.81
3720	Mfrs. of mixed fertilizers	62.22	71.07
3970	Signs and displays industry	21.62	30.39

Source: Canada, Consumer and Corporate Affairs, 1971, p. 38.

TABLE 2.14
Concentration ratios for regional industries (percent)

SIC Code	Industry	National CR₄ (1965)	Highest Regional CR₄ (1965)	Lowest Regional CR₄ (1965)
1010	Slaughtering and meat processing	58	96 (Sask.)	53 (Ontario)
1290	Bakeries	32	76 (N.B.)	24 (Quebec)
1410	Soft drinks	41	78 (Manitoba)	40 (Atlantic region)
2513	Sawmills and planing mills	16	23 (Prairie Region)	8 (Atlantic, Quebec, Ont.)
3080	Machine shops	8	55 (Sask.)	8 (Ontario)
3530	Stone products	22	80 (B.C.)	33 (Ontario)

Source: Canada, Consumer and Corporate Affairs, 1971, Table A-5.

competitive conditions. Some reduction in this percentage, though, has taken place since the data were compiled, because of partial deregulation in transportation, telecommunications, and finance. More important perhaps was the steadily rising competition from foreign trade which brought major improvements in the performance of Canadian firms.[24]

On the other hand, Table 2.10 shows some evidence of monopoly power at the level of individual products. A similar monopoly power may also arise because of the regionalization of industrial markets, as shown in Tables 2.13 and 2.14. Although this segmentation of national markets appears rather modest in manufacturing, it is quite substantial in other sectors. For instance, the newspaper industry and many services such as hotels, restaurants, and retail trade have purely local markets. All these effects are bound to reduce the competitiveness of Canadian industry in comparison to the picture that emerges from the national statistics. The conclusion, therefore, seems to be that the extent of competition in the Canadian economy remains substantially below that of the U.S., and that the encouraging trends that have emerged in recent years are not sufficient to set aside concerns about the concentration of market power in Canadian industry.

Conclusions

Market size and economies of scale, under the form of the minimum efficient scale or MES, determine how many firms of efficient size can function in the industry. This number, though, represents a theoretically optimal industry structure that need not have any correspondence with the actually-observed structure. It ranges between the polar-opposite cases of perfect competition and natural monopoly.

In the real world there are transient or dynamic factors that cause observed structures to diverge from optimal ones. These have to do with conditions of entry, foreign trade, and public policies concerning structure and conduct. Therefore, empirical studies seeking to explain observed industry structures must include these other factors as explanatory variables.

Several summary measures of industry concentration (used as a proxy for structure) have been developed, together with several methods for measuring MES. The application of these methods and measures to Canadian industry has detected the existence of suboptimally-sized firms in several sectors. Further, there is evidence of significant market power under the form of large concentration indices and/or public policies restricting competition. For these reasons microeconomic policy faces the dilemma of whether or not to pursue economies of scale at the expense of competition. No overall answer is available, and a case by case approach to each sector must be adopted.

Appendix 2A   MULTIPRODUCT FIRMS AND OPTIMAL INDUSTRY STRUCTURE

In recent years the theory of optimal industry structure was extended to multiproduct firms in a series of studies by W. Baumol and his associates, culminating in a major book by Baumol, Panzar and Willig (1982). This theory has already had some applications in public policy, especially in telecommunications; these will be reviewed in more detail in the next chapter. Here we give a summary of the principal concepts they developed for multiproduct firms, paralleling the analysis of a firm producing a single commodity that we saw in the main body of Chapter 2.

Although the extension of some of the single-output concepts to the multiproduct firm is obvious, other important concepts are not easy to visualize when more than one product exists. Concepts not easily visualized for the multiproduct firm are, for instance, the isoquants, the average cost (AC), and the expansion path. As with the single-output firm, the multiproduct firm can be examined both from the production as well as from the cost angles. We concentrate on the cost side, since this is the area where most applications have taken place.

Multiproduct Cost Functions

The presentation will be developed for the case of a firm with two inputs and two outputs. It can be easily extended to any number of inputs and outputs.

Let Q_1 and Q_2 denote the two output quantities, and X_1 and X_2 the inputs. An isoquant of a two-product firm is a set of input combinations capable of producing a given pair (Q_1^0, Q_2^0) of output quantities. It is a curve on an (X_1, X_2) diagram with the same properties as the single-output isoquant, namely, decreasing and convex to the origin.

However, a single isoquant map is no longer sufficient to describe the firm's production function. Any given input combination is capable of producing more than one combination of outputs. We need to describe how the outputs expand as we move from an isoquant to a higher isoquant in such a way that a single isoquant passes through any given (X_1, X_2) combination.

A two-output isoquant possessing this property can be constructed by a proportional expansion of both outputs. Thus in Figure 2A.1 the output pairs (Q_1^0, Q_2^0), (Q_1^1, Q_2^1), (Q_1^2, Q_2^2) represented by the three isoquants are such that

$$\frac{Q_1^1}{Q_1^0} = \frac{Q_2^1}{Q_2^0} \quad \text{and} \quad \frac{Q_1^2}{Q_1^0} = \frac{Q_2^2}{Q_2^0}$$

FIGURE 2A.1
Isoquants along a ray in output space

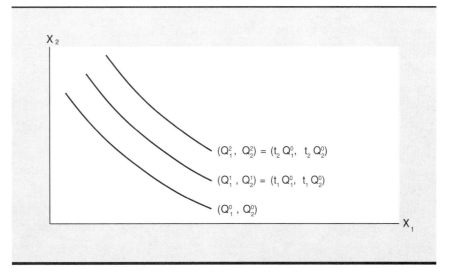

Alternatively, there exist constant numbers t_1 and t_2 such that $t_2 > t_1 > 1$, and $Q_1^1 = t_1 Q_1^0$, $Q_2^1 = t_1 Q_2^0$, $Q_1^2 = t_2 Q_1^0$, $Q_2^2 = t_2 Q_2^0$. Such proportional expansions of both outputs are sometimes known as *expansions along a ray in output space*.

Obviously, a given two-output production function must now be represented by an infinity of isoquant maps such as the one above. Each map is for a given relative proportion of output quantities, which is kept constant for every isoquant on the map. Every time this relative proportion is changed we get another isoquant map. The set of all such maps is sufficient to represent the technology of the two-output firm.

The optimal choice of inputs for the two-product firm is done in an identical manner with the single-product one. We simply replace the single-product isoquant map with maps of two-product proportionally increasing isoquants, one such map for each relative output proportion. The optimal input quantities are found by the tangency of the isocost to the corresponding isoquant. Figure 2A.2 shows three such isocost-isoquant pairs, as well as the expansion path for this particular output proportion or ray in output space. For instance, if $Q_1^0 = 3$, $Q_2^0 = 5$, all isoquants on the map have $Q_1/Q_2 = 3/5$. The second isoquant may have $Q_1^0 = 3.3$, $Q_2 = 5.5$, which implies $t_1 = 1.10$, and the third isoquant may have $Q_1 = 3.75$ and $Q_2 = 6.25$ with $t_2 = 1.25$.

The derivation of the cost function from a diagram such as Figure 2A.2 is done by plotting the cost values such as C_1, C_2 and C_3 against the corresponding output pairs (Q_1^0, Q_2^0), $(t_1 Q_1^0, t_1 Q_2^0)$ and $(t_2 Q_1^0, t_2 Q_2^0)$. Since there are two outputs

FIGURE 2A.2
The firm's expansion path along a ray

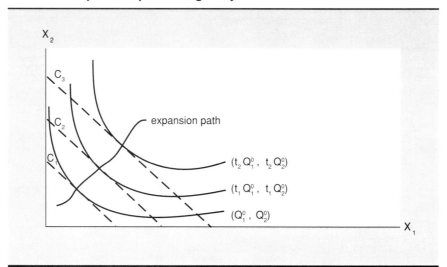

varying independently, the cost function for this firm is a function of the two output variables Q_1 and Q_2. It cannot therefore be plotted in a two-dimensional diagram. The plot derived from Figure 2A.2 will be that of values of the cost function along one ray in output space, i.e. for a proportional expansion of both outputs. The entire cost function can be derived from its values along each possible ray in output space.

Let $C(Q_1, Q_2)$ denote the total cost function for the two-product firm, i.e. the minimum cost necessary to produce the output quantities Q_1 and Q_2. This function gives rise to two marginal costs denoted by MC_1 and MC_2. They are the additional costs incurred by producing additional units of outputs Q_1 and Q_2 respectively, with the other output kept constant:

$$MC_1 = \frac{\partial C}{\partial Q_1} \quad \text{and} \quad MC_2 = \frac{\partial C}{\partial Q_2}$$

The concept of average cost, though, does not exist in the multiproduct firm in the same format as in the single-product one. Instead, we have the *ray average cost* or RAC. This is simply the total cost per unit of the distance travelled along the ray in output space.

Analytically, suppose that the output proportions used in Figure 2A.2 are represented by the ray R_1 shown in Figure 2A.3, in which $Q_1/Q_2 = 3/5$. The RAC along this ray are the costs such as C_1, C_2 or C_3 of Figure 2A.2 divided by the distance from the origin 0 along the line R_1. The question that arises is how to measure this distance, or what to use as the unit of distance. One possibility suggested is to use the intersection with the *unit simplex* as a unit of measurement. This is the line segment OA, where the ray R_1 intersects the 45° line with coordinates summing up to 1 at every point. For instance the coordinates of OA are $Q_1 = 0.375$ and $Q_2 = 0.625$, with $Q_1 + Q_2 = 1$. If the unit of measurement along R_1 is OA then the distance of any other point along the ray such as OA_1 will be equal to the sum of its coordinates. Thus it is easy to see that if A_1's coordinates are $Q_1 = 1.5$, $Q_2 = 2.5$ then $\frac{OA_1}{OA} = \frac{1.5}{0.375} = \frac{2.5}{0.625} = \frac{4}{1} = 4 = 1.5 + 2.5.$

The same is true for any other ray such as R_2, with proportion $\frac{Q_1}{Q_2} = \frac{3}{2}$. Suppose the intersection OB with the unit simplex is used as a distance unit, with coordinates $Q_1 = 0.6$ and $Q_2 = 0.4$. Then the distance OB_1 on the ray is equal to the sum of its coordinates, $1.5 + 1 = 2.5$. Therefore with such a specification the RAC in Figure 2A.2 are as follows:

$$\frac{C_1}{Q_1^0 + Q_2^0}, \quad \frac{C_2}{t_1(Q_1^0 + Q_2^0)} \quad \text{and} \quad \frac{C_3}{t_2(Q_1^0 + Q_2^0)}$$

FIGURE 2A.3
The unit simplex in output space

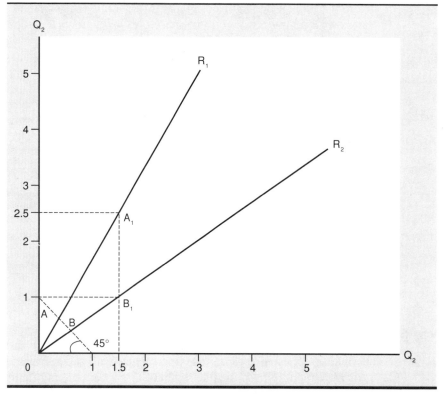

As a specific numerical example, consider the following two-product cost function:

$$C(Q_1, Q_2) = (3Q_1^3 + 5Q_2^3)^{1/3}$$

This cost function has the following marginal costs:

$$MC_1 = \frac{\partial C}{\partial Q_1} = 3Q_1^2 (3Q_1^3 + 5Q_2^3)^{-2/3} \quad \text{and} \quad MC_2 = \frac{\partial C}{\partial Q_2} = 5Q_2^2 (3Q_1^3 + 5Q_2^3)^{-2/3}$$

Its ray average costs are easy to find in this case for every ray. Let a ray be denoted by the constant ratio $Q_1/Q_2 = k$. Then the total costs along a ray are equal to $(3k^3 + 5)^{1/3}Q_2$ while the sum of the coordinates is equal to $Q_1 + Q_2 = (1 + k) Q_2$. Then for any given ray RAC $= \dfrac{(3k^3 + 5)^{1/3}}{1 + k}$, constant along each ray but differing between rays. Thus for $k = 1$ (the 45° ray in output space) we have $\text{RAC} = \dfrac{(3 + 5)^{1/3}}{2} = 1$. Consider $k = 0.6$ and $k = 1.5$, corresponding to the rays R_1 and R_2 of Figure 2A.3. The RACs become respectively $\dfrac{(5.648)^{1/3}}{1.6}$ and $\dfrac{(15.125)^{1/3}}{2.5}$.

The ray average costs are a generalization of the concept of average costs in single-product firms. Their behaviour for any given firm allows the testing for economies of scale in the domain of the cost function, in a manner similar to that for single output firms. Economies of scale, however, are only one of several related and interesting concepts in multiproduct firms.

Economies of Scale and Economies of Scope

As we saw in the single-product firm, economies of scale exist at a certain output level Q if the AC curve is decreasing, or $\dfrac{d\text{AC}}{dQ} < 0$. An equivalent statement is that economies of scale exist if the average cost exceeds the marginal cost MC, or AC > MC; this can also be stated as (total cost) > Q × MC, since AC is by definition equal to total cost divided by Q.

The major advantage of these definitions of economies of scale in the cost function domain is that they can be extended very naturally to the multiproduct case. To accomplish this it is sufficient to replace the average costs of single-product firms by the ray average costs or RAC of the multi-output firms. Specifically, the following statements of the existence of economies of scale at a given combination of output quantities (Q_1, Q_2) form counterparts to similar statements in single-output firms:

(i) Economies of scale exist at a certain pair of output quantities (Q_1, Q_2) if the RAC is decreasing along the corresponding ray in output space.
(ii) Economies of scale exist at (Q_1, Q_2) if the total cost exceeds $Q_1 \times MC_1 + Q_2 \times MC_2$, the product of each quantity multiplied by its respective marginal cost.

To apply statement (i) to a two-output cost function $C(Q_1, Q_2)$, we first express the RAC as a function of the position along the ray in output space "near" the output pair (Q_1, Q_2). Then for a proportional expansion (tQ_1, tQ_2) of the output quantities, the RAC must be a decreasing function of t for values of t "near" 1. Analytically, since $\text{RAC} = \dfrac{C(Q_1, Q_2)}{Q_1 + Q_2}$ economies of scale exist if

$$\frac{d}{dt}\left[\frac{C(tQ_1, tQ_2)}{t(Q_1 + Q_2)}\right] < 0 \qquad\qquad \textbf{Eq. (2A.1)}$$

where the derivative is evaluated at $t = 1$.

As a specific example consider the following two-product cost function:

$$C(Q_1, Q_2) = 30Q_1^{0.7}Q_2^{0.3} - 6Q_1 Q_2 + 0.5Q_1 Q_2^2$$

Suppose that we wish to test whether there are economies of scale at the output pair $Q_1 = 4$, $Q_2 = 4$. This is the ray that has equal output quantities. We first substitute $Q_1 = 4t$, $Q_2 = 4t$ in the cost function, and then divide the result by $t(Q_1 + Q_2) = 8t$. We get $\dfrac{C(tQ_1, tQ_2)}{t(Q_1 + Q_2)} = \dfrac{120t - 96t^2 + 32t^3}{8t} = 15 - 12t + 4t^2$. The derivative with respect to t is equal to $-12 + 8t$, which is negative at $t = 1$. Thus, RAC is declining at $Q_1 = Q_2 = 4$, and economies of scale exist. The same conclusion is derived by comparing $C(Q_1, Q_2)$ to $Q_1 \times MC_1 + Q_2 \times MC_2$ for $Q_1 = Q_2 = 4$: $MC_1 = 21Q_1^{-0.3}Q_2^{0.3} - 6Q_2 + 0.5Q_2^2 = 5$ and $MC_2 = 9Q_1^{0.7}Q_2^{-0.7} - 6Q_1 + Q_1 Q_2 = 1$. Then note that $Q_1 MC_1 + Q_2 MC_2 = 24$, while $C(Q_1, Q_2) = 56$.

The next important property that we'll examine in this section is the *subadditivity* of the cost function at a given output level. A particular form of it is also known as *economies of scope* in the case of multiproduct firms. It is related to the optimal industry structure for multiproduct firms.

We saw earlier that if it happens that the market can accommodate only one such firm then the industry is known as a natural monopoly. Its cost function, when evaluated at the total industry output, must present the subadditivity property. Thus at a given output quantity, any partition of that quantity among more than one firm yields a higher total production cost than if all output is produced by a single firm.

The situation becomes more complicated in the case of a multiproduct firm. Here the industry output consists of a vector of quantities, which can be partitioned in any number of ways. In the case of two outputs, one way of partitioning it is by concentrating all production of Q_1 in one firm and all of Q_2 in another one. If the resulting total cost from both firms exceeds the cost of producing them jointly in a single firm then we have *economies of scope*. Analytically, if $C(Q_1, Q_2)$ is the joint total cost, we have economies of scope at a given pair of values of Q_1 and Q_2 if

$$C(Q_1, Q_2) < C(Q_1, 0) + C(0, Q_2) \qquad \textbf{Eq. (2A.2)}$$

Such economies of scope arise because there are inputs which, once acquired to produce one output, become available for the production of other byproducts.

As a specific example of the existence of economies of scope, consider the cost function already examined earlier, $C(Q_1, Q_2) = (3Q_1^3 + 5Q_2^3)^{1/3}$.

If the industry output is $Q_1 = Q_2 = 2$, then $C(Q_1, Q_2) = [3 \times 2^3 + 5 \times 2^3]^{1/3} = 64^{1/3} = 4$, while $C(Q_1, 0) = [3 \times 8]^{1/3} = 2(3)^{1/3}$, and $C(0, Q_2) = [5 \times 8]^{1/3} = 2(5)^{1/3}$. It is easily seen that Equation (2A.2) holds, and economies of scope exist for this particular output pair.

By contrast, the cost function $C(Q_1, Q_2) = [3Q_1^{1/3} + 5Q_2^{1/3}]^3$ at the industry output $Q_1 = Q_2 = 1$ does not have economies of scope: $C(Q_1, Q_2) = [3 \times 1 + 5 \times 1]^3 = 8^3$, while $C(Q_1, 0) = 3^3$ and $C(Q, Q_2) = 5^3$. The sum of the last two is less than 8^3. Hence, in this last case it will cost less to produce the two outputs in separate firms.

Another useful concept for multiproduct firms is that of the *average incremental cost* or AIC for each product, and the related notion of *product-specific economies of scale*. In our notation the AIC_1 and AIC_2 for products 1 and 2, respectively, equal the following:

$$AIC_1 = \frac{C(Q_1, Q_2) - C(0, Q_2)}{Q_1} \;,\; AIC_2 = \frac{C(Q_1, Q_2) - C(Q_1, 0)}{Q_2}$$

Eq. (2A.3)

Their meaning is obvious. They are the extra cost per unit contributed by the addition of another product line to an existing one. Product-specific economies of scale exist for Q_1 (Q_2) if AIC_1 (AIC_2) declines as Q_1 (Q_2) increases, while the other output Q_2 (Q_1) remains constant. The conditions for the existence of product-specific economies of scale are as follows:

$$\frac{\partial(AIC_1)}{\partial Q_1} < 0 \quad \frac{\partial(AIC_2)}{\partial Q_2} < 0 \qquad \textbf{Eq. (2A.4)}$$

It can be shown that the multiproduct firm is a natural monopoly if both economies of scope and product-specific economies of scale for all products exist. However, a natural monopoly can also exist in other circumstances, as it was shown for a single-product firm.

Optimal Industry Structure

As we saw in the main body of the chapter, economies of scale are a sufficient but not necessary condition for a natural monopoly to exist: they imply a natural monopoly if present for the entire output range, but they are not implied by it. In multiproduct firms, by contrast, economies of scale along every possible ray in output space are neither necessary nor sufficient for the key subadditivity property of natural monopolies. To make matters more confusing, neither are economies of scale plus economies of scope sufficient to produce subadditivity.

Two sets of sufficient conditions were shown by Baumol *et al.* (1982) to create a natural monopoly. The first set, already mentioned, is economies of scope plus product-specific economies of scale for every product. The second set consists of economies of scale along every ray, plus a restriction on the shape of the cost function denoted as *transray convexity*.

In the two-product case, consider two different rays in output space, say $\hat{q} = (Q_1', Q_2')$ and $\bar{q} = (Q_1'', Q_2'')$. where $Q_1'/Q_2' \neq Q_1''/Q_2''$. Then the cost function exhibits transray convexity if for any pair of rays such as $\hat{q}$ and $\bar{q}$, and any θ between 0 and 1 we have:

$$C(\theta\hat{q} + (1-\theta)\bar{q}) < \theta C(\hat{q}) + (1-\theta)\,C(\bar{q})$$ **Eq. (2A.5)**

or, in more familiar notation:

$$C(\theta Q_1' + (1-\theta)Q_1'',\ \theta Q_2' + (1-\theta)Q_2'') < \theta\,C(Q_1',Q_2') + (1-\theta)\,C(Q_2'',Q_2'')$$

Diagrammatically, transray convexity implies in Figure 2A.4 that the cost evaluated at any point C along the line AB is lower than the combination of costs at points A and B, and that this occurs for every line such as AB. A cross-section of the cost surface along such a line must produce a convex curve, as shown in Figure 2A.4. Note that the application of (2A.5) to A, B and C of Figure 2A.4, with $\hat{q} = (0, Q_2^0)$, $\bar{q} = (Q_1^0, 0)$, yields $C((1-\theta)Q_1^0, \theta Q_2^0) < \theta\,C(0, Q_2^0) + (1-\theta)\,C(Q_1^0, 0)$.

The left-hand side of this expression implies jointly-produced output quantities, respectively smaller than Q_1^0 and Q_2^0; the right-hand side involves individually-produced outputs in larger quantities. The inequality states that the resulting economies of scope in joint production overcome the loss of economies of scale from the reduction of each product's quantity.

Transray convexity is a strong restriction on the shape of the multiproduct cost functions. It has, however, been weakened somewhat in many of the results in which it has been used. Further, it is a sufficient and not a necessary

FIGURE 2A.4
Transray convexity

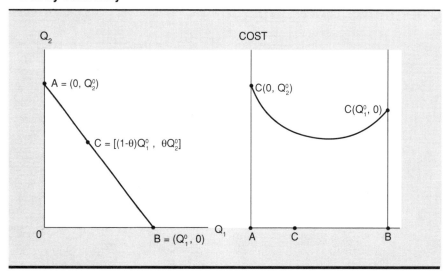

condition, implying that most of the properties, to which it is applied, hold also under more general conditions. This property will be used in the discussion of the multiproduct monopoly firms in the next chapter.

The next step is the extension of the concept of optimal industry structure beyond natural monopoly. This requires a multiproduct generalization of the U-shaped average cost curves that we saw in Figures 2.1 and 2.2. Such a generalization corresponds to the assumption that the RAC decreases along every ray in output space up to a certain length of the ray, and increases thereafter. Thus, the notion of MES level of production of the single-product firm is replaced by a set of vectors of products (one for each ray), each one of which represents the level at which a *constant proportions* production of all outputs exhausts all economies of scale along that ray. In the two-output case this set can be represented by a curve in product space; it becomes a surface in more than two dimensions. It was termed the *M-locus*.

Figure 2A.5 shows such an M-locus in the two-output case, an irregularly-shaped curve in output space. Points A and B, at which it intersects the two axes, correspond to separate production of each output; they are therefore the MES levels of the single-product case. Every other point such as C on the curve shows the minimum levels of jointly-produced Q_1 and Q_2 that minimize the

FIGURE 2A.5
The M-Locus and its convex enclosure

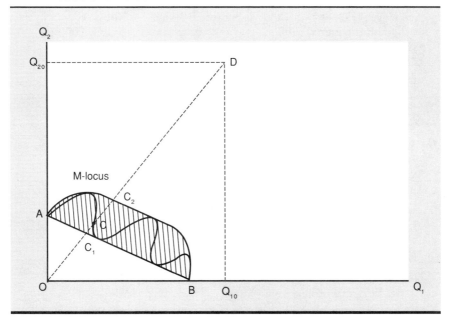

RAC, as long as the two products are produced in the constant proportions indicated by the corresponding ray such as OD.

Since the M-locus can have a very irregular shape, the relevant geometric area is not only the locus itself but its entire *convex closure*. This is the smallest convex region that contains the M-locus. It is represented by the cross-hatched region in Figure 2A.5. It is also assumed that cost subadditivity holds within that convex closure.

We are now ready to derive the optimal industry structure corresponding to a given set of outputs, such as the output pair (Q_{10}, Q_{20}) of the point D in Figure 2A.5. It can be shown that the number of firms in such a structure lies between an upper and a lower bound that depend on the lengths of the segments OC_1 and OC_2, relative to the length OD, where C_1 and C_2 are the intersections of the ray with the convex closure of the M-locus. Specifically, if $(OC_1) = \underline{t}(OD)$ and $(OC_2) = \bar{t}(OD)$, it can be shown that the number of firms that minimize the total cost of producing the output pair (Q_{10}, Q_{20}) lies between $\frac{1}{2\bar{t}}$ and $\frac{2}{\underline{t}}$. For instance, if $\underline{t} = .20$ and $\bar{t} = .25$ the optimal industry structure contains anywhere from 2 to 5 firms. If these bounds are not integers then they are replaced by the closest integers that are respectively larger and smaller than the lower and upper bound.

As we see from the example, the bounds are not particularly tight, yet they cannot be easily improved in a general case. Baumol *et al.* have presented examples in which the cost-minimizing structure contains a number of firms equal to one of the two bounds.[25] In spite of these, the analysis allows us to draw limited inferences about the desirable structure of a given multiproduct industry, based only on information about demand and the shape of the cost function around the M-locus.

Appendix 2B ECONOMIES OF SCALE AND THE FIRM'S COST FUNCTION

Let $Q = F(X_1, X_2)$ denote the firm's production function, and suppose that economies of scale exist locally for some input combination (X_1', X_2'). This means that for $\theta > 1$ we have $F(\theta X_1', \theta X_2') > \theta F(X_1', X_2') = \theta Q_1$, where Q_1 denotes the corresponding output. θ must also be very close to 1, so that we do not exceed the region of economies of scale. Hence we must have

$$\frac{F(\theta X_1', \theta X_2')}{\theta} > F(X_1', X_2')$$

when θ is very close to 1, or equivalently,

$$\frac{F(\theta X_1', \theta X_1')}{\theta}$$

must be increasing in θ at $\theta = 1$. Economies of scale at (X_1', X_2') are therefore equivalent to:

$$\frac{d}{d\theta} \frac{F(\theta X_1', \theta X_2')}{\theta}\bigg|_{\theta=1} > 0 \qquad \textbf{Eq. (2B.1)}$$

Let also $F_1 \equiv \dfrac{\partial F}{\partial X_1}$, $F_2 \equiv \dfrac{\partial F}{\partial X_2}$, the marginal products of the two inputs evaluated at $(\theta X_2', \theta X_2')$. Evaluating the derivative in Equation (2B.1) yields

$$\frac{[X_1'F_1 + X_2'F_2]\theta - F(\theta X_1', \theta X_2')}{\theta^2} > 0$$

which for $\theta = 1$ becomes

$$X_1'F_1 + X_2'F_2 > F(X_1', X_2') \qquad \textbf{Eq. (2B.2)}$$

where F_1 and F_2 are now evaluated at (X_1', X_2').

Let also W_1 and W_2 denote a pair of input prices, for which (X_1', X_2') represent the cost-minimizing input combination. Then if $C(Q)$ denotes the cost function, we have by definition $C(Q_1) = W_1X_1' + W_2X_2'$. Similarly, we have

$$\frac{F_1}{F_2} = \frac{W_1}{W_2} , \ \frac{W_1}{F_1} = \frac{W_2}{F_2} = \frac{dC}{dQ} \equiv C' \qquad \textbf{Eq. (2B.3)}$$

The first relation in (2B.3) is the familiar isoquant-isocost tangency necessary for cost minimization, while the second relation can be derived[26] from the relations $Q_1 = F(X_1', X_2')$, $W_1X_1' + W_2X_2' = C(Q_1)$ and $\dfrac{F_1}{F_2} = \dfrac{W_1}{W_2}$.

It will be shown that economies of scale imply that the average cost function $AC(Q) \equiv \dfrac{C(Q)}{Q}$ is decreasing at output Q_1 and vice-versa. Equivalently, it will be shown that $\dfrac{dAC(Q)}{dQ}\bigg|_{Q=Q_1} < 0$ or that $\dfrac{d}{dQ}\left[\dfrac{C(Q)}{Q}\right]_{Q=Q_1} = \dfrac{Q_1C' - C}{Q_1^2} < 0$ implying that

$$AC(Q_1) > \frac{dC}{dQ}\bigg|_{Q=Q_1} \qquad \textbf{Eq. (2B.4)}$$

the familiar result that average cost exceeds marginal cost. In other words, Equation (2B.2) yields (2B.4), and vice-versa.

We use the first relation in Equation (2B.3) to eliminate F_2 and place it into (2B.2): $F_2 = \dfrac{W_2F_1}{W_1}$ from which $X_1'F_1 + X_2'F_2 = F_1\left(X'_1 + \dfrac{W_2X_2'}{W_1}\right) = \dfrac{F_1}{W_1}(W_1X_1' + W_2X_2')$. This, however, is equal to $\dfrac{C(Q_1)}{C'}$ from Equation (2B.3). Replacing $\dfrac{C(Q_1)}{C'}$ into (2B.2) we get $\dfrac{C(Q_1)}{C'} > Q_1$, which is equivalent to Equation (2B.4). Conversely, we can show (2B.2) starting from (2B.4). Hence, (2B.2) and (2B.4) are equivalent statements of the existence of economies of scale at the point (X_1', X_2') of the production function.

Economies of scale exist as long as the average cost AC(Q) decreases. This implies that the minimum efficient scale is not reached as long as $\dfrac{dAC(Q)}{dQ} < 0$. If the cost function is available mathematically and the average cost function has the shape shown in Figures 2.2(a) and 2.2(b) then the MES is found by setting $\dfrac{dAC(Q)}{dQ} = 0$. For instance, suppose that $C(Q) = 30Q - 6Q^2 + 0.5Q^3$. Then $AC(Q) = 30 - 6Q + 0.5Q^2$, and $\dfrac{dAC(Q)}{dQ} = -6 + Q = 0$ implies that the MES is equal to 6.

Endnotes

1. See Statistics Canada Catalogue 31-402P, *Industrial Organization and Concentration in the Manufacturing, Mining and Logging Industries*, (1985), p. 59.

2. This because the firm's total and average costs of production are obviously dependent on the prices at which it purchases its inputs. See Appendix 2B for details of this dependence.

3. See Shepherd (1979), pp. 143-156; Scherer (1980), pp. 104-108; and Royal Commission on Corporate Concentration (1978), pp. 65-68. Basically, pecuniary economies of scale are discriminatory prices of inputs, with lower prices charged to large purchasers.

4. See the comments in Shepherd (1979), pp. 228-29 and 255-57.

5. For instance, the different types of steel products of a steel mill may be aggregated by weight.

6. A classic article that originally introduced this hypothesis is Averch and Johnson (1962). See also additional references in the next chapter.

7. See Eastman and Stykolt (1967).

8. For more details see Scherer (1980), pp. 145-150.

9. The smaller the inverse index is, the more concentrated is the industry.

10. Since

$$P_i = \frac{s_i}{\sum_{i=1}^{m} s_i} = \frac{s_i}{m\overline{S}}$$

it suffices to set $\frac{1}{m}\sum_{i=1}^{m} s_i^2 = \sigma^2 + \overline{S}^2$ and divide both sides by $m\overline{S}^2$.

11. For instance, the 1982 merger guidelines issued by the U.S. Department of Justice use the Herfindahl index to set thresholds of intervention.

12. Alternatively, the horizontal axis represents the cumulative percentage of firms, i.e. the number of firms divided by m.

13. Note that R can also be extracted from the Lorenz curve.

14. See Scherer (1980), p. 94.

15. See Scherer (1980), p. 93.

16. The study had covered a total of 12 industries, of which two (bearings and fabric weaving) have been omitted, since no comparable industry definition can be extracted from the SIC codes.

17. As Fuss and Gupta (1981) note, the Canadian steel industry is considered to be efficient by industry experts. Yet, if the MES estimates by the engineering method are to be believed, most of the industry uses plants of suboptimal scale.

18. See Green (1985), pp. 103-104.

19. See Fuss and Gupta (1981).

20. See Baldwin and Gorecki (1986), pp. 64-65.

21. Statistics Canada, Catalogue 31-402 (1983).

22. In other words, import prices adjusted for tariffs and transportation costs are used as upper limits on their own prices by domestic firms.

23. This was the opinion of Dr. R.S. Khemani, based on unpublished statistics collected by the Department of Consumer and Corporate Affairs. See also his comments in pp. 137-138 of his 1986 article.

24. See Chapter 11.

25. See Baumol *et al.* (1982), Ch. 5.

26. It suffices to differentiate the first two with respect to Q, yielding respectively $1 = F_1 \frac{\partial X_1'}{\partial Q} + F_2 \frac{\partial X_2'}{\partial Q}, W_1 \frac{\partial X_1'}{\partial Q} + W_2 \frac{\partial X_2'}{\partial Q} = C'$, and to use the first of these last two relations to eliminate $\frac{\partial X_1'}{\partial Q}$ from the second.

References

Averch, H. and L. Johnson. "Behavior of the Firm Under Regulatory Constraint," *American Economic Review*, 52 (December 1962), pp. 1053-1069.

Baldwin, J.R. and P.K. Gorecki. *The Role of Scale in Canada-U.S. Productivity Differences*, volume 6 of the research studies prepared for the Royal Commission on the Economic Union and Development Prospects for Canada. Toronto, Ont.: University of Toronto Press, 1986.

Baldwin, J.R., P.K. Gorecki, and J. McVey. "Imports, Secondary Output, Price Cost Margins and Measures of Concentration: Evidence for Canada, 1979," Discussion Paper 263. Ottawa, Ont.: Economic Council of Canada, 1984.

Baumol, W., J. Panzar, and R. Willig. *Contestable Markets and the Theory of Industry Structure*. San Diego, Cal.: Harcourt, Brace Jovanovich, 1982.

Department of Consumer and Corporate Affairs. *Concentration in the Manufacturing Industries of Canada*. Ottawa, Ont.: Minister of Supply and Services Canada, 1971.

Curry, B. and K.D. George. "Industrial Concentration: A Survey," *Journal of Industrial Economics*, 31, pp. 203-255.

Davies, S.W. "Measuring Industrial Concentration: An Alternative Approach," *Review of Economics and Statistics*, 62, pp. 306-309.

Eastman, H.C. and S. Stykolt. *The Tariff and Competition in Canada*. Toronto, Ont.: Macmillan, 1967.

Fuss, M. and V.K. Gupta. "A Cost Function Approach to the Estimation of Minimum Efficient Scale, Returns to Scale and Suboptimal Scale," *European Economic Review*, 15:2, pp. 123-135.

Gorecki, P. *Economies of Scale and Efficient Plant Size in Canadian Manufacturing Industries*, Research Monograph No. 1, Consumer and Corporate Affairs, Bureau of Competition Policy. Ottawa, Ont.: Minister of Supply and Services Canada, 1976.

Green, C. *Canadian Industrial Organization and Policy*. Toronto, Ont.: McGraw-Hill Ryerson, 2nd edition, 1985.

Hannah, L. and J.A. Kay. *Concentration in Modern Industry*. London, Eng.: Macmillan, 1977.

Khemani, R.S. "Extent and Evolution of Competition in the Canadian Economy," *Canadian Industry in Transition*, volume 2 of the research studies prepared for the Royal Commission on the Economic Union and Development Prospects for Canada. Toronto, Ont.: University of Toronto Press, 1986.

Marfels, C. "On Testing Concentration Measures," *Zeitschrift für Nationalökonomie*, 32:4 (1972), pp. 461-486.

McFetridge, D. "The Economics of Industrial Structure: An Overview," *Canadian Industry in Transition*, vol. 2 of the research studies prepared for the Royal Commission on the Economic Union and Development Prospects for Canada. Toronto, Ont.: University of Toronto Press, 1986.

Pratten, C.F. *Economies of Scale in Manufacturing Industry*. Cambridge, Eng.: Cambridge University Press, 1971.

Rosenbluth, G. *Concentration in Canadian Manufacturing Industries*. Princeton, N.J.: Princeton University Press, 1957.

Royal Commission on Corporate Concentration (RCCC). *Report*. Ottawa, Ont.: Minister of Supply and Services Canada, 1978.

Scherer, F.M. *Industrial Market Structure and Economic Performance*. Chicago, Ill.: Rand McNally, 2nd edition, 1980.

Scherer, F.M. *et al. The Economics of Multi-Plant Operation: An International Comparisons Study*. Cambridge, Mass.: Harvard University Press, 1975.

Shepherd, W.G. "Causes of Increased Competition in the U.S. Economy 1939-80," *Review of Economics and Statistics*, 64 (November 1982), pp. 613-626.

———. *The Economics of Industrial Organization*. Englewood Cliffs, N.J.: Prentice-Hall, 1979.

Statistics Canada, *Industrial Organization and Concentration in the Manufacturing, Mining, and Logging Industries*: Catalogue 31-402 (includes data until 1980, published 1983); Catalogue 31-402P (includes data for 1982, published 1985). Ottawa, Ont.: Minister of Supply and Services.

Stigler, G. "The Economies of Scale," *Journal of Law and Economics*, 1 (October 1958), pp. 54-71.

CHAPTER 3

The Theory

·································

# of Monopoly

·································

In the previous chapter it was established that the interaction between market size and economies of scale is one of the main determinants of the structure of the market. A market structure was named a natural monopoly when the size of the market is so small that the costs of production are minimized by concentrating all production in a single firm. In this chapter we examine the public policy framework and resulting firm behaviour of industries and markets that operate under monopoly structures. These sectors include but are not limited to most natural monopolies. Additional public policy issues pertaining to monopolies are analyzed in Chapter 10.

Monopolies have traditionally dominated the public utilities sector of the economy, primarily the transportation, energy and telecommunications industries. They are also found, however, in other areas, such as broadcasting, newspapers, and professional sports. Some of these monopolies are privately owned and protected by exclusive franchises against possible entry by competitors; in such cases they are also subjected to economic regulation. Other private monopolies are basically unregulated, with newspapers and professional sports being prime examples. In other sectors, such as mail distribution and electricity generation and distribution, the dominant mode is a public enterprise, which is also protected against entry. Last, private and public monopolies operate side by side in several important sectors of the Canadian economy, such as rail transport, telecommunications, and pre-deregulation airlines.

In this chapter the primary focus is on privately-owned regulated monopoly firms, such as Bell Canada, Canadian Pacific, and cable television companies. Much of the theory of monopoly was developed with precisely such firms in mind. As Table 2.9 showed, more than a third of total Canadian economic activity in 1980 originated in firms subject to some kind of regulation. Many of these firms were publicly owned monopolies; others belonged to oligopolistic sectors that were subjected to regulation for various reasons, mostly at their own request. Still others were deregulated after 1980. Nonetheless a regulated private monopoly is an obvious alternative to a public enterprise, while the behaviour of several of the oligopolies, whether regulated or not, is very similar to that of monopolies. For all these reasons the study of monopoly firms is an indispensable complement to the study of oligopolistic sectors, which together form the main topic of industrial organization.

In the first section we review briefly the microeconomic theory of the unregulated monopoly firm and examine the rationale for the dominant regulatory framework. The second section studies the behaviour of the single-product monopoly within that framework. The last two sections of the chapter are devoted to multiproduct monopolies and the intricate problems that arise during their regulation. One such problem, concerned with the establishment of the regulatory boundary or *frontier*, is dealt with in Appendix 3A.

The Desirable Behaviour of a Monopoly Firm

In a monopoly the firm and the industry coincide. In the absence of regulation, given that the monopolist is protected against entry by economic or public policy factors, the firm maximizes profits, depending on the industry demand curve and its own costs. Its choices determine the industry equilibrium.

Let $P = D(Q)$ denote the firm's demand curve in inverse form, if P is price and Q output; its sales revenue is therefore $R(Q) = QD(Q)$. If $C(Q)$ denotes the firm's cost function then the profit is $\pi = QD(Q) - C(Q)$. The optimal output choice, Q, maximizes profits, as shown in Figure 3.1.

The optimal Q, denoted by Q_M, corresponds to the maximum distance between $R(Q)$ and $C(Q)$. At Q_M the slopes of both curves are equal, yielding the familiar equality of marginal revenue MR and marginal cost MC, or MR = MC. Similarly, the marginal revenue is linked to the demand curve by the following relation: $MR = D(Q)[1 + 1/\epsilon]$, where ϵ is the price elasticity of demand.

At Q_M, where MR = MC, the marginal revenue must be positive, given that MC is always greater than zero. Hence, the quantity $1 + 1/\epsilon$ must be positive, implying that Q_M lies in the elastic portion of the demand curve. From

FIGURE 3.1
Monopoly profit maximization

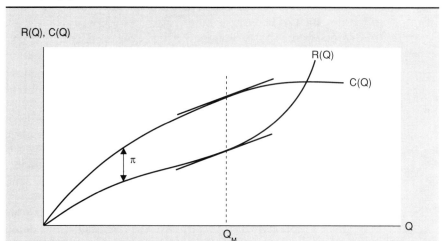

Q_M the equilibrium price P_M is now found from the demand curve. Figure 3.2 shows P_M and Q_M, as well as the resulting monopoly profits, represented by the cross-hatched rectangle.

The equilibrium state of the industry depicted in Figure 3.2 is clearly not desirable from the point of view of public welfare. Price is above marginal (and average) cost, economic profits accrue to the monopolist, output is curtailed, price is raised above its equivalent competitive level, and so on. A detailed examination of the inefficiencies due to monopoly will take place in Chapter 7, which deals specifically with performance. Even without a formal analysis, though, it appears obvious that a monopoly protected from competitors' entry should not be allowed to exploit its market power.

If, however, there are no formal obstacles to entry such as patents or exclusive monopoly franchises, then the realized profits would normally attract new firms to the industry. Such firms may or may not succeed in establishing themselves in the sector and transforming it into an oligopoly. In this chapter we shall initially assume that entry is completely free, and we shall deal with two important public policy issues: whether the monopoly can maintain its position without public protection from competition in the form of an exclusive franchise, the so-called *sustainability* issue; and what type of regulatory regime should be established if it is believed that an unregulated monopoly's behaviour is unfair and/or inefficient. As we shall see, the two issues are closely linked.

FIGURE 3.2
The monopolist's price, output, and profits

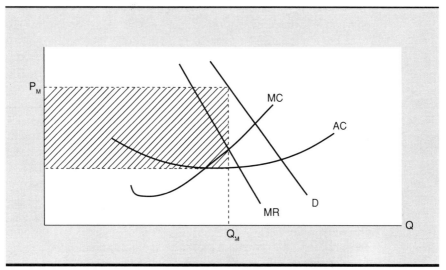

A monopoly is sustainable if it can establish a *sustainable* price, i.e. a price that covers its own costs, yet is sufficiently low to preclude any would-be entrant from undercutting it profitably. In other words, this price must be less than the unit cost of any firm that tries to undercut the monopolist by supplying a fraction of the market. If such a sustainable price exists then the monopolist does not need any protection, since it can charge this price and stay in business, while would-be entrants stay away from the sector.

At first glance it would appear, from the definition of a natural monopoly that we saw in the previous chapter, that such a monopoly would always be sustainable. After all, in a natural monopoly it is cheapest to concentrate all production in a single firm. Yet even for single product firms there are natural monopolies that are not sustainable under completely free entry conditions. Suppose, for instance, that the industry demand and average cost curves, D and AC respectively, are those shown in Figure 3.3, which reproduces Figure 2.5. Here the demand curve intersects the AC curve at output level Q_1, where there are diseconomies of scale ($Q_1 > Q_0$) but where it is still cheapest to have an industry consisting of a single firm.

The price P_1, at which D = AC, is not sustainable: an entrant can undercut it by charging a price between P_1 and AC_m and producing an output between Q_1' and Q_1, while still managing to cover its costs. This is not possible if the output level Q_1 that equates D and AC is less than or equal to Q_0, or if there are economies of scale or constant returns to scale at Q_1.

The non-sustainability of the natural monopoly shown in Figure 3.3 needs, however, to be qualified. As noted at the outset, it is assumed that entry is completely free. A market with completely free entry is one in which an entrant may enter and produce some output, sell it at a price below P_1 before the incumbent has had the time to retaliate, and then exit costlessly once the incumbent starts matching its price. Markets that exhibit these characteristics are known as *contestable*, and they are mainly distinguished by the absence of any sunk costs, i.e. costs which, once committed, cannot be recovered.[1] If any such costs are present they would be lost in the entry and subsequent exit process. Although it is probable that no perfectly contestable market exists, it is believed that markets for several transportation services such as airlines, trucking and taxicabs have characteristics that approach contestability. We shall return to this issue in more detail in Chapters 5 and 10.

A monopoly such as the one shown in Figure 3.3 is therefore unsustainable in a contestable market. By contrast, it would be sustainable if point Q_1, at which the demand curve intersects the AC curve, is at or to the left of the minimum efficient scale (MES) Q_0. The price level corresponding to that intersection point is sustainable, since it cannot be undercut profitably under any circumstances, even in a contestable market.

The situation is less clearcut if entry is not completely free. What happens in such a case depends, to a large extent, on the nature of the impediments. It is sufficient to say at this point that there exist several situations in which

FIGURE 3.3
An unsustainable monopoly

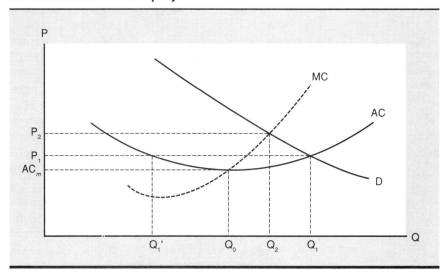

a combination of structural factors and firm behaviour can preserve some monopoly profits in the face of potential entry.

An unsustainable monopoly in an industry with completely free entry cannot persist in the long run. The industry structure that will emerge after a competitor's entry is not determined, but in most circumstances its welfare properties will be inferior to those of the monopoly. For this reason it would be better to prohibit entry in such natural monopoly industries. In such a case, however, the monopolist cannot be left to operate on its own, since it would then choose the profit-maximizing behaviour depicted in Figure 3.2. Hereafter, therefore, it will be assumed that the monopolist is subjected to the twin policies of protection from competition through an exclusive monopoly franchise, and curbs on allowable behaviour under the form of regulator-specified price(s) for its product(s). The monopolist is also obligated to satisfy all demand at that price level, an obligation that is known as the *common carrier requirement*. This is the regime under which most regulated industries operate, even though it is doubtful whether its establishment was initially motivated by unsustainability concerns.

Once the general features of the regulatory regime are agreed upon the question that arises is the specific price level that will be imposed upon the monopolist. Referring again to Figure 3.3, two obvious candidates suggest themselves: price level P_1, at which price is equal to average cost, the monopolist produces Q_1, and monopoly profits are zero; or price level P_2, with price equal to marginal cost and with the monopolist realizing positive profits. As we know from microeconomic theory, and as we shall see in more detail in Chapter 7, the necessary conditions for an optimal resource allocation imply both zero profits and a price equal to marginal cost for all firms. We are therefore obliged to sacrifice one of these two conditions.

The condition that will be sacrificed becomes obvious once we examine a natural monopoly, in which the MES level of Q_0 exceeds the intersection of the demand and average cost curves. Such a monopoly is shown in Figure 3.4. Here the demand curve intersects the marginal cost curve at output Q_2, at which marginal cost is less than average cost. The result is that the price-output combination P_2 and Q_2, which equates price and marginal cost while simultaneously satisfying all consumer demand, leaves the firm with economic losses equal to the cross-hatched area. There is therefore a need for a public subsidy to be granted to the monopolist to allow it to stay in business. Since such subsidies are not considered practical on economic or political grounds, it is price P_1, where demand intersects the AC curve, that is generally chosen for regulatory purposes.

The welfare consequences of setting price equal to average cost are not always desirable. For this reason there are more complex regulatory schemes, with allegedly superior welfare properties, that have appeared at times in the economics literature. For instance, *two-part tariffs*[2] are pricing rules in which

FIGURE 3.4
Possible regulated price levels for a monopolist

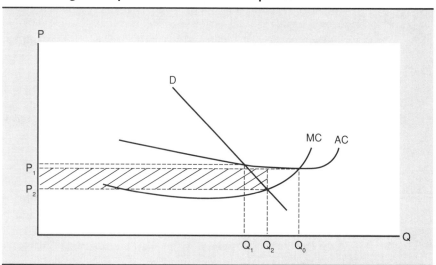

the consumer pays a lump sum fee for the right to receive service, plus a service charge that is proportional to the consumed amount; this latter charge can approximate marginal cost pricing. Such rules have not received much acceptance in North America, although they underlie the pricing of telephone service in several European countries.

In North America regulated monopoly prices are generally established on a cost recovery basis, i.e. by setting price equal to average cost. The revenues from such prices must be sufficient in order to cover all economic costs of the monopoly. This includes, in practice, all labour, materials, and other operating costs; all taxes; and all the costs of the capital invested in the business by the stockholders and bondholders of the regulated firm.

In Canada, most price regulation is undertaken by independent quasi-judicial bodies, of which the Canadian Radio-television and Telecommunications Commission (CRTC) and the Canadian Transport Commission (CTC) are the best-known. Prices are determined on the basis of open hearings initiated by the regulatory agency and/or the regulated firm. These hearings are quite often controversial, lengthy, and very expensive. More importantly, this type of regulation has generated persistent allegations that it induces inefficient behaviour on the part of the regulated firm. These allegations are examined in the next section.

The Behaviour of the Regulated Firm

In order to analyze firm behaviour it is appropriate to review the regulatory mechanism in some detail. When presenting a request for a price increase the regulated firm must justify it in terms of costs. It starts, therefore, by projecting product demand for the period for which the new price is requested. From these projections it then forecasts the operating costs likely to arise. To these it must add an allowance for the cost of capital invested in the business. This is done by including the actual cost of borrowed funds as well as an imputed cost for the stockholders' equity, the so-called *fair rate of return*. After adjusting for corporate income taxes, the total amount that results represents the necessary revenue for the firm to cover all its costs. The corresponding product price in a single-product firm can now be derived by dividing the required revenue by the projected demand. For multiproduct firms there is the added complication of apportioning this required revenue among the various products; this will be discussed in the next section.

Of all these steps the most controversial is the determination of the fair rate of return.[3] This rate should reflect the cost of keeping funds tied-up in the firm rather than in some other competing use. According to financial theory, this "cost of capital" should be equal to the rate of interest, which is the cost of riskless uses of funds, plus an allowance for risk. This risk depends on the type of business the funds are invested in. Herein lies the main problem faced by the regulators: a regulated monopoly firm is by definition unlike any other business in the country. Comparable objective standards of risk are therefore missing, leaving the regulators with very little to go on when deciding the fair rate of return.

The issue is resolved through hearings, during which the regulated company and the various intervenors present their own estimates of the fair rate of return. Not surprisingly, the firm has a tendency to exaggerate the risk of its operations in order to produce higher levels of regulated prices. Other intervening parties come up with lower estimates, with the result that the regulators are faced with estimates that differ by as much as 25 percent within the same hearings. For instance, during the 1982 rate-setting hearings for BC Tel, the telecommunications utility for British Columbia, the estimates of the fair rate of return offered by the various parties ranged from 15.25 to 19 percent.[4]

Two additional points deserve to be mentioned in the context of the fair rate of return. The first one refers to the mechanism of the regulatory process, which becomes itself a source of risk. Frequent changes in the regulated prices (as can happen, for instance, during inflationary periods), coupled with the uncertainty associated with the fair rate of return to be chosen by the regulators, make the firm's revenues unstable and risky. There is therefore a circularity involved in regulatory rate-setting which it is not possible to remove: the choice of the fair rate of return should reflect the firm's risk, which is itself a function of that choice.

The second issue concerns the size of this fair rate of return. Even if the firm's risk could be determined with precision, should the fair rate be exactly equal to the corresponding cost of capital? Alternatively, should the firm's revenues be exactly equal to its costs, or should the fair rate of return include a provision for some economic profit? In the former case it was pointed out by several researchers that the firm would have absolutely no incentives to operate efficiently: since all it can do is recover its costs, there is no reason why it should strive to minimize them.

Several studies therefore advocate a regulatory setting of the fair rate of return slightly above the exact cost recovery level.[5] A firm in that setting would be able to count on realizing some economic profit at a rate predetermined by the regulators. It would then choose its optimum inputs, given this rate. Unfortunately, this does not turn out to be true. This was first shown by Averch and Johnson (1962), and repeated in a large number of subsequent studies.

The Averch-Johnson Model

In this model the regulated firm chooses its labour L and capital K, as well as its output Q, by maximizing profits subject to a regulator-imposed constraint. This takes the form of an upper limit on the rate of return that it receives on its invested capital, which is, however, higher than the cost of that same capital, in line with our above discussion. Similarly, the choice of an output rate is constrained by the firm's production function, denoted by F(K,L).

Let s denote the upper limit on the rate of return and r the cost of capital. By assumption we have $s > r$. Let also D(Q) denote the firm's demand curve in inverse form, and w the unit cost of the labour input. The firm's profit π is therefore given by

$$\pi = QD(Q) - wL - rK$$

The regulated firm chooses K and L by maximizing π, subject to the production function Q = F(K,L), and the following rate of return constraint:

$$QD(Q) - wL \leqslant sK$$

This reflects the condition that the accounting profit rate, equal to the operating revenue per unit invested capital, or to $(QD(Q) - wL)/K$, must not exceed the upper limit s prescribed by the regulator. It is also assumed implicitly that either the constraint is effective, or that s is small enough to prevent the firm from attaining the choices it would have made in the absence of regulation.

In terms of the actual regulatory framework, the behaviour of the regulated firm implied by this formulation entails that the firm anticipates correctly the choice of the fair rate of return made by the regulatory commission. Given these anticipations, it then adjusts its own decisions optimally. While the earlier remarks on the uncertainty surrounding the determination of the fair rate of return seem to be at variance with this formulation, it must be remembered that most of this uncertainty arose out of the highly inflationary environment of the 1970s and early 1980s. At the time the Averch-Johnson study appeared the economic environment in both the U.S. and Canada was considerably more stable and predictable than in later years.

The solution of the constrained maximization problem contained in the Averch-Johnson model is presented in detail in Appendix 3B. Its main results can be stated under the form of a number of propositions, each one of which has been the focus of much discussion since the first appearance of the model:[6]

(i) The regulated firm will choose input proportions that do not minimize the cost of production.

(ii) The capital stock of the regulated firm will be larger than in the absence of regulation.

(iii) The capital-labour ratio of the regulated firm will be larger than the cost-minimizing level of that same ratio that corresponds to the chosen output level.

(iv) The chosen level of capital stock increases with the "tightness" of the regulatory constraint, i.e. it increases when the upper limit s on the rate of return decreases.

Figure 3.5 shows a geometric justification of the above results. Each one of the curves shown represents the values of the capital and labour inputs satisfying the rate of return constraint for a given s. They are derived by expressing the regulatory constraint as an equality and replacing the output Q by the production function F(K,L).

Analytically, suppose that we set $\pi = QD(Q) - wL - rK = (s-r)K$. Replacing Q by its equal, we get $F(K,L)D(F(K,L)) - wL - rK = (s-r)K$. This last equality represents, for any given value of s, a set of points in a (K,L) diagram. These points form a curve of the shape shown in Figure 3.5. Each such curve corresponds to a different value of s. Further, it can be shown that the curves move outwards as the constraint becomes tighter, i.e. as s decreases. The point denoted by π_M shows the limiting value of s, above which the constraint is no longer effective. This point also lies on the long-run expansion path of the firm, the set of cost-minimizing input combinations shown by the dashed curve.

For a given value of s the input choice of the regulated firm must lie on the corresponding curve. It is also the point on that curve that has the highest

FIGURE 3.5
The Averch-Johnson effect

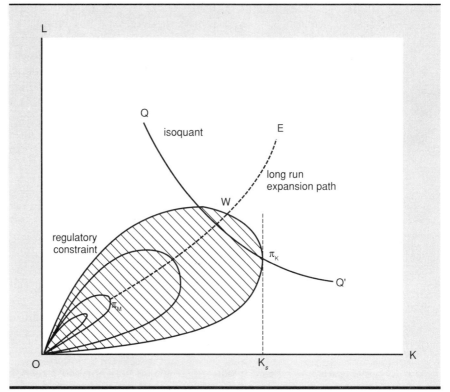

possible value of K, such as the point π_K shown in Figure 3.5, where the tangent to the curve is vertical to the K-axis; this because $\pi = (s-r)K$ is maximized when K is at K_s. It is clear from this figure, though, that such points lie to the right of the expansion path, since the corresponding isoquant has the well-known decreasing and convex shape. It is easy to see that Figure 3.5 embodies the four Averch-Johnson propositions stated above.

The Averch-Johnson results are quite disturbing, and for this reason they have been controversial since they appeared. Many subsequent studies examined the robustness of the results under relaxed assumptions concerning various aspects of the model. For instance, Peles and Stein (1976) and Perrakis (1976a and b) formulated the Averch and Johnson model under demand uncertainty, and studied the validity of the four propositions within this enlarged framework. They found that propositions 2, 3 and 4, the so-called *overcapitalization* results, were no longer true under demand uncertainty. Proposition 1, though, the main inefficiency implication of the model, was still valid under an even more objectionable format, which implied that the regulated firms engaged in deliberate cost padding when it became obvious that they were going to exceed the regulatory upper limit.

A more optimistic view of regulation was presented in other models, in which the basic regulatory constraint was somewhat relaxed in its application. Thus an important paper by Nerlove (1963), which appeared almost simultaneously with the Averch-Johnson study, assumed that regulation was concerned only with the price level without worrying about the rate of return considerations. In such a case the firm, faced with an exogenously fixed price and a market demand curve, will find it optimal to minimize costs for a given output, the latter being given by the demand curve and the regulated price. This eliminates the regulatory inefficiency, even though it may not always eliminate economic profits. The model, though, leaves in the dark the determination of the regulated price level. An intermediate position emerges from still another study by Bailey and Coleman (1971), in which it is assumed that regulation takes place with a lag. The regulatory constraint may be violated in the time period between rate-setting reviews, but price is set at the level that eliminates profits at each review point. In this specification the regulatory inefficiency disappears, since the firm adjusts its input choices to the cost-minimizing proportions between the rate reviews.

Given all these conflicting models and results, one would have supposed that empirical work would have helped clarify the issue. Yet the empirical results proved as ambiguous as the theoretical ones. While direct tests of the Averch-Johnson model by Boyes (1976), Courville (1974), Petersen (1975), and Spann (1974) claimed to have uncovered evidence of the model's predicted effects, econometric work on regulated industries continued to follow the Nerlove assumption of cost minimization for an exogenously given regulated price. Almost all these studies took place in the U.S. electric power generation industry. In that same industry a subsequent study by Perrakis and Zerbinis (1981) carried out a direct test of the two alternative specifications of the regulated industry, Averch-Johnson versus Nerlove. That study used an enlarged formulation in which demand uncertainty was explicitly incorporated. No evidence of the inefficiencies inherent in the Averch-Johnson results was uncovered.

In Canada econometric work on regulated industries took place mostly in telecommunications.[7] The regulated firm, Bell Canada, was modelled as producing more than one product. The studies followed mostly the Nerlove assumption, avoiding any considerations of the rate of return constraint. The main emphasis of recent studies has been the relative pricing of the various telecommunications services, which will be examined in the next section.

Despite these ambiguities, the possibility of inefficiencies associated with the regulatory process must be taken seriously. These inefficiencies cannot be easily avoided by changing the regulatory mechanism. As the models of regulation under uncertainty of Peles and Stein (1976) and Perrakis (1976a,b) showed, the precise form that these inefficiencies take depends very much on the type of information possessed by the regulators. This information is by necessity imperfect. Short of taking over the entire firm, the public authority in charge of regulation can only monitor certain aspects of the firm's performance. Given the different objectives pursued by firm and regulator, it is virtually impossible to design a form of regulation that avoids inefficiencies under all circumstances.

These issues have resurfaced in recent years in the United Kingdom, where several public utilities were privatized by the Thatcher government. These privatizations were prompted by the desire to improve the performance of the firms, although ideological considerations were probably at least as important. The public enterprise is an obvious alternative to the regulated privately-owned monopoly, although it has its own efficiency problems. It is not always clear which mode of ownership is preferable. At any rate, there are current attempts in the U.K. to devise regulatory mechanisms that result in efficient firm performance. One such example is the so-called RPI-X regulatory policy: a given weighted average of the prices of the regulated firm must fall by at least X percent per year in real terms until the next (predetermined) regulatory review. The key question, of course, is the selection of the average, as well as of the amount X. This policy, as well as other ones under discussion, is still in its infancy.[8] One cannot help but feel a certain amount of scepticism, however, on the ultimate outcome of these exercises, given the North-American experience with regulation.

As noted above, the main current issue in the regulation of Canadian telecommunications is the relative pricing of the various services. This can only be studied in a multiproduct context, which is examined next.

Multiproduct Monopolies and Relative Pricing

Most regulated firms produce more than one product. They must therefore determine more than one price. This creates major problems for their regulators which economic theory has only recently begun to tackle. These problems are related to the now familiar notion of the existence of a natural monopoly structure, as well as to its sustainability in the absence of public policy protection. A major complication not present in single-product monopolies is the extent of such protection: which products from the range produced by the regulated firm will be shielded from competition? This problem, known as the determination of the regulatory frontier, will be examined in Appendix 3A. In what follows we shall first consider the modifications to the single-product notions of subadditivity and sustainability, before approaching the policy issues of the relative pricing of the various products and the resulting firm behaviour.

As we saw in Chapter 2, the existence of a natural monopoly depends on the subadditivity of its cost function for the combination of output quantities that will be produced. This subadditivity implies by definition that it is cheaper to concentrate all production in a single firm. The alternative possibilities are much more varied in a multiproduct situation than when the firm produces only one product. Figure 3.6 shows a two-product case, in which public policy makers are considering the best structure to produce the output quantities represented by the coordinates of point A. Such a structure would be a natural monopoly if the value of the cost function at that point, $C(Q_{10}, Q_{20})$, is smaller than the sum of the costs corresponding to all possible partitions of the

FIGURE 3.6
Possible industry structures in two-product firms

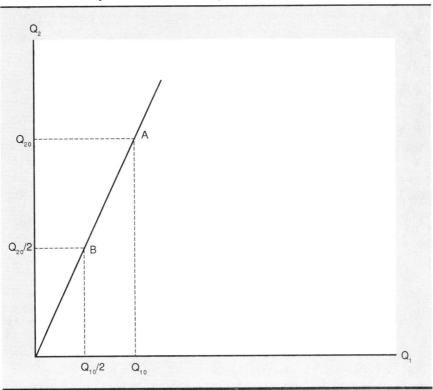

quantities Q_{10} and Q_{20} between more than one firm. Examples of two such possible partitions are the division of the total amounts in two equal parts corresponding to point B; and the complete specialization of production by producing Q_{10} in one firm and Q_{20} in the other. The resulting total industry costs of production are equal to $2C(Q_{10}/2, Q_{20}/2)$ and $C(Q_{10}, 0) + C(0, Q_{20})$ respectively. The subadditivity condition implies that both these costs must be larger than $C(Q_{10}, Q_{20})$ for a natural monopoly to exist. Needless to say, the verification of such an existence in real-life cases is quite difficult. Yet it cannot be avoided. The deregulation movement of recent years has prompted many would-be challengers to question the existence of a natural monopoly in several industries. The discussion of the case study in Appendix 3A illustrates such a challenge in the telecommunications industry.

Suppose now that we decide a natural monopoly exists in a given market for all conceivable quantities that we wish to produce. Is the monopoly sustainable, i.e. can it protect itself against entry, or does it need public protection in the form of an exclusive franchise? For a single-product firm we saw that sustainability required the existence of economies of scale at the industry output. For a multiproduct firm the answer is considerably more difficult. As shown in Appendix 2A economies of scale do not guarantee a natural monopoly, let alone sustainability, in a multiproduct firm. Under "free entry" conditions, as in contestable markets, we expect that a natural monopoly would need protection from entry. Otherwise we may not get a structure that produces the desired output, yet also minimizes the total costs of production.

There exists one set of natural monopoly conditions which, in combination with a particular set of regulated prices, guarantees sustainability. This set of conditions, which will be examined in the next section, is the existence of economies of scale along every ray,[9] plus the transray convexity property of the cost function examined in Appendix 2A. Before examining these conditions, however, we must turn to the issue of relative product pricing. For it turns out that the sustainable vector of product prices is also the same one that arises in another context. These prices are known as *Ramsey prices,* and they were first presented in a totally different context by F. Ramsey in 1927.

Ramsey Prices

Suppose that we have a regulator or planner who must determine the prices that the natural monopoly will charge for its various products or services. The firm must be allowed to raise sufficient revenue to cover all costs of production without any economic profit. In contrast to the single product case, this zero-profit condition does not determine a unique set of prices: there is an infinity of possible price combinations to choose from. One must therefore invoke some kind of social welfare objective for the regulator in choosing one particular price set.

The Ramsey prices are the prices chosen by maximizing the welfare criterion of *combined or total surplus* in the industry, subject to the zero-profit condition noted above. They are in other words prices that achieve the highest level of this given index of public welfare, while simultaneously allowing the firm to be self-financing without any excess profit. For these reasons their use in the relative pricing of the various products or services of a regulated company has been persistently advocated by several economists, in spite of their rather drastic implications concerning the realignment of existing prices in some regulated industries.

As we know from microeconomic theory, combined or total (consumer plus producer) surplus in a single-product firm is equal to the surface of the area between the demand curve, the price line and the vertical axis, plus the producer profits. Figure 3.7 illustrates this total surplus in a particular example, with the surplus shown as a cross-hatched area. The consumer surplus is the

FIGURE 3.7
Consumer and producer surplus

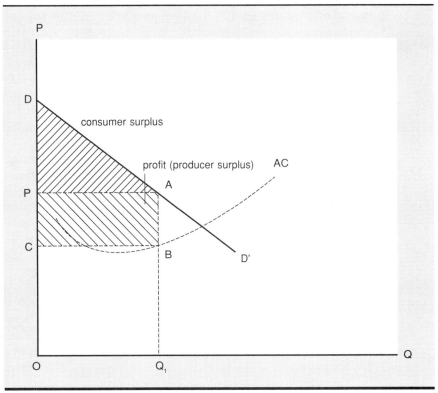

area DAP, while the producer profits are given by the rectangle PABC. An alternative representation that can be easily generalized for a multiproduct firm is to show the combined surplus as the difference of the areas (DAQ_10) and (CBQ_10). The latter is clearly the cost $C(Q_1)$, where $C(Q)$ is the firm's cost function. The former is the area under the demand curve, from the origin to the point Q_1. It can be easily shown that the maximization of the total surplus in such a single-product firm ends up with the familiar result that price is equal to marginal cost.

The use of the total surplus criterion as an index of social welfare has not always been generally accepted, even though it has been around for a very long time. It was only recently shown to be a good approximation to the "correct" welfare index in most cases of practical interest.[10] This approximation will be discussed in more detail in Chapter 7. At any rate, the total surplus is the main tool available to economists for the evaluation of alternative states at the level of individual industries.

The evaluation of the total surplus in a multiproduct monopoly firm follows the same analytical formulation as the one above. Suppose for instance that we have a two-product firm, with a cost function $C(Q_1,Q_2)$, and demand curves $D_1(Q_1)$ and $D_2(Q_2)$, which for simplicity are assumed independent of each other. For any level of industry production, i.e. for any pair of output values (Q_1', Q_2'), the total surplus is the sum of the areas under the two demand curves until the output levels Q_1' and Q_2', minus the cost $C(Q_1', Q_2')$. In other words, it is the sum of two areas similar to (DAQ_10) of Figure 3.6, minus the joint cost of producing both output levels. We want to determine the values of Q_1' and Q_2' that maximize this total, subject to a breakeven constraint that sets total profit equal to zero. This has the following form:

$$Q_1'D_1(Q_1') + Q_2'D(Q_2') - C(Q_1', Q_2') = 0$$

The maximization is carried out in Appendix 3B. The final expression that results is normally stated in terms of the price elasticities of the two demand curves, respectively denoted by ϵ_1 and ϵ_2, as well as the two prices P_1 and P_2 and the two values of the marginal cost MC_1 and MC_2. This expression, which is known as the *Ramsey rule*, states that the price-cost margins across the various products of a multiproduct firm must be inversely proportional to their price elasticities of demand.[11] Analytically this yields, for $i = 1,2$:

$$\frac{P_i - MC_i}{P_i} = \frac{k}{\epsilon_i}$$

where k is a proportionality constant. The expression is valid for any number of products, provided that the demands for each product are independent. A slightly more complex expression holds when this independence assumption is relaxed.

The policy implications of this pricing rule are quite major and somewhat controversial. In any multiproduct firm there are some costs that are directly attributable to individual product lines; other costs are common to all products. It is these latter costs that create problems in pricing. The Ramsey rule provides a method of allocating these common costs. This method says roughly that as demand becomes more inelastic (i.e. ϵ lowers in value), the more price exceeds marginal cost, and the more the product is burdened with common costs. Since products with inelastic demand are generally identified with necessities, the implication of the Ramsey rule is that the more of a necessity a particular product of a regulated monopoly is, the higher its relative price should be.

An immediate application of Ramsey pricing in the telecommunications industry concerns the allocation of the costs of the local telephone network among the various services produced by the telephone utility. These services are generally classified in three distinct categories: local voice messages; long-distance voice messages; and "other" services (a catch-all category that includes private lines and data transmission services in which the utility competes with other suppliers). All these services use the local telephone network. The Ramsey rule stipulates that the service with the most inelastic demand, in this case local voice messaging, must also carry the highest share of the costs of this local network. Needless to say, this requires a massive realignment of the relative rates. Such a realignment has been a standard request by Canada's main regulated private telecommunications company, Bell Canada, all through the late 1970s and early 1980s. It had not been accepted as of 1989.

Other Pricing Rules

Another rule for the allocation of the common costs is the so-called *fully distributed cost* rule. This rule allocates the common costs of the various products or services according to some criterion of relative usage. For instance, in the telecommunications example the costs of the local network would be allocated according to the intensity of traffic for each type of message travelling through a particular local network. The main drawback of this rule is the fact that it completely ignores demand considerations in pricing. Some of the opponents of its use have also stated that the resulting relative prices bear no relation to marginal costs.[12] This is not altogether true. In fact, it can be reasonably claimed that the long-run marginal cost of each product should also include some portion of the *congestion* that this product causes for the common facility. This congestion is reflected in the deterioration of the quality of all other products arising from the increase in production of a particular product. The fully distributed costs concept is an attempt to approximate the costs of congestion, since it can be reasonably assumed that congestion is proportional to the relative use of the common facility.

Two other methods for apportioning the common costs, proposed in economics literature, are both derived from the theory of multiproduct firms. These are the *incremental cost* and the *stand-alone* cost methods. The first concept, which was examined in Appendix 2A., measures the additional cost arising out of the introduction of a new product line. The second one measures the cost of supplying a particular product individually. For instance, in the two-output case with cost function $C(Q_1,Q_2)$, the stand-alone cost of product 1 is $C(Q_1,0)$, while its incremental cost is equal to

$$C(Q_1,Q_2) - C(0,Q_2)$$

According to Baumol and Willig (1986), the theory of contestable markets stipulates that the price of each product of a multiproduct firm should lie between a floor equal to its incremental cost and a ceiling given by the stand-alone cost.

Both these pricing concepts suffer from the same drawback as the fully distributed costs: they ignore demand. More serious, perhaps, is the fact that the range of prices implied by them is too wide to be of much use in most realistic applications. To demonstrate this, consider the telecommunications industry problem of allocating the costs of the local telephone network between the local and long-distance messaging services, assuming for simplicity that these are the only services produced by our telephone utility. The stand-alone cost of the local service is the cost of the local network, while that of the long-distance service is the cost of *both* the local and long-distance networks, since both are necessary for point-to-point long-distance voice communication. Similarly, the incremental cost of the long-distance service is the cost of the long-distance network, while that of the local service is zero, since it can be added at no additional cost if the point-to-point long-distance service is already available. Thus, the two pricing rules used together imply that the price of the long-distance messages should include anywhere from zero to 100 percent of the cost of the local network.

Nonetheless, the two cost concepts cannot be dismissed easily when considering relative prices in multiproduct regulated firms. At the very least, the bounds they imply cannot be violated with impunity. Part of the concerns of regulated telephone companies over the alleged high relative prices of long-distance messages has to do with the possible loss of revenue from large industrial users, who may find it more economical to build their own network. This would happen if the stand-alone cost of building and operating such a network is lower than the revenue extracted from the users by the regulated firm. Such a fragmentation of the telephone service would ultimately result in higher costs for providing the entire range of services, given the assumed natural monopoly property of the telecommunications industry.

As a general conclusion, therefore, one should note that no obvious solution to the problem of relative pricing in a regulated multiproduct industry exists. Each one of the pricing rules mentioned here has its own advantages and drawbacks. The Ramsey prices, which optimize the total surplus index of welfare, require information about price elasticities at every possible combination of quantities of the various products, which is not normally available. At best they may indicate the need for realignment, but not the necessary amount of realignment. The other rules are either imprecise or are valid only under special circumstances.

In the last section of this chapter we examine some additional important points that rise out of the contestable markets theory. These points are mostly theoretical, yet because of their policy implications they have provoked significant debate. They have to do with the old issues of sustainability and the need for an exclusive monopoly franchise.

Monopolies in Contestable Markets

In the single product case we saw that a natural monopoly is not sustainable unless it operates in the output region where economies of scale exist. Even in that case, the sustainable output price is greater than marginal cost, since the latter results in the firm being unable to cover its costs. In the multiproduct monopoly the socially optimal Ramsey prices are by definition sufficient to allow the monopolist to break even. The question that arises is whether these prices are also sustainable, allowing the firm to operate without protection from competitive entry. Recall that sustainability implies that the firm can successfully defend itself under perfectly free entry conditions, such as those present in contestable markets.

For such multiproduct monopolies a remarkable result was proven by Baumol *et al.* (1977) which is known as the *weak invisible hand theorem*. This result states that under certain assumptions, including a cost function exhibiting both scale economies and transray convexity, the Ramsey prices and their corresponding outputs form a sustainable industry configuration. These prices therefore allow the monopoly to operate without the protection of an exclusive franchise, even when its markets are perfectly contestable.

The policy implications of this theorem are indeed surprising. Suppose that we have markets for the monopoly's various products that are close to being perfectly contestable. The weak invisible hand theorem states that an incumbent natural monopolist may be able to operate under completely free entry conditions without any fear of competitor entry. It can protect itself only by choosing the particular vector of prices that maximize social welfare without enabling the firm to realize any economic profit. For such situations, therefore, completely free entry guarantees all the benefits of natural monopolies without any of the drawbacks associated with their regulation.

The questions that arise now concern the practical significance of this result. How close to perfect contestability are the real-life natural monopolies? How plausible are the sufficient conditions for the validity of the weak invisible hand theorem? If a natural monopoly is usually sustainable, as postulated in these sufficient conditions, then public policy can concentrate its efforts upon the removal of restrictions to entry instead of focusing on regulation. By contrast, the regulators would be faced with hard policy choices if it turns out that a natural monopoly's markets are contestable but no sustainable prices exist.

The answers to both questions are still shrouded in controversy. Starting with the second question, it is obvious that there would be unsustainable multiproduct monopolies, given that there are single-product natural monopolies that are unsustainable. As an additional illustration, we present here a well-known example, due to Faulhaber (1975), of a natural monopoly which possesses subadditive costs, but in which no price exists capable of protecting the firm against free entry.

Suppose that we have three communities that are to be supplied with water from the same plant. The cost of supplying any one of them, denoted by $C(1)$, is 300. The cost of supplying any two of these communities is $C(2) = 400$. The cost of supplying all three communities is $C(3) = 650$. It is easy to see that this cost is subadditive, and that the water supply is a natural monopoly: we have $C(2) < 2C(1)$, and $C(3) < C(2) + C(1) < 3C(1)$.

Nonetheless, there is no sustainable set of prices in this example. The stand-alone cost of each of the three different services is 300, and no community would be willing to pay more than this amount. Similarly, no pair of communities would be willing to pay more than 400, since they can obtain the service on their own for this amount. Since every one of the three possible pairs of cost allocations must be below 400, it can be easily shown that all possible three-way cost allocations must not exceed 600.[13] This is insufficient to cover the total cost of 650 for supplying all three communities with water. No matter how 650 is apportioned between the three firms, there would always be an incentive for two of them to go it alone and reduce their costs.

What this example shows is that even when a natural monopoly exists, it is conceivable that no prices exist that cover the costs while still remaining less than the costs of supplying only part of the total. Such prices, when they exist, are free of any *cross-subsidization* between the various classes of buyers of its products. Further, such prices have no necessary connection with the Ramsey prices. The latter depend upon both costs and demand, while subsidy-free prices are concerned only with the costs of the various alternative supply methods. Hence, for all its attractiveness and theoretical elegance, the weak invisible hand theorem cannot be assumed to hold in all realistic cases, such as the example presented above.

The next question concerns the contestability of real-life natural monopolies. Recall that the conditions for contestability are the absence of sunk costs and the "sluggishness" of retaliatory price reductions by incumbents in the event of entry. Neither condition is likely to be completely fulfilled in any practical situation. Most arguments concern whether they are approximately fulfilled. The areas in which contestability theory has been applied in practice are the transportation industries, namely airlines, trucking, and bus and taxi companies. In these areas the first contestability condition, the absence of sunk costs, is approximately valid given the ease of resale of most transportation equipment. It is the fulfillment of the second condition for which doubts have been raised by several opponents of contestability.

The essence of contestable markets is the feasibility of *hit and run* entry, in which a new firm can enter, realize profits, and then exit costlessly from the market. For such entry to be possible there must be a time interval during which the entrant can count on pre-entry incumbent prices staying the same. This is a restrictive condition, and unlikely to be fulfilled. It can be realized only if an incumbent's price adjustments are slow, giving sufficient time for the entrant to realize some profit. This is rather unrealistic, as several reviewers of the book by Baumol *et al.* (1982) that introduced contestability have pointed out.[14] More recently Schwartz (1986) has argued that even in the much discussed example of the airline deregulation, the supposed great success of contestability, incumbents have begun to change prices much more rapidly in recent years. The only reason they didn't do so before was because of the remnants of the regulatory system that continued to have some effect during the transition period.

In their most recent (1986) contribution, Baumol and Willig have admitted that airlines are rather less contestable than initially believed. They claimed, though, that the main reasons were shortages of airport and air control facilities as well as long delivery times for new aircraft. As a result, they believe that "trucks, barges and even buses may be more highly contestable than passenger air transportation."[15] They also point out that contestability theory, by its contributions in the areas of natural monopoly and relative pricing, has also been used as a benchmark for industries that are clearly not contestable. As an example, they cite the case of the railroad industry in the U.S., where recent regulatory decisions have used concepts borrowed from that theory.

These comments will close our discussion of multiproduct monopolies and contestable markets, to which we shall return in Chapter 10 (which deals with Canadian regulatory policies). There is little doubt that contestability theory has had a major impact on our thinking about monopolies and multiproduct industries. This theory has provided a benchmark for the regulation of natural monopolies similar to the standard of perfect competition for competitive industries. It has also had a significant impact in practice, being incorporated in regulatory thinking in several U.S. industries. Recently, though, the tide seems to be turning against more widespread applications of contestability, as we shall see in the second part of this book.

Conclusions

Several sectors of the economy must operate under a monopoly industry structure, given the existence of natural monopoly conditions. In the absence of any restrictions on their behaviour, these sectors will operate as profit-maximizing monopolists. The undesirable welfare consequences of such behaviour have prompted the search for regulatory mechanisms that are both fair and efficient. This search has not yet had a completely satisfactory outcome.

The dominant method of regulation has been the restriction of competitor entry coupled with a constraint on allowable profits. In single-product monopolies such a method has been shown to produce at times inefficient and non-cost minimizing choices of inputs. This result, though, is controversial, and has not been demonstrated empirically to everybody's satisfaction. Currently there is a search among economists for alternative regulatory mechanisms, coupled with the privatization of publicly-owned monopolies in the U.K.

In the area of multiproduct monopolies the most pressing current issue in Canada is the determination of the relative prices of the various products and services of the regulated firm. A set of prices that are alleged to maximize welfare, the Ramsey prices, have attracted much attention from theorists and practitioners alike. These prices, though, require massive realignment of existing rates in some regulated industries, and have not been implemented in Canada as yet.

In both single- and multi-product monopolies attention has been centered in recent years on entry conditions, were these to be allowed. A natural monopoly may or may not be able to protect its territory against would-be competitors under completely free entry conditions. Under such conditions, and for certain types of cost configurations of the monopolies, it can be shown that the resulting structure and conduct of the industry has very attractive welfare properties. These properties provide a standard for natural monopolies, similar to that of perfect competition in other industry structures. The realism, though, of both entry and cost conditions in cases of practical interest has been seriously questioned.

The lack of totally satisfactory solutions to the problems associated with the regulation of privately-owned monopolized industries has prompted a number of developments on the public policy front. One is the operation of the monopolies as public enterprises, as is currently the case in several important Canadian industries. These, however, have their own drawbacks from the point of view of efficiency. The other more recent development has been the so-called deregulation movement. This amounts to the removal of the twin restrictions of protection from entry and curbs on firm behaviour. The reasoning behind deregulation is that actual or potential competition from new entrants will force efficient behaviour on the monopolist.

The current status of deregulation in Canada will be surveyed in Chapter 10, together with other public policy issues associated with monopolies and/ or regulation. The next two chapters examine firms' conduct in oligopolistic industry structures. Chapter 4 focusses on the short run, while Chapter 5 deals with actual and potential entry into a sector. This latter chapter is also relevant to monopolies, since it analyzes entry conditions that are valid as well for monopolistic industries.

Appendix 3A THE FRONTIER OF A MULTIPRODUCT NATURAL MONOPOLY[16]

The deregulation movement of the late 1970s and 1980s in both the U.S. and Canada has raised persistent questions about the extent of public policy protection to be accorded to multiproduct monopolists. Is it desirable to provide all products or services under an exclusive monopoly franchise? Alternatively, should entry and competition be allowed in some of the submarkets served by a multiproduct firm? These questions are known as the problem of the determination of the regulatory frontier. This appendix describes the economic approach to the solution of this problem. While incomplete and at times ambiguous, this approach is nonetheless an indispensable complement to public policy decisions in several regulated industries.

The need for such decisions arises from requests by would-be competitors to enter and compete with the monopolist for the supply of some of its products or services. These requests are based on the claim that these products or services do not belong to the natural monopoly domain, given that the would-be suppliers are by themselves able to provide them at lower prices. The typical counterargument offered by the monopolists is that the entrants would be engaging in the so-called *creamskimming*. This argument is based on the alleged cross-subsidization of the costs of some of the products by the excess revenues raised from those products threatened by entry. According to the creamskimming arguments, the only reason profitable entry is possible is that public policy has imposed upon the monopolist the obligation to cross-subsidize certain products or services. Competition would destroy the excess revenues and render such cross-subsidization infeasible.

From the discussion in the main body of Chapter 3 it is possible to recast these arguments in terms of the concepts introduced in the context of pricing in multiproduct firms. The would-be entrants base their requests on the argument that prices exceed the stand-alone costs for some products, and hence the natural monopoly does not extend to these products. The incumbent monopolists counter that it is the relative prices that are incorrect, i.e. not based on the corresponding costs, and that a realignment of these prices would destroy all incentives for entry. Allowing such entry would, according to them, achieve two undesirable outcomes: eliminate the (presumably) socially desirable cross-subsidization; and increase the total cost of supplying the entire industry output, given the existence of a natural monopoly.

Both arguments hinge around the extent of the natural monopoly. If a natural monopoly exists in the provision of all products then industry costs are minimized by providing all of them through a single firm. If it does not exist then it is cheaper to allow entry. The question of relative pricing is not relevant to the basic policy issue of competitive entry. If cross-subsidization between different classes of consumers is considered desirable, it is still possible to achieve it even when entry is allowed. This can be done, for instance, by imposing a tax on entrants equal to the desired cross-subsidy.

Examples of industries in which these issues were raised are airlines, railroads, and (especially) telecommunications. For instance, cross-subsidization of low-density routes by the more popular routes has been offered as an argument against airline deregulation. In telecommunications the pressure to deregulate several of the services, such as private lines, data transmission, and long-distance voice messages, has been going on for many years in Canada, and for a much longer period in the U.S. It is the telecommunications industry that will be used as an example here, given the fact that deregulation remains a current issue and is likely to do so for the foreseeable future. The methodology, though, is clearly applicable to all multiproduct industries.

The basic method is easy to understand. Since the existence of a natural monopoly depends on the subadditivity property of the multiproduct cost function, it is important to develop estimates of this function. Once the functional shape of costs is known from these estimates it is relatively easy to test for subadditivity. The problems arise in practice from two sources: there is some disagreement on the appropriate estimation techniques, given the limited amount of data available to the econometricians; and the inferences drawn from the statistical tests depend very much on the specific structure of the hypotheses to be tested, and cannot provide firm proofs of the existence or not of a natural monopoly. This second problem is more serious than the first, since it means in practice that the argument will be lost by the party that was required by the regulator to provide the burden of proof.

Consider a two-product industry in which it must be ascertained whether a natural monopoly exists. The cost function depends on the industry output quantities Q_1 and Q_2 as well as the prices of the inputs. Suppose that we have three production inputs, capital K, labour L, and raw materials M, with corresponding prices W_K, W_L, and W_M. Then the cost function is a function of five variables: $C(Q_1, Q_2, W_K, W_L, W_M)$. As a first step we must therefore estimate this functional form from the available data. This means that we must find the best-fitting (in the statistical sense) function from a chosen class to the following cost relation:

$$C = C(Q_1, Q_2, W_K, W_L, W_M) \qquad \textbf{Eq. (3A.1)}$$

Here C is the total cost of production, and the other variables represent the observed values in time-series data.

The estimation must take into account the particular context in which the industry has been operating during the period covered by the data. Suppose for instance that both products have been covered by an exclusive monopoly franchise during the entire period. Suppose also that a would-be entrant challenges this industry structure by declaring its wish to compete with the incumbent for the supply of Q_2. Then the cost function will be estimated from the monopolist's observed cost, output levels, and input prices during a sufficiently long time period. This estimation must also be adapted in order to account for the existing regulatory regime.[17]

The effect of entry can be evaluated once the cost function is available in analytical form. This is done by projecting possible post-entry scenarios concerning the division of Q_2 between incumbent and entrant, as well as the probable values of the output levels and input prices. Suppose for instance that we estimate that the entrant will produce a share τ of the output of Q_2, with $1 - \tau$ going to the incumbent. We must examine whether cost subadditivity holds at these production levels. Neglecting for simplicity the dependence of cost on the input prices, we must test whether

$$C(Q_1, (1 - \tau)Q_2) + C(0, \tau Q_2) \geq C(Q_1, Q_2) \qquad \textbf{Eq (3A.2)}$$

for all plausible values of the entrant's market share τ.

The main difficulty in this test arises with the term $C(0, \tau Q_2)$. To evaluate it one must project the functional form estimated from Equation (3A.1) to the range of a zero value for Q_1. This range normally lies outside the observed data. There is therefore a question about the reliability of the tests, which it is not possible to resolve at the time the decisions must be taken.

A more fundamental question, though, is the meaning of the statistical test. Suppose that the basic hypothesis is that Equation (3A.2) holds with equality. If this hypothesis is rejected, we can safely infer that a natural monopoly exists and that entry should not be allowed. If, however, the tests fail to reject the hypothesis, we cannot assume that a natural monopoly does not exist. All that we can say is that the competitive alternative is not rejected by the data.

At this point the regulators must decide who will bear the burden of proof. If it is the monopolist which must demonstrate its alleged superiority, entry would be allowed. If, however, it is the would-be entrant which must prove that a natural monopoly does not exist, then entry would be rejected. Thus, the statistical tests may fail to provide a clear-cut answer, even after allowance for the estimation imperfections. Only in cases of obvious superiority of one structure over the other is such a clear-cut answer available.

Examples of such natural monopoly tests are to be found in the telecommunications industry in both Canada and the U.S. In Canada, Fuss and Waverman (1981) estimated a cost function for Bell Canada with three inputs and three outputs. The latter were basically the local and long-distance message services, the competitive services such as private line, and some other minor services. They then tested whether efficiency gains would result from concentrating the production of all competitive services into Bell Canada as well. The estimates of product-specific economies of scale failed to reject the hypothesis that private line services were produced under constant returns to scale, implying that the existence of natural monopoly could not be proven.

In the U.S. the estimates by Evans and Heckman reported in Evans (1983) used data from the Bell system over the 1947-1977 period. They distinguished three inputs, and two outputs (local and long-distance services). Their tests similarly failed to confirm the hypothesis that product-specific scale economies existed at the observed output levels. Since such economies are a sufficient condition for a natural monopoly, the existence of the latter could not be inferred.

In conclusion, therefore, the determination of the regulatory frontier is a mixture of value judgments and econometric estimates. The former hinge on who should bear the burden of proof, while the latter are objective examinations of the data to determine whether a clear picture emerges. While an element of arbitrariness remains in this procedure, the empirical work helps to sort out the cases where an objective decision can be made on economic grounds.

Appendix 3B THE MATHEMATICS OF MONOPOLY REGULATION

I) Unregulated Single-product Firm

If $D(Q)$ is the inverse demand curve and $C(Q)$ the cost function then profit $\pi = QD(Q) - C(Q)$ is maximized by setting $\frac{d\pi}{dQ} = 0$, or $\frac{d[QD(Q) - C(Q)]}{dQ} = 0$, yielding $MR = \frac{d[QD(Q)]}{dQ} = \frac{dC(Q)}{dQ} = MC$, Q.E.D. For a linear demand curve, $D(Q) = a - bQ$, $a > 0$, $b > 0$, we have $QD(Q) = aQ - bQ^2$, and $MR = \frac{d[QD(Q)]}{dQ} = a - 2bQ$.

Subadditivity   Suppose firms in the industry are characterized by a *quadratic* cost function, $C(Q) = d + cQ^2$, where d and c are > 0. The average cost function $AC(Q) = \dfrac{C(Q)}{Q} = \dfrac{d}{Q} + cQ$ is U-shaped, reaching its minimum at the MES level Q_0 at which $\dfrac{d[AC(Q)]}{dQ} = -\dfrac{d}{Q^2} + c = 0$, yielding $Q_0 = \left[\dfrac{d}{c}\right]^{1/2}$. It will be shown that subadditivity may hold for $Q > Q_0$.

Suppose the industry output Q_I is divided between two firms. One firm produces q and the other $Q_I - q$. The total industry cost of production, therefore, is $C(q) + C(Q_I - q) = 2d + cq^2 + c(Q_I - q)^2 = 2d + 2cq^2 + cQ_I^2 - 2cQ_Iq$.

The optimal partition of Q_I between the two firms is found by determining the value of q that minimizes $C(q) + C(Q_I - q)$ for a fixed Q_I. Differentiating and setting the derivative equal to zero is $\dfrac{d[C(q) + C(Q_I - q)]}{dq} = 4cq - 2cQ_I = 0$, which results in $q = Q_I/2$. Hence, the optimal duopoly is achieved by splitting Q_I in two equally-sized firms. This results in a total industry cost of $2\,C(Q_I/2) = 2d + 2c(Q_I/2)^2 = 2d + cQ_I^2/2$.

A monopoly can produce the industry output Q_I at a lower cost than the duopoly if $C(Q_I) < 2C(Q_I/2)$, or $d + cQ_I^2 < 2d + cQ_I^2/2$, from which we get $Q_I < \left[\dfrac{2d}{c}\right]^{1/2}$. This last quantity is larger than the value $Q_0 = \left[\dfrac{d}{c}\right]^{1/2}$, implying that subadditivity holds and the natural monopoly exists for $\left[\dfrac{d}{c}\right]^{1/2} < Q_I < \left[\dfrac{2d}{c}\right]^{1/2}$, even though economies of scale have been exhausted.[18]

II) The Averch-Johnson Model

Given the production function $Q = F(K,L)$, the demand curve $D(Q)$, the input prices r and w, and the rate of return constraint $QD(Q) - wL \leq sK$, where $s > r$, we must solve the problem:

$$\text{Max } \{QD(Q) - wL - rK\} \qquad \textbf{Eq. (3B.1)}$$
$$Q,L,K$$
$$\text{subject to } Q = F(K,L), QD(Q) - wL \leq sK^{19} \qquad \textbf{Eq. (3B.2)}$$

Substituting for Q from Equation (3B.2) in the revenue, we get $QD(Q) = F(K,L)D(F(K,L)) \equiv R(K,L)$, the firm's revenue as a function of the input quantities. The problem now becomes:

$$\text{Max } \{R(K,L) - wL - rK\}$$
$$L,K$$
$$\text{subject to } sK - [R(K,L) - wL] \geq 0$$

This problem in constrained maximization is solved by adjoining the constraint to the objective function with a nonnegative Lagrange multiplier λ. Hence, we now have, for $\lambda \geq 0$:

$$\text{Max } \{R(K,L) - wL - rK + \lambda(sK - R(K,L) + wL)\} \quad \textbf{Eq. (3B.3)}$$
$$L,K,\lambda$$

This yields the following system, if $R_L \equiv \dfrac{\partial R(K,L)}{\partial L}$, $R_K \equiv \dfrac{\partial R(K,L)}{\partial K}$:

$$(1-\lambda)\frac{\partial R}{\partial L} - w(1-\lambda) = 0 \text{ or } (1-\lambda)R_L = w(1-\lambda) \quad \textbf{Eq. (3B.4)}$$

$$\frac{\partial R}{\partial K}(1-\lambda) - r + \lambda s = 0 \text{ or } (1-\lambda)R_K = r - \lambda s \quad \textbf{Eq. (3B.5)}$$

$$\lambda(sK - R(K,L) + wL) = 0 \quad \textbf{Eq. (3B.6)}$$

If $sK > R(K,L) - wL$ then Equation (3B.6) implies $\lambda = 0$, which means that (3B.4) and (3B.5) now become $R_L = w$, $R_K = r$. These, however, imply that the marginal revenue products of both inputs are equal to their prices, which corresponds to the unregulated monopoly's input choices. If this solution is feasible then regulation is ineffective. We assume that s is sufficiently small to preclude this case. Then $\lambda > 0$ and $sK = R(K,L) - wL$.

Similarly (3B.5) implies that $\lambda \neq 1$, given that $r \neq s$. Hence, (3B.4) becomes $R_L = w$. The necessary conditions, therefore, become:

$$R_L = w \quad R(K,L) - wL = sK \quad R_K = \frac{r}{1-\lambda} - \frac{\lambda s}{1-\lambda} \quad \textbf{Eq. (3B.7)}$$

The solution of (3B.7) provides the values of K, L, and λ, corresponding to the optimal input choices of the regulated monopolist.

The four Averch-Johnson propositions follow from an analysis of (3B.7) under various "reasonable" restrictions on the shape of the demand and production functions. For instance, the first, second and fourth propositions are true if we assume that the revenue function QD(Q) has a unique maximum, defined by $\dfrac{d[QD(Q)]}{dQ} = 0$, or $D(Q) + QD'(Q) = 0$, with $\dfrac{d[QD(Q)]}{dQ}$ positive (negative) for Q smaller (larger) than at the maximum. It suffices to use the relation $R_L = w$ to define an implicit function L(K). Then it can be shown[20] that the curve $R(K,L(K)) - wL(K)$ also achieves a unique maximum as a function of K. The optimal choice K_s of K is the intersection of that curve with the line sK, as shown in Figure 3B.1.

By contrast, the optimal choice K_M of the unconstrained monopolist is at the point where the tangent to the curve has slope r, which is $< s$ by assumption. This proves that $K_s > K_M$, that K_s does not minimize cost (since K_M does), and that K_s increases as s decreases. As for the third Averch-Johnson proposition, that $K_s/L(K_s)$ exceeds the cost-minimizing proportion, it can also be shown to be true given that the capital-labour ratio decreases along an isoquant.[21]

FIGURE 3B.1
The regulated firm's capital stock

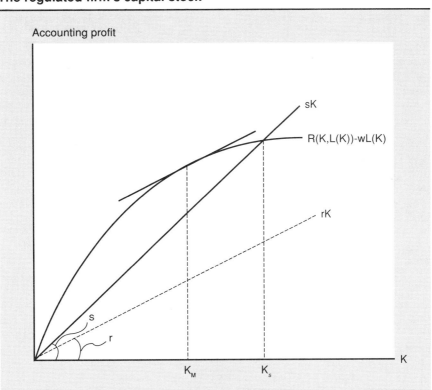

III) Determination of the Ramsey Prices

Given a two-output monopoly firm, with cost function $C(Q_1, Q_2)$, and demand functions (assumed separable) $D_1(Q_1)$ and $D_2(Q_2)$, we must determine the optimal quantities Q_1' and Q_2', and corresponding prices $P_1 = D_1(Q_1')$ and $P_2 = D_2(Q_2')$. These are chosen by maximizing total surplus

$$\int_0^{Q_1'} D_1(Q_1)dQ_1 + \int_0^{Q_2'} D_2(Q_2)dQ_2 - C(Q_1', Q_2') \qquad \textbf{Eq. (3B.8)}$$

subject to the breakeven constraint

$$Q_1'D_1(Q_1') + Q_2'D_2(Q_2') - C(Q_1', Q_2') = 0 \qquad \textbf{Eq. (3B.9)}$$

For the maximization we associate a Lagrange multiplier μ to (3B.9) and adjoin it to (3B.8). This yields:

$$\underset{Q_1{}', Q_2{}'}{\text{Max}} \left\{ \int_0^{Q_1{}'} D_1(Q_1)dQ_1 + \int_0^{Q_2{}'} D_2(Q_2)dQ_2 + \mu[Q_1{}'D(Q_1{}') + \right.$$

$$\left. Q_2{}'D(Q_2{}')] - (1+\mu)C(Q_1{}',Q_2{}') \right\} \qquad \textbf{Eq. (3B.10)}$$

The first-order conditions are:

$$D_1(Q_1{}')(1+\mu) + \mu Q_1{}'D_1{}'(Q_1{}') = (1+\mu)\frac{\partial C(Q_1{}',Q_2{}')}{\partial Q_1{}'} = (1+\mu)MC_1$$

$$\textbf{Eq. (3B.11)}$$

$$D_2(Q_2{}')(1+\mu) + \mu Q_2{}'D_2{}'(Q_2{}') = (1+\mu)\frac{\partial C(Q_1{}',Q_2{}')}{\partial Q_2{}'} = (1+\mu)MC_2$$

$$\textbf{Eq. (3B.12)}$$

together with the breakeven equation (3B.9), where we set $MC_i \equiv \dfrac{\partial C}{\partial Q_i{}'}, i = 1,2.$
Setting now $P_1 \equiv D_1(Q_1{}')$, $P_2 \equiv D_2(Q_2{}')$, and dividing (3B.11) and (3B.12) respectively by P_1 and P_2, we get after re-arrangement:

$$\frac{P_i - MC_i}{P_i} = -\frac{\mu}{1+\mu}\frac{Q_i{}'D_i{}'(Q_i{}')}{P_i} \quad i = 1,2 \qquad \textbf{Eq. (3B.13)}$$

If now we define the price elasticities of demand

$$\epsilon_i \equiv -\frac{P_i \partial Q_i}{Q_i{}' \partial P_i{}'} = -\frac{P_i}{Q_i{}'D_i{}'(Q_i{}')} \quad i = 1,2,$$

and set $k \equiv \dfrac{\mu}{1+\mu}$ then (3B.13) becomes the Ramsey rule:

$$\frac{P_i - MC_i}{P_i} = \frac{k}{\epsilon_i} \quad i = 1,2 \qquad \textbf{Eq. (3B.14)}$$

which is the relation shown in the text, Q.E.D.

Endnotes

1. The concept of contestable markets was introduced and developed in an important book by Baumol *et al.* (1982).
2. For a detailed examination of these tariffs see Phlips (1983), pp. 160-165.
3. For a detailed analysis of the issues involved in determining this fair rate of return see Robichek (1978).
4. See CRTC Telecom 82-5, *British Columbia Telephone Company: General Increase in Rates* decision, May 1982.
5. See, for instance, Averch and Johnson (1962), Baumol and Klevorick (1970) and Klevorick (1971). For differing views see Myers (1972) and Robichek (1978).
6. A summary of much of the early discussion is in Baumol and Klevorick (1970).
7. Examples of such work are Fuss and Waverman (1981), Breslaw and Smith (1982), and Denny, de Fontenay and Werner (1981).
8. For an economic analysis of such proposed policies under various assumptions see Guesnerie (1988), Rees (1988), and Vickers and Yarrow (1988).
9. Expansion along a ray in output space is a proportional expansion of all produced outputs. For instance, in Figure 3.6 the move from B to A is a 100% expansion along the corresponding ray.
10. This was done by Willig (1976).
11. The Ramsey rule was first introduced in the context of regulation by Baumol and Bradford (1971).
12. See Baumol and Willig (1986), p. 30.
13. Let A, B and C denote the three communities, and R(A), R(B) and R(C) the corresponding portions of the total costs that must be raised from each community. As noted, we must have R(A) + R(B) ≤ 400, R(B) + R(C) ≤ 400, and R(A) + R(C) ≤ 400. Summing all three and simplifying, we get R(A) + R(B) + R(C) ≤ 600, Q.E.D.
14. See the article by Dixit (1982), and the reviews by Perrakis (1982), and Spence (1982).
15. See Baumol and Willig (1986), p. 24.
16. Most of the material in this appendix is based on the collection of essays by Evans (1983), and the study by Fuss and Waverman (1981).
17. The estimates must also incorporate the possibility of a changing cost function, because of technological change in the industry during the period covered by the data.
18. The conditions for subadditivity under a general cost function are quite difficult; see Baumol *et al.*, Chapter 5, Appendix 2. The demonstration here is intended only as an illustration.
19. The mathematical proofs of this section are based on Perrakis (1976a).
20. By differentiating $R(K,L(K)) - wL(K)$ we get $R_K + (R_L - w)\dfrac{dL}{dK} = R_K$ given (3B.7).

However, $R_K = \dfrac{\partial}{\partial K}[F(K,L)D(F(K,L))] = [D + FD']\,F_K$ which has the same sign as $D + QD'$, given that $Q = F(K,L)$ and the marginal product F_K is positive.

21. Since, as shown in note 20, $R_K = (D+QD')\dfrac{\partial F}{\partial K}$ and, similarly, $R_L = (D+QD')\dfrac{\partial F}{\partial L}$, we get that $\dfrac{R_K}{R_L}$ is equal to the ratio of marginal products $\dfrac{F_K}{F_L}$ where $\dfrac{\partial F}{\partial K} \equiv F_K$ and $\dfrac{\partial F}{\partial L} \equiv F_L$. However, it is clear that $\dfrac{F_K}{F_L}$ is smaller at the point (K_s, L_s) than at (K_M, L_M), since R_K declines and R_L stays the same as K rises along the curve $(R(K,L(K))) - wL(K)$. The third proposition now follows, since $\dfrac{F_K}{F_L} = \dfrac{r}{w}$ at all cost-minimizing input combinations such as (K_M, L_M), and $\dfrac{F_K}{F_L}$ declines as K increases along an isoquant.

References

Averch, H. and L.L. Johnson. "Behavior of the Firm Under Regulatory Constraint," *American Economic Review*, 52 (Dec. 1962), pp. 1053-1069.

Bailey, E. and D. Coleman. "The Effect of Lagged Regulation in an Averch-Johnson Model," *Bell Journal of Economics and Management Science*, 2:1 (Spring 1971), pp. 278-292.

Baumol, W., E. Bailey, and R. Willig. "Weak Invisible Hand Theorems on the Sustainability of Prices in a Multiproduct Monopoly," *American Economic Review*, 67:3 (June 1977), pp. 350-365.

Baumol, W., J. Panzar, and R. Willig. *Contestable Markets and the Theory of Industry Structure*. San Diego, Cal.: Harcourt, Brace Jovanovich, 1982.

Baumol, W. and D. Bradford. "Optimal Departures from Marginal Cost Pricing," *American Economic Review*, 60:3 (June 1970), pp. 265-283.

Baumol, W. and A. Klevorick. "Input Choices and Rate-of-Return Regulation: An Overview of the Discussion," *The Bell Journal of Economics and Management Science*, 1:2 (Autumn 1970), pp. 162-190.

Baumol, W. and R.D. Willig. "Contestability: Developments since the Book," *Oxford Economic Papers*, new series, Vol. 38 Supplement (Nov. 1986).

Boyes, W.J. "An Empirical Examination of the Averch-Johnson Effect," *Economic Enquiry*, 14:1 (March 1976), pp. 25-35.

Breslaw, J. and J.B. Smith. "Efficiency, Equity and Regulation: an Optimal Pricing Model of Bell Canada," *Canadian Journal of Economics*, 15:4 (Nov. 1982), pp. 634-648.

Courville, L. "Regulation and Efficiency in the Electric Utility Industry," *The Bell Journal of Economics and Management Science*, 5:1 (Spring 1974), pp. 53-74.

Denny, M., A. de Fontenay and M. Werner. "Comparing the Efficiency of Firms: Canadian Telecommunications Companies," paper presented at the conference "Telecommunications in Canada," Montreal, March 1981.

Dixit, A. "Recent Developments in Oligopoly Theory," *American Economic Review* 72:2 (May 1982), pp. 12-17.

Evans, D.S., ed. *Breaking Up Bell*. Amsterdam, Neth.: North Holland, 1983.

Faulhaber, G. "Cross-Subsidization: Pricing in Public Enterprises," *American Economic Review*, 65:5 (December 1975), pp. 966-977.

Fuss, M. and L. Waverman. *The Regulation of Telecommunications in Canada*, Technical Report #7. Ottawa, Ont.: Economic Council of Canada, 1981.

Guesnerie, R. "Regulation as an Adverse Selection Problem: an Introduction to the Literature," *European Economic Review*, 32:213 (March 1988), pp. 473-481.

Klevorick, A. "The "Optimal" Fair Rate of Return," *The Bell Journal of Economics and Management Science*, 2:1 (Spring 1971), pp. 122-153.

Myers, S. "Finance Theory in Rate Cases," *The Bell Journal of Economics and Management Science*, 2:1 (Spring 1972), pp. 58-97.

Nerlove, M. "Returns to Scale in Electricity Supply," *Measurement in Economics*. C. Christ *et al.* eds. Palo Alto, Cal.: Stanford University Press, 1963, pp. 167-189.

Perrakis, S. Book review of Baumol *et al.* (1982), *Canadian Journal of Economics*, 15:4 (Nov. 1982), pp. 774-780.

————. "Rate-of-Return Regulation of a Monopoly Firm with Random Demand," *International Economic Review*, 17:1 (Feb. 1976), pp. 149-162.

————. "On the Regulated Price-Setting Monopoly Firm with a Random Demand Curve," *American Economic Review*, 66:3 (June 1976), pp. 410-416.

Perrakis, S. and J. Zerbinis. "An Empirical Analysis of Monopoly Regulation under Uncertainty," *Applied Economics* 13:1 (March 1981), pp. 109-125.

Peles, Y.C. and J.L. Stein. "The Effect of Rate-of-Return Regulation is Highly Sensitive to the Nature of Uncertainty," *American Economic Review*, 66:3 (June 1976), pp. 278-289.

Petersen, H.C. "An Empirical Test of Regulatory Effect," *The Bell Journal of Economics*, 6:1 (Spring 1975), pp. 111-126.

Phlips, L. *The Economics of Price Discrimination*. Cambridge, Eng.: Cambridge University Press, 1983.

Ramsey, F. "A Contribution to the Theory of Taxation," *Economic Journal*, 37 (March 1927), pp. 47-61.

Rees, R. "Inefficiency, Public Enterprise and Privatization," *European Economic Review*, 32:2/3 (March 1988), pp. 422-431.

Robichek, A. "Regulation and Modern Finance Theory," *Journal of Finance*, 33:3 (June 1978), pp. 693-705.

Schwartz, M. "The Nature and Scope of Contestability Theory," *Oxford Economic Papers*, 38, Suppl. (Nov. 1986), pp. 37-57.

Spann, R. "Rate-of-Return Regulation and Efficiency in Production: an Empirical Test of the Averch-Johnson Thesis," *The Bell Journal of Economics and Management Science*, 5:1 (Spring 1974), pp. 38-52.

Spence, M. "Contestable Markets and the Theory of Industry Structure: A Review Article," *Journal of Economic Literature*, 21:2 (Sept. 1983), pp. 981-990.

Vickers, J. and G. Yarrow, "The Regulation of Privatized Firms in Britain," *European Economic Review*, 32:2/3 (March 1988), pp. 463-472.

Willig, R. "Consumer Surplus Without Apology," *American Economic Review*, 66:4 (Sept. 1976), pp. 589-597.

The Theory of Oligopoly I:

....

Static Analysis

....

A s mentioned in the previous chapter, the size of the market in many Canadian industries is not sufficient to support more than a few firms operating at their minimum efficient scale. When this happens, the industry becomes an *oligopoly*. From its Greek roots, oligopoly literally means a market with few sellers. This chapter examines the behaviour of oligopolistic industries in the short run. It also examines the consequences of such behaviour for economic welfare. Specific policies designed to influence behaviour in oligopolies are studied in Chapter 9.

The Indeterminacy of Oligopolistic Behaviour

In the previous chapter we saw that perfect competition and monopoly are relatively simple and well-defined models. In their simplest forms these models have a unique and well-defined market equilibrium. However, an oligopoly does not have a unique outcome in either the short or long run.

If a small number of firms co-exist in the same market, they cannot help but be aware of their mutual interdependence. It is not clear, though, how these firms will exploit this interdependence. This is especially true since the rules governing their behaviour have been set by government policies. As a result, there has emerged a large variety of behaviour-predicting models in an oligopoly.

The resulting market equilibrium conditions differ widely among these models with respect to desirable attributes. It is the skill of the analyst that determines which model best fits a particular industry. Furthermore, this same industry can shift to behaviour described by a different model when external circumstances change.

The simplest type of oligopoly is a *duopoly*. This occurs when there are exactly two firms in the market, both of them of substantial size. As the number of sellers rises above two, and as the size of the largest seller shrinks, an industry moves towards the type of behaviour represented by competition. Between competition and duopoly, though, there is a large variety of intermediate oligopoly market structures.

For instance, there may be a market with only three or four large firms. An example of this is the North American automobile industry before the 1970s. Alternatively, there may be an industry with one or more large firms, together with numerous small fringe producers. An example of this is the computer industry. In the first example the firms are approximately equally important in shaping their interactions. In the second, however, the large firms are obviously the ones that establish the rules of the game.

Much of our analysis will be developed in terms of a duopoly market situation. This is sufficient to present most of the relevant concepts and problems, at least for the short-run analysis. The set of oligopoly models presented below does not pretend to be exhaustive, but it does cover the most important cases in theory and practice. Some of these, such as the Cournot model, have been around for a very long time; others, such as the conjectural variations approach, are very recent. They were developed in the late 1970s and early 1980s and are still at the frontiers of economic research.

The Competitive and Collusion Models

When only two firms are selling a homogeneous product in the market, there are a number of things that they can do. At one extreme they can be rivals. Each pursues its own self-interest while taking into account the competitor's actions. At the other extreme they can be perfect collaborators. They combine forces and share the market to their common advantage by jointly making important production and pricing decisions.

The first behaviour is described by the *Cournot and Bertrand duopoly models* first presented during the nineteenth century. The second behaviour is described by a *collusion model* or *cartel*.[1] Between these two extremes there are other varieties of behaviour that can become quite complex. For instance, there can be more than two firms in the market, or the product that each firm sells can be differentiated by brand-advertising or by small differences in quality. Alternatively, there may be asymmetries in firm behaviour, with one firm taking the initiative and the other firm(s) following, as in the *Stackelberg duopoly model* that will be examined in this chapter.

In the analysis below the results are sharper if the duopoly consists of two identical firms, selling their product in a single undifferentiated market. Hence, each firm faces the same market demand curve. The main decision variable that the firms choose is product quantity. This automatically determines the product price from the market demand curve once both firms' output has been determined.

The analysis is short-run. This means that the two firms ignore the possibility that other firms may enter the market and challenge them. The models are formulated in a simplified geometric presentation, while a rigorous treatment is reserved for Appendix 4A.

The Cournot Model

We distinguish the two firms by the subscripts $_A$ and $_B$. They choose to produce quantities q_A and q_B. The total quantity sold in the market is $q = q_A + q_B$. The price that will prevail in that market is given by the demand curve, $p = D(q)$. Each firm has a cost function that depends on its own output only: $C_A = C_A(q_A)$, $C_B = C_B(q_B)$.

The essence of the oligopoly problem is that under all circumstances the profit each firm will realize will depend not only on its own decisions, but also on those of its competitors. It is easy to see this. Firm A's profit is $\pi_A = R_A - C_A = pq_A - C_A$, where the revenue $R_A = pq_A$ depends on the amount q_B produced by the competitor, since the price $p = D(q) = D(q_A + q_B)$ is a function of q_B, as well as q_A.

In the Cournot model each firm decides its own level of production independently. It produces the "best" amount from its own point of view, in response to what its rival is doing. It does not take into account the fact that the rival may follow a similar logic. Consequently, the rival actions may not stay constant within the foreseeable future. If both rivals act according to the logic of the Cournot model, however, a unique market equilibrium will be reached.

The analytical determination of equilibrium in the Cournot model is made easiest by means of the concept of the *reaction function*. In a Cournot oligopoly there is one such function for each oligopolist. It gives its optimal output as a function of the output levels of all the other firms.

In our duopoly the Cournot reaction function is defined as follows. The profit π_A of firm A is equal to $\pi_A = pq_A - C_A = q_A \, D(q_A + q_B) - C_A(q_A)$. The optimal level q_A^* of firm A production is found by maximizing π_A with respect to q_A. The analytical details of this maximization are presented in Appendix 4A. Even without these details, however, it is easy to see that the resulting q_A^* depends on the level of output q_B produced by A's rival, given that q_B

influences the prevailing market price. This dependence is expressed in functional form by the Cournot reaction function: $q_A^* = F(q_B)$.

This reaction function can also be derived geometrically, by noting that each firm acts as a profit maximizing monopolist for every given level of the rival's output. Figure 4.1 illustrates this derivation in an example in which the market demand curve is $p = 90\,000 - 2(q_A + q_B)$, while firm A's cost function is quadratic: $C_A = 5q_A^2$. Two alternative levels of q_B, denoted by q_{B1} and q_{B2}, define two corresponding points q_{A1}^* and q_{A2}^* of the reaction function. For instance, for q_B fixed at $q_{B1} = 3\,000$, the demand curve $D_1 D_1'$ facing firm A is $p = (90\,000 - 2q_{B1}) - 2q_A = 84\,000 - 2q_A$. Profit maximization for this firm corresponds now to the familiar intersection of marginal revenue and short-run marginal cost curves MR_1 and SMC_A, where MR_1 was derived from the demand curve $p = 84\,000 - 2q_A$. This intersection yields q_{A1}^*. When q_B is equal

FIGURE 4.1
Geometrical derivation of the Cournot reaction function

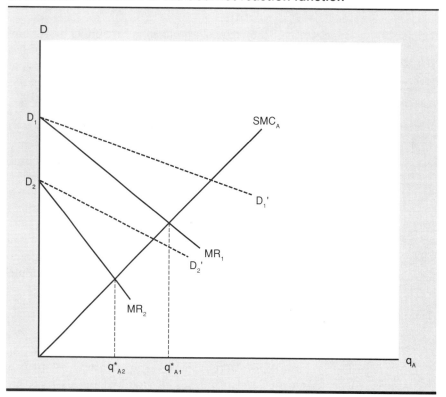

to $q_{B2} = 6\,000$, on the other hand, the demand curve D_2D_2 of firm A becomes $p = (90\,000 - 2q_{B2}) - 2q_A = 78\,000 - 2q_A$. This corresponds to the marginal revenue curve MR_2 whose intersection with SMC_A yields the point q_{A2} of the reaction function.

The complete reaction function for this example is plotted separately in Figure 4.2. It is derived analytically in Appendix 4A, where it is shown that it has the form $q_A^* = \dfrac{45\,000 - q_B}{7}$, which is the curve shown. It is a *decreasing* function, as is typically the case in Cournot models, implying that the firm finds it optimal to produce a lower amount when the rival increases its own output.

The curve shown in Figure 4.2 must be interpreted according to the basic assumption underlying the Cournot model. It gives the best response of firm

FIGURE 4.2
Firm A's reaction function

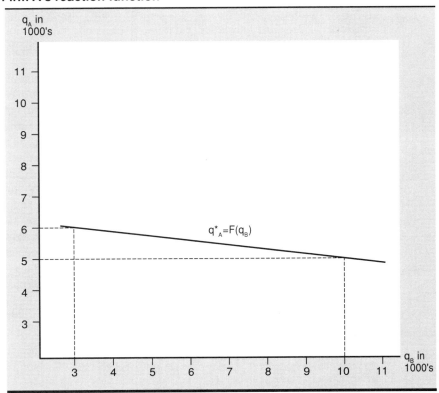

A to every production choice of firm B. For instance, for $q_B = 3\,000$ the ordinate of the curve is $q_A^* = \dfrac{45\,000 - 3\,000}{7} = 6\,000$; for $q_B = 10\,000$ $q_A^* = \dfrac{45\,000 - 10\,000}{7} = 5\,000$; etc. In all these choices firm A reacts automatically to what firm B does, without any consideration of the effect of its own actions upon its rival's behaviour.

Since both firms behave according to the Cournot model, firm B will also choose its optimal production level q_B as a reaction to the chosen level of q_A. When both firms have identical cost functions this optimal level q_B^* will be given by a reaction function $F(q_A)$ that is completely symmetric to $F(q_B)$. Hence, in our example if $C_B = 5q_B^2$ than $q_B^* = F(q_A) = \dfrac{45\,000 - q_A}{7}$. Its shape is also given by Figure 4.2, provided q_A and q_B are interchanged on the two axes.

Suppose that the two reaction functions are plotted on the same diagram, as in Figure 4.3. Suppose also that initially firm A produces 3 000 units and firm B 6 000 units per period, as in point 0. That point is not stable, given that each firm can unilaterally improve its own position if the rival's production remains unchanged. Suppose that it is firm A that moves first. According to the logic of the Cournot model, it will move to its optimal position given that $q_B = 6\,000$. This is point 1 on its reaction function, which is clearly a preferred position by the definition of the reaction functions.

Firm A will have no incentive to move from point 1 as long as q_B remains at 6 000 units per period. But now it is firm B that can improve its position unilaterally, by moving to point 2 on its own reaction function, which has the same q_A as point 1. The logic of the Cournot model unravels now inexorably. The successive moves of each firm to its preferred position will eventually converge to the point E_{CO}, where both reaction functions intersect. This is the *Cournot equilibrium point*. This point is stable. That is, none of the two firms will have an incentive to move unilaterally and independently, the only kinds of moves allowed by the Cournot model.

The determination of the Cournot equilibrium point is very simple in this case because of the symmetry between the two firms, which dictates that q_A must be equal to q_B in equilibrium. In the more general case, when the cost functions are not the same for both firms, the amounts are not going to be necessarily equal at the equilibrium point. The formal system that determines the equilibrium quantities is given in Appendix 4A.

In the numerical example given above, the Cournot equilibrium E_{CO} is found very simply by solving the system $q_A = \dfrac{45\,000 - q_B}{7}, q_B = \dfrac{45\,000 - q_A}{7}$, which yields $q_A = q_B = 5\,625$. In the Cournot equilibrium, therefore, the state

FIGURE 4.3
The equilibria of alternative duopoly models

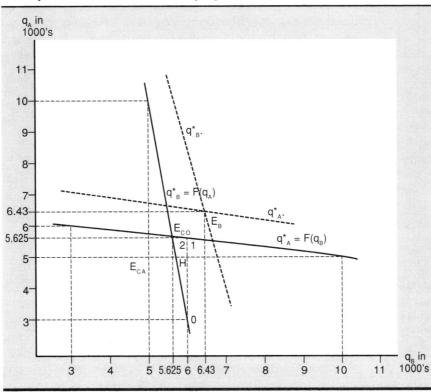

of the duopoly market is as follows: $q_A = q_B = 5\,625$ units $p = 90\,000 - 2(q_A + q_B) = 67\,500$ \$/unit, or $\pi_A = \pi_B = pq_A - 5q_A^2 = 221\,484\,375$ \$/period.

The Cournot equilibrium is the state that the duopoly industry will reach if the two firms compete against each other without any attempt to coordinate their activities. It is not, however, the only equilibrium point resulting from such competition. It was derived from the assumption that each firm acts always as if its opponent will keep its own output unchanged. Since the opponent will in fact react to such actions by changing its output, the Cournot model assumes that firms' actions are always based on erroneous predictions. The consistency of assumed and actual actions and reactions within the Cournot model can take place only under very special circumstances.[2]

The Bertrand Model

Suppose, in the previous example, that both duopolists continue to act independently of each other, but now choose their levels of production as if product price were constant. Since price is a decreasing function of total output $q_A + q_B$ this choice corresponds to a specific conjecture about the opponent's behaviour. It assumes in this case that the other firm will vary its output in the opposite direction and magnitude from one's own choice. Further, if price is assumed unchanged, the best each firm can do is to equate marginal cost to price. This leads us to the Bertrand equilibrium of the duopoly model.

The Bertrand duopoly equilibrium can also be represented by the intersection of two curves similar to the Cournot reaction functions. Indeed, if firm A equates product price to marginal cost, then its behaviour is represented by the relation $p = D(q_A + q_B) = \text{SMC}_A$. This relation contains both output quantities q_A and q_B. Hence, it can be rewritten as a function $q_A^{**} = G(q_B)$. A similar relationship holds also for q_B^{**}.

The intersection of these two functions yields the Bertrand market equilibrium E_B. This is shown in Figure 4.3 for the same numerical example as with the Cournot case. In Appendix 4A it is shown that the two reaction function-type curves corresponding to the Bertrand model in this example are $q_A^{**} = \dfrac{45\,000 - q_B}{6}$ and $q_B^{**} = \dfrac{45\,000 - q_A}{6}$. Their intersection E_B has coordinates given by the solution of the system $q_A = \dfrac{45\,000 - q_B}{6}$, $q_B = \dfrac{45\,000 - q_A}{6}$, which are $q_A = q_B = \dfrac{45\,000}{7} = 6\,429$ units. The corresponding market price is $p = 90\,000 - 2 \times \dfrac{90\,000}{7} = 64\,286$ \$/unit, while the profits turn out to be $\pi_A = \pi_B = pq_A - 5q_A^2 = 206\,630\,800$ \$/period.

The Bertrand equilibrium is stable, insofar as the market will converge to it as long as the basic behavioural rule of the Bertrand model is observed. No matter where the starting point is, the firms will eventually end up at E_B by successive moves. In each move the firms expand output if the prevailing price exceeds marginal cost, and reduce it if price is less than marginal cost. The only output decisions consistent with this behaviour are the ones corresponding to E_B, where they will ultimately converge.

A comparison of these results with those of the Cournot equilibrium shows that the Bertrand equilibrium corresponds to higher quantities and lower prices and profits for the industry.[3] In other words, it represents a more intense state of competition for the two firms. This is not surprising, given that the equality of price and marginal cost that results in this model is the very essence of competitive behaviour as we saw in previous chapters. The firms' decisions are shown in the three diagrams of Figure 4.4. The sum of the output quantities q_A^{**} and q_B^{**} in the marginal cost diagrams is equal to the output q of the demand diagram.

When the market is not homogeneous, the two firms' products are only imperfect substitutes for each other and no single demand curve exists. There is a separate demand curve facing each firm in such a case, which has both firms' prices as arguments. A Bertrand duopoly model in such a differentiated market corresponds to the behavioural assumption that each firm selects its own optimal price-quantity combination by maximizing profits under the conjecture that the rival keeps its own price unchanged. The solution is similar in spirit to our analysis of the Cournot model. It is found to be equating each firm's marginal cost to its marginal revenue, where the latter depends on the rival's price level.

The Bertrand equilibrium is another state that the oligopolists may reach in the absence of any attempts to coordinate their activities. It results from the assumption that firms act always as if the output price will remain constant. Since this price changes as a result of the firm's actions, the Bertrand model also results in inconsistency of assumed and actual actions, except under special circumstances.

FIGURE 4.4
The Bertrand duopoly equilibrium

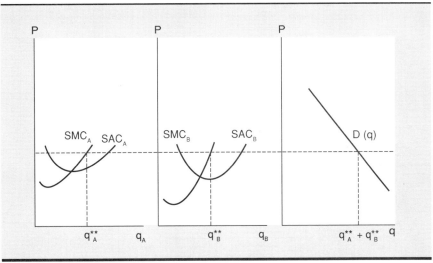

The Collusion Model

Sooner or later the Cournot or Bertrand oligopolists are going to realize that their behaviour will make the industry end up on the equilibrium points E_{CO} and E_B respectively. The question that arises then is whether each one can somehow improve its profit position by adopting a different type of behaviour. The simplest way for the rival firms to achieve such an improvement is by organizing and coordinating their output decisions. This is a perfectly collusive oligopoly or *cartel*.

A duopoly cartel chooses the output levels q_A and q_B by maximizing the sum of profits, $\pi_A + \pi_B$, with respect to both q_A and q_B. In other words, there is a simultaneous choice of the two firms' output levels. Adopting the same notation as before, choose q_A and q_B so as to maximize $\pi_A + \pi_B = q_A p + q_B p - C_A(q_A) - C_B(q_B) = qD(q) - C_A(q_A) - C_B(q_B)$, where $q = q_A + q_B$. That is, the cartel will maximize profits by operating as a multiplant monopolist. Hence, the first-order conditions that determine the quantities produced by the duopoly cartel are that the market marginal revenue must be equal to each firm's marginal cost, or that $MR = SMC_A$, $MR = SMC_B$, as shown in Appendix 4A.

The cartel's decision, denoted by E_{CA} in Figure 4.3, is shown in the three diagrams of Figure 4.5. It is the level of marginal revenue and marginal cost of each one of the two cartel members at which the sum of the output

FIGURE 4.5
The cartel solution in a duopoly

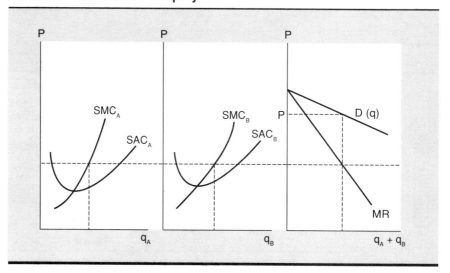

quantities $q_A + q_B$ on the marginal cost diagrams is equal to the output q on the marginal revenue diagram. It is clear from the diagram that the quantities produced by each cartel member are not going to be equal as long as the two firms' cost functions are not the same.[4]

In the example given earlier the two firms have identical cost functions, so that the system $MR = SMC_A = SMC_B$ has a solution in which $q_A = q_B$. This system is shown in Appendix 4A to yield the following solution, representing the state of the market in the cartel model:

$q_A = q_B = 5\,000$ units, $p = 90\,000 - 2(q_A + q_B) = 70\,000$ \$/unit

$\pi_A = \pi_B = 225\,000\,000$ \$/period

A comparison of this numerical result with the corresponding results under the Cournot and Bertrand equilibria shows that the cartel produces a lower industry output, which it sold at a higher price. The two cartel members reaped higher profits. This result is quite general. In oligopolies collusion brings higher prices and total profits and a lower industry output than any other behaviour. Hence, given the superior profit position for both firms, the participants in an oligopoly will tend to act as a cartel in the short run.[5] This tendency occurs provided the law gives the firms the right to form a cartel.

The matter, however, does not stop there. Suppose that the duopoly has reached smoothly the cartel agreement. That is, each firm has decided to limit production to 5 000 units each. Suppose also that firm A is "honest", meaning that it intends to stick with the agreement. Firm B, however, does not have any moral scruples to prevent breaking the agreement if it is in its interest to do so. Can it gain by breaking the agreement?

The answer to this question is "yes, provided the rival sticks to it." Indeed, by going back to Figure 4.3, note that if firm A sticks to its agreed-upon cartel production level represented by point E_{CA}, the "dishonest" firm B can unilaterally improve its position. It does this by increasing its own production to the level represented by point H on its reaction function. In other words, each member of the cartel has an incentive to break the agreement and increase production beyond the agreed level, provided all other cartel members respect the agreement. Otherwise, the industry will revert to the Cournot equilibrium E_{CO}.

This conflict between individually rational actions and the collective interest of the industry as a whole is a characteristic of a large class of behavioural models, whose implications transcend economic theory. Such models have been developed in the social sciences in order to represent situations of conflict and the incentives to form coalitions. They are known under the general term of *game theory*, while the specific class of models with results similar to the oligopoly is the *prisoners' dilemma* type of games. They are examined in some detail in Appendix 4B. In prisoners' dilemma games, each party to the conflict, by pursuing its own interests, ends up in a clearly inferior position with respect to some other achievable outcome. Conversely, if this optimal outcome is somehow reached each party has an incentive to violate it and go after its own objectives, hoping that the others will not detect it. The cartel model in an oligopoly is a typical example of such optimal outcomes where strong incentives exist for their violation.

For that reason, many legal cartels are plagued by frequent breakdowns of the collusion agreement. The more members in the cartel and the more varied their size and cost structure, the more serious are the breakdowns. In such cases the possibility that cheaters will be caught is sharply reduced. "Small" producers can cheat and increase their market share with relative impunity. They are confident that the larger sellers will not find it worthwhile to retaliate against them and risk a general breakdown in cartel discipline.

In a real-world situation, cheating by a cartel member often takes the form of undercutting the officially sanctioned cartel price. It does this to expand the amount that it can sell. Possibly the best-known cartel in recent years is the Organization of Petroleum Exporting Countries or OPEC. It was reported that at least one OPEC member, Nigeria, engaged in secret price cutting by reducing royalties and income tax for the oil companies working there.[6] The fact that Nigeria is not one of the major OPEC members was presumably responsible for the lack of retaliatory action on the part of the rest of the cartel.

The Stackelberg Model

We close this brief survey of duopoly models by presenting the asymmetric Stackelberg model of firm behaviour. This model may be a relevant description of market equilibrium in a duopoly when one firm accepts the role of a leader, while the other becomes a follower. Such a situation can arise if, for instance, the leader firm is larger than the other or has lower costs because of some technological or locational advantage. The Stackelberg model emerges if both firms accept their respective roles.

Suppose that firm A is the leader and B the follower. Then firm B accepts as given the other firm's output choices. It can, therefore, do no better than maximize profits in the spirit of a Cournot duopolist. The end result is that its output q_B would be given by the Cournot reaction $F(q_A)$ as a function of the leader's output q_A.

The leader, on the other hand, knows the follower's behaviour. It can therefore optimize its own choices by taking this behaviour into account. It maximizes its own profits with respect to q_A, by substituting the Cournot reaction function $F(q_A)$ in place of the follower's output q_B.

Analytically, using the same notation as before, the follower chooses q_B by maximizing $\pi_B = q_B\, D(q_A + q_B) - C_B(q_B)$, given q_A. This produces the Cournot reaction function $q_B^* = F(q_A)$. The leader, however, may now choose q_A by maximizing its own profits $\pi_A = q_A\, D(q_A + F(q_A)) - C_A(q_A)$, where the follower reaction has replaced the output q_B.

The equilibrium of the Stackelberg model has an elegant geometric representation, which is shown in Figure 4.6. The curves $\pi_A(q_A, q_B)$ are *isoprofit* curves, each one of which represents all points (q_A, q_B) yielding a constant level of firm A profit π_A. This level increases as the curves get closer to the q_A axis: in the diagram $\pi_A^3 \geqslant \pi_A^2 \geqslant \pi_A^1$. This is easy to see by noting that for any given level q_A the curve π_A^{i+1} has a corresponding higher q_B than π_A^i for $i = 1$, 2, yielding a lower product price and profit. Hence, the optimal leader choice must lie on an isoprofit as close to the horizontal axis as feasible. Since it must also lie on the reaction function $F(q_A)$, the Stackelberg equilibrium E_S, with coordinates q_A' and q_B', is the tangency point between $F(q_A)$ and an isoprofit curve, which is π_A^2 in the diagram. This property is also demonstrated rigorously in Appendix 4A.

As already noted, the Stackelberg model is not in general relevant when the duopoly is symmetric. It becomes important though when there are differences in the firms' cost functions, as discussed further on in this chapter. A

FIGURE 4.6
The Stackelberg equilibrium

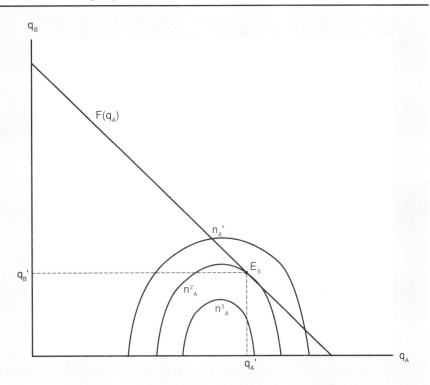

key assumption of this model is that both firms accept their respective roles. If both firms want to be followers the Stackelberg model collapses to the Cournot duopoly. If both firms want to be leaders then there is no equilibrium in the model. The Stackelberg model has also played an important role in representing entry of new firms, with an established firm playing the role of the leader.[7]

Oligopolistic Coordination and Price Leadership

As noted above, the characteristics of industry equilibrium under non-cooperative Cournot or Bertrand behaviour are lower prices and profits and a higher output than under the alternative collusive behaviour. In other words, the non-cooperative equilibria have more desirable properties from the point of view of social welfare than cartel behaviour has. Of course, the opposite is true if one considers the private welfare of the individual oligopoly members. It is therefore in society's interest to discourage joint decision-making in an oligopoly, just as it is in the oligopolists' interest to pursue it.

This conflict between private and social objectives has brought about two general results. First there is a body of law that prohibits outright price fixing and market share allocation agreements in most Canadian industries. Second this conflict has generated a large number of *indirect* methods of coordinating decision-making between members of an oligopoly.

The specific problems facing oligopoly firms and law enforcement agencies will be examined in Chapter 9. Here we shall review briefly some of the practices developed by firms in an oligopoly to approach conditions approximating cartel behaviour, while simultaneously keeping within the letter of the law. A subsequent section will examine the industry features that help or hinder the success of these efforts.

Even under the best of circumstances, when oligopoly members are maximizing joint profits, there is a need for a mechanism that will allow them to *revise* their pricing and market share decisions when underlying economic conditions change. The collusive solution to the oligopoly problem depends upon industry demand and the underlying cost functions of the member firms.

As time passes, these conditions change. Product demand may decrease or grow, depending on the state of the economy or the price changes of substitute products. Cost functions change when the prices of any one of the productive inputs change.

Every time such a change takes place, the optimal cartel price and production shares change. Thus, there is a periodic need to readjust their agreed-upon levels. Since formal consultations are prohibited by law, it is such readjustments that have generated the need for simple and legal coordinating mechanisms.

Another feature that may significantly complicate coordination in an oligopoly is the fact that in real life products are differentiated by brand or quality differences among oligopoly members. Even for such a simple product as crude petroleum there is enough quality heterogeneity among producers to create continuous friction within the cartel over the size of the price differentials corresponding to given differences in product quality. Thus heavier crudes or those that are less advantageously located with respect to markets command a lower price. However, the first price differential decreases when there is an unusually cold winter that stimulates heating oil demand. The second decreases when there is excess ocean tanker capacity that decreases freight rates.[8]

Coordination becomes considerably more difficult when the product sold has complex technical features that differ between suppliers. It is exacerbated even further when there is a fast pace of technological change in the industry that stimulates competition in product quality among members of the oligopoly. This is the situation that prevails now in technologically advanced industries such as aerospace and computers.

The best-known coordination mechanism is *price leadership*.[9] This is a pattern of price-setting in an oligopoly. One firm (the leader) takes the initiative in setting the price, while the other oligopolists match its action with a short time lag. There are two major types of price leadership patterns that have been observed in oligopolies in the past, *dominant firm price leadership* and *barometric price leadership*.

Dominant Firm Price Leadership

This pattern usually occurs in an industry that is tightly oligopolistic. Typically, it occurs where sellers' products are close substitutes, where there are barriers preventing entry of new competitors, and where demand for the industry's output is relatively inelastic.

The firm that acts as a leader is generally the largest in the industry. It may sometimes hold prices below the levels desired by the others if it enjoys cost advantages. For this reason it is also able to retaliate against recalcitrant followers. For instance it may initiate deep price cuts as a punitive measure whenever a member of the oligopoly is caught "cheating" in the implicit agreement to follow the leader.

Dominant firm price leadership in Canada has been found in industries as diverse as tobacco, oil, aluminum and cement, with Imperial Tobacco, Imperial Oil, Alcan and Canada Cement Ltd. playing the role of the corresponding leaders. A particularly well-documented case was that of Canadian General Electric (CGE), which was the undisputed price leader in the market for electric large lamps between 1959 and 1967.[10] In 1976 CGE, together with Westinghouse Canada and Sylvania Canada, were convicted of price fixing in that market. The three firms had a 95 percent share of the market, with CGE accounting for about half that share. The leading firm was responsible for the formulation of the first industry sales plan in 1959, as well as the publication of the revised price list in 1961; both were copied by the other two firms. Further, all three firms engaged in extensive consultations in policing the enforcement of the sales plans and price lists on the part of their wholesale and retail outlets.

Barometric Price Leadership

This is a much looser pattern of price leadership. Here the leader does no more than act as an indicator of changes in market conditions. The leader is not necessarily the largest firm in the industry. Furthermore, it may not always be the same firm.

Under barometric price leadership the leader lacks the power to enforce its own price decisions. The result is that these decisions may occasionally be rejected by the other members of the oligopoly. In such cases the leader has to rescind its initiatives. Quite often in the case of price reductions the leader does nothing more than make official what other firms have initiated through unofficial concessions.

An example of barometric price leadership can be found in the Canadian metal culvert industry during the 1960s. This industry produces metal culverts for drainage. Several of its leading firms had already pleaded guilty in 1959 to a charge of conspiring to fix and maintain uniform prices. In 1974, 10 firms in the industry were again convicted for price-fixing and received heavy fines. These two court cases produced a lot of evidence on the industry's pricing practices over a period of almost 40 years.[11]

The largest firm in that industry was Armco Canada Ltd., accounting for about 40 percent of industry shipments in the early 1950s. Armco was also the leading defendant in both court cases. Yet, it was another culvert producer, Robertsteel Canada, that took the initiative for price fixing during the early 1960s, by advocating an "open price policy", in which each firm would set out its prices and make them available to all customers and competitors. Robertsteel was also the first firm to publish such a price list, with the remaining firms, including Armco, following suit. Shortly thereafter firms in the industry started submitting identical bids to various Ontario local government bodies.

Price leadership, especially in its barometric form, has an excellent advantage as a device for coordinating oligopolists' actions. It is virtually indistinguishable from the normal phenomenon of price changes as a response to changing demand or cost conditions that occur under competitive behaviour. For this reason, price leadership belongs to the gray area of antitrust legislation. It allows the commission of an act that is illegal in its intent (price collusion) by actions that are perfectly normal economic behaviour. Chapter 9 discusses how policy-makers and legislators have coped with this problem.

In addition to price leadership a number of other coordinating devices are available to oligopolists, allowing them to vary prices in response to changes in cost and demand conditions without formal agreements.[12] Foremost among them stand simple product pricing rules. Such rules are known by a variety of names like cost-plus pricing, full-cost pricing, markup pricing, etc. All of them are variants of a simple procedure, in which estimated unit costs of production are increased by a desired profit margin in order to arrive at the product price. If all firms in the industry have adopted the same pricing rule, and if their costs are not too different, the pricing rule will insure that a common price will be maintained as costs or demand change. This price will be only approximately equal to the cartel's profit-maximizing price level. Nonetheless these pricing schemes provide simple and legal, though imperfect, coordination mechanisms that guarantee satisfactory profits over the long run.

Still other simple coordinating devices include the use of inventories and order backlogs as adjustments to short-term demand changes in order to avoid price fluctuations. Given the difficulties of agreeing on a price change, it is much simpler in an oligopoly to ignore the effects of short-term demand fluctuations. These fluctuations then show up as inventory accumulations or order backlogs.

One of the important results of the difficulties of coordinating the actions of oligopolies in the face of changing economic conditions and without formal agreements is that prices tend to fluctuate much less in such markets.[13] A price change, especially a price reduction, may be misunderstood as an attempt to expand the market share of a particular firm. Such a misunderstanding may easily bring a collapse of the collusive price. For this reason, firms refrain from changing prices in response to small changes in demand and cost conditions.

The Kinked Demand Curve Model

There is another theory that seeks to explain why oligopolists tend to refrain from frequent price changes. This is the kinked demand curve model, which was presented independently by Sweezy and by Hall and Hitch, both in 1939.

According to this model, the demand curve faced by an oligopolist does not have the same shape at price levels above and below the prevailing oligopoly price. If a firm in an oligopoly attempts to cut prices then its opponents will match the price cuts. The result is that the firm will maintain its share of the market, albeit at a lower price. By contrast, if this same firm raises prices above the current level then its competitors will refrain from matching these raises. The result is that the firm's share will decline sharply. This means that the demand curve facing the firm when it raises prices is considerably more elastic than the one corresponding to price cuts. This results in a kink at current prices.

Figure 4.7 shows the price and output behaviour of an oligopoly firm under the kinked demand curve model. Segments OA and AB of the demand curve correspond to price raises and price cuts, respectively. The kink of the demand curve at the current price level PA causes a discontinuity in the marginal revenue curves, with OC corresponding to price raises and DD′ to price cuts. The firm equates marginal revenue to short-run marginal cost, with the latter being at the position SMC_1 initially.

If the marginal cost curve now shifts to the position SMC_2, then the firm's level of marginal cost rises from point I to point II. However, both of these points correspond to the same level of current price, represented by point A on the demand curve. Hence, the oligopolist's price will not change in response to a cost shift such as the one shown. It will only change if the shift is much more substantial, raising the SMC curve above point C or lowering it below point D.

FIGURE 4.7
The kinked demand curve model

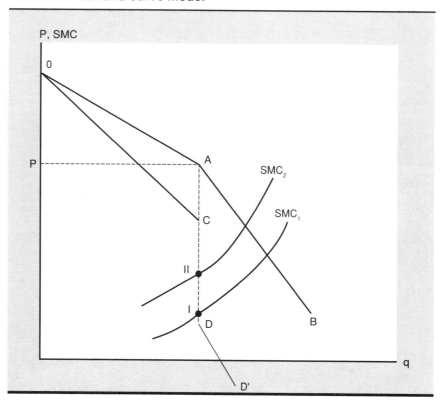

A similar pattern of price stability occurs when it is the demand curve that undergoes small changes. Suppose the demand curve shifts to the right (demand increases) or to the left (demand decreases). In such a case it is the vertical gap segment CD that is displaced right or left, while the curve SMC stays the same. The gap also shifts down slightly for a displacement to the right and up slightly for a displacement to the left.

The result, though, is the same. There is no change in product price as long as the curve SMC continues to intersect the marginal revenue curve at its point of discontinuity.

The main prediction of the kinked demand curve model is that prices in oligopolies tend to stay constant in the face of small changes in cost and demand conditions. This prediction is generally consistent with observed oligopoly behaviour. However, rigid prices also occur in practice in industries that are virtual monopolies, even though the kinked demand curve theory predicts that prices there should be much more responsive to demand or cost changes than in oligopolies. It should also be remembered from the previous section that there are alternative explanations, such as the difficulties of oligopolistic coordination, for the observed price rigidity in oligopolies.

Perhaps the most crucial shortcoming of the kinked demand curve theory is the fact that it does not explain how a particular price level is attained, but only why it stays rigid over time. For instance, suppose the SMC curves of all firms in the oligopoly shift upwards substantially so that they intersect the marginal revenue curve to the left of point C in Figure 4.7. Then all firms will have an incentive to raise prices. If all firms do raise prices, then every firm's pessimistic assumption that its rivals are not going to match price raises is contradicted. This violates the model's central hypothesis. As a result, the model is an incomplete description of firm behaviour in oligopolies.

Conditions Hindering and Helping Collusive Behaviour

Earlier sections of this chapter have established the desirability, from the oligopolists' point of view, of collusive behaviour. We have also seen why such behaviour is, in general, contrary to the public interest and hence is actively discouraged by legislation. This has resulted in a greater price stability in oligopolies than in competitive industries, as well as in the development of indirect coordinating devices that try to achieve the results of collusion without violating the letter of the law. Nonetheless, collusion is easier to achieve in some industries than in others. This section explores the aspects of an industry's structure that make it easy for the firms in the industry to coordinate their actions, with or without formal agreements.

One obvious feature of structure that affects the ability to collude is the number of firms in the industry. This is simply common sense: the more parties are involved the harder it is to reach an agreement in all circumstances. Further, the more parties to an agreement, the easier it is for a participant to violate the agreed-upon behaviour without immediate detection. The OPEC oil cartel example is a classic illustration of both these points. Lengthy negotiations in OPEC's headquarters in Vienna are necessary every time a new oil price is to be decided upon, an event that has been happening more and more frequently during the 1980s. Similarly, the necessity to accommodate the needs of the various oil producers in reaching an agreement, and the sanctions to impose when a member breaks the agreement, have been major sources of strife within the cartel, at times threatening its very existence. These difficulties have been exacerbated during the 1980s by a relative decline in the worldwide demand for oil and the increasing availability of oil from non-OPEC sources.

Yet, OPEC is a cartel in which all the preconditions exist for successful collusion. Public authorities are highly supportive; the industry produces a relatively homogeneous commodity, for which few substitutes exist in many important uses; reliable information on prices, costs and available quantities is plentiful; etc. In spite of these factors, agreement has been difficult to reach and maintain, especially under adverse conditions. One can imagine the difficulties of carrying on similar negotiations in an industry with as many members as OPEC, but in secrecy, against the force of the law, and with the likelihood of sanctions always present.

Within the Canadian context, the metal culvert industry in Ontario is a good example of the difficulties encountered by colluding firms. As already noted, the leading firms in the industry were convicted twice, in 1959 and 1974, of price-fixing behaviour. Between convictions, though, there were some short bouts of intense price competition, in addition to the price-fixing. These were stimulated by new entrants into the industry, which by 1962 already encompassed 22 firms. The formation in 1961 of a strong industry association, the Canadian Steel Pipe Institute, was an attempt to create a coordinating body that would be both legal and effective. It took two years, however, before price collusion took effect. This collusion was maintained until 1967, when a new supplier refused to adhere to it. Price competition in the industry resumed thereafter, due to the inability to enforce sanctions against those who broke the price agreement. The relative ease with which the cartel collapsed within four years should be contrasted with the situation prevailing in that same industry before 1959, the year of the first conviction. As the court documents made it amply clear, price collusion had started in the mid-1920s, and lasted till the mid-1950s. In those times, however, the industry was much more concentrated, with a CR$_4$ of 90 percent during the early 1950s, and with fewer participants.

The metal culvert case illustrates a number of other conditions necessary for the success or failure of oligopolistic coordination. These are the *ease of entry* in the industry, and the *similarity of costs* among the various producers. Clearly, the easier the entry of new firms into the sector, the harder it is to coordinate the price and quantity decisions of firms already in the industry. As we will see in the next chapter, the decision to enter into an industry is a function of the entrant's expected post-entry profits. These in turn depend on the current and expected actions of the existing firms. Oligopolistic coordination must therefore take such potential entry into account, and the easier the entry the harder it is to reach an agreement. The post-1960 difficulties encountered in the metal culvert industry are a case in point. It was the refusal of a new entrant to join the price-fixing agreement that eventually caused the resumption of price competition in that industry during the late 1960s. It became obvious at that time that maintenance of the agreement was no longer possible, given the entry conditions into the industry. As a result, the industry reverted to virtually competitive behaviour.

As we noted earlier, the agreement that was reached during the early 1960s in the metal culvert industry was not initiated by Armco, the largest firm and historical leader. In fact, Armco, which was the lowest-cost producer in the industry, was initially reluctant to join the agreement. This is not surprising, given the difficulty of reaching mutually-acceptable collusive price-quantity combinations whenever firms' costs are different. An example will illustrate this case.

Consider a duopoly with firms A and B, facing an industry demand curve $p = 10-2q$, where $q = q_A + q_B$ is the total quantity produced by both firms. The marginal revenue is therefore $10-4q = 10 - 4(q_A + q_B)$. The two firms have, however, different cost curves C_A and C_B, respectively given by $C_A = 3 + q_A + q_A^2$ and $C_B = 2 + 2q_B + q_B^2$. These correspond to marginal costs SMC_A and SMC_B, respectively equal to $SMC_A = 1 + 2q_A$ and $SMC_B = 2 + 2q_B$.

The various equilibria for this duopoly are derived in Appendix 4A. The results for the cartel are $q_A = 1.1$, $q_B = 0.6$, $p = 6.6$. The corresponding firm profits are $\pi_A = 1.1 \times 6.6 - (3 + 1.1 + 1.1^2) = 1.95$, and $\pi_B = 0.6 \times 6.6 - (2 + 2 \times 0.6 + 0.6^2) = 0.4$. This solution is very obviously not to the advantage of firm B, since firm A gets the lion's share of the total industry profits.

What are the alternative options for firm B? It can threaten to adopt Cournot behaviour. If both A and B act as Cournot players then the industry equilibrium is $q_A = 1.875$, $q_B = 0.9375$, $p = 5.75$, with corresponding firm profits $\pi_A = 1.23$, $\pi_B = 0.6367$. Here the total industry profits are much lower than in the cartel case, but firm B's individual position has improved. Firm A, however, can adopt the role of a Stackelberg leader, bringing the industry to the corresponding Stackelberg equilibrium. The results would be: $q_A = \dfrac{19}{14} = 1.357$, $q_B = \dfrac{37}{42} = 0.881$, $p = \dfrac{116}{21} = 5.524$, $\pi_A = 1.297$, $\pi_B = 0.329$. This represents a slight improvement and a sharp deterioration in the respective positions of firms A and B in comparison to the Cournot equilibrium. In both cases, however, the total industry profits are much lower than in the cartel solution.

For this reason it is in both firms' interest to bargain for a mutually advantageous sharing of the cartel profits. The other equilibria represent threats and counterthreats in establishing bargaining positions. The difficulties of reaching an agreement are clear, though, given the highly unequal division of the total cartel profits. That division is in turn a result of the cost differences between the two firms.

These difficulties of collusion are exacerbated when another type of condition is present, a *high proportion of fixed costs in the firm's total costs*. This condition makes oligopolistic coordination very difficult whenever it coincides with volatile product demand. Firms whose fixed costs are a large share of total costs typically rely on a high sales volume to cover their costs. When demand drops, the losses that such firms incur are particularly high, and the corresponding temptation to increase their sales at the expense of the other oligopolists is very strong. The difficulties of coordination are enhanced in such cases if there are also cost differences between firms, since the industry losses are going to be spread unequally between the various members of the cartel.

Another source of difficulties for colluders is the *heterogeneity of product*. As noted earlier, differences in product characteristics or quality are a standard feature of most industries. Such differences have multiple consequences for any attempts to coordinate the actions of the cartel members: they necessitate long and detailed price lists that set prices for the entire range of products produced by the industry; they increase the cost differences between producing firms, especially if each firm concentrates most of its production in a different subset of the industry's products; and they increase the likelihood of violations of the cartel agreements, since the firms have the possibility of increasing their market share by adhering to the agreed upon prices but improving the quality of their products. This last possibility is particularly pronounced whenever there is a high rate of technological change in the industry, as in computers and telecommunications.

The last category of conditions influencing the ability of oligopolists to coordinate their actions contains factors related to the *social structure* of the industry. Examples of such factors are the stability of the dominant firms in the sector, the tradition of secrecy or openness concerning relations with customers, the existence of a strong industry association, and the frequency with which industry executives interact on matters of common interest. For instance, the Canadian banking sector was until the 1980s a very cohesive group of companies, whose top executives participated very often in meetings presided over by the Governor of the Bank of Canada. This interaction dealt mainly with matters of Canada's monetary policy, but it did also create a favourable climate for the coordination of their pricing decisions. This sector has changed dramatically in recent years because of the introduction of competition by other financial intermediaries, as well as by foreign firms.

All conditions examined in this section refer to the ability of the firms in an oligopolistic sector to reach and maintain the cartel price. A different set of conditions governs the *long-run* stability of the oligopoly, given its collusive behaviour. Such conditions influence the ease of entry into the industry by new firms that are attracted into the sector by the cartel profits. As already noted, such entry will sooner or later destroy the oligopolists' ability to collude. Hence, oligopolistic coordination must take this entry into account. In the long-run, collusion may be sustainable or self-destructing, depending on various conditions. These will be examined in detail in Chapter 5, together with the strategies that oligopolists may follow in each case in order to preserve their cartel profits. It is sufficient to state here that the energy and vigour with which antitrust authorities should pursue colluding oligopolists is directly related to the sustainability of long-run collusion in the fact of new entry. For this reason, entry in an oligopoly has been attracting a lot of attention by economists and antitrust specialists in recent years.

Conjectural Variations

As we saw in the various models analyzed in the beginning of this chapter, the problem of equilibrium in an oligopoly does not have a unique solution. The differing predictions that arise out of the different models have as their root cause the differences in the oligopolists' perceptions of their rivals' actions and reactions. In recent years an interesting attempt has been made to unify all these different oligopoly models into a common formulation, by including a specific modelling of each firm's expectations about its rivals' actions. This has become known as the theory of conjectural variations.

Conjectural variations are a pair of functions attached to each pair of firms in an oligopoly. Each function represents the output response of a firm to a change in an opponent's output. In a duopoly with firms A and B the assumptions of firm A (B) about the behaviour of firm B (A) are represented by the conjectural variation r_{AB} (r_{BA}), the hypothesized change in the output of firm B (A) in response to a change in the output of firm A (B). Then the two firms maximize their respective profits by acting on the basis of their conjectures about their opponent's behaviour.

In Appendix 4A it is shown that with this formulation all duopoly equilibria can be represented by a single system, which contains the conjectural variations r_{AB} and r_{BA}. Such a system yields every one of the three symmetric models, Cournot, Bertrand, and collusion, given the appropriate specification of r_{AB} and r_{BA}. For $r_{AB} = r_{BA} = 0$ we get the Cournot model. For $r_{AB} = r_{BA} = -1$ we have the Bertrand equilibrium, while the collusion result corresponds to $r_{AB} = \dfrac{q_B}{q_A}$, $r_{BA} = \dfrac{q_A}{q_B}$. Each one of these pairs of conjectures would, when substituted into the general system, result in a pair of reaction functions. For instance, the demand curve $p = 90\,000 - 2(q_A + q_B)$ and the cost functions $C_A = 5q_A^2$ and $C_B = 5q_B^2$ result in the following pairs of reaction functions, as shown in Appendix 4A.

$$Cournot: \quad q_A = \frac{45\,000 - q_B}{7}, q_B = \frac{45\,000 - q_A}{7}$$

$$Bertrand: \quad q_A = \frac{45\,000 - q_B}{6}, q_B = \frac{45\,000 - q_A}{6}$$

$$Collusion: \quad q_A = \frac{45\,000 - 2q_B}{7}, q_B = \frac{45\,000 - 2q_A}{7}$$

Similar results hold for the Stackelberg model, with the difference that r_{AB} and r_{BA} have different forms.

An equilibrium with *consistent conjectures* is one in which the hypothesized conjectural variations used to solve the system do turn out to coincide with the actual conjectures derived from the reaction functions. Such an equilibrium is an attractive concept, insofar as hypothesized and actual behaviour are the same. In the above example none of the three equilibria has consistent conjectures, as can easily be seen by differentiating the appropriate reaction function and comparing it with the hypothesized values. Thus, the Bertrand equilibrium assumes $r_{AB} = \dfrac{\Delta q_B}{\Delta q_A} = -1$, while the reaction function yields $\dfrac{\Delta}{\Delta q_A}\left[\dfrac{45\,000 - q_B}{6}\right] = -\dfrac{1}{6}$. Similar results hold for the two other models.

In general, it can be shown that an equilibrium with consistent conjectures always exists. The form of the conjectures, though, depends on the specific expressions for the demand and cost functions. By an appropriate choice of the conjectures it is possible to generate any consistent conjectures duopoly equilibrium between the collusion and competitive points.[14]

Conclusions

Oligopoly is a market structure that results in a non-unique market equilibrium, depending on the behaviour of the firms in the industry. Such behaviour ranges from extreme rivalry to perfect cooperation. The model that correctly represents the state of the industry at any given time depends on the ability of the firms to pursue their interests.

The group view of the firms in the industry is that the perfectly cooperative equilibrium or cartel brings the best results. Such an equilibrium yields the highest price and lowest industry output. Hence, it is not considered desirable from the point of view of social welfare, and a body of law has been developed to prevent the successful achievement of cartel behaviour.

Nonetheless, it is believed that oligopolistic firms will always attempt to reach and maintain the cooperative equilibrium. Their efforts, though, will be complicated by the strong incentives that exist for every individual firm to violate the cartel agreement, provided all the others stick to it. Further, cost differences among firms necessitate side payments or other similar arrangements in order to accommodate high-cost producers. The result is that cartels are often plagued by instabilities and breakdowns, whose frequency of occurrence depends on industry characteristics.

The problems of cooperative oligopoly behaviour are exacerbated in the long run. In such a case the oligopolists must contend with possible new entrants to the industry as well as existing rivals. The impact of such entrants upon industry behaviour will form the topic of the next chapter.

Appendix 4A THE MATHEMATICS OF OLIGOPOLY PRICING

Since $p = D(q)$ denotes the inverse demand curve, and $q = q_A + q_B$ is the total industry output, we have the following systems for each type of equilibrium:

Cournot

We maximize π_A and π_B with respect to q_A and q_B with the other firm's output kept constant in each maximization. Since $\pi_A = pq_A - C_A(q_A)$, $\pi_B = pq_B - C(q_B)$, we get

$$\frac{\partial \pi_A}{\partial q_A} = \frac{\partial[q_A D(q_A + q_B)]}{\partial q_A} - \frac{dC_A(q_A)}{dq_A} = 0$$

$$\frac{\partial \pi_B}{\partial q_B} = \frac{\partial[q_B D(q_A + q_B)]}{\partial q_B} - \frac{dC_B(q_B)}{dq_B} = 0$$

Eq. (4A.1)

from which we get

$$D(q) + q_A \frac{dD(q)}{dq} = \frac{dC_A}{dq_A} = SMC_A$$

Eq. (4A.2)

$$D(q) + q_B \frac{dD(q)}{dq} = \frac{dC_B}{dq_B} = SMC_B$$

The solution of the Equation (4A.2) yields the Cournot equilibrium quantities q_A^* and q_B^*. The two equations represent the reaction functions $F(q_A)$ and $F(q_B)$.

From (4A.2) it is easy to get the Cournot equilibrium for the examples used in the text. In that first example $p = D(q) = 90\,000 - 2q = 90\,000 - 2(q_A + q_B)$, and $C_A = 5q_A^2$, $C_B = 5q_B^2$. We therefore have:

$$\frac{dD(q)}{dq} = \frac{d(90\,000 - 2q)}{dq} = -2 \quad \frac{dC_A}{dq_A} = SMC_A = 10q_A \quad \frac{dC_A}{dq_B} = SMC_B$$

The Equation (4A.2) therefore becomes $90\,000 - 2(q_A + q_B) - 2q_A = 10q_A$, $90\,000 - 2(q_A + q_B) - 2q_B = 10q_B$, yielding the two reaction functions $q_A^* = \frac{45\,000 - q_B}{7}$, $q_B^* = \frac{45\,000 - q_A}{7}$. The solution of this last system is $q_A = q_B = 5\,625$, $p = 90\,000 - 2(q_A + q_B) = 67\,500$ \$/unit.

Similarly, for the numerical example with $p = 10 - 2q$, $C_A = 3 + q_A + q_A^2$, $C_B = 2 + 2q_B + q_B^2$ we get from (4A.2) that $10 - 2(q_A + q_B) - 2q_A = SMC_A = \frac{dC_A}{dq_A} = 1 + 2q_A$, $10 - 2(q_A + q_B) = SMC_B = \frac{dC_B}{dq_B} = 2 + 2q_B$.

Solving this system yields $q_A = 1.1875$, $q_B = 0.9375$ and $p = 5.75$ \$/unit.

Bertrand

Here π_A and π_B are maximized under the assumption that the price p will remain constant, as in perfect competition. As we know from the first chapter, this yields

$$\frac{\partial \pi_A}{\partial q_A} = \frac{\partial [pq_A]}{\partial q_A} - \frac{dC_A(q_A)}{dq_A} = p - SMC_A = 0$$

$$\frac{\partial \pi_B}{\partial q_B} = \frac{\partial [pq_B]}{\partial q_B} - \frac{dC_B(q_B)}{dq_B} = p - SMC_B = 0$$

Eq. (4A.3)

which results in the equation:

$$D(q_A + q_B) = SMC_A = SMC_B \qquad \text{Eq. (4A.4)}$$

The solution of (4A.4) yields the Bertrand equilibrium quantities q_A^{**} and q_B^{**}. In our numerical example the Equation (4A.4) becomes $90\,000 - 2(q_A + q_B) = 10q_A = 10q_B$. The solution yields the Bertrand equilibrium $q_A = q_B = 6\,429$, $p = 64\,286$ \$/unit.

Collusion

As noted in the text, in this model firms maximize jointly the sum $\pi_A + \pi_B$ of their profits with respect to both q_A and q_B. Since $\pi_A + \pi_B = p(q_A + q_B) - C_A(q_A) - C_B(q_B) = (q_A + q_B)D(q_A + q_B) - C_A(q_A) - C_B(q_B)$, the first-order conditions become:

$$\frac{\partial[\pi_A + \pi_B]}{\partial q_A} = \frac{\partial[(q_A + q_B)D(q_A + q_B)]}{\partial q_A} - \frac{dC_A(q_A)}{dq_A} = 0$$

$$\frac{\partial[\pi_A + \pi_B]}{\partial q_B} = \frac{\partial[(q_A + q_B)D(q_A + q_B)]}{\partial q_B} - \frac{dC_B(q_B)}{dq_B} = 0$$

Eq. (4A.5)

from which we get

$$D(q_A + q_B) + (q_A + q_B)\frac{\partial D(q_A + q_B)}{\partial q_A} = D(q) + q\frac{dD(q)}{dq} = SMC_A$$

$$D(q_A + q_B) + (q_A + q_B)\frac{\partial D(q_A + q_B)}{\partial q_B} = D(q) + q\frac{dD(q)}{dq} = SMC_B$$

Eq. (4A.6)

where $q = q_A + q_B$. The Equation (4A.6) yields the quantities q_A and q_B corresponding to the collusion equilibrium.

Applying (4A.6) to the first numerical example we get $90\,000 - 4(q_A + q_B) = 10q_A = 10q_B$. The solution of this system yields the cartel equilibrium $q_A = q_B = 5\,000$, $p = 70\,000$ \$/unit. Similarly, when (4A.6) is applied to the asymmetric duopoly with $p = 10 - 2q$, $C_A = 3 + q_A + q_A^2$, $C_B = 2 + 2q_B + q_B^2$, we get the system $10 - 4(q_A + q_B) = 1 + 2q_A = 2 + 2q_B$, whose solution yields $q_A = 1.1$, $q_B = 0.6$ and $p = 6.6$ \$/unit.

Stackelberg

In this model the follower firm B acts as a Cournot duopolist, maximizing π_B with respect to q_B with q_A kept constant. Hence we have

$$\frac{\partial \pi_B}{\partial q_B} = 0, \quad D(q) + q_B\frac{dD(q)}{dq} = \frac{dC_B}{dq_B} = SMC_B \qquad \textbf{Eq. (4A.7)}$$

The Equation (4A.7), when solved with respect to q_B, yields the Cournot reaction function $q_B^* = F(q_A)$.

Firm A, now acting as a leader, maximizes π_A with respect to q_A, with output q_B being given by the reaction function. Since $\pi_A = q_A D(q) - C_A = q_A D(q_A + F(q_A)) - C_A$, we have

$$\frac{d\pi_A}{dq_A} = \frac{d[q_A D(q_A + F(q_A)) - C_A]}{dq_A} = 0$$

from which

$$D(q_A + F(q_A)) + q_A \frac{dD(q)}{dq} \frac{d(q_A + F(q_A))}{dq_A} = \frac{dC_A}{dq_A} = SMC_A \text{ and}$$

Eq. (4A.8)

$$D(q_A + F(q_A)) + q_A \frac{dD(q)}{dq} \left[1 + \frac{dF}{dq_A} \right] = SMC_A$$

The system (4A.7), (4A.8) yields the Stackelberg equilibrium.

It is also easy to see that the Stackelberg equilibrium corresponds to a tangency of the isoprofit with the reaction function, as represented in Figure 4.6. An isoprofit is a curve on a (q_A, q_B) diagram of the form $\pi_A = K$, where K is a constant. This curve is also a function $q_B(q_A)$; its slope $\frac{dq_B}{dq_A}$ is found by setting $\frac{d\pi_A}{dq_A} = 0$ (since π_A is a constant), from which $D + q_A D^1 \left[1 + \frac{dq_B}{dq_A} \right] = SMC_A$. Comparing this with (4A.8) we can easily see that the latter can be written as $\frac{dq_B}{dq_A} = \frac{dF}{dq_A}$, Q.E.D.

Applying (4A.7) − (4A.8) to the asymmetric duopoly $p = 10 - 2q$, $C_A = 3 + q_A + q_A^2$, $C_B = 2 + 2q_B + q_B^2$ we get from (4A.7) that $10 - 2(q_A + q_B) - 2q_B = 2 + 2q_B$, or $q_B = \frac{4}{3} - \frac{1}{3}q_A$, which is the follower's reaction function.

(4A.8) becomes $10 - 2(q_A + q_B) - 2q_A \left[1 - \frac{1}{3} \right] = 1 + 2q$, and the system yields $q_A = \frac{19}{14}, q_B = \frac{37}{42}, p = \frac{116}{21}$.

Conjectural Variations

Last we examine the unified treatment of equilibrium in a duopoly through the conjectural variations approach. The assumptions of firm A about the behaviour of firm B are represented by the conjectural variation $r_{AB} = \frac{\partial q_B}{\partial q_A}$. Similarly, $r_{BA} = \frac{\partial q_A}{\partial q_B}$ is the conjectured response of firm A to a change in firm B's output. Then the two firms maximize their respective profits by acting on the basis of their conjectures about their opponent's behaviour. We get

$$\frac{\partial \pi_A}{\partial q_A} = \frac{\partial [q_A D(q_A + q_B)]}{\partial q_A} - \frac{dC_A(q_A)}{dq_A} =$$

Eq. (4A.9)

$$D(q) + q_A \frac{dD(q)}{dq} \left[1 + \frac{\partial q_B}{\partial q_A} \right] - SMC_A = 0$$

and a symmetric relation holds for q_B. In deriving the second part of (4A.9) we used the chain rule of differentiation $\dfrac{\partial D(q_A + q_B)}{\partial q_A} = \dfrac{\partial D(q)}{\partial q}\dfrac{\partial q}{\partial q_A} = \dfrac{\partial D(q)}{\partial q}\left[\dfrac{\partial(q_A + q_B)}{\partial q_A}\right]$. The resulting duopoly equilibrium now becomes

$$D(q) + q_A[1 + r_{AB}]\frac{dD(q)}{dq} = SMC_A$$

$$D(q) + q_B[1 + r_{BA}]\frac{dD(q)}{dq} = SMC_B$$

Eq. (4A.10)

The interesting thing about the Equation (4A.10) is that it yields every one of the three symmetric models, Cournot, Bertrand, and collusion, given the appropriate specification of the conjectural variations r_{AB} and r_{BA}. Thus, a simple inspection shows that for $r_{AB} = r_{BA} = 0$ (4A.10) coincides with (4A.2) of the Cournot model. For $r_{AB} = r_{BA} = -1$ (4A.10) yields the Bertrand equilibrium of (4A.4), while the collusion result (4A.6) corresponds to $r_{AB} = \dfrac{q_B}{q_A}$, $r_{BA} = \dfrac{q_A}{q_B}$. Each one of these pairs of conjectures would, when substituted into (4A.10), result into a pair of reaction functions whose intersection determines the corresponding equilibrium. Similarly, the asymmetric Stackelberg model comes out of (4A.10) by setting $r_{BA} = 0$, $r_{AB} = \dfrac{dF(q_A)}{dq_A}$, which coincides with (4A.7), (4A.8).

Appendix 4B   OLIGOPOLY AND GAME THEORY

Oligopoly is an industry structure that results in an indeterminate behaviour, oscillating between conflict and cooperation between the firms. It cannot be adequately modelled by the conventional tools of microeconomic theory. Significant hopes for determinate solutions were raised by the appearance of *game theory*. It was developed by von Neumann and Morgenstern as a tool for the analysis of conflict situations. These hopes have not yet materialized. However, game theory has provided significant insights into oligopoly problems and has thus become an indispensable complement to the study of such problems.[15]

The simplest type of conflicts that can be analyzed by game theory are the so-called two-player *zero-sum* games. In such games the losses of one player are exactly equal to the gains of his opponent. A game of that type can be represented by the *payoff matrix*. In such a matrix the rows represent the strategies of one player and the columns the strategies of the other player. Each entry in the matrix is the payoff to the row player resulting from the choice of the corresponding row and column strategies. The payoff to the column player is the negative of the entry.

Figure 4B.1 shows the payoff matrix for a two-person zero-sum game with three strategies for each player.

The matrix entries show the payoffs to the row player A or the losses to the column player B. For instance the strategy pair a_1 and b_2 results in a loss of 7 for A and a corresponding gain of 7 for B.

For this type of game it can be shown that an equilibrium pair of strategies exists that guarantees for each player higher payoffs than any other strategies, assuming each player tries to maximize his payoffs. This pair is found if player A selects the strategy that maximizes his minimum gain (strategy a_2 in the example), while player B similarly selects the strategy that guarantees the smallest maximum loss (or the largest minimum gain), which is b_3 in the example. The circled entry in the matrix is the best that each player can do. It also represents a stable pair of strategies (an equilibrium), since no player can unilaterally improve his position by adopting another strategy.

Unfortunately this type of game is not generally representative of the types of situations that exist in oligopolies. The zero-sum assumption does not describe adequately the payoffs resulting from the oligopolists' strategies. The two-person, non-zero-sum game that comes closest to an oligopoly model is known in the literature as the *prisoner's dilemma* game. In this game two people,

FIGURE 4B.1
A two-person zero-sum game

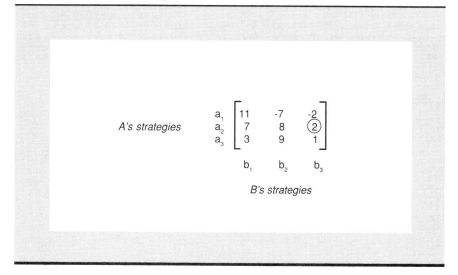

$$
\begin{array}{c}
\textit{A's strategies} \quad
\begin{array}{c}
a_1 \\
a_2 \\
a_3
\end{array}
\begin{bmatrix}
11 & -7 & -2 \\
7 & 8 & \boxed{2} \\
3 & 9 & 1
\end{bmatrix} \\
\qquad\quad b_1 \quad\;\; b_2 \quad\;\; b_3 \\[4pt]
\textit{B's strategies}
\end{array}
$$

A and B, are caught during the commission of a minor crime. They are suspected of a more serious crime, but the district attorney lacks proof. He therefore wants a confession from one of the suspects. The two suspects are separated and interrogated soon after they are caught. If one of them confesses and the other doesn't, they are told, then the one who confesses can turn state's evidence and go free. The other gets a ten-year sentence. If both of them confess they both get five years. If neither of them confesses they get one year each.

Figure 4B.2 shows the "payoff" matrix for this game. Each element of the matrix consists of a pair of negative numbers, representing years in prison for each player resulting from the corresponding strategy pair; player A's payoffs are listed first. It is clear from the matrix that for each player reasoning independently, the best strategy is to confess under all circumstances, since such a strategy yields the highest "payoff" (lowest sentence) in each case no matter what the other player does. The result is that the equilibrium point of this game is the pair of "confess" strategies, with each player getting five years.

This result makes both players much worse off in comparison to the "don't confess" pair, in which the suspects each get only one year in prison. If they could communicate with each other, there is little doubt that this is the equilibrium that they would reach. Hence, individually rational decisions that were reached independently by each player have resulted in a clearly inferior outcome.

FIGURE 4B.2
The prisoners' dilemma game

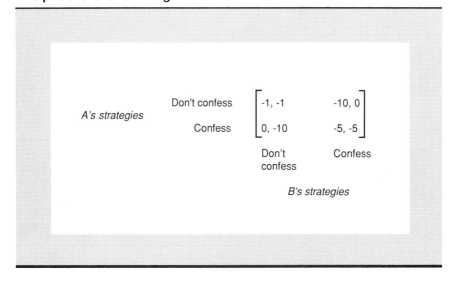

A duopoly market structure is very similar to the prisoner's dilemma game, at least in its static, single-move form. Consider again the two firms A and B of the numerical examples presented in Appendix 4A, with the market demand curve $p = 90\,000 - 2(q_A + q_B)$ and the cost functions $C_A = 5q_A^2$, $C_B = 5q_B^2$. We concentrate on the two alternative strategies derived from the Cournot and collusion models, i.e. with production levels of 5 625 and 5 000 respectively. In a game matrix, Figure 4B.3 shows the payoffs (profits) to the two, rounded off to the nearest million dollars. It is clear that in this game the Cournot strategy of each firm producing 5 625 units is a dominant one. It results in higher payoffs no matter what the other firm does. Yet, as we saw earlier, the collusion strategy of each firm producing 5 000 units is a superior one. It yields higher profits for both firms, provided it can be reached and maintained as the underlying conditions change.

The similarity between static oligopoly and the prisoners' dilemma game conceals important differences in the dynamics of the situation. The two firms don't play a one-shot game, and their opportunities for indirect communication are much greater than those of the two prisoners. Hence, the duopoly must be modelled as a multiperiod game, in which each successive strategic move by a player takes into account the opponent's reactions in subsequent periods.[16] Such models may generate the collusive outcome as an equilibrium solution under certain circumstances, at least in the initial stages of the game.

FIGURE 4B.3
The duopoly in a prisoners' dilemma game format

		q = 5 000	q = 5 625
A's strategies	q = 5 000	(225, 225)	(219, 229)
	q = 5 625	(229, 219)	(221, 221)

B's strategies

The duopolists acquire an incentive to collude because they know that any failure to adopt cartel behaviour would provoke retaliation in subsequent periods.

The predictions of such multiperiod games depend very much on the specifics of the situation. The existence of uncertainty in the economic environment, the nature of the information available to the two players, and the type of retaliatory moves allowed in the model become major determinants of the outcome. As a result, such an approach has not yet generated any firm conclusions. It is difficult to formulate models that can predict the circumstances under which collusion or competition will prevail. In spite of this, game theory has provided valuable insights to oligopoly pricing problems. It has identified general situations where conflict coexists with incentives for cooperation.

A more recent application of game theory has been in the modelling of long-run oligopoly behaviour in the face of entry. In these applications the dominant firm or oligopoly is in conflict with some unspecified entrant. The conflict takes place over time and the main strategic decisions may involve variables other than product price, such as installed capacity, plant location, or innovative activity. Such models are very popular in the current economic literature.[17] They will be examined briefly in the next chapter.

Endnotes

1. See the 1963 translation of Cournot, which appeared originally in 1838. The Bertrand model, originally appearing in 1883, is better known through its subsequent development by Edgeworth (1925, pp. 111-142). The collusion model was suggested by Chamberlin (1929).

2. See Bresnahan (1981), and Boyer and Moreau (1983).

3. Note, however, that this is true only for a homogeneous product. If the market is differentiated so that the two firms may charge different prices, the Bertrand model need not produce a "more competitive" outcome than Cournot behaviour.

4. The same is true of the two firms' profits. In fact, collusion maximizes the sum of the two firms' profits, without necessarily improving the profit position of any single firm as compared to, for instance, the Cournot equilibrium.

5. If one of the cartel's firms has lower profits by being in the cartel than it can achieve at the Cournot point then the other cartel members will have to accommodate it. They can do this by kicking back some of their own profits or by small deviations from the collusion prices and quantities. Otherwise, that firm will have no incentive to adhere to the cartel.

6. *Wall Street Journal*, September 8, 1981.

7. See Spulber (1981), and Perrakis and Warskett (1983).

8. See Scherer (1980), pp. 202-203.

9. This price leadership, which is simply a device for moving from the old to the new cartel solution, should not be confused with the Stackelberg model, which aims at a different market equilibrium.

10. See Green (1985), p. 171.

11. The two cases are *R.V. Armco et al.*, 1959 and 1974. An excellent summary is in Green (1985), pp. 175-177.

12. An extended treatment of such devices is in Scherer (1980), Chapter 6.

13. This is also confirmed by empirical evidence. For instance, a U.S. study by Carlton (1986) found that as the industry concentration rose the interval between price changes tended to lengthen.

14. For a proof see the article by Boyer and Moreau (1983).

15. The applications of game theory to oligopoly and other areas of economics were surveyed and extended in Telser (1972) and Friedman (1977). See also Bacharach (1977) and Scherer (1980), pp. 160-164.

16. Examples of such work are in Green and Porter (1984), and Rotemberg and Saloner (1986).

17. Recent examples are Kreps and Wilson (1982), Milgrom and Roberts (1982) and Perrakis and Warskett (1983).

References

Bacharach, M. *Economics and the Theory of Games*. Boulder, Colo.: Westview Press, 1977.

Boyer, M., and C. Moreau. "Consistent versus Non-Consistent Conjectures in Duopoly Theory: Some Examples," *Journal of Industrial Economics*, 32 (September 1983), pp. 97-109.

Bresnahan, T.F. "Duopoly Models with Consistent Conjectures," *American Economic Review*, 71:5 (Dec. 1981), pp. 934-945.

Carlton, D.W. "The Rigidity of Prices," *American Economic Review*, 76: 4 (September 1986), pp. 637-658.

Chamberlin, E.H. "Duopoly: Value Where Sellers Are Few," *Quarterly Journal of Economics*, Vol. 43 (Nov. 1929), pp. 63-100.

Cournot, A. *Researches into the Mathematical Principles of the Theory of Wealth*, translated by N.T. Bacon. Homewood, Ill.: Irwin, 1963.

Edgeworth, F.Y. *Papers Relating to Political Economy*. London, Eng.: McMillan & Co., 1925.

Friedman, J.W. *Oligopoly and the Theory of Games*. Amsterdam, Neth.: North Holland, 1977.

Green, C. *Canadian Industrial Organization and Policy*. Toronto, Ont.: McGraw-Hill Ryerson, 2nd edition, 1985.

Green, E.J., and R.H. Porter. "Non-cooperative Collusion Under Imperfect Price Information," *Econometrica*, 52 (Jan. 1984), pp. 87-100.

Hall, R.L., and C.J. Hitch. "Price Theory and Business Behaviour," *Oxford Economic Papers*, Vol. 2 (May 1939), pp. 12-45.

Kreps, D., and R. Wilson. "Reputation and Imperfect Information," *Journal of Economic Theory*, Vol. 27 (1982), pp. 253-279.

Milgrom, P., and J. Roberts. "Limit Pricing and Entry Under Incomplete Information: an Equilibrium Analysis," *Econometrica*, 50: 2 (March 1982), pp. 443-459.

Neumann, J. von, and O. Morgenstern. *Theory of Games and Economic Behavior*. Princeton, N.J.: Princeton University Press, 1944.

Perrakis, S., and G. Warskett. "Capacity and Entry Under Demand Uncertainty," *Review of Economic Studies*, Vol. 50 (July 1983), pp. 495-511.

Rotemberg, J.J., and G. Saloner. "A Supergame-Theoretic Model of Price Wars During Booms," *American Economic Review*, 76:3 (June 1986), pp. 390-407.

Scherer, F.M. *Industrial Market Structure and Economic Performance*. 2nd ed., Chicago, Ill.: Rand McNally, 1980.

Spulber, D.F. "Capacity, Output, and Sequential Entry," *American Economic Review*, 71:3 (June 1981), pp. 503-514.

Sweezy, P. "Demand Under Conditions of Oligopoly," *Journal of Political Economy*, Vol. 47 (Aug. 1939), pp. 568-573.

Telser, L.D. *Competition, Collusion and Game Theory*. Chicago, Ill.: Aldine-Atherton, 1972.

CHAPTER 5

The Theory of Oligopoly II:

Long Run Analysis

The analysis of firm conduct carried out in the previous chapter took for granted the existing dimensions of industry structure, namely the number and relative size of firms in the industry. In other words, it was an analysis focussed mostly on the short run, implying a time period not long enough to allow "significant" entry or exit of firms in the industry. This chapter, by contrast, is concerned with such a process of gradual change in industry structure over time. We examine here the determinants of entry for firms in an industry, the consequences of such entry on industry structure, and the role played by public policies that enhance or prevent entry in given sectors. Of particular interest are the implications that potential entry of new competitors has upon the behaviour of existing firms in an industry. As we shall see, the possibility of new entry brings at times crucial modifications upon the conduct of incumbent firms. For these reasons no analysis of industry structure, conduct, and performance is complete without a detailed examination of the conditions of firm entry.

Oligopolies in the Long Run: Entry and Industry Structure

The main reason that firms may wish to enter into an industry is to make profits. Accordingly, the decision to establish a new firm in a given market must always start with some forecast of the demand and costs associated with production in that market. Since the firm to be established does not exist as yet, the information contained in these forecasts is derived by observing the firms that already exist in the industry. It is the profits realized by these firms that attract new entrants.

Economic theory stipulates that under perfect competition this process of entry will continue to the point where no profits remain to firms in the industry apart from the "normal" remuneration of invested capital. In an oligopoly, however, such an elimination of "excess" profits does not always take place in practice. Entry may not be possible to the point where no profits remain. Conditions exist under which new firms would be deterred from entering the industry even when the incumbents realize substantial profits. Such conditions are known as *barriers to entry* .

The precise definition of a barrier to entry has been somewhat controversial. The definition implied in the previous paragraph is that a barrier to entry is a set of conditions preventing the entry of new firms into the industry even when incumbent firms realize profits, i.e. when product price exceeds average cost. This definition, which is the one most widely accepted, was originally due to Bain (1956). By contrast, Stigler (1968) has adopted a somewhat more limited definition, according to which a barrier is a disadvantage faced by prospective entrants that incumbent firms do not have to face. The main difference between the two definitions is in the treatment of economies of scale, which are included in the list of barriers under Bain's but not under Stigler's definition.

An even more recent approach to the barriers to entry problem is via a set of duopoly models, in which an incumbent firm interacts with a potential entrant in a formulation that uses the general framework of game theory. A barrier to entry exists in such a setting when the incumbent can adopt policies that will render entry unprofitable, while simultaneously preserving some positive profits for itself. This set of models, while consistent with Bain's general approach, has altered some of his original results while uncovering new sources of entry barriers. It is known under the general title of *strategic entry deterrence.*[1]

Since barriers to entry tend by definition to promote a less competitive industry structure, one would have expected that public policies would be aimed at reducing or eliminating them. Indeed, we saw in the Ontario metal culvert industry example in Chapter 4 how an industry, in which entry was relatively free of barriers, was forced towards competitive behaviour in spite of the existence of a tradition and a mechanism for collusion. This is mostly true of the general thrust of public policy, but there are two major sets of exceptions in Canada. The first exception stems from "legitimate" reasons, when it can be shown that barriers to entry tend to promote general welfare in the long run. An example of such a policy is the granting of protection to new products or processes through long-lived patents or trademarks. The second exception is less defensible in many cases, and is associated with entry restrictions in the so-called *regulated* sectors. These are sectors in which the market mechanism is not allowed to function in its entirety. Incumbent firms accept some limitations on their freedom to choose the levels of several economic variables in exchange for protection against competition from new entrants. Barriers to entry in such sectors take the form of quotas, licenses, or other entry restrictions. While such regulated sectors are traditionally associated with natural monopolies, as we saw in Chapter 3, they have also been established in some otherwise competitive industries.

Some economists such as Demsetz (1982) have placed particular emphasis on entry barriers created by public policy. They tend to stress the beneficial effects of entry restrictions due to patents, trademarks, or exclusionary clauses, and the need for incumbent firms to acquire the cooperation of public policy in enforcing these restrictions. In this chapter we shall spend comparatively little time on the welfare effects of entry restrictions, reserving the discussion for the policy chapters in the second part of this book.

In what follows we shall first examine the classical approach to entry barriers that emphasizes structural factors. Then we proceed to the conduct aspect of this approach by examining the limit-entry pricing theory. The more recent behavioural and strategic treatment of entry barriers comes next, while the final section contains the empirical evidence on the effects of barriers to entry in Canada.

Barriers to Entry

As already noted, barriers to entry in the Bain definition include all types of conditions that may deter entry into an industry. Such conditions may arise from the cost side, from the product demand side, or from public policies. All these barriers, though, can be ultimately treated as if they resulted from the cost side, i.e., as if they conferred a unit cost advantage to an incumbent firm vis-à-vis a new entrant. Figure 5.1 shows this advantage in a hypothetical situation, with AC_E representing the entrant's average costs.

This unit cost advantage is sometimes referred to as the height H of the barrier. It represents a competitive situation, in which the incumbent firm may lower the price to a level at which the entrant would be incurring losses, while the incumbent would still be operating profitably. Potential entrants, recognizing such competitive situations before they occur, would elect to stay out of the industry rather than engage in a hopeless rivalry.

Absolute Cost Advantages

The simplest type of a barrier to entry occurs when incumbent firm(s) have lower unit costs than any would-be entrants because of privileged access to one or more production inputs. Such an access may be due to their location, with respect to either the source of these inputs or to the product markets. It

FIGURE 5.1
Cost advantages as a barrier to entry

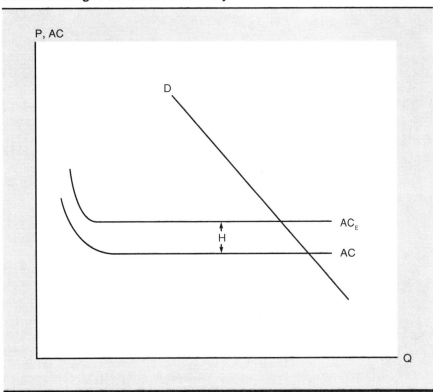

may also be due to circumstances that existed at the time they were established, but are no longer in existence.

This type of barrier to entry is very common in Canada, especially in agriculture. Climatic and soil conditions make entry into the market for many agricultural commodities, including most fruits and many vegetables, totally infeasible for Canadian producers. Conversely, the privileged access of Canadian farmers to plentiful supplies of a key agricultural input, land, has given Canadian grain producers a strategic advantage in the world grain markets. In both examples these barriers to entry have been overcome, even though temporarily, by government intervention: Canada produces wine, its climate and soil notwithstanding; Europe produces and exports cereals, in spite of its limited supplies of arable land. Yet these interventions have not succeeded in creating any permanent situation, and in both instances it is necessary to continue inputs of tariff protection or price supports to domestic producers.

Similarly, barriers to entry arising out of absolute cost advantages exist in the mining and natural resources industries. Control over a particularly rich mineral deposit constitutes a barrier to entry in the market for that particular commodity. For instance INCO, the International Nickel Company, held a quasi-monopoly in the world supply of nickel for much of the first half of the 20th century, because of its control over particularly rich ores in Northern Ontario.[2] Until very recently few producers would challenge Middle-Eastern countries in the world oil markets, given the much lower oil exploration and extraction costs in those countries. A similar dominant position over world supplies of particular commodities has been associated at times with individual countries: tin with Bolivia, copper with Chile, gold with South Africa, etc. Other suppliers may enter these particular markets only if the corresponding commodity prices rise sufficiently and for a "long" time period, in order to overcome the cost handicap of the new suppliers.

Patents

A patent is a license by which a firm acquires exclusive control over a particular technology or production process. To the extent that such a process is a more economical way of producing a given commodity, the patent confers to its holder an absolute cost advantage in the market for that commodity. It therefore constitutes a particularly powerful and effective method of preventing entry in that market.

Patents are especially important in some industries such as pharmaceuticals and the "high tech" group (computers, communications and aerospace). Patented products and processes are either produced directly by the patent-holder, or are produced by licensees after payment of a royalty while the patent is in force. After expiration of the patent anyone may use the patented technology without reference to the patent holder. Nonetheless, it is believed that benefits from the patent continue accruing to the original producer long after the patent has expired, especially in an industry such as pharmaceuticals: a patented product becomes differentiated in the eyes of consumers, who accept paying a higher price for it than for otherwise identical substitutes.[3] Thus, patents create barriers to entry that may last long after their expiration.

While the barrier to entry implications of patents are of course undesirable from the public interest point of view, it is believed that the financial incentives to innovation provided by the patent system produce technological developments that would not otherwise be forthcoming. These incentives are greater the longer the period of patent protection, implying that longer-lived patents produce more innovations. On the other hand, a longer patent protection also implies less competition in the market for that particular product. The actual length of patent protection is a compromise between these two opposite points of view.[4]

Figure 5.2 illustrates the benefits conferred by a patent to its holder. These benefits are a function of the alternative pre-patent technology, which allows production at unit costs of P_1, under the assumptions of constant marginal and average costs and a competitive market structure. The new technology reduces these costs to the level P_2. The patent holder would like to price the product at P_3, defined as shown, at the intersection of the marginal revenue and marginal cost curves. The old technology, however, provides a ceiling of P_1 to the possible price. The patent-holder, therefore, can either drive the other firm out of business and price the product at a slightly lower level than P_1, or it can license the patent to another producer for a royalty payment of $(P_1 - P_2)$ \$per unit. The *value* of the patent would then be equal to the discounted sum of these royalties over the length of the patent protection. For instance, if the patent lowers the unit costs by \$1 over the previous technology, the licensee produces 1 000 000 units per year, the interest rate (adjusted for risk) is 8 percent per year, and the patent still has 10 years to expiration, then

the value of the patent is $1\ 000\ 000 \times \sum_{t=1}^{10} \dfrac{1}{(1.08)^t} = \$6\ 710\ 000.$

FIGURE 5.2
Patented innovation as a barrier to entry

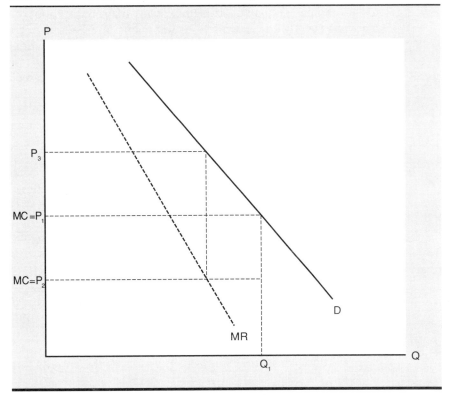

It is clear from this illustration that the value of a patent is very much dependent on its length, which becomes therefore a crucial public policy decision. This decision is bound to be controversial: too short a patent raises questions about the incentives to innovate and the size of R&D spending; if the patent life is lengthened the consumers are saddled with higher prices for a longer period, given that competition is prevented from forcing the product price down. The optimal patent length is by necessity a compromise between these two contradictory effects, and will be reviewed in detail in Chapter 11.

Another factor that plays a major role in the value of a patent is the unit cost of alternative technologies or close substitute products. This cost constitutes the ceiling on the royalty rate that the patent holder may extract. The difference between old and new cost (the $1 in the example above) represents the *height* of the entry barrier produced by the patent: it is equal to the maximum losses per unit product that a patent holder or its licensee may inflict on would-be entrants while continuing to realize profits.

Given the importance of alternative technologies, it is in the interest of the patent holder to insure that the height of the entry barrier is at a maximum. This height can be increased if the patent holder controls not only the lowest-cost production process, but also the processes with slightly higher unit production costs. Conversely, the competitors are spurred to R&D activity in order to "get around" the patent. This R&D rivalry may produce a lot of "imitative" innovation, with little payoff from the public interest point of view. Thus, critics of the patent system have alleged that patents tend to drain inventive resources away from truly significant innovations, and towards purely imitative or defensive R&D. It is nonetheless difficult to envision a replacement of patents with a better system, one that would diminish the patents' anti-competitive role while preserving its incentives for innovation and R&D.

Product Differentiation

Product differentiation through brand-name advertising can be described as the creation of buyer perceptions about differing product qualities for a given brand compared to other competing brands. Such perceptions define an individual demand curve for the differentiated product, distinct from that of its competitors. It is then possible to charge a higher price for the differentiated product without losing the entire market share, thus creating a certain amount of market power for the producing firm.

Figure 5.3 shows the impact of product differentiation as an entry barrier. The demand curve for the incumbent's differentiated product is denoted by D, while D_e is the demand for a potential entrant. Both firms' products are close substitutes, with the result that a change in the price level of one product changes the location of the other's demand in the same direction as the price change. Thus, when the incumbent's price is P_1 the entrant demand is D_e^1, while this demand shifts down to D_e^2 when the price drops to P_2. Both firms produce under identical technologies, implying that their unit cost curves AC (assumed constant after the minimum efficient scale) are the same.

As drawn in Figure 5.3, profitable entry is possible when the incumbent prices its product at P_1: there exists a portion of the entrant demand D_e^1 that lies above the unit cost curve AC. At P_2, though, the demand curve has shifted down at D_e^2, so that it now lies entirely below AC. The potential entrant has no profit opportunities left since all price and output combinations would create losses. The incumbent, however, continues to enjoy positive profits equal to the level H per unit output. This level now constitutes the *height* of the entry barrier due to product differentiation.

Product differentiation, carried out of the point where it constitutes an entry barrier, is quite frequent in certain industries and products. Differentia-

FIGURE 5.3
Product differentiation as a barrier to entry

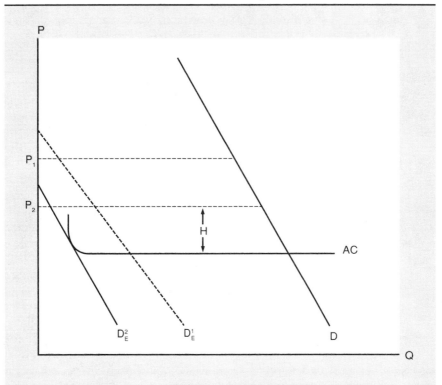

tion may be initially due to an identification of the product with the first producer's brand, especially when this first producer has operated under an exclusive patent for a certain time. It is very easy to think of such situations, especially in an industry such as pharmaceuticals: Aspirin and Valium have become synonymous with the drugs that bear their names. As Schmalensee (1982) has pointed out, such differentiation is not necessarily just due to consumer misperceptions about the advantages of the pioneering brands; it may also reflect uncertainty about product quality, with the established brands being considered more reliable. Nonetheless, the magnitude of the differentiation effect exceeds any conceivable real quality differences, especially in view of the rigorous testing that takes place for all pharmaceutical products. As McRae and Tapon (1983) pointed out, the brand name products have managed to maintain most of their share in the market for Canadian pharmaceuticals in spite of the huge difference in price, even after they lost their patent protection. It took public intervention, under the form of compulsory use of the lowest cost supplier in all publicly-funded medical insurance plans, in order to bring a reduction in prices consistent with competitive conditions.

Product differentiation need not be initiated by a patent. Advertising can also be used in order to create the perception of superior quality for a certain brand. Once the first firm to be established in a given market has created such perceptions for its own products, it acquires a built-in advantage against new entrants, as illustrated in Figure 5.3. While these new entrants can also try to advertise in order to neutralize this advantage, the first mover has certain factors in its favour in the ensuing rivalry, as we shall see in more detail later in this chapter. Indeed, advertising costs are by and large sunk, implying that once committed, they can never be recaptured. Hence, the incumbent need not concern itself with these costs, while the entrant must incorporate them in its decision-making. This asymmetry is at the heart of the various strategic entry-deterrence models, examined in a later section.

The *value* of this barrier to entry due to product differentiation can also be estimated in a manner similar to that of a patent, even though the data for such an estimation may not be as easily obtainable. It is also equal to the discounted sum of the product of: the height of the barrier H times the volume of production, over the number of years that the barrier would persist. This height may at times be observed as the excess price charged by brand-name products over their unknown competitors (provided such competitors exist), or by the cost at which brand names or trademarks are licensed. What is not always observable is the "economic life" of the differentiation effect, i.e. the time during which the barrier exists. This barrier is generally treated as an investment, implying that it is subject to depreciation over time, unless new investment in advertising is forthcoming.[5] Its accounting treatment is in conformity to these principles, since it is quite often capitalized as "goodwill" and subjected to depreciation. It should be noted, though, that the "goodwill" account represents in general the combined effects of all barriers to entry, and not just those due to product differentiation. The latter's effects can only be separated if some reasonable assumptions can be made about its persistence such as, for instance, that it will persist perpetually with a "normal" amount of advertising.

Economies of Scale

In Chapter 2 we introduced the concept of minimum efficient firm scale or firm-level MES, defined as the smallest volume of production at which all unit cost savings at the firm level are exhausted. This MES is also the output at which the average cost (AC) curve reaches its minimum. In what follows it will be assumed that beyond this output volume (denoted by Q_0) the average cost curve stays horizontal for a "large" range of output values. As noted in Chapter 2, such a cost structure is thought to characterize many production processes.

The idea underlying the view of economies of scale as an entry barrier is quite simple. A challenger wishing to enter a given market and compete with an incumbent firm must do so at a sufficiently large scale, above Q_0, in order to take advantage of the lower costs due to scale economies. The addition of Q_0 to the incumbent firm's production, though, is bound to reduce the prevailing market price in order to allow for the sale of this extra output. Such a price reduction may render the entry unprofitable. Recognizing this, the potential entrant may choose to stay out, thus establishing the entry barrier.

Figure 5.4 illustrates this effect. The unit cost curve AC drops quite sharply for Q less than the output level Q_0 of the MES, so that entry below MES is not profitable. The incumbent firm is able to price its product at a level P_L above unit cost AC, with market output Q_L, and still be protected from entry. The addition of an output equal to MES to Q_L will bring the market price down to AC, since the total industry output will be Q_I after entry, the output at which the demand curve D intersects the AC curve. This will wipe out all industry profits. It suffices, therefore, for the incumbent to set prices just a shade below P_L in order to be protected from entry, since the incumbent would realize that the *post-entry* state of the industry will not be conducive to profits.

The analysis is essentially unchanged even if the AC curve does not drop as sharply as in Figure 5.4. The height H of the barrier is lower in such a case. In Appendix 5A it is shown that the limit-entry output must satisfy a condition, according to which the entrant's best prospects must be such that the post-entry price is barely sufficient to cover the unit costs. The conditions defining this output are shown in Appendix 5A to correspond to the situation represented in Figure 5.5. The best the entrant can do is at the output Q_E, where the average cost curve has the same slope as the post-entry demand. It can be easily seen that the difference $Q_I - Q_L$ is smaller in this case than in the

FIGURE 5.4
Economics of scale as a barrier to entry

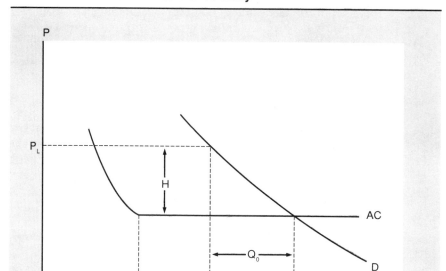

situation depicted in Figure 5.4, yielding a lower entry barrier. This may tend to weaken somewhat the barrier effect of economies of scale, given that in several industries average costs increase fairly slowly for outputs below MES. Table 5.1 shows the rise in AC at output equal to $Q_0/3$ or $Q_0/2$ for several industries, from studies carried out during the late 1960s in several countries. It is clear from this data that the rate at which unit cost rises below MES can have a major impact on the importance of economies of scale as entry barriers, over and above the size of MES relative to industry output.

Public Policies Preventing Entry

The simplest system of a publicly-erected barrier to entry is through a transferable quota. Each incumbent producer receives a certain allocation of product, for which it acquires absolute property rights. This allocation must be enforced through an agency, whose decisions have the force of law. For a new producer

FIGURE 5.5
Barrier to entry when costs rise slowly below MES

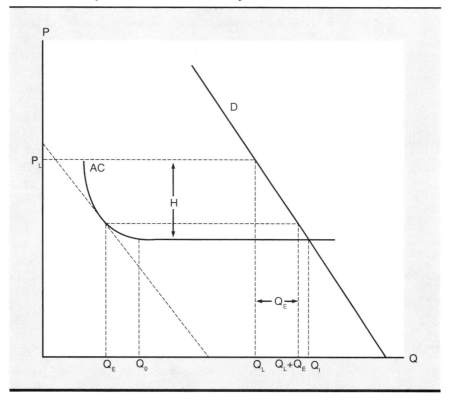

TABLE 5.1
Cost disadvantages of plants below MES, selected industries

Industry	Percent Unit Cost Rises at $\frac{1}{3}$ MES	Industry	Percent Unit Cost Rises at $\frac{1}{2}$ MES
Beer brewing	5.0	Flour mills	3.0
Cigarettes	2.2	Bread baking	7.5
Paints	4.4	Printing paper	9.0
Petroleum refining	4.8	Sulphuric acid	1.0
Nonrubber shoes	1.5	Synthetic rubber	15.0
Glass bottles	11.0	Detergents	2.5
Portland cement	26.0	Bricks	25.0
Integrated steel	11.0	Machine tools	5.0

Source: F.M. Scherer *et al.* (1975), pp. 80-94; R.T. Masson and P.D. Qualls, eds. (1975), pp. 128-31.

to enter the industry there must be a quota available, which generally must be purchased from an existing firm. The cost of that purchase is an additional cost to new entrants, which was not borne by those initially in the industry.

Such quotas exist in several agricultural commodities such as eggs, milk, poultry, and tobacco, as well as in offshore fishing. In the latter market the purpose of the quota system is the protection of the fish stocks, while the other markets were transformed through lobbying into what in fact amounts to a producer cartel. The economic consequences of this cartelization will be examined in more detail in Chapter 10, given that these sectors are most often referred to as "regulated industries."

Alternatively, entry may be prevented in certain industries through a licensing system. New would-be producers must acquire a licence before entering the industry. This licence is either purchased from an existing firm, or is awarded by a licensing body following lengthy and costly procedures in which the new entrant must demonstrate that there is a need for the product or service to be provided. Needless to say, incumbent firms have a strong incentive to oppose the granting of the licence, and they often act as hostile parties to the application.

Licensing systems exist in most transportation sectors such as airlines, taxicab services, and trucking. They also normally form part of the so-called regulated industries, and they will therefore be examined in more detail in Chapter 10. Some of these sectors, such as airlines and trucking, have become the focus of deregulation in recent years, although the situation is not completely resolved as of this writing. Until now licences in these industries have been extremely effective barriers to entry, contributing to high industry prices and to a host of other economic developments, which are examined in later chapters.

Still other sectors subjected to entry barriers are broadcasting and cable TV, and telecommunications. In the former, entry takes place through a system of transferable licences, while the latter is an industry operating under a monopoly franchise. Entry of new firms is completely blocked for many products of the telecommunications industry, while licences for broadcasting and cable TV may be purchased from existing producers.[6] Lastly, other sectors where public policies restrict entry are those such as electricity generation and distribution, which are dominated by a publicly-owned firm.

As the above discussion makes clear, public policies preventing entry are almost always associated with regulated industries. This is no accident. As we saw in Chapter 3, the essence of regulation is the acceptance, on the part of the regulated firm, of some restrictions on economic freedom in exchange for protection from additional competition. Barriers to the entry of new firms are essential components of this protection.

Still another, subtler type of barrier to entry is that created by public policies that discriminate between existing firms and potential new entrants.

Such policies are quite common in environmental protection regulation. They are essentially "grandfather" clauses, giving existing firms time to catch up with newly-perceived environmental hazards when old plants are scrapped. For instance, the Pulp and Paper Regulations under the Fisheries Act allow existing plants to exceed the pollution standards for new paper mills by about thirty percent. To the extent that it is cheaper to pollute than to not do so, this differential standard constitutes an absolute cost advantage-type of barrier to entry.

Barriers to entry are highly desirable for incumbent firms. It is therefore natural for them to invest money in erecting, enhancing, or preserving them. The question that arises is whether firms are able to do so. Before examining this question, though, we turn to the role played by barriers in firm conduct, which is known as the limit-entry pricing theory.[7]

Limit-Entry Pricing

Up till now we have examined only the structural aspects of barriers to entry. Yet, as we noted at the beginning of this chapter, it is the implications of the barriers for the conduct of incumbent firms that are perhaps their most important feature. Of the two different classes of models that we have on this topic, the limit-entry pricing models tend to emphasize price or output as the incumbent's strategic variable. The second category of models, collectively known as strategic entry deterrence, pay much more attention to the behavioural aspects of the incumbent-entrant interaction.

The idea behind limit-entry pricing is very simple. Potential entrants are attracted to the sector by high profits, which are themselves the consequences of high prices. Firms would do well therefore to reduce these prices voluntarily to the level at which new entrants would elect to stay out. By doing so, the incumbents will ultimately end up with higher profits over the long run than if entry had taken place.

It is important to highlight the assumptions about firm behaviour implied by this conduct. All models of firm entry must start from a description of the prospective entrant's conjectures about the post-entry incumbent reactions. Limit-entry pricing adopts a Cournot-type assumption, namely that entrants believe that incumbents will continue producing the same output following entry that they produced before. This assumption is known as the *Sylos postulate*, after P. Sylos-Labini (1962). It is also assumed in all these models that the incumbent(s) is either a monopoly or a perfectly colluding oligopoly. Hence, the analysis is valid for both monopolistic and oligopolistic market structures.

With these assumptions the logic of the limit-entry pricing model follows very simply. The incumbent strategy depends on the combined height H of the entry barriers. The smallest output that it will conceivably produce is the monopoly output Q_M, sold at the corresponding price P_M. If the excess of this price over average cost AC is less than H then the incumbent can act as an unconstrained monopolist, and entry is *blockaded*. If, on the other hand, $(P_M - AC)$ is greater than H, the incumbent has the choice of reducing price (expanding output) to the limit-entry level P_L (Q_L), sacrificing current monopoly profits to forestall entry; this is known as *effectively impeded entry*. An alternative decision (*ineffectively impeded entry*) is to continue charging the monopoly price, accepting its eventual reduction due to new firms' entry.

An illustration of this choice can be obtained by referring to Figure 5.6 below. This figure is very similar to Figure 5.4 insofar as the industry exhibits significant economies of scale and thus entry barriers. The AC curve rises very steeply, and entry cannot take place profitably at any level below the MES value of Q_0. An incumbent monopolist who ignores the threat of entry would charge the monopoly price P_M, from the intersection of marginal revenue and

FIGURE 5.6
Limit-entry pricing

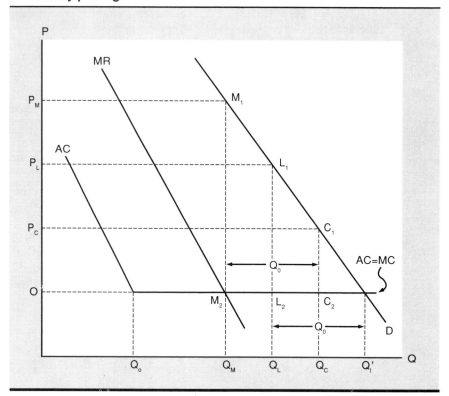

marginal cost, and produce the corresponding output of Q_M. This pricing policy, though, leaves room for a new entrant, who may enter at the MES level of Q_0 and force down the industry price to the level P_c. By contrast, a limit-entry pricing policy would have the incumbent adopt a price just a shade below the level of P_L with output Q_L. The addition of a firm producing the MES to the pre-entry industry output Q_L would now generate a total industry output exceeding $Q_I{'}$ and force the price below the unit cost level of AC.

Thus, the two alternative policies facing the incumbent firm may be summarized as follows according to the limit-entry pricing argument:

(i) Charge the monopoly price P_M initially (until entry takes place), and the price P_c subsequently.
(ii) Charge the limit-entry price P_L from the outset.

The choice between these two policies would depend on a number of factors affecting the comparison of the sum of discounted profits produced by the two alternatives. These are the following:

(i) Area (P_M M_1 M_2 0) initially, area (P_c C_1 C_2 0) after entry.
(ii) Area (P_L L_1 L_2 0) from the outset.

Clearly, the longer it takes for a new firm to enter, the more policy (1) is favoured. Similarly, the higher the discount rate, the more policy (1) appears more profitable, since the quick monopoly profits are discounted less heavily than the distant eventual superiority of the limit-entry pricing policy (2).

For a numerical illustration of this policy choice consider an incumbent monopoly firm with demand curve given in inverse form by $p = 80 - 3Q/1\,000$. The average cost curve is horizontal at the level of \$8 per unit provided the firm's annual production exceeds the MES level of 10 000 units. This AC curve rises very steeply below that level of production, making it uneconomical to operate below MES. As shown in Chapter 3, the level of production of a profit-maximizing monopolist when entry is ignored is given by the equality of marginal revenue (MR) and marginal cost (MC). Since the MR curve is given by the relation MR $= 80 - 6Q/1\,000$, the monopoly output Q_M is found by setting MR $= 80 - 6Q/1\,000 =$ AC $= 8$, yielding $Q_M = 12\,000$ units,

$$p = 80 - \frac{3 \times 12\,000}{1\,000} = 44 \ \$/\text{unit}.$$

If the incumbent produces 12 000 units per year sold at 44 \$/unit, however, it will invite entry. A new entrant may easily enter at a level of 10 000 units annual production, and still realize economic profits. The total industry output after entry, corresponding to Q_c in Figure 5.6, is equal to $Q_M + Q_0 =$ 12 000 + 10 000 = 22 000, and the industry price is $p = 80 - \dfrac{3 \times 22\,000}{1\,000} =$

\$14, which is amply sufficient to cover the unit cost of \$8.

Suppose, by contrast, that the incumbent were to practice limit-entry pricing by expanding production to a level Q_L and charging a price P_L, so that if new entry at the level of Q_0 takes place the industry price would fall below the AC level of 8 \$/unit. To find the upper limit on P_L (or the lower limit of Q_L) we find the output Q_I, at which the demand curve intersects the AC line, and subtract Q_0. This is done analytically by equating the expressions for the inverse demand and average cost curves, and solving for the resulting output. This is done in Equations (5A.4) - (5A.5) of Appendix 5A for linear demand and constant AC curves. Applying (5A.5) with $a = 80, c = 8, b = 3/1\,000$ and $Q_0 = 10\,000$, we find $Q_L = 14\,000$ and $P_L = 80 - \dfrac{3 \times 14\,000}{1\,000} = \$38$. An incumbent production level slightly above 14 000 (sold at a price slightly below \$38) would preclude post-entry profits for any potential entrants. Hence, the two alternative policies now become in this example:

(i) $p = P_M = \$44$, $Q = Q_M = 12\,000$ before entry; $p = P_c = \$14$, $Q = Q_c = 12\,000$ after entry
(ii) $p = P_L = \$38$, $Q = Q_L = 14\,000$.

The corresponding profits are:

(i) $\pi_M = (44-8) \times 12\,000 = \$432\,000$ pre-entry; $\pi_c = (14-8) \times 12\,000 = \$72\,000$ after entry
(ii) $\pi_L = (38-8) \times 14\,000 = \$420\,000$ always.

The firm will then choose policy (1) or (2) by comparing the discounted series of π_M and π_c to the capitalized stream of π_L. For instance, if it is estimated that it would take 4 years for a new firm to enter, the discount rate is 10 percent and the incumbent firm plans by looking ahead at a 15-year horizon, policies (1) and (2) produce the totals of $432\,000 \sum\limits_{t=1}^{4} \dfrac{1}{1.10^t} +$ $72\,000 \sum\limits_{t=5}^{15} \dfrac{1}{1.10^t} = 1\,688\,844$, and $420\,000 \sum\limits_{t=1}^{15} \dfrac{1}{1.10^t} = 3\,194\,520$ respectively, with policy (2) the clear winner.

The dependence of the policy choice on the discount rate appears clearly in this example. An increase in this rate would tend to reduce the total corresponding to policy (1) less than the other sum. Similarly, the existing barrier to entry plays a major role in the policy choice. For instance, suppose that the MES level of Q_0 were to fall to 8 000 from 10 000 in this example. Then the size of the barrier to entry decreases. By repeating the earlier computations we find that $Q_L = 16\,000$, $P_L = \$32$ and $\pi_L = \$336\,000$, while the post-entry price is $P_c = \$20$, with incumbent profits $\pi_c = \$144\,000$. This tends to work against the limit-entry pricing policy.

As the above example shows, the limit-entry pricing policy choices are crucially dependent on the validity of the Sylos postulate. If the incumbent can easily vary post-entry output from Q_M to Q_L or vice-versa, then there is little basis for the entrant's belief that this output will remain constant. In such a case it would make no sense for the incumbent to adopt the limit-entry pricing policy (2). Such a policy would not be credible unless accompanied by other features. It is these features that delineate the strategic entry deterrence models from limit-entry pricing.

The probable ineffectiveness of limit-entry pricing can be easily ascertained by referring to the above numerical example with $Q_0 = 10\,000$. Suppose that the incumbent has already decided to adopt the limit-entry pricing policy (2), producing an amount in excess of $14\,000$, say $15\,000$, and charging a price equal to $80 - \dfrac{3 \times 15\,000}{1\,000} = \$35$. A new entrant, producing the MES volume of $10\,000$, would drive the market price down to $80 - \dfrac{3 \times (25\,000)}{1\,000} = \$5$, which is below the unit cost of \$8, provided the incumbent continues to produce a post-entry output of $15\,000$. If, however, the incumbent can be persuaded to curtail its own output, then the entrant can be accommodated and both firms can realize profits.

Suppose that the entrant were to call the incumbent's bluff and enter the sector in spite of the limit-entry price. According to the accommodation viewpoint, the incumbent would automatically restrict its output provided that this action also reduces costs proportionately. Otherwise both firms would suffer instead of realizing profits. Hence, under these circumstances a limit-entry pricing strategy is not a credible deterrent to entry. The next section examines models that deal explicitly with this credibility issue.

Strategic Entry Deterrence

The lack of credibility of limit-entry pricing demonstrated in the previous section is derived from the incumbent's ability to reduce its costs by varying its post-entry output. If this ability is missing, or in other words, if the expansion of output to the limit-entry point entails some *irrecoverable or sunk costs*, then the credibility of entry deterrence is restored. The incumbent will find it profitable to adopt the Sylos postulate as a behavioural rule. The essence of strategic entry deterrence models is that entry is deterred by the pre-commitment of irrecoverable resources on the part of the incumbent, rather than by the voluntary limitation of its prices and profits.

Sunk costs are present in almost every industry, and the only question is how important they are. For instance, all advertising, exploration, R&D, and much of construction and installation costs cannot be recovered once spent. Many of these costs must be committed upon entry. Similarly, expansion of output to a given level entails an irreversible expansion of a large part of these costs. Such an expansion lends credibility to entry deterrence, since subsequent output contraction cannot reduce these costs.

The oil industry during the mid-1980s is a good example of the importance of sunk costs when an industry attempts to curtail its output. During the beginning of that period the industry was plagued by a worldwide excess of production over demand at the then-prevailing high prices. The ensuing collapse of the world price of oil led to persistent attempts by the OPEC cartel of oil exporters to reduce output in order to raise prices. Yet these attempts proved futile over the short run. The nature of most of the costs in the oil industry is sunk—literally, as well as figuratively—since they consist of drilling and exploration expenses. These costs won't go away if oil production is curtailed, while any excess of the oil price over the operating expenses would help recover them. Hence, the only possible correction of the low oil prices is in the long run, through the cessation of both exploration and drilling of new wells.

More generally, the choice of credible entry-deterring policies can be represented schematically by the diagram of Figure 5.7. The incumbent may remain passive and accept entry, or alternatively commit resources irreversibly in order to fight entry. In each case the entrant has the choice to enter or stay out of the sector. Given entry, the incumbent has a choice of sharing the market (i.e. reducing its output to raise price above average cost), or fighting the entrant in an attempt to force it out of business, by keeping output constant. The

FIGURE 5.7
Strategic entry deterrence

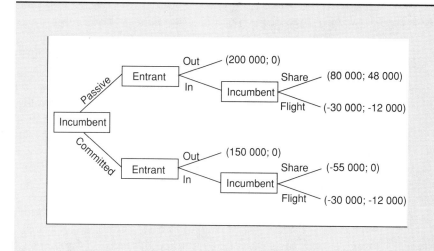

terminal payoffs (profits) will ultimately determine the strategic choices of the two firms. They are shown as a pair of numbers at each terminal state.

For a numerical example similar to the one provided above, consider an industry demand curve $p = 100 - 2Q/1\,000$, and a constant unit cost $AC = \$60$, as long as the firm's production volume is at least equal to the MES value of 6 000 units per year. The two incumbent strategies, "passive" and "committed", refer to monopoly and limit-entry pricing respectively. Suppose also that of the \$60 per unit of total cost only \$5 is variable and may be avoided by curtailing production. The remaining \$55 consists of advertising and capital costs that cannot be recovered once committed. Last, the incumbent's choice of pre-entry production level implies that this level acts as a constraint on any subsequent output choices. In other words, the choice of pre-entry production level is equivalent to a choice of *capacity to produce*, which may not be exceeded in the short run.

Given these specifications, consider first the passive incumbent strategy. This is the choice of pre-entry monopoly output, which equates marginal revenue to the marginal cost of \$60 : $10 - \dfrac{4Q}{1\,000} = 60$, yielding $Q_M = 10\,000$ units, $P_M = \$80/\text{unit}$, and profits $\pi_M = \$200\,000$. Post-entry, however, the incumbent must contend with an extra 6 000 units of output supplied by the entrant: its residual demand curve is $p = 100 - \dfrac{2(Q + 6\,000)}{1\,000} = 88 - \dfrac{2Q}{1\,000}$. The incumbent's relevant marginal cost is now only \$5, since this is the only variable portion. Hence, it has no incentive to reduce production in order to accommodate the entrant: its marginal revenue at the pre-entry output of 10 000 (the maximum possible) is $88 - \dfrac{40\,000}{1\,000} = 48$, which is far in excess of the marginal cost of \$5. Hence, the post-entry price and incumbent profit are $P_c = 100 - \dfrac{2(10\,000 + 6\,000)}{1\,000} = \$68$ and $\pi = (68 - 60) \times 10\,000 = 80\,000$, while the entrant realizes a profit of $(68 - 60) \times 6\,000 = 48\,000$. This is the outcome of the "passive" strategy for the incumbent, who is unable to fight entry due to the existing capacity constraint.

The "committed" strategy, on the other hand, involves expanding capacity and output above the limit-entry volume of $Q_L = 14\,000$ units (since $p = 100 - \dfrac{2(14\,000 + 6\,000)}{1\,000} = AC = 60$). Suppose that the firm commits enough funds to produce 15 000 units/year,[8] charging a price of \$70 and realizing a profit of $\$(70 - 60) \times 15\,000 = \$150\,000$ in the absence of entry. Here entry at the MES level of 6 000 will produce the following results for the incumbent:

Share: $p = \$60$, $Q = 14\,000$, $\pi = 60 \times 14\,000 - (55 \times 15\,000 + 5 \times 14\,000) = -\$55\,000$

Fight: $p = 100 - \dfrac{2(15\ 000 + 6\ 000)}{1\ 000} = \$58, \pi = 58 \times 15\ 000 - 60 \times 15\ 000 = -\$30\ 000.$

It follows that the committed incumbent would be better off fighting than sharing (reducing its output to accommodate the entrant in the case of entry).

Similarly, the logic of the lower part of Figure 5.7 is that the entrant would elect to stay out once it realizes that the incumbent is "committed" irreversibly to an output of 15 000 units, for in such a case entry would bring forth the superior (for the incumbent) "fight" outcome. Hence, a committed incumbent would realize a profit of $150 000 without having to share the market. By contrast, the upper part of Figure 5.7 yields the conclusion that the entrant would enter, and the passive incumbent would be forced to share the market. The logic derived from the entire Figure 5.7, therefore, is that the incumbent will end up with $150 000 profit if committed, and $80 000 profit if passive.

In general, it can be shown that sunk costs upon entry, combined with the necessity to enter at least at MES, are sufficient to produce economic profits from entry deterrence.[9] The entry-deterring output Q_L is the same as in the analysis of limit-entry pricing, i.e. it is equal to the output at which the demand curve intersects the average cost, minus the MES level of Q_0. The credibility of maintaining post-entry the output Q_L, though, is crucially dependent on the existence and importance of sunk costs. The necessary conditions are given by equations (A.7) and (A.8) in Appendix 5A. For $b = 2/1\ 000$, $Q_0 = 6\ 000$, $a = 100$, $d = 5$, $r = 55$, it is easily seen that (A.8) is satisfied. If, however, with the same total average cost of $60 the sunk component is reduced below $28, then (A.8) is violated, and entry deterrence is no longer credible. The incumbent is better off charging the monopoly price and accepting the eventual loss of its monopoly position.

Although the logic underlying the credibility of entry deterrence is the same for all types of firms and markets, there are differences in practice in the specific form taken by the commitment of resources. The example presented above has the form of *excess capacity* (or excess investment): irreversible investment, in excess of what is profitable, is committed and is sufficient to deter entry.[10] It is a costly commitment, given that it reduces the monopoly profits from $200 000 to $150 000 in the example. It is also detrimental to public welfare: it insures that the incumbent's dominant position will persist, and that profits and consumer prices will remain high. For instance, if sunk costs did not exist the example shown above would end up with three firms in the sector, producing the MES level of 6 000 units and charging a price of $64, instead of $70.

While excess investment is the only possible form of commitment in a homogeneous single location market, there are other alternatives in products differentiated by location or quality. The commitment to entry deterrence is signalled for such products in a similar way as for the homogeneous ones, but the specific form that it takes differs according to the circumstances. Two particular case studies that have surfaced in recent economics literature will be examined below.

Brand Proliferation

In a market for products that are differentiated by quality characteristics, interfirm rivalry may take place along both price and quality dimensions. A new firm may compete with incumbent(s) either by undercutting the price for an existing quality level, or by supplying a new product variety at prices comparable to those of existing firms. Entry deterrence in such cases would involve an incumbent's choice of providing a combination of product qualities and corresponding prices such that new entry would not bring profits to the entrant. These incumbent choices must also entail an irreversible commitment of resources, so that according to the logic of Figure 5.7 it would not be profitable for the incumbent to share the market in the event of entry. This commitment may be a combination of capacity investment and brand advertising, such that capital is not resaleable once invested.

This type of entry deterrence in a differentiated market resulted in a court action in the U.S. that lasted for ten years before being terminated in the beginning of 1982. The action was brought by the U.S. Federal Trade Commission (FTC) against the four (later reduced to three) main U.S. manufacturers of ready-to-eat breakfast cereals, led by the Kellogg Corporation. The suit involved many complaints, but we shall concentrate here on the allegations concerning the leading firms' attempts to deter entry through brand proliferation and "excessive" advertising.[11] Even though the FTC decided to stop the action after a ten-year litigation, that decision was taken after a vote that was split along partisan lines. It does, therefore, represent a significant interest. The issues raised in it were novel and likely to resurface in the future. The erection of barriers to entry by dominant firms or cartels is very difficult to detect and/or prevent with the normal tools of competition policy. Firm conduct in many such cases is virtually indistinguishable from conventional competitive behaviour, and neither American nor the much weaker Canadian law can deal with it effectively.

Ready-to-eat cereals have a number of product quality characteristics that differentiate them in the eyes of the consumers. Some of these are sweetness, protein content, shape, grain base, vitamin content, fibre content, etc. It also seems likely that quality competition between brands is localized, with each brand having only a few direct competitors among brands that are similar in most characteristics. If prices are equal, then a specific consumer would choose the brand that corresponds most closely to his preferences with respect to the quality characteristics. The more brands there are in the market differing in these characteristics, the less easy it will be for a competitor to introduce a new brand profitably. Since a new firm needs several brands in order to establish itself at minimum efficient scale, a strategy of brand proliferation is likely to be an effective deterrent to entry.

The brand proliferation strategy involves heavy advertising and little price competition. As a leading government witness showed in his testimony, it is in many cases a better strategy for dominant firms than price competition. The dominant firms can keep the monopoly price unchanged and simply increase the number of marketed brands to the point at which it wouldn't pay for a would-be competitor to introduce a new brand at the existing price. The leading firms incur a cost to do this. The amount of necessary advertising for all these brands exceeds the amount that maximizes the monopoly profits if no possibilities for entry existed. Nonetheless, the brand proliferation strategy is a credible instrument of entry deterrence, according to the terminology used earlier. A brand, once introduced with certain quality characteristics, cannot change these characteristics without substantial additional costs. The sunk cost component of the introduction of a brand is significant, and the likelihood that the incumbents will accommodate the entrant is rather low.

Further, it was argued in that same testimony that this type of rivalry through non-price instruments such as product quality is not the type that maximizes social welfare, even though it is optimal from the leading firms' point of view. The brand proliferation strategy has two welfare effects. One is positive, giving the consumers more choice; the other negative, yielding higher costs and prices. In this case it was argued that more price competition, even though it may be at the expense of the total available product variety, would increase consumer welfare. As a result, two of the proposed remedies were that the leading firms create new competitors by divesting themselves of certain brands and trademarks; and that they license their existing trademarks to other firms on a royalty-free basis, provided these firms respect quality standards.

These arguments, as already noted, were insufficient to win the case for the FTC. The new (1981) U.S. administration abandoned the action after a ten-year litigation. Part of the objections to further prosecution involved the proposed remedies, which amounted to a restructuring of the breakfast cereals industry. It was alleged that such restructuring was beyond the mandate of the FTC.[12] It is also questionable whether the welfare benefits of reducing prices at the expense of restricting the number of available product qualities could be proven with the standards expected in a court action. Nonetheless, the issue of whether the public interest would be advanced by attempting to intervene in cases such as the breakfast cereals industry remains open at this point. The key policy issue is how to balance the interests of the community against the normal safeguards for firms' and individuals' rights that are expected in a democratic environment.

Locational Preemption

Geographical location can play the same role in deterring entry that product quality characteristics play in the breakfast cereals industry. Incumbents choose the combination of locations and corresponding prices that insure the failure of new entrants. Although no judicial action is associated with locational preemption, there exists a case study by West (1981a and b) of entry deterrence in the supermarket industry on the Canadian West Coast, and in particular in the city of Vancouver. This deterrence was achieved through the leading firms' practice of "packing" the city's geographical space with stores in a systematic pattern that left little space for profitable entry or expansion by competitors.

The theoretical analysis of this case is very similar to that of the breakfast cereals industry. Price competition is avoided, and new entry is deterred at "high" prices by making it unprofitable for a new firm to locate itself anywhere in the market. In the supermarket case, the hypothesis of market preemption was tested statistically in the greater Vancouver area market. This hypothesis was shown to be consistent with the data.

Under market preemption the leading firms would divide the market among themselves into territories. Then, each firm would pack its territory with supermarket outlets. No new entrant would find it profitable to enter. This is because consumers are supposed to patronize the store that is located closest to them, provided no price differences exist. Hence, if market preemption exists, the outlets of the leading firms would tend to have stores owned by the same firm as direct locational neighbours. Furthermore, each firm's stores should be clustered in a territory.

Both predictions are testable with relatively simple statistical methods. The tests first showed that the ownership of supermarket outlets in the greater Vancouver region was not randomly distributed across all existing stores. Second, it was shown that there was a strong tendency for any given store owned by a leading firm to have stores of the same ownership as neighbours. Finally, it was shown that within the city of Vancouver the establishment of new stores by the two leading firms in the post-1940 period followed an established pattern. That pattern was consistent with the hypothesis that one leading firm preempted locations by building new stores in the western sector and the other leading firm preempted locations in the eastern sector.

This type of inter-firm rivalry, which promotes non-price competition to achieve the combined goals of profit-maximization and restriction of entry by new firms, poses significant challenges to economists and policy-makers. As already noted in the breakfast cereals case, the effect of such rivalries upon social welfare are mixed. The public policy goals have to balance the benefits of increased consumer choice with the drawbacks of higher prices stemming from lack of price competition. No satisfactory solutions to this public policy dilemma have been developed as yet.

Sunk costs also play the reverse role from the point of view of entry barriers. In other words, their absence from a certain industry means that entry barriers are going to be very difficult to sustain. Markets in which there are no sunk costs when establishing a new firm are known as contestable,[13] and were already examined briefly in Chapter 3.

Contestable Markets

The concept of the contestability of a market is a generalization of that of perfect competition. Market equilibrium in a contestable market has all the desirable properties of a perfectly competitive equilibrium: prices are as low as possible, subject to firms covering their costs; costs are minimized and profits are zero. These properties are achieved without any need for the existence of a large number of firms in the industry. In theory, this highly desirable market equilibrium can be achieved with only two firms in the industry. It is the potential entry of new competitors that forms the mechanism through which contestable markets reach their equilibrium.

For a market to be contestable, entry must be perfectly and costlessly reversible, meaning that the entering firm must be able to exit the sector without suffering any losses. Entry can then take place whenever a profit opportunity arises. The entering firm may then realize these profits and get out of the sector as soon as the profits disappear. Such an entry is known as *hit-and-run entry*.

As already noted, contestable markets must have no sunk costs for entering firms, since these costs are lost once entry occurs. Similarly, entering firms must be able to count upon a time period during which the pre-entry prices prevailing in the industry will remain unchanged, so that they have the chance to reap their profits. This can happen if, for instance, long-term binding contracts between sellers and buyers can be negotiated prior to a firm's entry into the industry; such contracts may not always be feasible in real-life markets. If a market displays these characteristics then incumbent firms would be prevented from setting prices above marginal costs by the possibility of hit-and-run entry, thus insuring the attractive industry equilibrium state mentioned above.

Markets approaching contestability are thought to exist in many industries that were once subjected to regulation in the U.S., most of which are still regulated in Canada. Airlines, taxicab companies, and trucking are the most obvious examples. In these industries the necessary equipment for entering the market can easily be resold in the second-hand market with little loss of capital. Hit-and-run entry is therefore possible, at least in principle. The contestable state of these markets gave a great deal of impetus to the deregulation movement of the late 1970s and early 1980s. Nonetheless, the issue is not completely resolved as of this writing. The recent wave of mergers in the U.S. airline industry, and the increased sophistication of incumbent airlines in fighting off new entrants (while raising prices once these entrants have gone out of business), have raised some questions about the contestability of this industry. We shall return to these questions when we examine deregulation in Chapter 10.

Reputation

Although the breakfast cereals and supermarkets cases were similar in the nature and form of entry deterrence, there were some important differences between the two. In the breakfast cereals case there was an unmistakable irreversibility in the commitment of resources (primarily advertising) every time a new brand was marketed by an incumbent firm. There was less irreversibility involved, by contrast, in opening a new supermarket, given the ease with which the facility could be reconverted to a different type of store. In other words, the crucial irreversible commitment feature of entry deterrence was not as conspicuously present in the supermarkets case as in breakfast cereals. Why then did an entrant not call the bluff of the dominant incumbent firms? Alternatively, why did these firms persist in entry-deterring schemes that were as damaging to themselves as to their potential rivals?

The answer to these questions was provided in a series of new contributions to economic literature during the early 1980s.[14] These contributions deal with what has become known as *reputation* in the entry deterrence arguments. Specifically, these studies have shown that in many instances it may be in the interest of incumbents to fight rather than to share a particular market, even when irreversible commitments do not exist. For this profitability of rivalry two conditions must exist: the incumbent(s) must have more than one market to protect from new entry, and/or there must be considerable uncertainty concerning the nature of the irreversible commitments, the incumbent costs of production, or the profit consequences of alternative policies. Potential entrants use the threat of entry in order to resolve such uncertainty, depending on the incumbents' reactions. Incumbents, on the other hand, may use these reactions in order to send signals that may or may not present a true picture of the situation. The purpose of these signals is to create an image (*reputation*) of commitment and willingness to fight entry that may or may not be true. This image then may act as a barrier to entry, since potential entrants may not be willing to incur the costs of testing its truth to the ultimate conclusion, except in the most perfectly contestable markets.

The literature on reputation is still relatively new, and few empirical studies on the subject exist as yet. Its behavioural foundations, though, are solidly grounded in models of interfirm conflict similar to the ones presented earlier in this section. The costs of engaging in a mutually disadvantageous fight may be viewed as an investment in entry deterrence: by fighting a given entry incumbents invest in reputation, i.e. in building an image of a firm that does not tolerate invasion of its territory. For such an investment to be worthwhile there must be considerable uncertainty about the benefits and costs of the various incumbent policies concerning entry. Once this image has been created it can act as a barrier to entry just like product differentiation or economies of scale.

Entry and Industry Structure in Canada: Empirical Evidence

As the brief review of the theoretical studies on barriers to entry and their effects shows, many important new insights have appeared on these topics in recent years. These insights have greatly increased our knowledge about firm entry and its consequences on industry structure and conduct. They have also had a significant impact on public policy, especially in the deregulation area, through the contestable markets literature.

The empirical work, though, has not as a whole kept pace with the theory. Most empirical studies of structure, conduct, and performance have paid at least lip service to barriers to entry, by including proxy measure of some of them among their explanatory variables. These inclusions, though, were almost always done on an *ad hoc* basis, with little link to the underlying theoretical models. This is not intended as a criticism of the empirical studies, given the complexity of the theory, but their shortcomings should serve as a reminder of the comparatively low degree of reliability of the results.

The Measurement of Entry Barriers

The barriers to entry that are most often included in empirical studies are those stemming from economies of scale and product differentiation. Variables measuring R&D intensity (as a proxy for patent activity and/or sunk costs) are also used quite frequently, as are absolute capital requirements. The latter were part of Bain's original work on barriers to entry, but have played little role in the literature since then.

Other sources of barriers to entry are almost always ignored in empirical work. For instance, sunk costs are perhaps the single most important factor of the strategic entry deterrence aspect of entry barriers. Yet these costs are not part of the type of data normally available to economists, and consequently they are omitted from the list of entry barriers in most studies.

Typically, an empirical work uses statistical estimation techniques to fit industry or firm data to one or more functional relationships of the form:

$$\pi = F(X_1, X_2, \ldots, X_n)$$

In the studies that interest us the dependent variable π may represent one of the following: structure measured by concentration indices; performance measured by price-cost margins, profits, or rate of return; or conduct, measured by price inflation or entry rates. Among the independent variables $X_1, \ldots, X_n$, there are several that measure barriers to entry: the ratio of MES to industry shipments for economies of scale; advertising expenses as a proportion of industry sales for product differentiation; etc.

A factor that significantly complicates the measurement of entry barriers and their effects is the non-linearity of the impact of each possible source of entry barriers. For instance, economies of scale are usually evaluated according to the methods examined in Chapter 2, by the ratio of MES to market size as a proxy variable. This is, however, insufficient, since we also need a measure of the cost disadvantage experienced by plants of suboptimal scale. The proxy used in practice is a "good" indicator of the importance of scale economies in the sector, but only if the cost disadvantage is important; otherwise, suboptimally small plants can also enter and survive in the sector, and scale economies are not a sufficiently powerful entry barrier. Similarly, the intensity of advertising in the sector is sometimes taken as an indicator of product differentiation and hence of entry barriers. Nonetheless, this intensity of advertising (which is traditionally measured by the share of advertising expenses in total sales), is larger for convenience goods than for other consumer goods; therefore the absolute numbers are meaningful only in relation to the sector that they refer to. Further, as shown in the empirical studies discussed below, these advertising expenses are *ceteris paribus* higher in Canadian firms under U.S. control than in the purely domestic ones.

Many of these problems are overcome by a variety of techniques that bear testimony to the ingenuity of the researchers. Samples are stratified according to type of product, firm ownership, or size of independent variable; barriers to entry variables are introduced in a nonlinear way in the statistical estimation; proxies for the cost disadvantage below MES are included in some studies; etc. It is not possible to do full justice to these efforts in this brief review. Yet it is also impossible to dispel lingering doubts about the robustness of the model specification in each case. These doubts should be kept in mind when reviewing the studies' results.

Empirical Studies of Barriers and their Effects

Relatively few studies of firm entry and exit in Canada have appeared in the recent economics literature. The creation and scrapping of plants is not part of the published economic statistics, and special data aggregation is needed for any such studies. On the other hand, most empirical studies of Canadian industry do include variables representing the entry barriers, given their importance for industry structure, conduct, and performance. Thus, the study by Eastman and Stykolt (1967), already discussed in Chapter 2, presented evidence on the sources of barriers to entry and their impact on industry prices, profits, and costs. That study had classified a sample of industries into a number of categories, depending on the source and the importance of entry barriers. As noted in the earlier chapters, the presence of high entry barriers and the lack of competition from imports were essential for the effects of high concentration (high prices and profits, but also higher costs due to X-inefficiency or to the presence of suboptimal firms) to manifest themselves.

Barriers to entry were also examined in an important study by Caves *et al.* (1980). That study was based on a specially constructed data base that differentiated between firms under Canadian and U.S. ownership. It was mostly concerned with firm behaviour, and an attempt was made to include most types of barriers to entry in the empirical work. Proxy variables attempting to measure economies of scale, the cost disadvantage of plants of suboptimal scale, advertising (as an index of product differentiation), and sunk costs were used as explanatory factors for industry structure, conduct, and performance, separately for Canadian and foreign firms. Last, the effects of foreign trade, in the form of tariff protection, competition from imports, or participation in export activity were also taken into account.

The results of that study confirmed the theoretical predictions about the effects of entry barriers on industry structure as measured by concentration ratios. Thus, economies of scale and the structure of capital costs turn out to be highly significant determinants of concentration, albeit in a nonlinear way. The influence of product differentiation through advertising is somewhat weaker, but it still has the expected positive sign. Further, product differentiation is shown to counteract somewhat the negative effect of small scale on the survival ability of suboptimal firms.

Other important results of this study concerned the impact of the large foreign presence in Canadian manufacturing, chiefly under the form of subsidiaries of U.S. multinationals. This presence was found to be unevenly distributed across Canadian industries, with the differences arising largely in response to the differential advantages enjoyed by the multinationals: heavy advertising and R&D, and heavy use of sophisticated managerial personnel. The multinationals dominate the sector where these advantages are important, while Canadian-owned firms are prevalent where these advantages are unimportant, or where the flexibility associated with small size and local contacts is a distinct asset. Last, from the point of view of profit performance the differences between Canadian and U.S.-owned firms were also quite sharp, with Canadian firms' profits being strongly related to the existence of market power (high concentration ratios). The subsidiaries' profits, on the other hand, were very difficult to explain by the conventional market structure variables, suggesting that their actual profit stream may have been poorly measured by the variables used.[15]

Such differentiated results were also found in earlier studies, but with a somewhat different emphasis. Thus Gorecki (1976) confirmed the differential response of Canadian and U.S.-owned firms to incentives and barriers to entry. His study found that Canadian firms respond only weakly to incentives to entry such as profitability and growth, but react strongly (and negatively) to the presence of entry barriers. Foreign ownership, on the other hand, has exactly the opposite effect: strong response to incentives, but a weak response to entry barriers.

These findings, though, were not altogether confirmed in the most recent study of the entry and exit process by Baldwin and Gorecki (1983), carried out on behalf of the Economic Council of Canada. That study used a specially created data base to examine the process by which Canadian manufacturing firms entered, expanded, contracted or exited from specific sectors in the 1970-79 period. Entry into a sector was separated according to its manner of occurrence, whether by building a new plant or by acquiring an already existing establishment. Likewise, exiting firms were identified as either scrapping or divesting themselves of their producing facilities. Last, the ownership of the firm (Canadian or U.S.) was used to divide the empirical results into two subgroups.

The purpose of that study was to examine the adaptation of the Canadian manufacturing sector to the growing liberalization of foreign trade that occurred during the decades of the late 1960s to early 1980s. During the period covered by the study, exports as a percentage of domestic production rose from 23.3 percent in 1970 to 28.0 percent in 1979, while the corresponding proportions for imports were 21.7 percent and 27.2 percent. Tariffs fell by 30 percent between 1966 and 1978 as a result of international agreements in the 1960s and 1970s. These reductions were not spread uniformly over all sectors. Some industries saw their protection reduced much faster: in the food and beverage group the average tariff declined from 21.1 percent in 1966 to 11.2 percent in 1975, while the comparable proportions for all manufacturing were 11.9 percent and 8.8 percent. The study covered the firm entry and exit processes that occurred, in part as a result of the foreign trade changes.

The results of the study showed a high degree of entry and exit in the Canadian manufacturing sector over the 1970-79 period. On average, 14.0 percent of an industry's sales in 1979 were accounted for by new entrants that built plants during the decade, while 16.2 percent of 1970 sales were by firms that subsequently exited by scrapping their plants. Hence, on average entry and exit balanced one another, implying a relatively painless transition. Nonetheless there were many surprising results. Thus, the difference between fast and slow-growing industries manifested itself primarily in differences in firm birth rates, while the rate at which firms were exiting remained fairly constant across industries. In declining industries exits were substantially higher than entries, but there was nevertheless a significant number of entries even in such industries.

From the point of view of barriers to entry and exit and their impact on the corresponding processes, the study turned out a number of interesting differences. Plant scale and concentration had a negative effect on both entry and exit, but this effect was relatively weak in both cases. By contrast, advertising (product differentiation) and R&D had a much stronger and significant influence on both entry and exit. Thus, advertising reduced both entry and exit by new firms, while R&D led to less entry and more exit by both new and continuing firms. For this latter type of firms the effect of advertising was similar to that of R&D, i.e. it caused less entry and/or more exit.

Last, the study highlighted a number of important differences between domestic and foreign firms. Thus, domestic firms were shown to respond strongly to industry size (number of firms), profitability, domestic sales growth, and export growth. By contrast, foreign firms responded strongly only to the existence of other foreign firms, and they responded to growth and profitability only if they were already established in Canada. In other words, entering foreign firms do not respond to the same entry incentives as domestic firms, but once they are established they tend to behave in a similar way. The consequence of this differential response was that Canadian firms entered into sectors previously dominated by foreign firms and underwent a rationalization process that should have bolstered their competitive position.

On balance, therefore, this brief review must close on a rather optimistic note. The Canadian manufacturing sector seems to have adapted quite well to the major liberalization of foreign trade that occurred over the last two decades. It responded to trade and growth opportunities by entering into new sectors and closing down unprofitable plants, and it managed to do so without losing ground to firms under foreign ownership. This adaptation confirms the beneficial effects of free trade for industry performance, to which we shall return in Chapter 11.

Conclusions

In the long run, industry structure, conduct, and performance are strongly influenced by the conditions governing entry of new firms into the industry. These conditions are known as barriers to entry. They influence firm conduct and performance both indirectly, through their effect on structure, but also directly, because of the possible behaviour that they induce from incumbent firms.

Barriers to entry are mostly elements of industry structure that allow incumbent firms to enjoy positive profits, while guaranteeing that new firms won't find it profitable to enter the industry. As such, they are considered quite desirable by incumbents, but less so by public policy-makers. The latter, though, have few weapons at their disposal, given the difficulty of separating desirable and undesirable features of entry barriers. These mixed aspects of the barriers are partly the result of the type of strategic conduct that they produce upon incumbent firms. Such strategies often have both positive and negative aspects for public welfare, and it is not always clear which one will predominate.

Nonetheless, public policy cannot afford to ignore entry barriers. For one thing, the effectiveness of collusion and consequently the necessity for vigorous antitrust enforcement depend very heavily on their existence. Conversely, when the entry barriers can be shown to be low, and/or when they can be weakened by public actions, as with deregulation in contestable markets, competition policy can rely on entry to do its job. The results in selected sectors in Canada and the U.S. will be reviewed in more detail in Chapter 10.

Appendix 5A   THE MATHEMATICS OF ENTRY DETERRENCE

Let $p = D(Q)$ denote the inverse demand curve. The average cost curve of firms in the industry is denoted by $AC(Q)$, and it is decreasing for $Q \leq Q_0$ and thereafter constant and equal to c, where Q_0 denotes the MES output. Hence, $C' \equiv \dfrac{dAC}{dQ} < 0$ for $Q \leq Q_0$, $\dfrac{dAC}{dQ} = 0$, $Q > Q_0$. The marginal cost is also equal to c for $Q \geq Q_0$.

Monopoly Price and Output, P_M and Q_M

From Chapter 3, this is found by solving the equation $QD' + D = c$ (marginal revenue = marginal cost). For a linear demand $D(Q) = a - bQ$, $QD' + D = a - 2bQ = c$, and $Q_M = \dfrac{a - c}{2b}$, $P_M = a - bQ_M = \dfrac{a + c}{2}$.

Limit-entry Price and Output, P_L and Q_L

Let Q_E denote the potential entrant's output. The total industry output after entry is $Q_L + Q_E$, with corresponding price $D(Q_L + Q_E)$. Q_L must be selected in such a way that the post-entry price $D(Q_L + Q_E)$ must be less than or equal to the entrant's unit cost $AC(Q_E)$ for all possible Q_E. Hence, we must have:
Entrant profit $\pi_E = Q_E D(Q_E + Q_L) - Q_E AC(Q_E) = 0$, implying

$$D(Q_L + Q_E) = AC(Q_E) \qquad \textbf{Eq. (5A.1)}$$

Q_E maximizes π_E, implying $\dfrac{\partial \pi_E}{\partial Q_E} = 0$,

$$\frac{\partial[Q_E \, D(Q_L + Q_E) - Q_E \, AC(Q_E)]}{\partial Q_E} = 0 \text{ or}$$

$$D(Q_L + Q_E) + Q_E \frac{\partial D}{\partial Q_E} = AC(Q_E) + Q_E \frac{dAC}{dQ_E} \qquad \textbf{Eq. (5A.2)}$$

(A.1) and (A.2) taken together imply that

$$\frac{\partial D}{\partial Q_E} = \frac{dAC}{dQ_E} \qquad \textbf{Eq. (5A.3)}$$

or that the slope of the demand at $(Q_L + Q_E)$ equals that of the average cost at Q_E. In turn, these two relations imply the situation shown in Figure 5.5.

If now the average cost curve $AC(Q)$ rises very steeply (more steeply than the demand curve) for $Q < Q_0$ then (5A.3) can hold only when $Q_E = Q_0$. Then the limit-entry output is simply given by (5A.1) for $Q_E = Q_0$, or

$$D(Q_L + Q_0) = AC(Q_0) = c \qquad \textbf{Eq. (5A.4)}$$

In the linear demand case, (5A.4) yields $a - b \, (Q_L + Q_0) = c$, or

$$Q_L = \frac{a - c}{b} - Q_0 \qquad \textbf{Eq. (5A.5)}$$

Credibility of Entry Deterrence

Let the average cost c for $Q \geq Q_0$ be decomposable into a recoverable and a sunk component, i.e. $c = d + r$, where d is recoverable and r is sunk. Then entry deterrence at the limit output Q_L is credible if the incumbent finds it more profitable to continue producing Q_L post-entry, rather than curtail output. The incumbent profit π is:

$$\pi = Q_L [D(Q_L + Q_0) - d] - rQ_L \qquad \textbf{Eq. (5A.6)}$$

where rQ_L is constant post-entry, i.e., it cannot be recovered if Q_L is reduced; hence, it is ignored in decision-making. For entry-deterrence to be credible we must have $\frac{\partial \pi}{\partial QL} > 0$, implying that output contraction is unprofitable. Hence

$$\frac{\partial \pi}{\partial Q_L} = \frac{\partial\{Q_L[D(Q_L + Q_0) - d]\}}{\partial Q_L} = D(Q_L + Q_0) + Q_L \frac{\partial D}{\partial Q_L} - d \geq 0, \text{ yielding}$$

$$D(Q_L + Q_0) + Q_L \frac{\partial D}{\partial Q_L} \geq d \qquad \textbf{Eq. (5A.7)}$$

For a linear demand curve this becomes $a - b(Q_L + Q_0) - bQ_L \geq d$ or, using (5A.5), setting $c = d + r$, and eliminating Q_L, we get after simplification:

$$bQ_0 \geq a - d - 2r \qquad \textbf{Eq. (5A.8)}$$

which forms the credibility condition.

Endnotes

1. See Salop (1979) and Dixit (1982).
2. See Scherer (1980), p. 241.
3. See Schmalensee (1982), and McRae and Tapon (1983).
4. The pioneering treatment of this issue is by Nordhaus (1969). See also Scherer (1972). A summary of their work is in Chapter 11 of this book.
5. See Caves and Porter (1976), p. 45.
6. See Perrakis and Silva-Echenique (1983, 1985).
7. The initial analysis of limit-entry pricing is due to Bain (1956) and Sylos-Labini (1962).
8. In fact, it can be shown for this example that any production above the limit output of 14 000 would produce the entry deterrence results. The amount of 15 000 is chosen simply as an illustration.
9. See Schmalensee (1981) and Perrakis and Warskett (1986). The latter study has developed credibility conditions under demand uncertainty and shown that such uncertainty increases the profits from entry deterrence.
10. Excess capacity was first presented by Wenders (1971), and analyzed in detail by Dixit (1980), Spulber (1981), and Perrakis and Warskett (1983, 1986). A different approach, but with similar results, was taken by Eaton and Lipsey (1980).
11. The classic treatment of this topic is by Schmalensee (1978), who was a witness for the U.S. government in the breakfast cereals case described here.
12. See the relevant articles in the *New York Times*, Sept. 11, 1981 and Jan. 16, 1982.
13. The term was first presented and analyzed in detail in Baumol *et al.* (1982). See also the discussion by Dixit (1982) and Perrakis (1982).
14. The basic references on the reputation model are by Kreps and Wilson (1982), and Milgrom and Roberts (1982), both of which use the formal structure of game theory.
15. This can happen if, for instance, the subsidiaries have "transferred" part of their profits to the parent companies by paying inflated transfer prices for any products or services that they may acquire from the parent company.

References

Bain, J.S. *Barriers to New Competition*. Cambridge, Mass.: Harvard University Press, 1956.

Baldwin, J., and P. Gorecki, with J. McVey and J. Crysdale. *Entry and Exit to the Canadian Manufacturing Sector: 1970-1979*, Economic Council of Canada Disc. Paper #225, February 1983.

Baumol, W., J. Panzar and R. Willig. *Contestable Markets and the Theory of Industry Structure*. San Diego, Cal.: Harcourt, Brace Jovanovich, 1982.

Caves, R.E., and M. Porter. "Barriers to Exit," *Essays on Industrial Organization in Honor of Joe S. Bain*, R.T. Masson and P.D. Qualls, eds. Cambridge, Mass.: Ballinger, 1976.

Caves, R., M. Porter, M. Spence, and W.J.T. Scott. *Competition in the Open Economy.* Cambridge, Mass.: Harvard University Press, 1980.

Demsetz, H. "Barriers to Entry," *American Economic Review,* 72:1 (March 1982), pp. 47-57.

Dixit, A. "The Role of Investment in Entry Deterrence," *Economic Journal,* 90 (March 1980), pp. 95-106.

———. "Recent Developments in Oligopoly Theory," *American Economic Review,* 72:2 (May 1982), pp. 12-17.

Eastman, H., and S. Stykolt. *The Tariff and Competition in Canada.* Toronto, Ont.: Macmillan, 1967.

Eaton, B.C., and R.G. Lipsey. "Exit Barriers are Entry Barriers: the Durability of Capital as a Barrier to Entry," *The Bell Journal of Economics,* 11:2 (Autumn 1980), pp. 721-729.

Gorecki, P.K. "The Determinants of Entry by Domestic and Foreign Enterprises in Canadian Manufacturing Industries: Some Comments and Results," *Review of Economics and Statistics,* 58 (November 1976), pp. 485-488.

Kreps, D., and R. Wilson. "Reputation and Imperfect Information," *Journal of Economic Theory,* Vol. 27 (1982), pp. 253-279.

McRae, J.J., and F. Tapon. "Post-Patent Barriers to Entry in the Canadian Pharmaceutical Industry and Olson's Hypothesis about the Rise and Decline of Industries," paper presented at the 1983 meetings of the Canadian Economics Association, Vancouver, B.C., May 1983.

Masson, R.T., and P.D. Qualls, eds. *Essays on Industrial Organization in Honor of Joe S. Bain.* Cambridge, Mass.: Ballinger, 1975.

Milgrom, P., and J. Roberts. "Predation, Reputation and Entry Deterrence," *Journal of Economic Theory,* Vol. 27 (1982), pp. 280-312.

Nordhaus, W. *Invention, Growth and Welfare: A Theoretical Treatment of Technological Change.* Cambridge, Mass.: Massachusetts Institute of Technology Press, 1969.

Perrakis, S. Book Review of Baumol *et al.* (1982), *Canadian Journal of Economics,* 15:4 (November 1982), pp. 774-780.

Perrakis, S., and J. Silva-Echenique. "The Profitability and Risk of CATV Operations in Canada," *Applied Economics,* 15: 6 (December 1983), pp. 745-758.

———. "The Profitability and Risk of Television Stations in Canada," *Applied Economics,* Vol. 17 (August 1985), pp. 745-759.

Perrakis, S., and G. Warskett. "Capacity and Entry Under Demand Uncertainty," *Review of Economic Studies,* 1983, pp. 495-511.

———. "Uncertainty, Economies of Scale and Barriers to Entry," *Oxford Economic Papers,* Vol. 38, Supplement (November 1986), pp. 58-74.

Salop, S. "Strategic Entry Deterrence," *American Economic Review,* 69:2 (May 1979), pp. 335-338.

Scherer, F.M. *Industrial Market Structure and Economic Performance*. Chicago, Ill.: Rand McNally, 2nd edition, 1980.

Scherer, F.M., A. Beckenstein, E. Kaufer, and R.D. Murphy. *The Economics of Multi-Plant Operations: an International Comparisons Study*. Cambridge, Mass.: Harvard University Press, 1975.

Scherer, F.M. "Nordhaus' Theory of Optimal Patent Life: a Geometric Reinterpretation," *American Economic Review*, 62:3 (June 1972), pp. 422-427.

Schmalensee, R. "Entry Deterrence in the Ready-to-eat Breakfast Cereal Industry," *The Bell Journal of Economics*, 9:2 (Autumn 1978), pp. 305-327.

————. "Economies of Scale and Barriers to Entry," *Journal of Political Economy*, 89:6 (December 1981), pp. 1228-1238.

————. "Product Differentiation Advantages of Pioneering Brands," *American Economic Review*, 72:3 (June 1982), pp. 349-365.

Spulber, D.F. "Capacity, Output, and Sequential Entry," *American Economic Review*, 71:3 (June 1981), pp. 503-514.

Stigler, G.J. *The Organization of Industry*. Homewood, Ill.: Irwin, 1968.

Sylos-Labini, P. *Oligopoly and Technical Progress*. Cambridge, Mass.: Harvard University Press, 1962.

Wenders, J.T. "Excess Capacity as a Barrier to Entry," *Journal of Industrial Economics*, Vol. 20 (1971), pp. 14-19.

West, D.S. "Tests of Two Locational Implications of a Theory of Market Preemption," *Canadian Journal of Economics*, 14:2 (May 1981), pp. 313-326.

West, D.S. "Testing for Market Preemption Using Sequential Location Data," *The Bell Journal of Economics*, 12:1 (Spring 1981), pp. 129-143.

CHAPTER 6

Other Topics in Monopolies

·····

and Oligopolies

·····

T his chapter provides the theoretical framework for a number of important policy issues in industrial organization that do not fit into traditional monopoly or oligopoly theories. These issues arise because of particular structural or behavioural features of real-world firms and markets that have been mostly ignored in the simplified and stylized models that we saw in the previous chapters. While there are many such features that have been omitted for simplification purposes, we focus here on two particular assumptions that have been made in much of our analysis until now: the homogeneity of markets and the homogeneity of products.

A firm's market is homogeneous if all buyers of its product are broadly similar in nature, with the result that the seller is unable to distinguish between them. In reality, most firms' customers differ in tastes, income, geographical location, or other attributes. Often a firm may be able to divide its market into segments corresponding to different classes of buyers. It may then find it profitable to practice *price discrimination*, by selling the same product at different prices to different classes of customers without any difference in costs. Such discrimination takes various forms in practice; some of these forms are legal, while others are prohibited by our competition legislation.

The lack of homogeneity of the various products sold in a given market has already been mentioned repeatedly throughout the previous chapters. Most firms produce and sell a variety of products, differentiated by type or quality. Similarly, there are differences in the products sold by the various participating firms in any given market, with the result that these products are only imperfect substitutes for each other. As we saw in Chapter 5, this type of differentiation can have important barrier to entry effects.

In this chapter we focus on the means by which firms can differentiate a product that may otherwise be virtually indistinguishable from that of their competitors. This is the issue of *advertising*, which is a major dimension of conduct in the modern corporation. Through its differentiation effect, advertising has important structural implications, with attendant consequences for conduct and welfare. We present here a brief economic analysis of advertising, together with some empirical evidence of its effects on the Canadian economy.

Last, this chapter contains a brief analysis of a particular type of structure in a market for differentiated products, that combines features of perfect competition and market power. This is known as the theory of *monopolistic competition*, developed by Chamberlin in the early 1930s. While this theory has been attacked on methodological grounds by several economists associated with the Chicago School of economic thought, it has recently attracted attention because of the emphasis it places on product differentiation. Several of its results have been incorporated into other influential models in industrial organization.

Price Discrimination

Price discrimination can take many forms and is frequently encountered in practice. The most obvious case occurs when the same commodity is sold at different prices to different classes of customers. Another type of price discrimination occurs when the same commodity is sold in two different markets at the same price, in spite of the fact that the costs of serving the two markets are different. Still another form of discrimination takes place when the price of the product or service differs according to the time of day or the season, even though the costs are again identical.

You have probably already recognized several real-life examples of discriminatory pricing conforming to the above descriptions. Children and senior citizens frequently pay lower ticket prices than adults for movies and other forms of entertainment. The price of the basic telephone service is the same in rural and urban areas, in spite of the higher costs of serving the former. Electricity is priced lower outside the peak usage periods. All of these examples are common and legal types of price discrimination which are generally accepted without much controversy.

Other discriminatory pricing tactics, though, may not be legal. For instance, a firm may charge different prices for the same product in two different markets because it faces competition in the lower-priced market. If this lower price is predatory in nature it may run afoul of the law.

Discriminatory pricing is only possible under a number of conditions. The most obvious one is that buyers or markets must be separated. Otherwise it is possible to have the so-called commodity *arbitrage*, meaning that low-price buyers can sell their purchases to high-price buyers, thus eliminating the price differential. The separation of markets may occur because of the nature of the product, as with electricity supply to individual customers or personal services applied directly to the purchaser (such as physicians, dentists, etc.). Alternatively, the markets may be separated geographically, in which case the price differential between them cannot exceed the unit transportation costs.

A second set of necessary conditions for price discrimination is the existence of differing demand elasticities for the classes of customers that one wishes to discriminate between. Further, it must also be possible for the seller to identify the demands corresponding to these classes. Different demand elasticities may arise because of differences in tastes, income, availability of substitutes, or many other reasons. For instance, a dentist may choose to charge different fees to rich and poor customers, given the higher elasticity of demand for his services on the part of the poor customers. The discriminatory pricing of movie theatre tickets on the basis of age is also partly based on demand elasticity differences arising from income differences, given the often-limited incomes of young people and senior citizens.

Last, price discrimination can be practiced only if the seller has some market power. In a perfectly competitive market the price is outside the control of individual firms, thus removing their capacity to discriminate. As the movie theatre and dentist examples show, market power need not be very extensive, and may arise solely because of slight product differentiation.

The traditional analysis of price discrimination classifies it into three categories, depending on the ability of the seller to distinguish between customer classes. These are known as first, second, and third degree price discrimination, following their classic treatment by Pigou (1920).

First degree price discrimination is also known as perfect discrimination by a monopolistic firm, which manages to extract the highest possible level of profits from its monopoly power. This is achieved by selling each individual unit of the product at the highest possible price at which a buyer is willing to purchase. This price is known as *reservation price*, and it must be established through individual bargaining with each customer. An alternative and more realistic way of practicing such discrimination, even when all buyers in the market have the same demand curve, is by selling them each individual units of the commodity at progressively decreasing prices.

Figure 6.1 shows the revenue extracted by the seller with such a perfectly-discriminating pricing scheme. The unit denoted by dQ is sold at the price P, which is found from the corresponding ordinate of the demand curve DD'. The corresponding revenue is equal to the cross-hatched trapeze, which is

FIGURE 6.1
First degree price discrimination

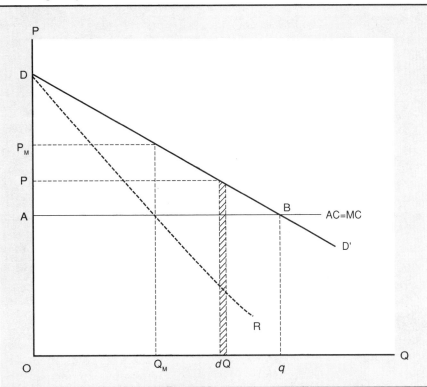

approximately equal to P times dQ. The sum of the revenues derived from the sales of all such units is equal to the area of ODBq. The price at which the monopolist will stop selling corresponds to the horizontal line at A, where it becomes equal to marginal cost. In the diagram it has been assumed without loss of generality that marginal and average costs are constant and equal. Hence, the total cost is equal to the area of OABq, and the firm's profit is the area of the shaded triangle ABD. This, as we know, is equal to the corresponding total consumer surplus.[1] Thus perfect price discrimination allows the firm to extract under the form of profit the entire surplus that would normally have accrued to the consumer.

From the above discussion it would seem that such price discrimination is highly undesirable. This may perhaps be true on equity grounds, but it should be noted that the efficiency properties of perfect price discrimination have many attractive features, at least in comparison to the non-discriminating monopolistic alternative. The equilibrium of such a firm is at the price P_M and quantity Q_M, found from the intersection of marginal cost with the marginal revenue DR. In fact, the quantity produced by the discriminating monopolist is identical to the corresponding equilibrium under perfect competition.[2] In theory, therefore, first-degree price discrimination, combined with a profit tax that transfers the monopoly profits back to the consumers, can achieve the attractive welfare properties of perfect competition. This improvement in general welfare as a result of price discrimination is found in many cases, with the result that the legal treatment of discriminatory pricing is considerably more ambivalent than, say, price collusion.

First degree price discrimination is rarely found in practice, due to the difficulties and costs of segregating buyers by their reservation prices. The example that is most often cited as coming closest to it is Xerox Corporation during the 1960s, which used a customer self-selection mechanism.[3] The company leased its photocopying machines on the basis of a monthly flat rate, but it also charged a fee that varied linearly with the number of copied pages. Hence, the monthly rental of the machine was much higher for high- than for low-use customers. The firm managed to separate the customers according to their willingness to pay by installing a meter on the machine that measured the number of copies made every month.

Second degree price discrimination is basically an attempt to approximate perfect discrimination by separating customers into a discrete number of classes according to their reservation prices, and charging a uniform price for each class. Figure 6.2 shows the case of a firm practicing discrimination of the second degree, with four classes of buyers. A customer in the ith class is charged price P_i, $i = 1, \ldots, 4$, with P_i declining as i increases. The firm profits, for constant average and marginal costs, are given by the shaded area bounded by the vertical axis, the cost line, and the irregular line ABCGEF. Clearly, the more classes it is possible to discriminate between, the higher the profits and the closer the approximation to perfect discrimination. This type of discrimination is found frequently in pricing by electric utilities, in which the unit price of energy declines as consumption increases, in a number of discrete steps.[4]

Last, we have *third degree* price discrimination, which is the one found most commonly in practice. This type of discrimination is very much like the second degree, insofar as the total demand is again split into classes. These, however, no longer correspond to reservation prices, but to some observable buyer characteristic such as age, location or income. Each one of these demand segments has its own price, chosen on the basis of the maximization of total profits.

Figure 6.3 shows third degree price discrimination practiced by a monopolist selling in two separate markets, with demand curves D_1D_1' and D_2D_2'. The corresponding marginal revenue curves are MR_1 and MR_2. The firm's average

FIGURE 6.2
Second degree price discrimination

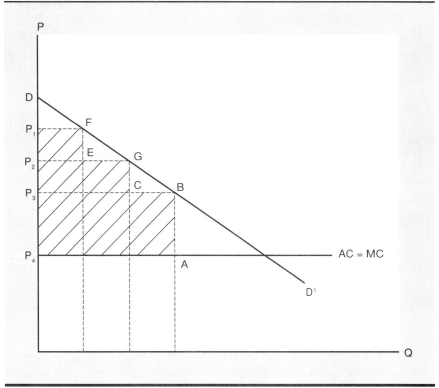

and marginal costs AC and MC are again assumed to be constant and equal. In Appendix 6A it is shown that the optimal quantities that can be sold in both markets are the ones that equate the marginal revenues to each other, and to marginal cost. These are denoted by Q_1' and Q_2', yielding market prices P_1 and P_2. At these profit-maximizing prices the price is higher in market 2, with the more inelastic demand. It can also be easily seen that price P_2 is so high that no sales would take place in market 1 if it were to prevail there as well.

As already noted, the difference between the two prices must not exceed the transportation costs between the two markets in case of resaleable commodities. If price discrimination were to be abolished then the two markets must be combined, and a common price charged in both of them. Such a price would lie between P_1 and P_2, increasing the burden to the customers in market 1, with the higher demand elasticity. Hence, the welfare effects of price

FIGURE 6.3
Third degree price discrimination

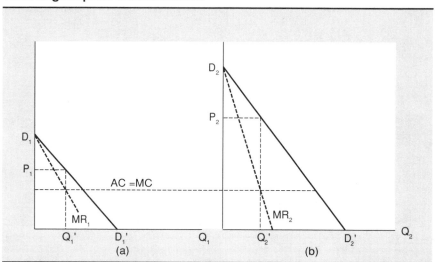

(a)   (b)

discrimination must by necessity be ambiguous, since it is by no means clear that it is better, on equity grounds, to have equal prices in both markets.[5]

Third degree price discrimination is quite frequent. Public utilities practice such discrimination almost routinely in energy and telecommunications. For instance, the charges for basic telephone service are much higher for business than for private subscribers. Conversely, industrial users of electricity pay less for energy than private consumers. In both cases it is the customers with the more inelastic demand who pay the higher price. Similarly, there is third degree price discrimination in several business practices, frequently hidden under the form of quantity discounts offered to key customers. An obvious example is the substantial discount offered to university professors when purchasing books or magazine subscriptions.

Public policy attitudes towards price discrimination have been somewhat ambivalent. Generally, the tendency has been to allow it, except when it is clearly predatory in purpose. In the U.S. the so-called Robinson-Patman Act of 1936, which outlaws such price discrimination, was introduced during the Great Depression as a reaction to widespread business failures by independent retailers who could not compete with chain stores. It is a piece of legislation that has been widely applied, but also one that has been much criticized by economists and legal scholars.[6] In Canada, by contrast, there have been very few cases brought up under the relevant section of the competition law, which will be reviewed in more detail in Chapter 9.

Peak-load Pricing

In Chapter 3 we saw that the accepted method of regulating a monopolist is to charge a product price that equates total revenues to total costs, while simultaneously satisfying all demand. We also saw some of the difficulties arising when this method is applied to monopolies producing more than one product. Peak-load pricing is a similar type of problem: the firm or its regulators must determine the appropriate prices for selling a single, non-storable commodity at two (or more) different times. The prices must cover all costs without any profit, given different market demand curves at both times. The ability of the firm to satisfy the demand during each time period depends on the invested capacity. Hence, the peak-load pricing problem amounts to a simultaneous determination of optimal capacity and prices during each period, so that all costs are covered and no profit remains.[7]

Peak-load pricing is a standard practice in public utilities, amounting to differential pricing of services across the different times of day. For instance, telephone utilities charge lower rates for long-distance calls outside normal business hours. Similarly, electric utilities have lower charges for energy consumption that takes place at off-peak hours. To the extent that demand is reduced by higher prices, such differential pricing would result in shifting consumption from peak to off-peak hours. In turn this would allow the utility to reduce invested capacity, which must be sufficient to satisfy the peak consumption.

The optimal peak and off-peak prices are determined under the assumption that unit operating and capacity costs are constant,[8] respectively denoted by c and C. The long-run marginal cost curve is discontinuous at the level K of invested capacity, with heights of c and $c + C$ respectively to the left and right of K. The off-peak and peak demand curves are denoted by DD' and $D_1 D_1'$, with the second lying above the first. It is assumed for simplicity that both peak and off-peak periods are of equal length. Figure 6.4 shows the resulting configuration of demand and costs for a given capacity K, with the peak price equal to $c + C$.

In the solution shown in this figure the peak period customers must pay for the entire capacity cost, while off-peak price is only equal to unit operating cost. The off-peak quantity Q_1 is below capacity. The optimal capacity K is found by setting the peak price equal to $c + C$.

The total consumption is Q_1 during off-peak and K during peak periods. Hence, the total operating costs are $c(Q_1 + K)$. The total capacity costs are CK, which are collected only during peak periods; hence, C must be redefined as twice the unit capacity costs. This ensures that the total revenues $cQ_1 + (c + C)K$ collected during both periods cover costs exactly, without any economic profits.

This solution, however, is not always feasible. Suppose, for instance, that

FIGURE 6.4
Peak-load pricing for "low" capacity cost

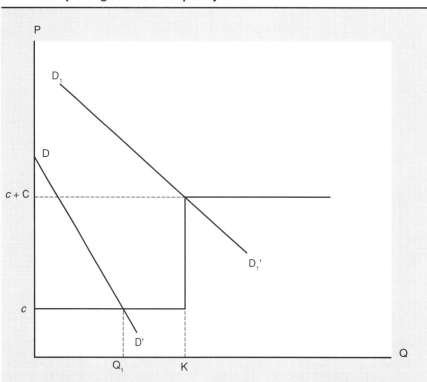

peak demand is not excessively larger than off-peak, but that capacity costs are significantly larger than operating costs. Then it is possible that setting a peak price equal to $c + C$ and an off-peak price equal to c would yield a lower demand for peak than for off-peak hours. The higher peak price reduces demand so much that off-peak and peak consumptions are now of inverse order of magnitude. Clearly, it is no longer fair or efficient to charge all capacity costs to peak period customers.

This situation is shown in Figure 6.5. A peak period price of $c + C$ yields a demand of Q_1, while an off-peak price of c corresponds to a higher demand of Q_2. As the diagram shows, it is optimal in this case to charge peak and off-peak prices P_1 and P_2 that equalize demands in both periods. This means that both classes of customers, and not just the peak period ones, pay a share of the capacity costs. The prices and capacity are found from the requirements that demands be equal to K and to each other, and that the corresponding

FIGURE 6.5
Peak-load pricing for "large" capacity costs

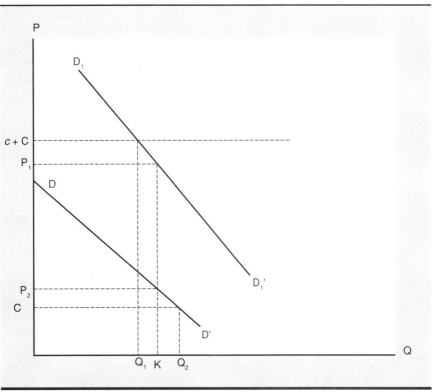

revenues be sufficient to cover all operating and capacity costs. Hence, the system determining K, P_1 and P_2 consists of the two demand curves linking K to P_1 and P_2, and of the equation between the total revenues of $K(P_1 + P_2)$ and the total costs $(2c + C)K$.

With peak-load pricing, the class of peak-period consumers pay higher prices than the off-peak ones. Yet there is no question that these prices are also efficient, given that they reduce capacity costs. A single price system for both periods will invariably increase the costs of serving both markets, by raising the capacity requirements to those of peak-hour consumption. Hence, it can also be argued that such a uniform pricing system would be unfair, insofar as it would force off-peak customers to pay for capacity they do not need. It should be noted that the non-storability of output is crucial to the formulation of the problem, since otherwise it would be easy to produce output during off-peak hours, store it, and then use it to satisfy peak-load demand.

Advertising

Advertising and, more generally, selling and promotional efforts, are attempts by the firm to alter the demand for its product(s). Stated more simply, advertising is an investment in improving the firm's demand. Like all investments, it must be carried out only to the point where it is profitable. Since it is a technique available to every firm in a given industry, advertising has consequences for industry structure and performance. Such consequences have attracted increasing attention in recent years.[9]

Advertising can be informative or persuasive. The former brings to the consumer's attention information about product availability and price or quality characteristics. By reducing the consumer's costs of searching for the product most closely suited to his or her needs, informative advertising is generally beneficial to economic welfare.

Persuasive advertising is aimed at creating images or perceptions about a particular product, generally with the purpose of differentiating it from close competitors. The informational content of such advertising is insignificant, and its impact is felt on consumer tastes rather than search costs. Typical examples of persuasive advertising are the various cigarette or liquor advertisements, in which the product is promoted through the creation of an appealing consumer image. This type of advertising is not always desirable. As we saw in the previous chapter, it can be a source of barriers to entry, through its product differentiation effects. However, such effects can also allow a new competitor to penetrate a particular market.

Most advertising is generally a mixture of the informative and persuasive types. Factual material about a product typically coexists with subtle image-creating messages. Similarly, the net effect of advertising on industry structure can be either pro- or anti-competitive. The final verdict will depend on the empirical evidence.

The economic analysis of advertising is carried out in detail in Appendix 6A. This analysis assumes that the industry structure is a monopoly or oligopoly, perhaps as a result of advertising. In other words, each firm in the industry must be facing a downward-sloping demand curve. This demand is now a function of the amount of advertising messages that the firm purchases, as well as of product price. An increase in the amount of advertising produces an upward shift in the firm's demand curve.

Profit maximization is carried out under the assumption that the cost of each message is constant. The optimal firm decisions involve both product price and quantity of advertising. The final result ends up with a relationship between advertising expenditures and demand elasticities that has become known as the *Dorfman-Steiner* rule, after the classic 1954 paper by these two authors. This rule states that the ratio of optimal advertising expenses to total sales is equal to the ratio of demand elasticities with respect to advertising and price. In other words, if *a* denotes the relative change in demand per unit relative change in advertising, ϵ is the price elasticity of demand, AM is the total advertising expenditure, and PQ denotes the firm's total revenue, the optimal choice of price and advertising must satisfy

$$AM/PQ = a/\epsilon \qquad \textbf{Eq. (6.1)}$$

Several implications of the Dorfman-Steiner rule are consistent with observed business practices. For instance, if the ratio of elasticities in Equation (6.1) is approximately constant, as it happens with well-established products, then the rule predicts that firms would spend a constant share of their receipts on advertising. Similarly, the share of advertising in total sales revenue is expected, on the basis of (6.1), to be higher for products with a high responsiveness to advertising (a high a) as compared to price. Such products are those in which image is important, such as jewellery, women's clothing, perfume, or cosmetics. Both predictions have been broadly verified in empirical surveys, even though there are several other factors that affect advertising expenditures as well as demand elasticities.

In an oligopoly a firm's optimal choice of advertising is going to be affected by the anticipated rivals' reaction to it. An increase in the amount of advertising by a firm's competitors will have a depressing effect on its own demand. On the other hand, an increase in the total amount of advertising by all firms in the market tends to shift upwards the market demand curve. The key question is the impact of market structure on advertising. As argued in Chapter 4, price competition increases as the number of firms in the market goes up. This also tends to reduce advertising intensity.[10] Hence, one expects that advertising would increase with concentration. On the other hand, in an oligopoly with a small number of firms each firm expects its rivals to match its own spending; this may lead it to curtail advertising beyond a certain amount in order to preserve the collusive equilibrium.[11]

For all these reasons several authors have postulated a nonlinear relationship between market concentration and advertising. The ratio AM/PQ, the advertising to sales ratio, would increase at low levels of concentration and then start decreasing beyond a certain point. A possible form of such a relationship is shown in Figure 6.6.

Such a relationship was tested in Canada in an important empirical study by Caves *et al.* (1980), already cited in Chapter 5. The sample consisted of 123 three-digit industries, for which data on various aspects of structure, conduct, and performance during the 1960s were collected. A subsample of these industries was individually matched with comparable U.S. industries, in order to investigate differences in the behaviour of comparable firms between the two countries. The industries were classified into producer and consumer goods, and the latter were further subdivided into non-convenience and convenience goods.[12]

The results derived from the entire sample gave support to the collusion hypothesis regarding advertising. In other words, highly concentrated

FIGURE 6.6
The relationship between concentration and advertising intensity

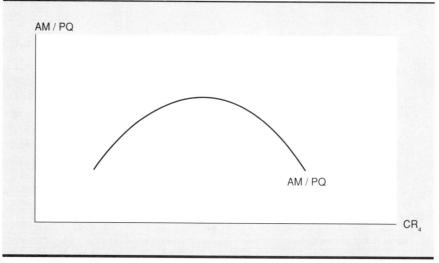

industries showed less advertising intensity than those of medium concentration, with four-firm concentration ratios between 40 and 70 percent. Further,
competitive conditions in the industry, whether international through exports
and imports or domestic through a low concentration ratio, also had a negative
influence on advertising. Last, a significant presence of foreign-controlled
firms in a Canadian industry was generally associated with a high advertising
intensity. This presumably reflected the different patterns of firm behaviour
in Canada versus the U.S.

A comparison of the Canadian and U.S. results showed that advertising
intensities were similar on average between the two countries for each industry
subgroup, in spite of the vast differences in concentration. With the exception
of the non-convenience goods subgroup, the U.S. industries tended to have
slightly higher advertising-to-sales ratios. In spite of these similarities, the
concentration ratios played a far from unimportant role, being responsible for
whatever differences existed. In general, when all other factors were taken
into account, industrial concentration was found to have the nonlinear effect
on advertising intensity shown in Figure 6.6, first increasing and then decreasing it.

As already noted, advertising can be a source of barriers to entry, through
its product differentiation effects. A new entrant challenging an established
firm faces a lower demand curve for its product, even when the products are
relatively homogeneous. This handicap can presumably be overcome by heavy

advertising on the part of the entrant. The barrier to entry is created by the fact that the cost of advertising is sunk. It is also magnified in some cases by the identification of the product with the incumbent's brand or trademark, as in the case of new drugs. The empirical studies on barriers to entry in Canada that were surveyed in the previous chapter generally found that advertising had a negative effect on entry, although the strength of this effect was not the same in all studies.

Beyond the barrier to entry effect, however, there are other consequences of advertising whose impact may favour competition. This is particularly true of informative advertising, which may be used to make customers aware of alternative products in challenging an established firm's monopoly position. Similarly, in markets with many sellers advertising may bring lower prices, by informing prospective buyers of the prices charged by the various competing firms. This would tend to increase the elasticity of the market demand curve. It is interesting to note in this context that this pro-competitive effect of advertising may be the motivating factor in the persistent opposition to advertising by the legal profession in most parts of Canada.

The impact of advertising on firm and industry sales volumes may also be positive even in the case of purely persuasive advertising. Figure 6.7 shows the case of a firm that operates initially in a competitive industry without any advertising. In the long run its price P_0 is equal to average cost AC, corresponding to a volume of Q_0. If advertising, under the form of an increase in the fixed costs, is now introduced into the industry, then the firm's demand curve DD' is no longer horizontal and the total cost curve is raised to the level AC'. The firm now produces at the level Q_1, equating marginal revenue MR to marginal cost MC, and charging a higher price P_1. The net effects of advertising have been increases in the amount produced by the individual firm and in the price level, as well as in the minimum efficient scale of the firms in the industry.

The end result, however, is still not clear. Whether the final quantity sold in the industry will rise or fall as a result of advertising depends on a number of industry-wide structural factors. If all firms engage in advertising and acquire downward-sloping demand curves, then the industry demand curve will also shift to the right as a result, at least up to the point at which consumers become saturated. It is thus possible to have an increased aggregate sales volume by all firms in the industry, in spite of the higher costs and prices. On the other hand, the final equilibrium will also depend on the entry conditions in the industry following the introduction of advertising. These entry conditions will generally become more difficult, due to the barriers to entry effect of advertising. Nonetheless, if such an effect is not present, and if the entry conditions remain easy, then a different long-run equilibrium will emerge. This equilibrium corresponds to a market structure known as *monopolistic competition*, identified and studied by Chamberlin in the early 1930s. Due to its historical interest, this structure is examined in a separate section.

FIGURE 6.7
The introduction of advertising in a competitive industry

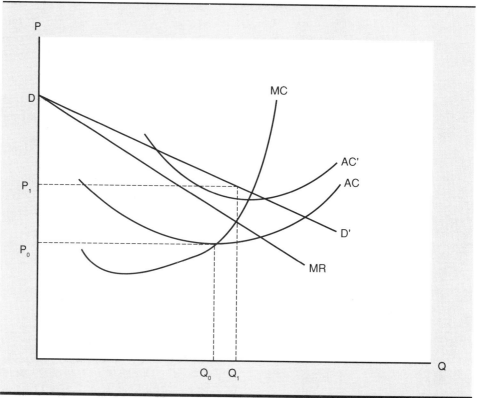

Monopolistic Competition

In monopolistic competition there is a sufficiently large number of firms in the industry for each one to believe that it can ignore the effects of its own actions on market equilibrium. On the other hand, each firm possesses some market power, thus facing a downward-sloping demand curve. While the industry products are differentiated by the seller, they remain close substitutes. The production technology and input prices are identical among firms, so that each firm faces the same cost curve. Last, entry conditions are easy, as in perfect competition.

The distinctive features of monopolistic competition are its demand assumptions and the type of industry equilibrium that they lead to. Each firm maximizes profits by equating marginal revenue to marginal cost, with the other firms' output taken as given, as with the Cournot oligopoly. However, since products are not homogeneous, variations of its own output have a much stronger effect on its product price than those of each competitor's output. Since, however, there are many competitors, the cumulative effect of their actions on the firm's demand is far from insignificant. The net result is that at each price level the firm faces two intersecting demand curves: one that represents variations of its output level alone, and another one that embodies identical variations in the levels of all firms in the industry. The two curves intersect only at the current price and output levels.

Figure 6.8 shows the short-run equilibrium of a firm in a monopolistically-competitive market. The demand curve DD' and corresponding marginal revenue MR are the curves that the firm uses in deciding its own output level Q_1, which is found by the intersection of MR with the short-run marginal cost curve SMC. D_1D_1' is the demand curve that it effectively faces when all

FIGURE 6.8
Short-run equilibrium under monopolistic competition

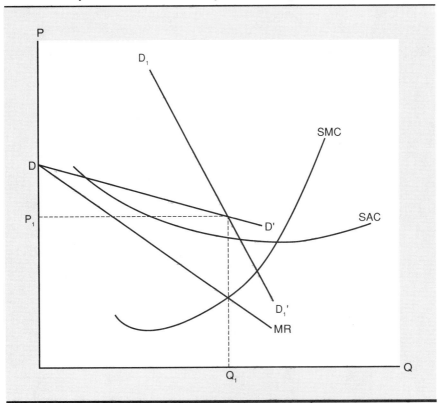

firms in the industry vary their output levels. The equilibrium price-output combination is therefore constrained to be on D_1D_1'. The two demand curves intersect at the equilibrium price level P_1.

In the long run the profits realized by firms in the industry are bound to attract new entrants. Since entry conditions are easy and all firms produce close substitutes, each entrant will cause a shift to the left of the firm's demand curves. Entry takes place until all profits are eliminated, implying that price must be equal to average cost. Hence, the demand curve DD' at the firm's long-run equilibrium must be tangent to its average cost curve. All other positions of DD' yield either losses or profits, which are both inconsistent with long-run equilibrium and the absence of entry. The situation is depicted in Figure 6.9.

An important feature of this long-run equilibrium is that the tangency point A is to the left of the minimum efficient firm size, represented by the lowest average cost at output Q_0. This implies that monopolistic competition

FIGURE 6.9
Long-run equilibrium under monopolistic competition

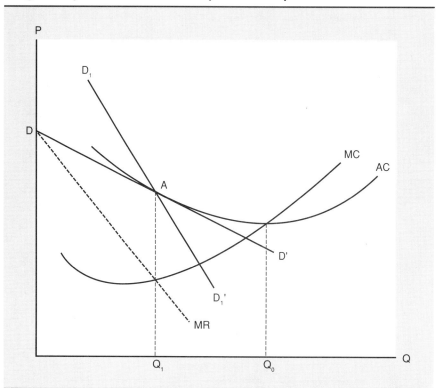

results in a suboptimal firm size, with firms producing a smaller output Q_1 at a higher unit cost than in a perfectly competitive market. On the other hand, free entry brings economic profits down to zero.

The monopolistic competition model has generated a lot of controversy, much of which is still going on today. It has come under attack from several economists, especially those associated with the Chicago School of economic thinking, on both methodological and analytical grounds.[13] There is little doubt that it is flawed in many important respects. For instance, it combines heterogeneous products with identical cost and demand curves for all firms in the market. Similarly, the relationship between the two intersecting demand curves is not specified precisely. Yet when it appeared it represented a pioneering analysis and a focussing of attention to several real-life features of business firms that were omitted by the more conventional models of monopoly and perfect competition. These features were (in addition to product differentiation) the emphasis placed on oligopoly, the role of new entry, and the definition of an industry. Each one of these topics has become a thriving area of research in the more than fifty years since the appearance of Chamberlin's work.

Conclusions

With the exception of passing references to multiproduct firms and differentiated markets, most of the material examined in this text until now has dealt with homogeneous single-product markets. Each market was characterized by a demand curve representing all prospective buyers of the single traded commodity, which was taken as a given by all producers in that market. These assumptions were relaxed in this chapter in two important dimensions: the market was disaggregated by different classes of buyers; and through advertising firms were able to alter the nature of the demand that they faced.

When the market can be split into distinct segments without any possibility of arbitrage, it is optimal for the firm to practice price discrimination. The size of the profits that it derives depends on the feasibility of partitioning the market into as many segments as possible. Such partitioning is generally costly, so that there are practical limits to the profitability of discrimination. The finest partition corresponds to price discrimination of the first degree, which is very rarely encountered in practice. Discrimination of the second and (especially) the third degree is on the other hand quite common. It is generally a legal business practice, in spite of a section in the competition legislation that prohibits it. It may become illegal only when it is clearly predatory in intent.

Peak-load pricing is a special type of price discrimination, in which customer purchases are differentiated with respect to the time period at which they occur. The aim of such pricing is to reduce the costs of serving the demand over the entire cycle. By charging higher prices for peak than for off-peak demand periods, the firm achieves an optimal choice of installed capacity sufficient to serve both periods. The form that this type of pricing takes depends on the relative sizes of peak and off-peak demands, as well as on the relationship between operating and capacity costs.

Advertising, whether of the informative or the persuasive kind, shifts upwards the demand curve facing a firm. Its optimal choice is derived from the profit maximization conditions, and depends on the elasticities of the firm's demand curve. In an oligopoly such a choice is also contingent on the anticipated reactions of the firm's competitors, who are expected to match any increases in the chosen amount in order to preserve their own market share. For this reason it is hypothesized that the intensity of advertising initially increases with market concentration, but then starts decreasing once such concentration exceeds a certain level.

The welfare effects of advertising are ambiguous. Informative advertising reduces consumer search and improves welfare. Persuasive advertising increases total costs and may have anticompetitive effects. Perhaps the most important of these adverse effects is the barrier to entry that may be created by the product differentiation consequences of persuasive advertising. Since most advertising is a mixture of the informative and persuasive types, public policies have had little interest in advertising except when it is fraudulent or misleading.

Product differentiation in a market with many sellers and comparatively easy entry may create a market structure known as monopolistic competition. Such a structure combines aspects of both monopoly and competition. It is primarily of historical interest, being associated with the beginnings of industrial organization as a field of economic science.

Appendix 6A THE MATHEMATICS OF PRICE DISCRIMINATION AND ADVERTISING

Price Discrimination

Let $D(Q)$ denote the monopolist's demand curve, and assume that average and marginal costs AC and MC are constant and equal to c. Under first-degree price discrimination each output unit dQ is sold at its reservation price $p = D(Q)$, yielding a revenue of $D(Q)dQ$. Hence, the total revenue is equal to $\int_0^q D(Q)dQ$, where q is the total quantity sold by the firm. Profit maximization

therefore implies a choice of q maximizing the profit $\pi = \int_0^q D(Q)dQ - cq$.
Setting $d\pi/dQ = 0$, we find $D(q) = c$, corresponding to point B in Figure 6.1 where the demand curve intersects the AC line. It is also easy to see that the profit is equal to the area of the triangle (ABD).

For third-degree price discrimination we assume that demand can be separated into two different submarkets, with demand curves $D_1(Q_1)$ and $D_2(Q_2)$. Let also $C(Q)$ denote the firm's cost function, where $Q = Q_1 + Q_2$ is the total industry output. Then profit $\pi = Q_1D_1(Q_1) + Q_2D_2(Q_2) - C(Q_1 + Q_2)$ is maximized by setting $\dfrac{\partial\pi}{\partial Q_1} = \dfrac{\partial\pi}{\partial Q_2} = 0$, yielding $\dfrac{d[Q_1D_1(Q_1)]}{dQ_1} \equiv$

$MR_1 = \dfrac{d[Q_2D_2(Q_2)]}{dQ_2} \equiv MR_2 = \dfrac{dC}{dQ} = MC.$

Advertising

Let A denote the amount of advertising messages purchased by a monopoly firm at a cost of \$M per unit. The firm's demand curve is $Q = Q(P,A)$, where P is the product price. This curve is increasing in A and decreasing in P, i.e. $\dfrac{\partial Q}{\partial A} > 0, \dfrac{\partial Q}{\partial P} < 0$. Let also ϵ and a denote the elasticities of demand with respect to P and A respectively:

$$\epsilon = -\frac{\partial Q}{\partial P}\frac{P}{Q} \quad a = \frac{\partial Q}{\partial A}\frac{A}{Q} \qquad \textbf{Eq. (6A.1)}$$

The firm's production cost function is $C(Q) = C(Q(P,A))$, and its total cost (including advertising) is $C(Q(P,A)) + AM$.

The choice of the product price P and the volume of advertising A are carried out by maximizing the profit $\pi = PQ(P,A) - C(Q(P,A)) - AM$ with respect to P and A. The first-order conditions become:

$$\frac{\partial\pi}{\partial P} = Q\,(P,A) + \frac{P\partial Q}{\partial P} - \frac{\partial C}{\partial Q}\frac{\partial Q}{\partial P} = 0 \qquad \textbf{Eq. (6A.2)}$$

$$\frac{\partial\pi}{\partial A} = \frac{P\partial Q}{\partial A} - \frac{\partial C}{\partial Q}\frac{\partial Q}{\partial A} - M = 0 \qquad \textbf{Eq. (6A.3)}$$

Rewriting (6A.3) under the form $\left(P - \dfrac{\partial C}{\partial Q}\right)\dfrac{\partial Q}{\partial A} = M$, and multiplying both sides of this last relation by $\dfrac{A}{PQ}$ we get:

$$\frac{1}{P}\left(P - \frac{\partial C}{\partial Q}\right)\frac{A}{Q}\frac{\partial Q}{\partial A} = \frac{AM}{PQ} \qquad \textbf{Eq. (6A.4)}$$

However, from (6A.2) we can easily see, by re-arranging, that

$$\frac{1}{P}\left(P - \frac{\partial C}{\partial Q}\right) = -\frac{Q(P,A)}{P} \times \frac{1}{\frac{\partial Q}{\partial P}} = \frac{1}{\epsilon}$$

Hence, (6A.4) can be simply rewritten as $\frac{AM}{PQ} = \frac{a}{\epsilon}$ which is Equation (6.1) in the text, the Dorfman-Steiner rule.

Suppose now that we have an oligopoly with m firms, and let A_i, $i = 1, \ldots, m$ denote the amount of advertising purchased by the ith firm. Let also

$$A = \sum_{\substack{j=1 \\ i \neq j}}^{m} A_j$$

be the aggregate amount of advertising purchased by the other firms in the industry. The industry demand curve is $Q = Q(P, A + A_i)$, while each firm faces a demand curve that depends on its own price and advertising, as well as on the amount of advertising purchased by each competitor. Assume, for simplicity, that all firms are identical, so that each firm charges the same price and purchases the same amount of advertising. Then the ith firm's demand curve is $Q_i = Q_i(P, A_i, A)$, while its cost is $C(Q_i) + MA_i$.

The profit-maximization conditions involve the simultaneous determination of price and advertising. The choice of price depends on the type of behaviour adopted by the oligopoly (Cournot, Bertrand, collusion, or any in-between case), as examined in Chapter 4; it will be ignored here, since it is not affected by advertising.[14] Hence, we maximize $\pi_i = PQ_i(P, A_i, A) - C(Q_i) - MA_i$ with respect to A_i. This maximization yields:

$$\frac{\partial \pi_i}{\partial A_i} = \left(P - \frac{\partial C}{\partial Q_i}\right)\left(\frac{\partial Q_i}{\partial A_i} + \frac{\partial Q_i}{\partial A}\frac{\partial A}{\partial A_i}\right) - M = 0 \qquad \textbf{Eq. (6A.5)}$$

However,

$$\frac{\partial A}{\partial A_i} = \sum_{\substack{j=1 \\ j \neq i}}^{m} \frac{\partial A_j}{\partial A_i}$$

where the terms $\frac{\partial A_j}{\partial A_i}$ represent the conjectural variations, the assumptions made by firm i about the reactions of firms $j = 1, \ldots, m, j \neq i$ to its own choice of advertising. It is reasonable to assume that $\frac{\partial A_j}{\partial A_i} > 0$ for all $j \neq i$, and that $\frac{\partial Q_i}{\partial A} < 0$. These assumptions imply that firms react to a competitor's increase in advertising by raising their own message purchases, and that a rise in aggregate spending on competitors' advertising has a depressing effect on a firm's demand.

From (6A.5) we can, by moving M to the other side and multiplying both sides by $\dfrac{A_i}{PQ_i}$, derive a modified version of the Dorfman-Steiner rule. Let $a_i \equiv \dfrac{\partial Q_i}{\partial A_i} \dfrac{A_i}{Q_i}$ be the elasticity of the ith firm's demand with respect to its own spending, ignoring the conjectural variations effect. Then we have:

$$\frac{1}{P}\left(P - \frac{\partial C}{\partial Q_i}\right)\left(a_i + \frac{A_i}{Q_i}\frac{\partial Q_i}{\partial A}\frac{\partial A}{\partial A_i}\right) = \frac{MA_i}{PQ_i} \qquad \textbf{Eq. (6A.6)}$$

This expression is similar to (6A.4), except that instead of the elasticity of demand with respect to advertising in the left-hand side (LHS) we now have the sum in the second parenthesis in (6A.6). Since, as argued above, $\dfrac{\partial Q_i}{\partial A} < 0, \dfrac{\partial A}{\partial A_i} > 0$, this sum is less than a_i, implying that the share of advertising in total spending will be smaller than implied by (6A.4).[15]

Endnotes

1. See Chapter 2.
2. As shown in Appendix 6A, a perfectly discriminating monopolist equates price to marginal cost, as in a competitive firm.
3. See Greer (1984), pp. 312-313.
4. Such energy prices are known as *block rates*.
5. For a welfare analysis of third-degree price discrimination between geographically separated markets see Phlips (1983), pp. 51-63.
6. For a summary of these criticisms see Greer (1984), pp. 322-336.
7. The economic analysis of peak-load pricing was initially done in two studies that appeared almost simultaneously, by Boiteux (1949) and Houthakker (1951). For a more detailed analysis see Phlips (1983), pp. 134-143.
8. For instance, in electricity generation c may represent the cost of the fuel needed to produce a unit of energy, while C may be a weighted average of the unit costs of the generating plant and the labour needed to operate it, under the assumption that these inputs vary proportionally to the installed capacity.
9. Important contributions to the economic analysis of advertising are by Dorfman and Steiner (1954), Nerlove and Arrow (1962) and Telser (1964). See also the monographs by Schmalensee (1972), Ferguson (1974), and Lambin (1976). A good summary is in Clarke (1985), Chapter 6.
10. This is a consequence of the Dorfman-Steiner rule, since a firm's individual demand curve becomes more elastic as the industry becomes more competitive.
11. See Equation (6A.6) in the Appendix.
12. Convenience goods are those sold at convenience stores such as drugstores, supermarkets and gasoline retailers. Non-convenience goods are more expensive and less frequently purchased items such as appliances, furniture and clothing.
13. See Chamberlin's (1957) reply to his Chicago critics. An excellent survey of the monopolistic competition debate is in Hay and Morris (1979), pp. 10-20.
14. However, a complete formulation and solution of the model would yield a simultaneous determination of price and advertising levels.
15. Note that the analysis has ignored the effect of advertising on total industry demand.

References

Boiteux, M. "La Tarification des Demandes en Pointe," *Revue Générale de l'Electricité*, 58, (1949), pp. 321-340.

Caves, R.E., M.E. Porter and A.M. Spence, with J.T. Scott. *Competition in the Open Economy: a Model Applied to Canada*. Cambridge, Mass.: Harvard University Press, 1980.

Chamberlin, E.H. *The Theory of Monopolistic Competition*. Cambridge, Mass.: Harvard University Press, 1933.

———. "The Chicago School," Essay #15 in *Towards a More General Theory of Value*. New York, N.Y.: Oxford University Press, 1957.

Clarke, R. *Industrial Economics*. Oxford, Eng.: Basil Blackwell, 1985.

Dorfman, R., and P.O. Steiner. "Optimal Advertising and Optimal Quality," *American Economic Review*, 44, (1954), pp. 826-836.

Ferguson, J.M. *Advertising and Competition: Theory, Measurement, Fact*. Cambridge, Mass.: Ballinger, 1974.

Greer, D.F. *Industrial Organization and Public Policy*. New York, N.Y.: Macmillan, 2nd Edition, 1984.

Hay, D.A., and D.J. Morris. *Industrial Economics: Theory and Evidence*. Oxford, Eng.: Oxford University Press, 1979.

Houthakker, H.S. "Electricity Tariffs in Theory and Practice," *Economic Journal*, 61, (1951), pp. 1-25.

Lambin, J.J. *Advertising, Competition and Market Conduct in Oligopoly Over Time*. Amsterdam, Neth.: North Holland, 1976.

Nerlove, M. and K.J. Arrow. "Optimal Advertising Policy Under Dynamic Conditions," *Economica*, 29 (1962), pp. 129-42.

Phlips, L. *The Economics of Price Discrimination*. Cambridge, Eng.: Cambridge University Press, 1983.

Pigou, A.C. *The Economics of Welfare*. London, Eng.: Macmillan, 4th Edition, 1920.

Schmalensee, R. *The Economics of Advertising*. Amsterdam, Neth.: North Holland, 1972.

Telser, L.G. "Supply and Demand for Advertising Messages," *American Economic Review*, Papers and Proceedings, 56 (1966), pp. 457-466.

CHAPTER 7

Performance

....

Standards

....

This chapter examines the performance dimension of the structure-conduct-performance (SCP) model, which was taken for granted until now. Indeed, we seem to have tacitly accepted in the five previous chapters that perfect competition is a desirable state in any given industry, serving as the focus of public policy initiatives. The time has now come to submit this implied assumption to the critical evaluation of economic theory. To what extent is the achievement of perfect competition possible or desirable in any given case? How "perfect" should this competition be? How are we to recognize it when we are confronted with it?

The answers to these key questions are an indispensable prerequisite to the second part of this book, which deals with public policy. Such policy is embodied in institutions, laws, and regulations, which must be designed to carry out certain predetermined objectives. Although economists have not always been consulted when economic policies were being formulated, their influence has been increasing in recent years. This chapter examines their ability to provide simple and clear guidelines to policy design and implementation by means of the SCP or any alternative economic model. These contributions can only be made when economists are themselves confident about the objectives and standards that policies must pursue.

The Objectives of Public Policy

The branch of economic theory that deals with the performance of an economic system is known as welfare economics. This part of microeconomics is essentially centred around the general equilibrium of a perfectly competitive economy. This equilibrium has some very attractive properties. Unfortunately, there are many reasons why no economy can ever achieve a perfectly competitive state. The question that arises, therefore, is whether it is still worthwhile pursuing perfect competition in that part of the economy where it is feasible, or whether some other arrangement is preferable. A related question asks what should be done about the sectors where perfect competition is for some reason impossible.

As we shall see in this chapter, and as you may already suspect from theory courses, no hard and fast answers exist to these questions. In other words, for just about every policy prescription it is possible to provide counter-examples where a different course of action would be preferable. Nonetheless, a certain consensus has been emerging among economists in recent years concerning broad policy initiatives and the manner of their application. Some such policies, such as the prohibition of price collusion, are generally accepted as being at worst redundant, and at best highly beneficial to general welfare. Others, such as curbs on horizontal mergers, are more ambiguous in their results, depending on the structural characteristics of the sector and of the merging firms. It is, however, still possible to develop rules distinguishing desirable from undesirable mergers. It should be kept in mind that, when designing appropriate policies for such ambiguous cases, inaction should also be considered a policy initiative whose consequences must be evaluated like those of any other. The burden of proof in choosing a given policy should lie with the course of action (or inaction) that is "most often" detrimental to public welfare.

This existence of a general consensus among economists, however, should not be exaggerated. For instance, we noted in the first chapter that there are sharp divisions of opinion concerning the appropriateness of using the SCP model for policy purposes. Most economists do agree, more or less, on the proper methodology and tests that should be used in any given case. Such agreement became possible when a piecemeal approach to policy evaluation was developed, which could be applied at the level of individual industries or markets. This made it feasible to combine broad policies designed to enhance competition throughout the economy with more precise evaluations of individual actions when it came to apply these policies to concrete cases. The main drawback of this piecemeal approach is that it demands a high degree of sophistication on the part of the judges or civil servants who are entrusted with policy application.

Before proceeding with our examination of the various economic performance criteria, it is appropriate to issue a warning about other possible dimensions of performance. Economics is not the only set of guidelines to public policies affecting business. The main economic criteria, efficiency in production and resource allocation, must be supplemented with considerations such as equity, justice, individual and collective security, and the enhancement of our democratic values. These criteria are most often ignored by economists, who consider them subjective and controversial. They are fond to point out that efficiency, by contrast, can be objectively defined and tested.

Needless to say, such views are rather shortsighted. We saw in the previous chapters that equity considerations are at least as important as efficiency in several policy issues such as the regulation of monopolies, the treatment of barriers to entry, and predatory price discrimination. In some of these cases there is no conflict between the efficiency and equity criteria, while in others one of the two must be sacrificed. Economists who ignore non-economic objectives run a well-deserved risk of having their opinions treated as irrelevant.

Nonetheless, there is still ample space for economic analysis even when other objectives predominate. To begin with, it is preferable to choose economically efficient policies aimed at such objectives. Most important, though, is the role that economic analysis can play in evaluating the fulfillment of intended goals. Many policies that start with very commendable purposes end up benefiting those who least deserve it on equity grounds. Several such examples will be provided in subsequent chapters.

The first sections of this chapter review the general case for pro-competitive policies, as it emerges from economic theory. This case is centred around the theory of general equilibrium and the concept of Pareto optimality. Next, there is a brief survey of the reasons why the perfectly competitive standard is not achievable in practice. This survey is extended to cover alternative theories about the behaviour of a business firm when it operates in a non-competitive environment. A subsequent section examines the theoretical justification for a piecemeal approach to economic policy through the criterion of the maximization of total surplus. The chapter concludes with a review of the empirical evidence concerning the link between structure and performance in the context of the SCP model, and the on-going debate about the use of this model for public policies concerning structure.

The Standard of Perfect Competition

The basic postulates concerning the efficiency of perfect competition at the level of an individual market were already presented in Chapter 2. Figure 7.1 summarizes the results of that earlier discussion. In a competitive market structure, the equilibrium price P_0 is equal to the long run average and marginal

FIGURE 7.1
Competitive market equilibrium

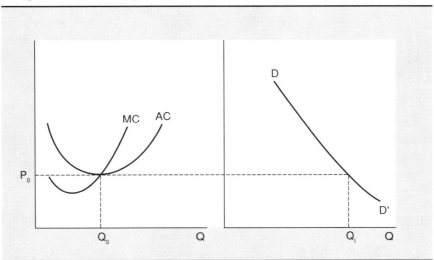

cost, and each firm produces the output Q_0 corresponding to the minimum efficient scale (MES). This equilibrium is reached by firm entry in response to the presence of profits, which ceases when these profits are eliminated. The industry output Q_I is found from the demand curve DD', corresponding to the equilibrium price P_0.

This equilibrium is static in nature. The basic conditions (demand, costs, entry, and some other requirements discussed below) determine the competitive structure of the market; this structure in turn yields the equilibrium shown. Market power, under the form of monopoly or oligopoly structures, produces distortions in the equilibrium of the types examined in Chapters 3 to 6. Hence, the first requirement for a perfectly competitive equilibrium in the entire economy is that the MES be "small" in relation to the entire market for every sector, and that the average cost start increasing very soon after this MES has been reached.

Under perfect competition, product market equilibrium must be supplemented by equilibrium in the factor markets, and by consumer equilibrium given the prevailing market prices.[1] In the factor markets the price of each factor equalizes total demand to total supply. For the primary factors such as capital and labour, the total supply is derived from the exogenously given initial factor endowments. In that factor market equilibrium the profit-maximizing choice of each input implies that its price will equal the value of its marginal product. Hence, at equilibrium the marginal rate of technical substitution of any pair of factors (the ratio of their marginal products) is equal to the ratio of their prices. This equality guarantees that the cost of production is minimized for the given factor prices and output level.

Last, at the perfectly competitive equilibrium all consumers in the economy must be completely "satisfied", in the sense that their utility is at a maximum given the prevailing prices. Otherwise, they would readjust their purchases, and this may alter the product market equilibrium. This utility maximization is obtained when the marginal rate of substitution (the ratio of marginal utilities) for each pair of purchased products is equal to the ratio of the corresponding product prices. This obviously implies that the ratio of marginal utilities for any pair of products is the same for all consumers in the economy. Figure 7.2 shows the familiar indifference map diagram and the equilibrium of a representative consumer, given the product prices P_1 and P_2 and the consumer's budget constraint.

In such a perfectly competitive equilibrium throughout the entire economy, the number of necessary conditions is sufficient to determine all relevant

FIGURE 7.2
Consumer utility maximization

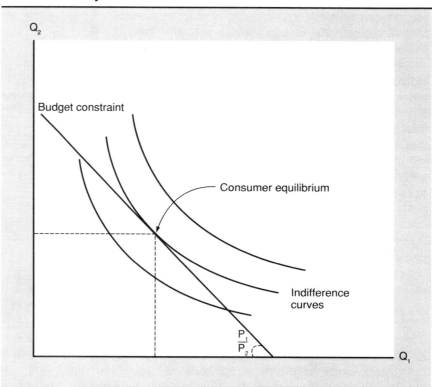

economic variables. These are the prices and quantities traded at each factor and product market, the amounts produced by each firm in the economy, the quantities purchased by each consumer, and the factors used by each firm in its production process. The exogenous data used in the solution of these necessary conditions include, in addition to each firm's production technology and each consumer's utility function, the number of consumers in the economy and the initial factor endowments of each of them. Hence, a given competitive equilibrium is a function of these data and depends therefore on the initial situation of every consumer.

As it has already been noted in several earlier chapters, the perfectly competitive equilibrium has many attractive welfare properties. By definition, it maximizes the satisfaction of every consumer, given his/her initial resource endowments, and it does this in an efficient manner in the allocation of resources to production. Thus, it possesses a property known as *Pareto optimality*: in a Pareto optimal state it is not possible to improve the welfare of a particular consumer without worsening that of somebody else. This is clearly a powerful concept, but one that may not always be useful in practice. In particular, to every possible initial resource endowment there is a corresponding perfectly competitive equilibrium, and all of these equilibria are Pareto optimal; there is no way of distinguishing among them unless one introduces concepts such as fairness or equity.

This brief reminder of the necessary conditions for perfectly competitive equilibrium closes with a summary of the assumptions used in its derivation. These assumptions start with the fundamental postulates of microeconomics: consumers maximize utility and firms maximize profits; all markets clear, with no unsold quantities and no shortages; all product and factor markets are perfectly competitive; and there are no externalities in production or consumption.[2] The perfectly competitive market assumption is by itself a summary of a number of conditions that must hold for each such market: price-taking behaviour (no market power) on the product or factor sides; perfect mobility of resources and economic agents; and perfect information by all participants about present and future conditions.

All these conditions are very strong, and it is easy to see that their simultaneous fulfillment is unlikely in any real-world economy. The question that arises is what will happen to the perfectly competitive equilibrium when one or more of them is violated, as they are bound to be. The next section summarizes the most frequently observed violations and their consequences.

The Limits to Perfect Competition

The first requirement of a perfectly competitive equilibrium is, by definition, that the structure of all production be perfectly competitive. This in turn presupposes that the MES be small in relation to the size of the market. This condition is not fulfilled in a large segment of the Canadian economy, as it was made clear in Chapter 2. Consequently, a realistic formulation of general policies must contend with the fact that the Canadian economy (or, indeed, any economy) will always contain an important non-competitive segment, in which market power will be present.

The distortions produced by such market power fall into two broad categories, both of which are sufficiently important to warrant separate treatment in subsequent sections. The more obvious one concerns *allocative efficiency*: by raising product price and curtailing output, market power triggers a series of developments that alter the distribution of income and output in comparison with the competitive standard. More subtle, though, are the alleged effects of market power on *productive efficiency*. These strike at the heart of the basic economic theory postulates, for they raise questions about profit-maximizing behaviour by firms in non-competitive sectors. They gave rise to an entire set of theories, collectively known as *managerial* or *behavioural* theories of the firm, which will be discussed in the next section.

Other limitations to perfect competition arise from market failures due to the existence of public goods and common property resources. A public good is a product or service that once produced becomes available for consumption to everybody without possibility of exclusion; radio and television broadcasting, justice, and security are obvious examples of public goods in our society. Clearly, these goods are not marketable since everybody can obtain them at zero cost once they are produced. A common property resource, on the other hand, is an essential production input of some sector that belongs to the community at large. Therefore, anyone can access the resource unless a specialized allocation system is devised. Our forests, fishing stocks, broadcasting spectrum, and offshore mining rights are obvious examples of such common property resources. Free entry is not desirable in such sectors as long as the resource remains in short supply, since it may lead to the complete exhaustion of the resource or to interference with other producers.

Market power or *monopsony* can also exist on the buyer side. It is found most often in the factor markets. For instance, there are many relatively remote communities in Canada in which a large local firm is the only important source of employment; a monopsony exists in the labour market of such communities. A different example of monopsony is to be found in some agricultural processing industries such as sugar refining and tobacco. There the main ingredient is supplied by many small farmers, but there is substantial market power on the part of the processors. All these examples are violations of the perfectly competitive model.

Other limits to perfect competition appear even in competitive sectors. A very important set of assumptions that are violated almost everywhere is that each consumer or firm incurs all costs and derives all benefits arising from its respective consumption or production activities. In fact, many economic activities have external effects, i.e. costs and/or benefits accruing to other parties. These external effects imply that the private costs or benefits of these activities are not equal to their "true" social costs. A polluting activity is an obvious example of a social cost that a producer or consumer may impose upon the community at large. Many industries pollute the air or water around their location; so do car drivers and cottage dwellers. Conversely, there may be external benefits, as when a firm builds a road in an area for its own activities but it is also available for use by others.

The presence of externalities violates a fundamental condition of the efficiency of perfect competition. The prices established via a market mechanism reflect only the private and not the total marginal costs. Many public policy efforts to adjust costs under the form of taxes, subsidies, and regulatory rules have been made in recent years, but their results have not always been effective or consistent. These rules sometimes also have unintended anticompetitive effects by creating barriers to entry. At any rate, the presence of externalities is an obvious constraint to both the feasibility and the desirability of perfect competition.

The existence of advertising may also be incompatible with the perfectly competitive equilibrium. As we saw in the previous chapter, some types of advertising are purely persuasive, implying that they are aimed at changing the demand for the firm's product by altering the consumers' tastes (utility functions). These functions were exogenous data in establishing the competitive equilibrium. If firms can change them through advertising then a circularity is being introduced in the definition of the equilibrium: the resource allocation system, whose aim was supposedly the maximization of consumer utilities, in fact changes the nature of the maximands. This raises doubts about the ultimate efficiency of the system.

Last, one should note the static nature of the perfectly competitive model. Its equilibrium is compatible with a stagnating economy in which the firms' production functions remain the same over the long run. In such an economy there is a total absence of technological change through which production functions may evolve over time. In the perfectly competitive model such change is usually exogenous. In reality, however, technology evolves in part because of R&D spending by private firms. Such spending is also crucially influenced by public policies in the areas of patent protection and taxation. These policies may not favour competition in the short run. Similarly, there are reasons to believe that market structure is not unrelated to innovation and R&D activities. As with externalities, these effects of technological change cast doubts upon both the feasibility and the desirability of universal perfect competition.

Overall, therefore, perfect competition must by necessity be excluded from part of the economy. This also implies that the necessary conditions of the perfectly competitive equilibrium cannot be fulfilled everywhere. The key question that arises is whether it is still worthwhile to pursue them wherever they are feasible, or whether a "piecemeal" sector-by-sector approach to public policies towards competition is desirable.

Over the past few decades, there has been a long debate among economists on this question, which is generally known as the problem of the *second best*.[3] The necessary conditions for a Pareto optimal allocation are the *first best*. Are they still desirable wherever possible if they are infeasible everywhere? Is there another second best set of conditions to be preferred? This point will be discussed more extensively in a subsequent section, where the criteria for a sector-by-sector approach to public policies will be examined. For the moment, it suffices to state that the answer the majority of economists would give to both questions is a qualified "yes": competition should be promoted wherever possible, and second best conditions should be applied if competition is infeasible in a given sector. This stems in part from the severe drawbacks that may accompany the absence of competition. These drawbacks are the subject of the next two sections.

The Limits to Profit Maximization

Firms vary in size and organizational structure, from single proprietorships and partnerships on one hand, to complex multinational corporations at the other extreme. Single proprietorships or partnerships, in which the firm is managed by its owner(s), are to be found in only the smallest production units. Most medium to large firms are managed under some form of corporate structure, in which there is in most cases separation of ownership and day-to-day decision-making. Such firms are typically run by professional managers, subject to a rather distant supervision by the owners (stockholders). What is the form that profit maximization takes in such firms? What are the incentives for the managers to advance the interests of the owners as embodied in profit-maximizing behaviour? What role does market structure play in these incentives? These are the obvious questions to be raised once it becomes apparent that the simple models of owner-managed firms from microeconomic theory courses are no longer adequate to represent the complex reality of modern corporations.

The first two questions have produced a significant volume of literature, most of it by critics of the traditional economic postulate about profit maximization. These criticisms follow two distinct strains, one of which is centred on the descriptive realism of the postulate and the other on the managerial motives issue. The first one is relatively settled now, with most economists accepting the orthodox position. The debate on the second set of criticisms, however, is very much alive today under a variety of forms.

The realism of profit-maximizing behaviour (even when managers are honestly disposed to pursue it to the best of their abilities) has been questioned by several critics on the grounds of the complexity of the necessary actions. This complexity is especially pronounced in the presence of uncertainty about the economic environment. For instance, Scherer (1980) has pointed out that in choosing between alternative courses of action in the presence of risk, managers need information about owners' attitudes towards risk. Such information, however, is not easy to get. Further, decision-making under risk is by itself quite complex, requiring knowledge both of the chances that a given situation will prevail, as well as of the impact of that situation on the firm's financial position.[4]

These criticisms have been answered with a variety of counterarguments. The consensus about the proper decision-making rule in the presence of risk seems to be that managers' actions must strive to maximize the value of the stockholders' wealth. Modern financial theory has shown that this is the equivalent to profit maximization in the presence of uncertainty and the financial markets in which the firm's common stock is traded. As for the complexity arguments, these were answered with a famous analogy by Machlup (1946). He pointed out that profit maximization by a manager is no more difficult in practice than driving a car is for a motorist: the latter can easily perform motions that can only be described by complex laws of physics and differential calculus. Similarly, the manager need not be aware of the complex estimates necessary for profit maximization in order to undertake the necessary actions.

A different type of attack on the descriptive realism of the traditional approach is embodied in the so-called *behaviouralist* view.[5] Behaviouralists consider the firm as the sum of its human components, each one of whom has its own goals and aspirations. The resulting organizational structure and behaviour is the product of political bargaining and compromise. A key to such compromise is the so-called *satisficing* behaviour, which is qualitatively different from the maximization of profits, or indeed from any other single-minded objective. A typical satisficer has a set of performance variables, each one of which must be kept above a corresponding minimum level. These may include, in addition to profits, market share, price-cost margins, stability of production, etc. The firm monitors these variables and institutes special procedures every time one of them falls below its specific target.

As a description of actual firm behaviour, the behaviouralist approach is certainly more accurate than profit maximization. Indeed, much of it has been incorporated into standard courses on organizational behaviour taught in business schools. It has not, however, found much acceptance among economists. The complexity of firm conduct that it predicts makes it rather unsuitable for empirical validation, notwithstanding its realism. As Milton Friedman stated in a famous article, "The Methodology of Positive Economics" (1953), a theory need not be descriptively realistic as long as it is testable and has predictive power. One need not go as far as that in order to recognize that behaviouralism, for all its accuracy, has fallen far short of the theory standards normally expected in the economics discipline.

The question of managerial motives, however, is not so easily disposed of. Managers, like consumers and firm owners, are rational economic agents aiming at maximizing their own utility. There are no a priori reasons why the necessary actions for such maximization should coincide with profit-maximizing behaviour. In fact, there are excellent reasons for them to differ.[6]

Most managers receive a large part of their remuneration under the form of salary. Their compensation is broadly related to the size of the firm that they manage, measured by sales, number of employees, or value of assets. Hence, managers' actions should be geared towards maximizing one or more of these size dimensions, rather than stockholder wealth; the two sets of actions are definitely not identical.

The defenders of the traditional position have pointed out that managers who concentrate on empire-building to the exclusion of stockholder interests will soon find themselves out of a job.[7] Although the control exercised by the annual stockholder meeting is not very effective, there are other mechanisms that can be used to discipline greedy managers. Perhaps the most effective of them is the hostile takeover: dissatisfied owners would produce depressed share prices, which will trigger a takeover attempt by an outsider group. The first action of such a group when it gains control is to get rid of the top managers. The latter have therefore a significant stake in keeping their stockholders happy. An added incentive is the fact that in many corporations the top managers receive part of their compensation under the form of stock options or dividends; this effectively transforms them into stockholders.

An interesting compromise between the profit and sales or revenue maximization points of view has been proposed by W. Baumol (1959). His model recognizes that managers would rather pursue maximum sales, since this is more in line with their own interests. Nonetheless, the need to keep their stockholders happy makes them include a *minimum* profit constraint into their objectives. Figure 7.3 shows the firm equilibrium in the Baumol model. Point A represents the profit-maximizing output, at which the distance between the revenue and cost curves TR and TC is largest. Point C is the output yielding maximum revenue whose corresponding profit, however, lies below the minimum target T. Hence, the firm would be forced to operate at the intermediate point B, at which the profit constraint is satisfied with equality. This corresponds to the maximum sales revenue that guarantees the achievement of the minimum profit level.

Other objectives that are thought by some authors to be more closely correlated with managerial motivation than profits are growth, non-salary benefits of top executives (the so-called "perks"), and risk-avoidance. These objectives do not necessarily correspond to a different output choice than profit maximization. In particular, growth of output must be preceded by the

FIGURE 7.3
Sales maximization with a profit constraint

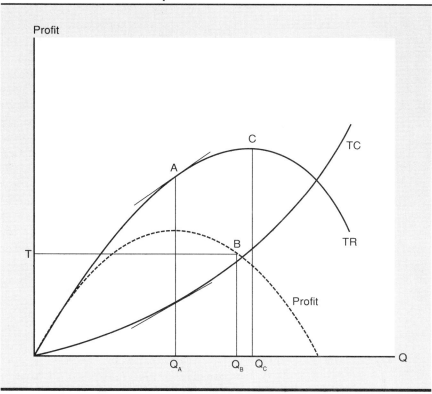

expansion of invested capacity, which is most often financed by retained profits. Similarly, the reduction of risk forms part of the objectives of profit maximization when uncertainty is incorporated into the firm's decision-making. As for the executive perks, there is no reason why they should have any effect on output choice; they do, however, result in lower profits, since they do not come for free. In fact, such perks are a subset of the waste normally associated with market power that we have already seen under the name of *X-inefficiency*.[8] This is sufficiently important to warrant special treatment in the next section.

There have been several empirical studies of the managerial motives hypothesis about firm behaviour. Some of these studies compare performance between firms, classified by the type of managerial control. According to the managerial motives argument, profits should be higher for owner-managed firms than for those controlled by professional managers. This does turn out to be the case in most such studies, although several of them found no significant difference between the two groups. Perhaps a more important finding was that the difference in profit rates was strongest where monopoly power was present. A study by Palmer (1973) found that profit rates were on average higher by 0.70 percent under owner management when market power was low (10.59 percent versus 9.89 percent under managerial control), but that this difference rose to 3.36 percentage points (14.77 percent and 11.41 percent) when a high monopoly power existed. The latter difference was highly significant statistically, while the former was not.

In support of traditional theory, on the other hand, one should cite the fact that most studies did not find sales maximization dominating profit considerations as managerial objectives.[9] In fact, executive compensation was found to be more closely associated with profit than with sales in many studies, thus undermining the basic tenet of the managerial motives approach. Similarly, little empirical evidence was found in support of the Baumol sales-maximizing model in the presence of a profit constraint. Other studies did, however, uncover plenty of "excess" managerial perks, especially under market power.

In summary, therefore, the traditional economic approach to the theory of the firm through profit maximization seems to have emerged relatively intact from its various attackers. There is sufficient justification for its adoption even in complex modern corporations, especially in its demand and pricing dimensions. Some departures from it have been documented, however, on the cost side under market power, and are examined in the next section.

More recently the conflicting objectives of firm owners and managers have become the subject of an extensive literature focussed on what is known as the *principal-agent* problem.[10] In general terms an agent is a person who takes actions on behalf of someone else (the principal). These actions affect the principal's welfare, but their monitoring is both costly and difficult, especially in the presence of uncertainty about the outcomes of specific actions. The losses incurred by the principal are known as *agency costs*. Principal-agent literature has obvious relevance to diverging stockholder-manager goals. Its main interest has been its design of effective contracts and incentive schemes for agents, which encourage them to pursue the same objectives as the owners.

Managerial Slack and X-Inefficiency

Inefficiency due to managerial slack should be viewed as similar to excessive management perks. To the extent that cost-reducing efficiency requires effort, which decreases managers' utility, it is preferably avoided if possible. In other words, managers gain a perk in extra leisure. Needless to say, this is only possible if there is not much pressure from competition; otherwise, high-cost firms would be eliminated by more efficient competitors.

It is important to realize that X-inefficiency is qualitatively different from excess cost due to insufficient scale or improper choice of technology. Basically, X-inefficiency exists when the chosen input combination produces a lower output than is feasible under the current state of the arts. Inputs are wasted because of error, inertia, carelessness, or any other type of incompetence. In more precise language, the X-inefficient firm does not operate on the production and cost functions corresponding to current technology and the prevailing input prices.

It is easy to see why such inefficiency is impossible in competitive sectors. By definition, firms in such sectors have zero profits. Any managerial slack would therefore produce negative profits, which in the long run would force the firm out of business or its managers out of a job. By contrast, by producing some profit in spite of the higher cost, market power may allow X-inefficient firms to stay in business depending on entry conditions.

The concept of X-inefficiency is closely linked to the behavioural theories about managerial motives, and like them it has been controversial among economists from the outset. For instance, Stigler (1976) has suggested that X-inefficiency is no different from agency costs, the costs and difficulties of monitoring performance and enforcing contracts that we saw in the principal-agent problem.[11] Nonetheless, X-inefficiency predicts that these costs are going to be higher when market power exists. For this reason it is difficult to deny either its plausibility on common sense grounds or the mounting empirical evidence in its favour. Such evidence comes from two sources: anecdotal accounts of managerial wastefulness in large firms, often associated with changes of management as a result of takeovers; as well as a few systematic empirical studies.

Documented cases of excessive management perks or other types of waste generally associated with market power are plentiful in business literature. They may appear as accounts of successful reorganization plans in business magazines such as *Fortune*, *Forbes*, or *Business Week*, as parts of industry studies, or as parts of the autobiographies of successful businessmen.[12] What is not clear from these accounts is the generality of the practices and the real costs that they impose on the economy as a whole. For these one needs to turn to systematic studies, of which there have been only a few. The difficulties of isolating X-inefficiency from other cost-increasing factors such as small scale or high input prices are presumably responsible for the scarcity of evidence. Nonetheless, there are some statistical approaches that manage to overcome these difficulties.

One of these approaches is the already-mentioned comparison of cost or profit performance between firms in the same industry, separated into groups under stockholder and manager control, respectively. For instance, the previously-cited study by Palmer (1973) found significant differences in profit rates between owner- and manager-controlled firms only when market power was present. Another method is the comparative cost performance of firms in the same industry, divided into groups differing by market power; X-inefficiency would show as higher costs for the more concentrated markets. An example of such a study is the comparison of matched Canadian and U.S. industries by Bloch (1974). In that study, a sample of 20 manufacturing industries were divided into 4 groups according to their concentration and tariff protection. For each such group the study estimated the price P, unit cost AC, and profit per unit output π/Q relative to the corresponding U.S. measures. The results are shown in Table 7.1.

These results provide support to the X-inefficiency view of monopoly power. Industries which are highly-concentrated and highly-sheltered from foreign competition are also the highest-cost producers relative to their U.S. counterparts. Competition, on the other hand, whether from domestic firms or from imports, suffices to bring Canadian costs more or less in line with the U.S. The study provides only weak evidence for X-inefficiency, however, since it does not control other possible reasons for the observed differences in cost performance. These may be due to differing input prices, plant size, or technology between the two countries.

Other studies were more precise in this respect. For instance Primeaux (1977) compared the costs of electricity production between cities in the U.S., classified according to whether the market structure was a monopoly or a duopoly. Overall, he found that the average cost was reduced by more than 10 percent in the duopoly case, which he attributed to the efficiency gained through competition.

Perhaps the most persuasive evidence in favour of the existence of X-inefficiency is the one provided by the deregulation movement in the U.S.,

TABLE 7.1
Comparative performances, 20 Canadian manufacturing industries (U.S.=100)

Industry type	P	AC	π/Q
High concentration, high tariff	111.6	119.3	117.3
High concentration, low tariff	104.4	100.3	121.6
Low concentration, high tariff	99.8	102.8	91.2
Low concentration, low tariff	101.6	105.9	79.9

Source: Bloch (1974), p. 604

in particular with respect to the airline industry. The deregulation of that industry corresponded almost to a controlled experiment, in which the only significant change that could account for observed differences in performance was the change in market structure, which became competitive within a relatively short time. There is no question that cost performance in airlines improved spectacularly following deregulation, and that a significant part of that improvement was due to better managerial efforts under the prod of competition. Baumol and Willig (1986) have given a good summary of the relevant industry studies. While part of the cost reduction was achieved at the expense of wages, or was brought about by the increased traffic and load factors, other improvements were due to better routing procedures and reduced overhead that should be attributed solely to better managerial control over costs.

In summary, therefore, the X-inefficiency view of monopoly power is a powerful argument in favour of policies to promote competition, and has been gaining a somewhat grudging acceptance by most economists. It is also being used as an argument for a more permissive attitude towards mergers and takeovers, as we shall see in Chapter 8. Yet, for all its merits this reasoning has its limitations, given the high transactions costs involved in hostile take-overs and the range of weapons available to the threatened managers. Hence, the reduction in managerial slack provided by the takeover mechanism is bound to be imperfect. That X-inefficiency has not been even more widely accepted by conventional economic theory can only be due, as Galbraith (1988) put it in his inimitable style, to economists' tendency to subordinate inconvenient circumstance to theoretical convenience.

As already noted, however, competition cannot be imposed in every sector in the economy. We need, therefore, a tool for the evaluation of the benefits of a change in the structure of an individual industry towards more or less competition. This brings us to the sector-by-sector approach to economic policy.

Consumer Surplus as an Index of Welfare

The piecemeal approach to public policy is based on partial equilibrium methods applied to individual industries or markets. For instance, it is forecasted that a certain public policy geared towards a given industry will bring changes to the prices and quantities prevailing there, as well as those other sectors linked to it on the demand or supply sides. Suppose that these changes can be estimated accurately. Can we then compare the changes in welfare with and without the policy by focussing on the affected sectors alone? As we noted earlier, the answer to this question is a qualified "yes", but it took some time before a consensus was reached among economists.

In its initial formulation, the theory of the second best that we mentioned earlier was perceived as being very destructive of any public policy initiatives aimed at promoting competition. This theory examined general equilibrium in an economy in which monopolistic deviations from the necessary conditions for Pareto optimality existed in a number of sectors. It then went on to show that achieving a competitive solution in one part of the economy was not necessarily an improvement in welfare if monopolistic distortions continued to exist elsewhere. Since competition everywhere is infeasible, this seemed to kill any economic rationale for using public policies to promote competition. Such policies had a long tradition of acceptance in many countries, including the U.S. and Canada, even before the Pareto optimality properties of the perfectly competitive model had been demonstrated.

Fortunately, the theory of the second best turned out in the end to be considerably more constructive than it was initially thought. While it does not support an uncritical application of perfect competition everywhere, it has also provided an important tool for the evaluation of sector-by-sector policies on second best considerations. This tool is the consumer surplus, which we saw briefly in Chapter 3. It can be used for the evaluation of welfare changes in moving from one industry equilibrium to another. Its use tends to support the argument that competition in a given sector would generally improve welfare even in the absence of X-inefficiency, unless there are other considerations such as economies of scale or vertical effects on other sectors.[13]

Figure 7.4 demonstrates such a use of the consumer surplus. The curve DD' is the demand of an individual consumer for the product of the sector under review. Initially, the market price and corresponding quantity are P_1 and Q_1. It is estimated that a given policy-related event (for instance, a merger) will raise the price to P_2 and bring a drop of consumer purchases to Q_2. As a result, the consumer surplus is reduced by the amount indicated by the cross-hatched area. Is this a "good" measure of the consumer's loss in welfare as a result of the price change?

As discussed in Appendix 7B, the answer to this question depends on the marginal utility of income along the demand curve. As we know from our theory courses, a demand curve such as DD' for any given good is derived under the assumption that the consumer's money income stays constant, while his/her utility varies. The area P_1ABP_2 is an accurate indicator of the consumer's change in welfare only if the marginal utility of the income left over after the expenditures on the good stays approximately constant along DD'. In general, there is no reason for this to happen. However, it was shown by Willig (1976) that even when the marginal utility changes along AB the change in consumer welfare can still be approximately measured by the cross-hatched area of Figure 7.4 as a function of the income elasticity of demand along AB.

The Willig results are presented in some detail in Appendix 7B. The accu-

FIGURE 7.4
Change in consumer surplus resulting from a price rise

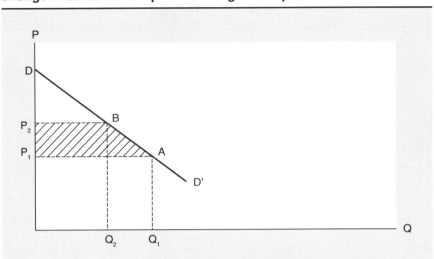

racy of the measurement of the welfare change by the area P_1ABP_2 depends on the maximum and minimum values that the income elasticity of demand assumes along the segment AB of the demand curve. If these values are close to each other, then the cross-hatched area combined with the consumer's money income can be used to derive a good approximation to the money income supplement necessary to keep the consumer's utility unchanged in spite of the rise in price. As shown in Appendix 7B, for a normal good this income supplement, known as the *compensating variation*, is equal to (P_1ABP_2) plus a small correction approximately equal to one-half of the product of the income elasticity times the ratio of (P_1ABP_2) to consumer income. For most commodities and prospective price changes this correction is very small and can be ignored as a first approximation. This implies that (P_1ABP_2) can give a good approximation to the loss of utility, measured in money terms, stemming from the price change.

This result has important implications for welfare economics. To begin with, it can be used to give an empirical content to the theoretical measures of individual welfare. While consumer utility is not observable, consumer demand curves and income elasticities are, as well as consumer incomes. Hence, the observable cross-hatched area in Figure 7.4 can be used according to the expressions provided in Appendix 7B in order to evaluate the impact on the consumers, in money terms, of any policies that would result in a price rise from P_1 to P_2. Since the impact of these same policies on the producers can be measured by the change in their profits, we have acquired monetary measures of the policy results upon all affected groups.

There are also other implications of the use of consumer surplus and profits to measure welfare. Satisfaction, as expressed by utility, is an individual concept that cannot be aggregated across different individuals. The same is not true with money, however, and both profit and consumer surplus are monetary measures. Hence, the total impact of the price rise in our example can be evaluated in money terms by the change in *total surplus*, computed by adding all changes in consumer surplus and all changes in profits. If this total change is positive then one can be fairly confident that the policy is beneficial to society as a whole. It is possible to impose countervailing taxes and subsidies that redistribute the income changes from those who gained to those who lost, so that everybody is at least as well off as before.

The policy evaluation does not stop with the sector at which it takes place. The price change will bring a reallocation of consumer purchases and/or producer decisions, resulting in price changes in all markets. In theory, therefore, the estimation carried out for the single consumer market shown in Figure 7.4 must be extended to every such market in the economy. In practice, however, the task is not as formidable as it sounds. Only the markets for goods with significant cross-elasticities of demand and supply need to be examined, and there is only a limited number of such markets for any conceivable policy.

The total surplus criterion therefore provides a useful performance standard to evaluate proposed policies directed towards a given sector. Examples of such policies are pricing in regulated industries, as we saw in Chapter 3, and public attitudes towards a proposed merger, which we shall examine in Chapter 8. Another interesting application of the total surplus concept is in the measure of the welfare distortions brought about by the introduction of monopoly in a given sector. This has been extended to measure the total economic losses due to the existence of monopolies in the economy.

Welfare Loss Due to Monopoly

The comparison between alternative monopoly and competitive market structures is shown in Figure 7.5. It has been simplified by assuming that the average cost curve is horizontal within the relevant range. In such a case, marginal and average costs, MC and AC, are equal to each other and to product price P_C under perfect competition. The competitive industry output Q_C is found from the corresponding point of the demand curve DD'. By contrast, a conversion of the industry into a monopoly would result into a curtailment of output to the level Q_M, where marginal revenue MR is equal to marginal cost. This produces a monopoly price P_M, and economic profits equal to the rectangle $P_M ABP_C$.

FIGURE 7.5
Deadweight loss due to monopoly

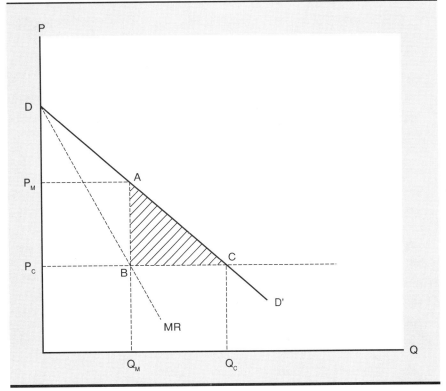

Under perfect competition the total surplus consists of the area DCP_C, the consumer surplus, given that profits are zero. Under monopoly the consumer surplus shrinks to the area DAP_M, to which one must add the profit P_MABP_C to arrive at total surplus. Hence, the total surplus in going from competition to monopoly has been reduced by the area of the triangle ABC, in addition to the transfer of surplus from the consumers to the firm's owners represented by the profits. The triangle ABC, the pure loss in surplus, is known as the *deadweight loss* due to monopoly, and its estimation provides a measure of the allocative inefficiency created by the monopolization of that particular sector of the economy.

The size of the deadweight loss, denoted by W, is a function of the price and quantity changes and the price elasticity of demand. The area of the triangle is equal to $1/2(\Delta P)(\Delta Q)$, where ΔP and ΔQ denote $P_M - P_C$ and $Q_C - Q_M$, represented by the lengths AB and BC in the diagram. Setting the relative price change $\Delta P/P$ equal to t, and the price elasticity of demand $(\Delta Q/\Delta P)(P/Q)$ equal to ϵ, we can easily see that the deadweight loss becomes equal to $1/2(\Delta P)(\Delta Q) = 1/2Q_C(\Delta P/P_C)(P_C\Delta Q/Q_C) = 1/2Q_C P_C(\Delta P/P_C)^2(P_C\Delta Q/Q_C\Delta P) = 1/2\epsilon P_C Q_C t^2$. This quantity is measurable, since the data needed consist of the price rise above the competitive level, the total revenue, and the price elasticity of demand.

Estimates of W were carried out by several authors, mainly in the U.S. under a variety of assumptions. The first estimate was by Harberger (1954), with data from the U.S. manufacturing sector in 1924-28. He assumed a value of 1 for the elasticity of demand, and computed the relative excess price t by using the ratio of excess profits to sales for each individual industry. Excess profits, on the other hand, were considered to exist when the industry profit rate exceeded the average for all manufacturing. He found that the sum of the deadweight losses for all sectors was very small, not exceeding 0.1 percent of GNP.

This optimistic result on the unimportance of monopoly in the U.S. economy has not withstood the test of time, due to its sensitivity to changes in its basic assumptions. There is no consensus on what the aggregate welfare loss due to monopoly actually is, with estimates ranging up to 4 percent and even as high as 10 percent of GNP for the U.S. This range of estimates was created by studies that altered somewhat the expression yielding W. Thus, Cowling and Mueller (1978) argued that since Q_M is equal to $1/2Q_C$, $\Delta Q/Q_C$ is approximately 1. Hence t should be equal to the reciprocal of the price elasticity of demand, which would make W equal to $1/2P_C Q_C t$. Using firm data, they found an aggregate W on the order of 4 percent of GNP for the U.S. and 10 percent for the U.K. Other authors have argued that even this figure is an underestimate, given that it ignores inefficiencies on the cost side. On the other hand, there have also been other studies that found low estimates similar to Harberger's.

The omission of excess costs of production from the welfare losses of monopoly is potentially a serious downwards bias to the measures of W. Such excess costs include the higher agency costs or any other sources of X-inefficiency, as well as possible overpayments to factors of production like managerial perks. Similarly, any costs involved in securing a monopoly position through government licensing, or through the erection of any other "wasteful" barrier to entry, must also be added to the excess costs. Although reliable measures of the total loss when all these are taken into account do not exist, it can be easily seen how one can arrive at the figure of 10 percent of GNP if some extreme assumptions are used.

In Canada there is an added factor that plays a role in estimating the welfare loss due to monopoly. This is the existence of imports which compete with the products of the monopolized domestic sector. Stegeman (1984) modified the estimation of W shown in Figure 7.5, by taking into account the fact that monopolies, by raising prices, will also create a market share loss to imports. The size of this loss depends on a number of factors such as product differentiation and the size of the importing economy. The argument will be re-examined in Chapter 11, which discusses the role of foreign trade in structure and performance. At any rate, even if this extra welfare loss is ignored it is highly probable that the total loss will be higher in Canada than in the U.S., due to the much more pervasive existence of market power.

Dynamic Considerations

The analysis of performance carried out thus far is essentially static in nature, in both global and piecemeal formulations. There are, however, many important dynamic effects that may require public policy attention. Some of these effects, such as predatory pricing, advertising, and excess capacity, were examined in previous chapters. Our discussion of performance standards in a dynamic context will be rather brief, given the lack of clarity in public policy guidelines when one goes beyond the static framework.

The complications brought about by the introduction of the time factor in dynamic models of the firm affect particularly the non-price dimensions of conduct. Investment, quality choice, advertising, and R&D are basically long-run decisions, which may bring changes to future industry structure. A number of questions arise in connection with the public policy attitudes that should be adopted towards these decisions. We shall restrict ourselves to a brief discussion of two points: is static competition compatible with long-run efficiency objectives? should public policy be concerned with conduct that may be anti-competitive in the long run?

The second point has already been answered in the affirmative in previous chapters. We saw that firms may find it profitable to adopt conduct whose only purpose is the creation of monopoly power in the long run. Such conduct consists basically of the erection of entry barriers through a variety of means: excess capacity, excessive advertising, brand proliferation, strategic location, etc. It comes under the general term of predatory conduct, and it includes predatory pricing whose aim is the creation of reputation factors. Unfortunately, we also saw that there is very little that can be done about such conduct with the currently available public policy tools. The dividing line between predatory conduct and vigorous competition is not easily distinguishable given the current state of the art, a point that will be made repeatedly in the policy chapters that follow. For this reason, judicial cases dealing with predatory conduct belong to the frontiers of antitrust policy, even in the U.S.[14]

The compatibility of the static competitive model with long-run dynamic efficiency is also not a simple issue. The most obvious example of a contradiction between short-run competitive performance and long-run efficiency objectives is in the public policies that should be adopted with respect to patents. As we saw in Chapter 5, a patent is a barrier to entry created by public policy. The longer the period of patent protection the more effective the barrier would be, but the incentives to innovate grow as well. The optimal patent length should clearly be a compromise between the two contradictory points of view.

Such conflicts between static and dynamic objectives are at the root of the reverse structure-performance model that we saw briefly in the first chapter. According to that model, it is long-run differences in performance that are responsible for monopolistic structures in the absence of government intervention. Such differential performance can arise from successful innovation, superior management, accurate market forecasts, or any other type of good performance. The policy implications that stem from this model are sufficiently important to warrant a special section at the end of this chapter. Outside the reverse model, dynamic factors bring few modifications to static competitive objectives with a few obvious exceptions (such as patents).

Workable Competition

We may now summarize the conclusions of our discussion about the economic rationale for competition policy. It started with general equilibrium and Pareto optimality, and the supposed efficiency of global perfect competition. The impossibility of achieving such a standard, and the destructive result of the second best, forced us to turn to the piecemeal, sector-by-sector approach to competition. Here the justification for competition is productive inefficiency, under the form of excess production costs or X-inefficiency, and allocative inefficiency based on the deadweight monopoly loss. This piecemeal approach allows for relaxation of the competitive standards when conditions warrant it, as in the case of a natural monopoly.

Still, even for such a piecemeal approach the formulation of public policy needs some general framework within which one may examine each individual sector. The concept of workable competition, originally formulated by Clark (1940) in a general equilibrium context, may provide such a framework. It has since been modified to incorporate the sector-by-sector approach. Although it suffers from a degree of imprecision that many economists find unacceptable, it has been very popular, especially among policy makers.

Workable competition essentially amounts to a set of basic rules intended to set the limits of acceptable structure, conduct, and performance. Public policy intervention is triggered when such limits are exceeded. The main purpose of the rules, however, is to define the appropriate climate within which competition may flourish. In other words, it is hoped that the private sector will reach an efficient performance without public intervention.

The criteria for workable competition were summarized by Sosnick (1958), who surveyed the relevant literature.[15] They cover separate requirements for structure, conduct, and performance, elaborated under the form of qualitative norms as follows:

A) *Structure*
   (i) A substantial number of firms, consistent with economies of scale; no firm must dominate the market.
   (ii) No artificial barriers to entry.
   (iii) Adequate access to buyer information.
   (iv) Moderate, price-responsive quality differentials in the supply of products in the relevant markets.

B) *Conduct*
   (i) Some uncertainty among rivals about whether price changes will be followed.
   (ii) No collusion.
   (iii) No predatory, exclusionary, coercive, or otherwise unfair tactics.
   (iv) No misleading advertising.
   (v) No persistent price discrimination.

C) *Performance*
   (i) Efficient operations.
   (ii) No excessive selling and promotional expenses.
   (iii) Profits that are just sufficient to reward investment and encourage efficiency and innovation.
   (iv) Price fluctuations should not contribute to instability and inflation.
   (v) Quantity and quality of output responsive to consumer demand.

The vagueness of most of these criteria needs few further comments. Ideally, a set of criteria should prescribe thresholds of policy intervention to modify unacceptable structure or conduct, so that the performance norms would be met. The criteria listed above fall far short of such an ideal. For instance, how does one decide that there is enough uncertainty about price responses? How well-informed should buyers be?

In spite of these drawbacks, the workability criteria of structure and conduct reflect more or less most of the efficiency goals that were expressed in the previous sections. There is clearly an attempt to include dynamic considerations, macroeconomic concerns, and non-price dimensions of firm conduct. Probably the most useful approach to workably competitive criteria, however, was the one expressed by Markham (1950), which is more in line with the piecemeal view of public policy. He suggested that each sector be examined on its own merits, and be declared "workable" if no policy change can bring clear improvements. This approach, coupled with the quantitative criterion of maximizing total surplus, can provide simple and pragmatic policy rules applicable to any given situation.

This brief survey of performance standards completes the economic case for pro-competitive policies. It is not a very strong case, riddled as it is with qualifications and ambiguities. It can be strengthened with non-economic factors such as equity and justice, but many economists consider these subjective and value-laden. The alternative to public policies promoting competition is a laissez-faire attitude, with minimal public intervention. The economic case for such an approach relies mainly on dynamic efficiency considerations, as embodied in the reverse structure-performance model. The empirical evidence for the validity of this model will be surveyed in some detail in the last section of this chapter.

The Structure-Performance Relationship

According to the traditional SCP model, there is a causal link between firm profitability and industry structure through firm conduct. A concentrated structure facilitates collusion and produces high prices and profits. Hence, such a structure is undesirable on allocative efficiency grounds as long as it does not promote economies of scale or any other contributions to productive efficiency.

Suppose, however, that there are cost advantages to some firms in an industry, whether because of better management, conventional economies of scale, or any other factors. Then most of the oligopoly models surveyed in Chapter 4 predict that such low-cost firms would have in equilibrium both high market shares and high profits. Further, it can be shown that the Herfindahl index would have a higher value than if all firms had identical costs, and that this value is positively related to the average profitability of the industry.[16] Here, however, the causal link between concentration and profitability has been reversed: it is profitability, itself due to efficiency advantages, that increases market concentration and not vice-versa. This in turn has policy implications with respect to structure that differ drastically from those of the conventional SCP. If concentration is not a causal factor of market power but a result of superior efficiency, then public policy has no reason to worry about it, nor to interfere whenever it may increase because of a merger or takeover.

As we saw in Chapter 1, this benign view of concentrated market structures has become known as the reverse structure-performance model, while the mainline SCP view has been named by Demsetz (1973a) the *market concentration doctrine*. Given the important policy implications stemming from these two contrary views, a survey of the empirical evidence is in order. The number of relevant studies has mushroomed in recent years, but their results have not been conclusive. Nonetheless, they have managed to instill at least some doubt among economists and policy-makers about the validity of that particular part of SCP.

Most of the earlier empirical studies of the profit-concentration relationship were based on industry data. The dependent variable was a profit measure, denoted by π. It was regressed against a set of explanatory variables across a sample of industries. These variables were intended to capture the effects of structure, of barriers to entry, and of demand. Examples of such studies are the pioneering work of Bain (1956) in the U.S. and the studies of McFetridge (1973) and Jones *et al.* (1973) for Canada.

With the passage of time better data became available, with the result that more precise testing also became possible. Thus, when company (rather than industry) data was used, the firm's market share was introduced as an explanatory variable. More recently, a number of U.S. surveys of large multiproduct firms made it possible to use profitability and market share data on every individual industry in which a firm participates. This increased both the power and the sophistication of the tests, but it still did not provide any firm conclusions.

The difficulties inherent in the empirical work stem from the simultaneity of many of the underlying relationships. Suppose, for instance, that we take the simplest model and denote by X_c, X_b and X_d the independent variable(s) measuring respectively collusion, barriers to entry, and demand. Then the regression to be estimated would have the form:

$$\pi = a_0 + a_1 X_c + a_2 X_b + a_3 X_d$$

In many studies the exogenous variables used as proxies for X_b, X_c, or X_d are not truly exogenous, but are themselves determined by fundamental conditions. For instance, if X_c is measured (as is very often the case) by some measure of market concentration, then the SCP model specifies that it should be determined endogenously by economies of scale and demand. These, however, are included separately in the regression, in X_b (as a barrier to entry) and X_d respectively. Hence, the true impact of structure on profitability may be hidden by these parallel effects. This problem is further accentuated because there is often little available data on several crucial variables, such as demand elasticity, which are therefore omitted. Such an omission may bias the estimates of the effects of the exogenous variables.

Other problems likely to be faced in empirical research concern the choices of appropriate measures for the dependent and independent variables. One of the most controversial of such variables is profitability, for which a number of alternative measures have been proposed. These include rate of return on assets, rate of return on equity, price-cost margin, and more recently, the ratio of stock market value to the book value of the firm, also known as Tobin's q. Each one of these measures has its own drawbacks, some of which may introduce systematic biases in the results. A most extreme position on these imperfections, articulated (among others) by Fisher and McGowan (1983), goes as far as denying the validity of any empirical results on the relationship between profitability and market structure or firm size. If this position is accepted then there is no way of choosing between the SCP and the reverse structure-performance model.

Still, empirical research has made a valiant effort to overcome these problems. Proxies such as advertising intensity, the average share of the largest firms, and capital intensity were included as measures of the barriers to entry. Exogenous variables were entered non-linearly in the regressions when there was reason to believe that their effect was not linear. Simultaneous equation models were used in order to separate the different effects. Only a few of these studies are summarized below.[17]

The studies that appeared during the 1960s and 1970s were overall supportive of SCP, insofar as they found a significant relationship between structure and profitability. Such important studies, based on cross-sectional data across individual industries in the U.S., were those by Mann (1966), Collins and Preston (1968, 1969), and Weiss (1974). All these studies confirmed the findings of Bain's earlier work, according to which concentration and entry barriers were significant determinants of industry profitability. Their results were consistent with similar studies in the U.K. by Philips (1972) and Hitiris (1978), and with the two Canadian studies, McFetridge (1973) and Jones *et al.* (1973), cited earlier.

Things started getting more complicated once firm-level data on profitability and sales became available. It was then found in the cross-sectional studies that a firm's size was a much stronger determinant of profitability than concentration or barriers to entry. These were the results of Hall and Weiss (1967), in which firm asset size was a more important determinant of profitability than concentration, and of Shepherd (1972), in which a firm's market share was more closely associated with profits than either concentration or entry barriers. Such results are also consistent with the reverse structure-performance model, even though there were still significant market structure effects on profits.

Demsetz (1973b) proposed to test the two competing models by examining the association between profit and firm size within an industry. If it is concentration that causes high profits by facilitating collusion, then both large and small firms (as long as they exceed the MES) should benefit, and there is no reason to observe a correlation between profit and market share. If it is efficiency differentials that bring high concentration and high market shares and profits to efficient firms then large firms should show higher profits than small firms in concentrated industries. Hence, the significance of market share as a determinant of intra-industry profitability differentials can only be due to differences in efficiency between firms.

This finding, however, is still not sufficient in order to establish the validity of the reverse structure-performance model. One must also determine the reasons for such efficiency differentials, especially if they are not due to economies of scale. Is it superior management that makes large firms prosper? Do such firms possess advantages in production methods or market selection? If so, why is it that other firms do not imitate them to emulate their success? In other words, if it is not management that is responsible for the success of these firms, then there is also a need to articulate the type of entry barriers that preserve the dominant firms' superiority.

As we already noted, the most recent studies on market structure and profitability have had contradictory results. Gale and Branch (1982) used firm data disaggregated by individual product markets, drawn from the Profit Impact of Market Strategy (PIMS) program of the Strategic Planning Institute. They find that concentration is completely dominated by market share as an explanatory variable of profitability. Similar results were found by Ravenscraft (1983), and by Smirlock *et al.* (1984). By contrast, Salinger (1984) found a significant effect of concentration on profits, while Schmalensee (1987) found that the conventional SCP model was more consistent with the data than the reverse model for one of the two years that he examined, while neither model performed well for the other year.

These U.S. results must be supplemented with studies from other economies. In the U.K., a study by Clarke *et al.* (1984) found no general evidence for efficiency effects for the years in their data (1971 and 1977). Market share was important only in a subsample of 29 industries, but even there the authors of the study argue that the evidence is also consistent with market power effects on profitability. In Canada, the major study on market structure and performance that uses firm level data is the one by Caves *et al.* (1980), that has been cited repeatedly in earlier chapters. That study used a complex simultaneous equation model, in which both market concentration and entry barriers emerged as significant determinants of profitability, albeit in a highly nonlinear form.

Perhaps the most systematic testing of the various competing hypotheses in the structure-performance relationship was carried out by Schmalensee (1985). That study used a very simple framework which analyzed profitability along the firm and industry dimensions. Specifically, if r_{ij} denoted the profit (measured by the accounting rate of return) realized by firm i through its operations in industry j, then this profit was subjected to an analysis of variance model as follows:

$$r_{ij} = m + a_i + b_j + cS_{ij} + e_{ij}$$

In the above equation, a_i and b_j respectively denote firm and industry effects, while S_{ij} is the corresponding market share and e_{ij} a random term.

The analysis was carried out with 1975 data collected by the U.S. Federal Trade Commission (FTC) under a highly controversial Line of Business program that surveyed a sample of large firms in a detailed manner over three years.[18] Those same data had also been used in the study by Ravenscraft

(1983), cited earlier, which is all the more surprising given the contrary results obtained in this case. Indeed, the analysis finds that firm effects are completely non-existent, while market share effects are significant but rather small. By far the most important influence on profitability, however, is the industry effect, thus yielding strong support to the conventional SCP model. Further, and somewhat surprisingly, market share turns out to be negatively correlated with the industry effects, a fact that helps explain the contradiction between the Schmalensee and Ravenscraft results.

The insignificance of the firm effect in the Schmalensee study basically means that successful performance in one industry does not predict a firm's success elsewhere. It also tends to suggest that managerial factors at the firm level may not be responsible for high performance outside each firm's narrow industry range. It is, however, consistent with differences in profitability within an industry, coupled with a stable industrial composition of a firm's range of activities. Thus, it does not completely contradict the reverse structure-performance model, but it is much more supportive of traditional SCP.

What is one to conclude from this wealth of contradictory results? What is the meaning of the one piece of evidence that was produced by the more recent studies: the significance of market share as a determinant of profitability? There are two alternative interpretations. The first is that large firms have superior efficiency in accordance with the reverse structure-performance model. The second is a market power model: the superiority of large firms may be due to product differentiation and barriers to entry created because of market power, together with possible reputation factors. While the two interpretations are not necessarily inconsistent, they have fundamentally different policy implications.

In choosing to follow the traditional SCP model, as has been done throughout this text, neither one of these competing explanations was discarded. There are feedback effects from performance to structure in the basic diagram that introduced SCP, Figure 1.1. There are also feedback effects from conduct to structure, in accordance with the market power interpretation of the link between market share and profitability. There is ample evidence, both theoretical and empirical, for the two feedback effects in the recent literature. The two competing models ignore one of the effects or the other in order to focus on the policy implications. In our opinion much of this focus has to do with ideological considerations about the proper role of government in the regulation of economic activity.

Such considerations need not concern us here. It is sufficient to say that current mainstream economic thought accepts that it is proper for governments to intervene in individual markets in order to improve their performance, in accordance with some version of the SCP model. This would accept that dominant firms and monopolistic structures may be initially established because of genuine efficiency advantages. They also have, however, the potential to transform themselves into self-perpetuating monopolies or cartels long after these advantages have disappeared. It is the role of public policy to distinguish the latter cases from the former in its interventions.

Perhaps the best justification for the use of the traditional SCP model is the emphasis that it places on the industry as the unit of analysis. As we saw in Chapters 1 and 2, most economic data is collected at that particular level. By contrast, the reverse model is centered on the firm, for which little data is publicly available. As Schmalensee (1985) noted, this emphasis of the traditional SCP is also in accordance with the dominant role that the industrial specialization of firms plays in determining performance. Thus the traditional SCP emerges as the "natural" paradigm of industrial organization on legal and practical grounds, without necessarily diverging from economic theory.

Conclusions

Public policies to promote competition throughout the economy were established basically on non-economic grounds. In both the U.S. and Canada the first antitrust legislation predated by several years the systematic formulation of general equilibrium and Pareto optimality conditions. This non-economic case for competition was therefore strong enough on its own grounds to justify pro-competitive public policies.

Economists' contributions in the policy area mostly took the form of formulating economic performance standards, against which the results of any given policy could be evaluated. Such standards basically ignore anything that lies beyond efficiency in production and resource allocation. They can, however, be justified as indispensable complements of policy evaluation if one keeps in mind their limited scope.

The basic performance standards to emerge from economic theory were the general justification of competition as the best possible regime, based on the Pareto optimality concept, and the more recent maximization of total surplus criterion for any sector-specific policy. The first line of approach can be rigorously justified on theoretical grounds only if perfect competition is established everywhere in the economy. The impossibility of doing this, coupled with the theoretical attack on the partial fulfillment of the Pareto optimality conditions of the theory of the second best, constitutes a serious limitation on the economic case for competition.

On the other hand, a public policy of inaction in the face of market power does not have much to commend it either, if it is not justified on the grounds of superior performance. The theoretical justification for inaction, as formulated in the reverse structure-performance model, invokes precisely such grounds as an explanation of the emerging market structure. Most proponents of that model, however, would still accept policy intervention to curb abuses of dominant firm conduct. The empirical evidence in support of the reverse model is at best weak, while its most serious deficiency is the denial of possible structure-altering conduct by dominant firms. Nonetheless, the debate is still far from over in the choice between the two models when formulating public policy.

Other important elements that should play a role in establishing performance standards for policy evaluation are behavioural and dynamic considerations. The former are mostly embodied in the concept of X-inefficiency associated with market power; they are strongly supportive of competitive policies. The latter form the cornerstone of the reverse model, but they may also be used in support of public intervention in the case of predatory conduct.

Overall, the picture that emerges from this brief survey of the economic case for competition policies must by necessity rely more on pragmatic grounds than on rigorous theoretical analysis. The best argument that one can make for competition is that the weight of evidence seems to favour it most of the time over its alternatives. Anyway, if there is any suspicion that competition may not be the best solution for a given industry, there is the total surplus tool to build a case for a different approach.

This is the core of the philosophy that is embodied in the current approach to public policy in Canada. It means basically that competition is desirable everywhere unless one can make a case against it on some grounds. Several such exceptions have been explicitly recognized in the legislation. Unfortunately, there have also been many cases where competition has been deliberately suppressed, notwithstanding the unanimous contrary verdict of economic analysis. These can presumably be justified on non-economic grounds, although for some of them equity is clearly not a relevant argument. The policy chapters that follow will highlight some such examples.

Appendix 7A NECESSARY CONDITIONS FOR PARETO OPTIMALITY

Suppose we have an economy with two produced and traded goods, denoted by x and y, which require labour l and capital k as production inputs. The economy has $I + 1$ consumers and $2J$ firms, respectively denoted by the indices i and j. The production functions are $F^x(l, k)$ and $F^y(l, k)$ for x and y respectively. We assume, without loss of generality, that firms $1, \ldots, J$ produce x, while firms $J + 1, \ldots, 2J$ produce y.

The assumption of perfect competition everywhere implies that there are uniform prices for x, y, l and k, denoted by P_x, P_y, w and r. The ith consumer has an initial endowment (x_{i0}, y_{i0}, k_{i0}) of x, y and k, as well as a maximum endowment l_0 of labour, assumed the same for all consumers.[19] The consumer's income m_i therefore is given by:

$$m_i = P_x x_{i0} + P_y y_{i0} + r k_{i0} \qquad \textbf{Eq. (7A.1)}$$

The utility function $U^i(x_i, y_i, l_i)$ is maximized by the consumer where $U_x^i > 0$, $U_y^i > 0$, $U_l^i < 0$, $U_{xx}^i < 0$, $U_{yy}^i < 0$, $U_{ll}^i < 0$, and the subscripts denote the first and second partial derivatives with respect to the corresponding variables.

We start from the definition of a Pareto-optimal allocation of consumption. Suppose that the minimum levels of utilities of consumers $i = 1, \ldots, I$ are fixed at the levels U_0^i while the utility of consumer $I + 1$ is being maximized. The total consumption of commodities x and y, as well as the total supply of labour in the economy, are fixed: $\sum_i x_i = X$, $\sum_i y_i = Y$, $\sum_i l_i = L$. Hence, we have the following maximization problem:

$$\underset{x_{I+1}, y_{I+1}, l_{I+1}}{\text{Max}} \quad \{U^{I+1}(x_{I+1}, y_{I+1}, l_{I+1})\}$$

subject to: $U^i(x_i, y_i, l_i) \geqslant U_0^i$, $i = 1, \ldots, I$. $\displaystyle\sum_{i=1}^{I+1} x_i = X$, $\displaystyle\sum_{i=1}^{I+1} y_i = Y$, $\displaystyle\sum_{i=1}^{I+1} l_i = L$.

If we attach Lagrange multipliers λ_i, $i = 1, \ldots, I$ to the utility constraints, and multipliers α, β, and γ correspondingly to the other three constraints, then we have to maximize the following expression:

$$U^{I+1}(x_{I+1}, y_{I+1}, l_{I+1}) + \sum_{i=1}^{I} \lambda_i \left[U^i(x_i, y_i, l_i) - U_0^i \right] + \alpha \left[X - \sum_{i=1}^{I+1} x_i \right] +$$

$$\beta \left[Y - \sum_{i=1}^{I+1} y_i \right] + \gamma \left[L - \sum_{i=1}^{I+1} l_i \right]$$

The maximization is with respect to the $3(I + 1)$ terms, x_i, y_i, and l_i, $i = 1, \ldots, I + 1$ and the multipliers α, β, γ and λ_i, $i = 1, \ldots, I$. It is easy to see that the first-order necessary conditions take the form:

$$\lambda_i U_x^i = \alpha \ , \ \lambda_i U_y^i = \beta \ , \ \lambda_i U_l^i = \gamma \ , \ i = 1, \ldots, I$$

$$U_x^{I+1} = \alpha \ , \ U_y^{I+1} = \beta \ , \ U_l^{I+1} = \gamma \qquad \textbf{Eq. (7A.2)}$$

$$U^i = U_0^i \ , \ i = 1, \ldots, I, X = \sum_i x_i \ , \ Y = \sum_i y_i \ , \ L = \sum_i l_i$$

These necessary conditions are sufficient to determine all variables. From Equation (7A.2) one may easily derive the following:

$$\frac{U_x^i}{U_y^i} = \frac{U_x^{I+1}}{U_y^{I+1}} \ , \ \frac{U_l^i}{U_x^i} = \frac{U_l^{I+1}}{U_x^{I+1}} \ , \ i = 1, \ldots, I \qquad \textbf{Eq. (7A.3)}$$

Hence, in a Pareto-optimal allocation, the ratio of marginal utilities (or marginal rate of substitution) of any pair of commodities is the same for all consumers in the economy.

Equation (7A.3), together with the last set of equations in (7A.2), provide a set of $3I + 3$ equations with as many unknowns. Their solution yields a consumption allocation that maximizes the utility of consumer $I + 1$ while maintaining the other consumers' utility at the given levels, and with fixed total amounts of goods x and y and labour l. This maximization takes place by pure exchange operations, without any production. It is also dependent on the fixed utility levels U_0^i, which act as constraints on the maximum utility that can be achieved by consumer $I + 1$.

Next we consider Pareto optimality in production. Suppose that the total available input quantities $\sum_{j=1}^{2J} l_j$ and $\sum_{j=1}^{2J} k_j$ are fixed at corresponding levels L and K, where l_j and k_j represent the inputs used by firm j. Suppose also that the total output Y is fixed, and that we want to find the maximum possible output $\sum_{j=1}^{J} x_j$ that can be produced from the available inputs. Since all firms producing x or y are assumed identical, they also use the same amounts of labour and capital. Let, therefore, (l_1, l_2) and (k_1, k_2) denote l_j and k_j for $j = 1, \ldots, J$ and $j = J + 1, \ldots, 2J$ respectively. Then $Jl_2 = L - Jl_1$, or $l_2 = \dfrac{L}{J} - l_1$, and similarly $k_2 = \dfrac{K}{J} - k_1$. The corresponding output produced by any firm $j = J + 1, \ldots,$ 2J is fixed and equal to $\dfrac{Y}{J} = F^y \left(\dfrac{L}{J} - l_1, \dfrac{K}{J} - k_1 \right)$.

A Pareto-optimal input allocation is one that maximizes the output x_j produced by any firm with index $j = 1, \ldots, J$, for fixed total output Y and total available input quantities L and K. Since all x-producing firms are assumed identical, it suffices to consider only one of them, with production function $x_j = F^x(l_1, k_1)$. We must, therefore, solve the problem:

$$\text{Max} \{JF^x(l_1, k_1)\}$$
$$l_1, k_1$$

subject to $Y = JF^y \left(\dfrac{L}{J} - l_1, \dfrac{K}{J} - k_1 \right)$. If α denotes as before a Lagrange multiplier,

then the maximization equates to zero the partial derivatives with respect to l_1, k_1 and α of the following expression:

$$JF^x(l_1, k_1) + \alpha \left[JF^y \left(\dfrac{L}{J} - l_1, \dfrac{K}{J} - k_1 \right) - Y \right]$$

If the subscripts 1 and 2 denote partial differentiation with respect to labour and capital then the first-order necessary conditions become:

$$F_1^x = \alpha F_1^y \; , \; F_2^x = \alpha F_2^y \; , \; JF^y = Y.$$

From these we get:

$$\frac{F_1^{\,x}}{F_2^{\,x}} = \frac{F_1^{\,y}}{F_2^{\,y}} \qquad\qquad \textbf{Eq. (7A.4)}$$

Hence, a Pareto-optimal allocation of inputs to production equates the ratios of marginal products (the rate of technical substitution) of any pair of inputs across all firms in the economy.

Last, we have the general case of Pareto optimality in a simultaneous allocation of resources to production and consumption. This case will be covered more briefly, since it is basically a synthesis of the other two. As before, we must find the allocation that maximizes the utility U^{I+1}, given minimum levels U_0^i of utilities $U^i, i = 1, \ldots, I$. The maximization is constrained by the total available resources, which are owned by the consumers. The relevant constraints are $\sum\limits_{i=1}^{I+1} k_{i0} = J(k_1 + k_2)$ and $\sum\limits_{i=1}^{I+1} l_i = J(l_1 + l_2)$. There are also two more constraints which specify that what is consumed must also be produced. Hence, we must have $\sum\limits_{i=1}^{I+1} x_i = JF^x(l_1, k_1), \; \sum\limits_{i=1}^{I+1} y_i = JF^y(l_2, k_2)$.

As before, we attach Lagrange multipliers to each constraint and maximize the resulting expression with respect to $x_i, y_i, l_i, i = 1, \ldots, I+1$, as well as the inputs $l_j, k_j, j = 1, 2$. The maximization generates the previously-found conditions (7A.3) and (7A.4), as well as the following new condition for $i = 1, \ldots, I+1$:

$$\frac{U_x^i}{U_y^i} = \frac{F_1^y}{F_1^x} = \frac{F_2^y}{F_2^x} \; , \; F_1^x = -\frac{U_l^i}{U_x^i} \; , \; F_1^y = -\frac{U_l^i}{U_y^i} \qquad \textbf{Eq. (7A.5)}$$

In other words, in a Pareto-optimal allocation the marginal rate of commodity substitution for any pair of commodities and any consumer is equal to the inverse ratio of the corresponding marginal products of any factor of production. This definition covers also the second set of conditions if we note that the products x and y can be treated as factors of production, whose marginal product is equal to one.

Equations (7A.3), (7A.4), and (7A.5) are the necessary conditions for a Pareto-optimal allocation. It can be shown that if a single one of them is violated then it is possible to improve at least one consumer's utility while leaving everybody else at least as well off. It remains to show that equilibrium under perfect competition produces a Pareto-optimal resource allocation.

Under perfect competition consumers maximize their utilities $U^i(x_i, y_i, l_i)$, $i = 1, \ldots, I+1$, subject to their budget constraint. In the latter their total purchases are limited by the income that they earn by working, as well as by their initial endowment (7A.1). Hence:

$$x_i P_x + y_i P_y = m_i + wl_i \qquad \textbf{Eq. (7A.6)}$$

As we know from consumer theory, this maximization yields the familiar equality of marginal rates of substitution to the corresponding price ratios for every pair of consumed commodities. Hence:

$$\frac{U_x^i}{U_y^i} = \frac{P_x}{P_y} \qquad \frac{U_1^i}{U_x^i} = -\frac{w}{P_x} \qquad i = 1, \dots, I+1 \qquad \textbf{Eq. (7A.7)}$$

Since under perfect competition the prices and wage rates are the same for all consumers, we get (7A.3) from (7A.7), Q.E.D.

Next we have the competitive equilibrium in production. Since this is well-known, we shall simply state the relevant results. Each firm chooses its inputs by maximizing profits. Under perfect competition, input and product prices are given and the maximization produces the following results:

$$P_x F_1^x = w \ , \ P_x F_2^x = r \ , \ P_y F_1^y = w \ , \ P_y F_2^y = r \qquad \textbf{Eq. (7A.8)}$$

From (7A.8) we immediately get (7A.4) by observing that the ratio of marginal products equals the input price ratio for both firms x and y, Q.E.D.

Similarly, (7A.7) and (7A.8) can be easily seen to yield (7A.5). It suffices to rewrite (7A.8) as $F_1^x = \dfrac{w}{P_x}, F_1^y = \dfrac{w}{P_y}, F_2^x = \dfrac{r}{P_x}$ and $F_2^y = \dfrac{r}{P_y}$. It follows that $\dfrac{F_1^x}{F_1^y} = \dfrac{P_y}{P_x}$, which, combined with (7A.7), yields the first part of (7A.5) while the second part of that same relation is derived directly from the marginal products expressed as price ratios, Q.E.D.

A perfectly competitive equilibrium in the economy therefore produces a Pareto-optimal resource allocation to production and consumption. Such an allocation is crucially dependent on the distribution of initial resource endowments among the $(I + 1)$ consumers in the economy. A redistribution of these endowments will produce a different perfectly competitive equilibrium, which will also satisfy the criteria for Pareto efficiency. Hence, many economists believe that it is better to pursue social objectives such as equity and protection of the economically disadvantaged through income redistribution via the fiscal system, rather than distortions in the market mechanism.

Nonetheless, the perfectly competitive equilibrium is possible only if the various necessary conditions enumerated in the text are *all* true simultaneously. If at least one of them is violated for some reason, then it is no longer necessarily true that the satisfaction of the remaining conditions will constitute a Pareto-optimal allocation. Suppose, for instance, that the two first conditions in (7A.8) are violated because the market for product x is a natural monopoly. Then the product price P_x exceeds the marginal cost $\dfrac{w}{F_1^x} = \dfrac{r}{F_2^x}$; assume that $P_x = \alpha \frac{w}{F_1^x}$ where $\alpha > 1$. Then it is easy to see that (7A.7) can no longer be satisfied, which in turn implies that (7A.5) cannot be satisfied either.

The theory of the second best can be formulated analytically by accepting the postulated violation, and then going on to maximize utility as before, *but* with the violation included now as an additional constraint.[20] In the above example this means that too little of x will be produced (and consumed) by assumption, implying that the values of U_x^i are larger than implied by (7A.7). By constraining these marginal utilities to these larger values and then applying the Pareto optimality analysis, we can find the second best conditions, which now involve higher-order partial derivatives of the utility functions. Therefore, the original Pareto conditions have little meaning in a second best analysis, unless one can argue that these higher-order terms are unimportant. This is the implicit assumption that is more or less adopted in applying the total surplus concept in the piecemeal approach.[21]

Appendix 7B CONSUMER SURPLUS AS A MEASURE OF WELFARE

As noted in the text, the welfare effects of a given sector-specific policy are evaluated in terms of the change they bring to total surplus. Specifically, this surplus is estimated under the new sector equilibrium that emerges after the policy has been implemented; the result is then compared to the pre-policy situation. This comparison is extended to other sectors that are directly linked to the one subjected to the policy. In this section we justify the use of the consumer surplus as an index of welfare, following the analysis by Willig (1976).

Let m_0 denote the consumer income, and P_1 and P_2 respectively the prices prevailing in the sector before and after the policy was implemented, with $P_2 > P_1$. The consumer demand curve is DD', and the area $P_1 abP_2$, shown in Figure 7B.1, is the corresponding change in consumer surplus. It will be shown that this area, denoted by A, represents an approximate measure of consumer welfare lost by the price rise.

The *maximum* utility achieved by the consumer when the price is P_1 is denoted by $V(m_0, P_1)$.[22] This utility is reduced to $V(m_0, P_2)$ when the price rises. We define the *compensating* and *equivalent* income variations, respectively C and E, as follows:

$$V(m_0, P_1) = V(m_0 + C, P_2) \; ; \; V(m_0 - E, P_1) = V(m_0, P_2) \textbf{ Eq. (7B.1)}$$

In other words, C and E are income changes that bring the consumer to the utility levels that he/she can achieve at (m_0, P_1) and (m_0, P_2) under the price levels P_2 and P_1 respectively. Our purpose is to show that the unobservable amounts C and E, representing the "true" loss in welfare (measured in income terms), can be approximated by the observable A, the change in consumer surplus.

As we know from consumer theory, when the price rises from P_1 to P_2 the consumers reallocate their purchases. This reallocation can be decomposed into income and substitution effects. The amounts C and E are measures of income effects. On the other hand, at any point along the consumer's demand curve DD', the consumer equates the ratio of marginal utilities, with respect to any pair of commodities, to the corresponding price ratio. Suppose that money income m is one of those commodities[23] whose price is equal to unity. Then, if $U(Q,m)$ denotes the consumer's utility, we have along any point (P, Q) of the demand curve DD': $\dfrac{\partial U}{\partial Q} = \dfrac{P \partial U}{\partial m}$. By integrating this relation along the demand curve between 0 and Q_2 and 0 and Q_1 respectively, we can find the levels of utility corresponding to prices P_2 and P_1. These will be respectively equal to $\displaystyle\int_0^{Q_2} P\dfrac{\partial U}{\partial m}dQ$ and $\displaystyle\int_0^{Q_1} P\dfrac{\partial U}{\partial m}dQ$. If $\dfrac{\partial U}{\partial m}$ (the marginal utility of money)

FIGURE 7B.1
Equivalent and compensating variations compared to the change in consumer surplus

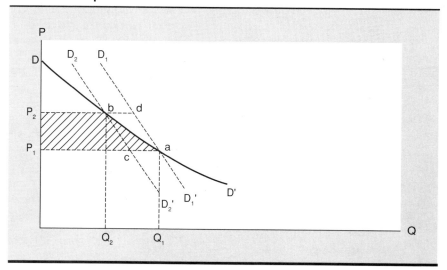

stays approximately constant along DD', then we can easily see that the two utility levels are proportional to the consumer surpluses at price levels P_2 and P_1. There is, however, no reason for $\frac{\partial U}{\partial m}$ to stay constant along DD'.

Nonetheless, it can still be shown that the consumer surplus A is a "good" indicator of C and/or E. For this it suffices to draw the compensated demand curves through points a and b, respectively D_1D_1' and D_2D_2'. These are constant utility demand curves that for a normal good have the relative positions shown in Figure 7B.1. D_1D_1' (D_2D_2') is the demand curve corresponding to a utility level equal to $V(m_0, P_1)$ ($V(m_0, P_2)$) everywhere. Further, it can be shown that C and E are equal to the areas (P_1adP_2) and (P_1cbP_2) respectively, and that $E \leqslant A \leqslant C$ for a normal good.[24]

The relationship between the observable A and the unobservables C and E was shown by Willig to be as follows. Let η denote the income elasticity of demand, $\eta \equiv \frac{\partial Q}{\partial m}\frac{m}{Q}$, and let $\underline{\eta}$ and $\overline{\eta}$ be respectively the lowest and highest values of η along the segment ab of the curve DD'. Then, if $\frac{\overline{\eta}|A|}{m_0}$ is "small" (say less than 10 percent), the following approximate relations hold for a normal good, with A being positive (negative) for a price increase (decrease):

$$\frac{\underline{\eta}|A|}{2m_0} \leqslant \frac{C-A}{|A|} \leqslant \frac{\overline{\eta}|A|}{2m_0} \; , \; \frac{\underline{\eta}|A|}{2m_0} \leqslant \frac{A-E}{|A|} \leqslant \frac{\overline{\eta}|A|}{2m_0} \qquad \textbf{Eq. (7B.2)}$$

Otherwise, if $\frac{\overline{\eta}|A|}{m_0}$ is large, there are more complex expressions yielding lower and upper bounds to $\frac{C-A}{|A|}$ and $\frac{A-E}{|A|}$, which are functions of $\underline{\eta}$, $\overline{\eta}$ and $\frac{A}{m_0}$.[25]

For a numerical application of (7B.2), suppose that for a given commodity the reduction in consumer surplus as a result of a price increase is $\frac{A}{m_0} = .04$. The income elasticity of demand has a highest value $\overline{\eta} = 1.10$, and a lowest value $\underline{\eta} = .70$, along the segment ab of the demand curve between the initial and final prices. Then (7B.2) implies that $0.14 \leqslant \frac{C-A}{|A|} \leqslant .022$, $.014 \leqslant \frac{A-E}{|A|} \leqslant .022$, from which $1.014 \leqslant \frac{C}{A} \leqslant 1.022$, $.978 \leqslant \frac{E}{A} \leqslant .986$. If, instead of (7B.2), the exact bounds on $\frac{C-A}{|A|}$ and $\frac{A-E}{|A|}$ are used then for these values of $\underline{\eta}$, $\overline{\eta}$ and $\frac{A}{m_0}$ these bounds are again .014 and .022.[26]. Hence, the approximation provided by (7B.1) is very good for most "realistic" values of the parameters.

The area A is approximately equal to $Q_2(P_2 - P_1) + \frac{1}{2}(Q_1 - Q_2)(P_2 - P_1)$, or if ΔP and ΔQ represent the changes in price and in consumer purchases, to $(Q_2)(\Delta P) + \frac{1}{2}|\Delta P||\Delta Q|$. For most commodities, most realistic price changes, and most consumers, this amount is expected to be a "small" percentage of total consumer income, far below the four percent used in the numerical illustration. This will bring the bounds in (7B.2) very close to each other. Hence, in most practical applications both C and E are going to be very close to A, thus justifying the use of the change in consumer surplus as a monetary equivalent to the change in consumer welfare.

Endnotes

1. A rigorous formulation of the properties of general equilibrium under perfect competition is in Appendix 7A.

2. In other words, production or consumption by some economic agents does not provide costs or benefits to other agents.

3. The original formulation of this concept was by Lipsey and Lancaster (1956/57).

4. See Scherer (1980), p. 30.

5. This view has been articulated by March and Simon (1958), Cyert and March (1963), and Simon (1979). A discussion of this approach in contrast with traditional economic theory is in Machlup (1967).

6. For an early systematic formulation of a managerial utility maximization model of the firm see Williamson (1967).

7. For an extended survey of the debate centred on managerial motives, see Scherer (1980), pp. 31-41.

8. The term was coined by Leibenstein (1966).

9. See Greer (1984), pp. 222-224, for a summary and contrast of the results of the relevant studies.

10. See, for instance, Jensen and Meckling (1976), and Holmstrom (1979).

11. See also the reply by Leibenstein (1978).

12. For an example of such accounts, see Greer (1984), pp. 229-230, and Galbraith's review of several autobiographical books by eminent businessmen and public servants (1988).

13. A good theoretical exposition of these arguments is in Harberger (1971).

14. See the discussion of the IBM and breakfast cereals cases in Caves (1987), pp. 95-96.

15. See also Scherer (1980), pp. 41-44.

16. For a rigorous demonstration of this development, see Clarke (1985), pp. 100-102.

17. A more extensive survey is in Green (1987).

18. Several of these firms had gone to court to try to avoid participating in this costly survey.

19. This acts as a constraint on the amount of labour supplied by each consumer; it will be assumed that this constraint is satisfied in the analysis that follows, and hence it will be ignored.

20. For an example, see Henderson and Quandt (1971), pp. 286-288.

21. For a more extended, rigorous treatment of the subject, see Henderson and Quandt (1971), Chapter 7.

22. This is also called the *indirect utility function*.

23. In other words, $m = m_0 - PQ$, the income left over after the expenditures PQ on the good.

24. The inequality is reversed for an inferior good.

25. See Willig (1976), pp. 594-596.

26. See Willig (1976), pp. 594-596.

References

Bain, J.S. *Barriers to New Competition*. Cambridge, Mass.: Harvard University Press, 1956.

Baumol, W.J. *Business Behavior, Value and Growth*. New York, N.Y.: Macmillan, 1959.

Baumol, W.J. and R.D. Willig. "Contestability: Developments since the Book," *Oxford Economic Papers*, 38 (Supplement) (1986), pp. 9-36.

Bloch, H. "Prices, Costs and Profits in Canadian Manufacturing: the Influence of Tariffs and Concentration," *Canadian Journal of Economics*, 7 (1974), pp. 594-610.

Caves, R.E. *American Industry: Structure, Conduct, Performance*. Englewood Cliffs, N.J.: Prentice-Hall, 6th Edition, 1987.

Caves, R.E., M.E. Porter, and A.M. Spence, with J.T. Scott. *Competition in the Open Economy: A Model Applied to Canada*. Cambridge, Mass.: Harvard University Press, 1980.

Clark, J.M. "Toward a Concept of Workable Competition," *American Economic Review*, 30 (1940), pp. 241-56.

Clarke, R. *Industrial Economics*. Oxford, Eng.: Blackwell, 1985.

Clarke, R., S.W. Davies, and M. Waterson. "The Profitability-Concentration Relation: Market Power or Efficiency?" *Journal of Industrial Economics*, 32 (1984), pp. 435-50.

Collins, N.R. and L.E. Preston. *Concentration and Price-Cost Margins in Manufacturing Industries*. Berkeley, Cal.: University of California Press, 1968.

————. "Price-cost Margins and Industry Structure," *Review of Economics and Statistics*, 51 (1969), pp. 271-286.

Cowling, K. and D.C. Mueller. "The Social Costs of Monopoly Power," *Economic Journal*, 88 (1978), pp. 727-748.

Cyert, R.M. and J.G. March. *A Behavioral Theory of the Firm*. Englewood Cliffs, N.J.: Prentice-Hall, 1963.

Demsetz, H. *The Market Concentration Doctrine*. Washington, D.C.: American Enterprise Institute for Public Policy Research, Aug. 1973, pp. 1-30.

————. "Industry Structure, Market Rivalry and Public Policy," *Journal of Law and Economics*, 16 (1973b), pp. 1-9.

Fisher, F.M. and J. McGowan. "On the Misuse of Accounting Rates of Return to Infer Monopoly Profits," *American Economic Review*, 73 (1983), pp. 82-97.

Friedman, M. "The Methodology of Positive Economics," *Essays in Positive Economics*. Chicago, Ill.: Chicago University Press, 1953.

Galbraith, J.K. "Big Shots," *The New York Review of Books*, 35:8 (1988), pp. 44-47.

Gale, B.T. and B.S. Branch. "Concentration Versus Market Share: Which Determines Performance and Why Does It Matter?" *Antitrust Bulletin*, 27 (1982), pp. 83-105.

Green, C. "Industrial Organization Paradigms, Empirical Evidence, and the Economic Case for Competition Policy," *Canadian Journal of Economics*, 20:3 (1987), pp. 482-505.

Greer, D.F. *Industrial Organization and Public Policy*. New York, N.Y.: Macmillan, 2nd Edition, 1984.

Hall, M. and L.W. Weiss. "Firm Size and Profitability," *Review of Economics and Statistics*, 49 (1967), pp. 319-331.

Harberger, A.C. "Monopoly and Resource Allocation," *American Economic Review*, Papers and Proceedings, 44 (1954), pp. 77-87.

———. "Three Basic Postulates for Applied Welfare Economics: An Interpretive Essay," *Journal of Economic Literature*, 9 (1971), pp. 785-797.

Henderson, J.M. and R.E. Quandt. *Microeconomic Theory*. New York, N.Y.: McGraw Hill, 2nd Edition, 1971.

Hitiris, T. "Effective Protection and Economic Performance in UK Manufacturing Industry, 1963 and 1968," *Economic Journal*, 88 (1978), pp. 107-120.

Holmstrom, B. "Moral Hazard and Observability," *Bell Journal of Economics* 10 (1979), pp. 74-91.

Jensen, M.C., and W.H. Meckling. "Theory of the Firm: Managerial Behavior, Agency Costs and Ownership Structure," *Journal of Financial Economics*, 3 (1976), pp. 305-360.

Jones, J.C.H., L. Laudadio, and M. Percy. "Market Structure and Profitability in Canadian Manufacturing," *Canadian Journal of Economics*, 6 (1973), pp. 356-368.

Leibenstein, H. "Allocative Efficiency vs. X-efficiency," *American Economic Review*, 56 (1966), pp. 392-415.

———. "X-Inefficiency Xists — Reply to an Xorcist," *American Economic Review*, 68 (1978), pp. 203-211.

Lipsey, R. and K. Lancaster. "The General Theory of the Second Best," *Review of Economic Studies*, 24 (1956/57), pp. 11-32.

Machlup, Fritz. "Marginal Analysis and Empirical Research," *American Economic Review*, 36 (1946), pp. 521-522.

———. "Theories of the Firm: Marginalist, Behavioral, Managerial," *American Economic Review*, 57 (1967), pp. 1-33.

Mann, H.M. "Seller Concentration, Barriers to Entry, and Rates of Return in Thirty Industries, 1950-60," *Review of Economics and Statistics*, 48 (1966), pp. 296-307.

March, J.C. and H.A. Simon. *Organizations*. New York, N.Y.: John Wiley & Sons, 1958.

Markham, Jesse W. "An Alternative Approach to the Concept of Workable Competition," *American Economic Review*, 40 (1950), pp. 349-361.

McFetridge, D.G.A. "Market Structure and Price-cost Margins: an Analysis of the

Canadian Manufacturing Sector," *Canadian Journal of Economics*, 6 (1973), pp. 344-355.

Palmer, John. "The Profit-Performance Effects of the Separation of Ownership from Control in Large U.S. Industrial Corporations," *Bell Journal of Economics and Management Science*, 4 (1973), pp. 293-303.

Philips, A. "An Econometric Study of Price-fixing, Market Structure and Performance in British Industry in the Early 1950s," *Market Structure and Corporate Behaviour*, K. Cowling, ed. London, Eng.: Gray-Mills, 1972.

Primeaux, Walter J. "An Assessment of X-Efficiency Gained Through Competition," *Review of Economics and Statistics*, Vol. 59 (Feb. 1977), pp. 105-108.

Ravenscraft, D.J. "Structure-profit Relationships at the Line of Business and Industry Level," *Review of Economics and Statistics*, (1983), pp. 22-31.

Salinger, M. "Tobin's *q*, Unionization, and the Concentration-Profits Relationship," *Rand Journal of Economics*, Summer (1984), pp. 159-170.

Scherer, F.M. *Industrial Market Structure and Economic Performance*. Chicago, Ill.: Rand McNally, 2nd Edition, 1980.

Schmalensee, R. "Collusion Versus Differential Efficiency: Testing Alternative Hypotheses," *Journal of Industrial Economics*, 35 (1987), pp. 399-425.

————. "Do Markets Differ Much?" *American Economic Review*, 75 (1985), pp. 341-351.

Shepherd, W.J. "The Elements of Market Structure," *Review of Economics and Statistics*, 54 (1972), pp. 25-38.

Simon, Herbert A. "Rational Decision Making in Business Organizations," *American Economic Review*, 69 (1979), pp. 493-513.

Smirlock, M., T. Gilligan, and W. Marshall. "Tobin's *q* and the Structure Performance Relationship," *American Economic Review*, 74 (1984), pp. 1051-1060.

Sosnick, Stephen. "A Critique of Concepts of Workable Competition," *Quarterly Journal of Economics*, 72 (1958), pp. 380-423.

Stegemann, K. "The Social Costs of Monopoly in an Open Economy," *Canadian Journal of Economics*, 17:4 (1984), pp. 718-730.

Stigler, George J. "The Xistence of X-efficiency," *American Economic Review*, 66 (1976), pp. 213-216.

Weiss, L.W. "The Concentration-profits Relationship and Antitrust," *Industrial Concentration: the New Learning*, Goldschmid *et al.*, eds. Boston, Mass.: Little, Brown, 1974.

Williamson, O. *The Economics of Discretionary Behavior: Managerial Objectives in a Theory of the Firm*. Chicago, Ill.: Markham Publishing, 1967.

Willig, Robert D. "Consumer's Surplus without Apology," *American Economic Review*, 66 (1976), pp. 589-597.

CHAPTER 8

Public Policy I:

The Control of Structure

The previous chapter concluded the first part of this text, containing the theory underlying the structure-conduct-performance (SCP) model. Throughout that first part, mention was made repeatedly of public policies within the context of this model. The remaining chapters are devoted to these public policies as they appear in the recent Canadian experience. The aim of this second part is to provide illustrations of the manner in which specific policies and decisions of the various layers of the Canadian government can be analyzed by means of the SCP model.

The design and evaluation of public policies belongs to the common domain of varying disciplines such as law, political science, and economics. Each one of these disciplines has its own role to play in the public policy context. In particular, economics is concerned with the consequences of public policies for equity and efficiency, along the lines outlined in the previous chapter. Such consequences may or may not have been intended during the phase of policy design and implementation.

The four policy chapters that form the bulk of the second part of this text are divided along principles derived from the SCP model. Chapters 8 and 9 deal with policies pertaining to specific parts of this model, referring respectively to structure and conduct. Chapter 10, on the other hand, examines policies associated with real or alleged cases of market failure, in which administrative decisions are substituted for the normal economic determination of quantities such as prices, output, or investment. Last, Chapter 11 deals with economic policies that are not specifically tied to the SCP model but nonetheless have important consequences for it. Examples are policies pertaining to foreign trade, patents, and foreign investment.

As already noted in Chapter 2, policies aiming to affect the structure of specific markets or sectors form the rules of the game under which the evolution of the structure of these sectors takes place. These policies are primarily those affecting mergers and acquisitions. Their purpose is to prevent or mitigate the anticompetitive effects of such mergers, according to the performance objectives analyzed in Chapter 7.

Two particular aspects of public policies concerning mergers deserve to be singled out in any survey of the topic. The first was already noted and discussed extensively in the previous chapter; it has to do with the reverse structure-performance model, and it raises questions about the philosophical underpinnings of any public attempts to control industry structure. If concentrated structure is the result of superior performance, what right does public policy have to interfere with this "natural selection" feature of the economic process that allows the fittest to survive and prosper? Why should successful corporations be prevented from swallowing up or otherwise eliminating their less efficient competitors, and reaping the rewards of their success? Even if one does not accept the reverse model in its entirety, it is important that any of its implied positive aspects of mergers be recognized and preserved in the design and implementation of public policies.

The second aspect of merger policies was mentioned briefly in Chapters 2 and 7. It is particularly important in the Canadian context, and it refers to the ever-present dilemma between economies of scale and competition. As we noted in the earlier chapters, there is a substantial body of evidence showing the presence of suboptimally-sized firms in many sectors of the Canadian economy. These firms must grow to their minimum efficient size, or otherwise merge with other firms to create larger and more efficient entities. The decision on whether to block or allow a given merger must therefore begin with an examination of whether or not economies of scale will be realized as a result of that merger. Given such economies, it must then be ascertained whether they are sufficiently important to counteract the possible anticompetitive effects of the mergers. As we shall see, the total surplus test implies that a strong a priori presumption exists in favour of the economies of scale effect.

The next section of this chapter examines the motives and effects of the three types of mergers, horizontal, vertical, and conglomerate. Horizontal mergers, which most public policies refer to, are discussed in the following three sections in terms of policy dilemmas, the law, and some recent case studies.

Economic Motives for Mergers

As already noted in previous chapters, the various types of mergers have different effects upon the SCP model. Horizontal mergers affect the structural component of this model directly. Vertical mergers may have an effect on industry structure, under certain circumstances. Conglomerate mergers, on the other hand, lie almost completely outside the model.

There is no question that horizontal mergers affect industry structure by increasing concentration and potentially reducing competition. As we saw in Chapter 2, the Herfindahl index of a sector in which a merger takes place increases. For this reason, given that public policy has as a general objective the enhancement of competition in the economy, major mergers have traditionally come under the scrutiny of the public agencies overseeing competition policies. The questions that arise are multiple. What are the benefits of any given merger? When should such a merger be prevented? How can public policy balance the need to preserve the economic freedom of the parties that wish to merge, and the need to prevent adverse effects upon other parties (such as workers, consumers, and minority stockholders) that are likely to be adversely affected by the merger?

The different types of mergers stem from varying motives and have differing benefits. For horizontal mergers, for which the anticompetitive effects are likely to be most pronounced, the most obvious benefit is the achievement of economies of scale, examined in detail in the next section. One less obvious benefit, however, which is also present in conglomerate mergers is the imposition of performance standards upon the managers of firms.

The argument surrounding this second benefit was already noted in earlier chapters, and may be summarized as follows. Inadequate managerial performance that fails to maximize the profits of the firm will depress the value of the firm's stock. This creates incentives for outsiders to acquire control over the firm and remove the inept management. Stock values can then be increased by improving the performance of the firm with new managers. Such takeovers are hostile, since existing managers have powerful incentives to block them. They are nonetheless commonplace, and they form perhaps one of the most effective instruments of monitoring and disciplining managerial performance. However, the transaction costs of such unfriendly takeovers are quite high, and existing managers have many effective instruments for blocking or delaying them. The available evidence on the hypothesis that the primary motive for mergers is the elimination of inefficient firms or managers is at best weak.[1] The fact that most mergers tend to occur in waves while managerial inefficiency is presumably randomly distributed through time is also proof that not all mergers should be viewed as beneficial.

The last and perhaps most prevalent motive for horizontal mergers is the achievement of market power. This is precisely the motive that is considered most objectionable by antitrust law. By merging or acquiring a competitor a major firm in an industry can build up a position as a monopolist or as a dominant firm in a tight oligopoly. It may then use that position to raise prices and curtail output in order to reap economic profits. Such undesirable conduct can be prevented by blocking mergers whose anticompetitive effects are their dominant if not their sole motive. This therefore forms the rationale for public policy interventions in the area of mergers and acquisitions.

A vertical merger is the acquisition by a firm of another firm involved in a preceding or successive stage in production. Such acquisitions, respectively denoted as upstream and downstream vertical integration, may alter the structure of the sector of one or both of the merging firms. The question of whether vertical mergers should be the object of scrutiny by antitrust law enforcers has been the subject of some debate in economics.[2] To date they have mostly been ignored in Canada, except in the case of regulated industries.

There are, however, several instances in which vertically-integrated firms have at times occupied centre stage in public policy debates in Canada. For instance, many oil-producing firms are completely vertically integrated, from exploration to refining to marketing to final consumption stages. In telecommunications, Bell Canada has integrated upstream by acquiring control of Northern Electric. Some pulp-and-paper firms have integrated upstream into forest products, and some automobile producers have integrated downstream into dealership networks. All these cases may in theory extend market power from an upstream to a downstream sector or vice-versa, thus raising public policy questions.

The reasons that have been advanced for vertical integration have been multiple and varied. One category of motives for vertical integration centres around economic efficiency. By integrating upstream or downstream, firms in an industry are able to replace external market transactions by internal decision-making. If external transactions costs (search, information, negotiations, etc.) exist, and if they exceed the costs of decision-making, then integration improves efficiency. Other gains in efficiency may come from the reduction of risk that follows from the elimination of price fluctuations and the security of supply or distribution channels.

Other motives, though, may be less pure. Suppose for instance that the upstream market has a non-competitive structure, say a tight oligopoly. Then downstream integration may be used as an instrument in converting a previously competitive market into an oligopoly by squeezing out the non-integrated sellers. This may be done, for instance, by refusing to sell to them, or by raising the input prices while holding the downstream prices constant. Such behaviour is alleged to have taken place in the petroleum and steel products industries in the U.S., although its success in the petroleum industry is doubtful.

Still another reason for integration is when one of the industries consists of a single firm, which is a regulated monopoly. As we saw in Chapter 3, such a firm is normally subjected to limits on its profits. However, the firm may overcome such limits by integrating vertically with one of its input suppliers, and purchasing inputs from this supplier at inflated prices. Thus the firm may effectively evade all regulatory restrictions by transferring the profits to the upstream firm. While there are regulatory policies that can nullify this profit-shielding, such policies are almost always difficult to enforce or administer, and thus unlikely to be very effective.[3]

To summarize, vertical integration by a firm in an industry may affect the industry's structure for two main reasons. If there are substantial efficiency gains from integration, then the effect of integration is similar to the effect of economies of scale upon firms of suboptimal scale. In other words, it is a handicap that diminishes the performance of the non-integrated firms relative to their competitor. If, on the other hand, the integrated firm wishes to acquire market power, there must be such power at least at one of the two stages, upstream or downstream. Some of this power may perhaps be transferred to the other stage, depending on conditions of entry at that stage; this in turn can endanger the situation of competing firms at that stage.

Last, we have conglomerate mergers, in which the merging firms belong to different product lines or geographical markets. Here the dominant motive is that of diversification, i.e. of the reduction of risk by putting one's eggs in more than one basket. Diversification is based on the premise that the forces responsible for the fluctuations of the demand or costs are not closely correlated across different products or markets. In this way a decline in demand for a particular product line need not have a major impact on the total sales revenues of a well-diversified firm, since it will not in general be accompanied by corresponding declines in demand for other products of the same firm. Conglomerate mergers are popular instruments for such diversification. Since they have no impact on market structure, they tend to be ignored by public policy makers.

Overall trends in merger activity are broadly similar in the U.S. and Canada. This means that the observed merger "waves" are roughly coincident in the two countries. This appears very clearly in the two curves of Figure 8.1, which depict the total number of mergers in the U.S. and Canada in recent years.

It is clear from Figure 8.1 that merger activity is relatively much more pronounced in Canada than in the U.S. From 1970 until 1986 there were between three and five times as many mergers in the U.S. as in Canada. The Canadian economy and population, however, are roughly only 10 percent of those in the U.S. The higher Canadian frequency of mergers is observable in years of low merger activity, as well as in the more recent mid-1980s period when U.S. mergers exhibited a sharp upward trend.[4] Part of this difference may reflect the influence of the strict U.S. merger law, which must be con-

FIGURE 8.1
Mergers and acquisitions 1970-1988, Canada and the U.S.

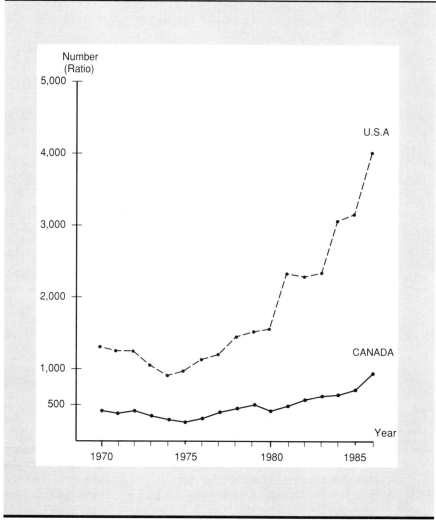

Source: Marfels (1988), p.84

trasted with the totally ineffective pre-1986 Canadian legislation (see below).

Recent trends in the U.S. point to the growing importance of conglomerate mergers as a percentage of total merger activity. By contrast, horizontal mergers, which earlier formed the majority of U.S. mergers, have declined in importance in recent years. In 1973-1977 they represented only 15.1 percent of total U.S. merger activity in contrast to the 79.1 percent of conglomerate mergers during that same period.[5]

In Canada, on the other hand, horizontal mergers have continued to form a majority of total mergers in most years throughout the mid- to late-1980s, as shown in the data of Table 8.1. Hence, concerns about the effect of mergers on industry structure are likely to be more justified in Canada than in the U.S., given the much greater share of horizontal mergers. On the other hand, the smaller Canadian market justifies an optimal industry structure with much fewer minimum efficient sized firms than in the U.S. Thus, it is possible that horizontal mergers are used to eliminate inefficiently small firms and realize economies of scale. For instance, mergers and acquisitions formed an important component of the entry and exit processes in Canadian manufacturing in the study by Baldwin and Gorecki (1983), which was cited extensively in Chapter 5.

A careful analysis of Canadian merger activity during 1976-83 was carried out by Eckbo (1986). His study used the same primary data base as Table 8.1, but the cases included in the sample contained much interesting information on the details of the economic activities of the acquiring and target firms. For

TABLE 8.1
Mergers and acquisitions in Canada, 1970-1986

Year	Number	Horizontal[a]	Others[a]	% Horizontal
1970	427	224	203	52.5
1971	388	215	173	55.4
1972	429	238	191	55.5
1973	352	227	125	64.5
1974	296	158	138	53.4
1975	264	179	85	67.8
1976	313	214	99	68.4
1977	395	261	134	66.1
1978	449	231	218	51.4
1979	511	290	221	56.8
1980	414	220	194	53.1
1981	491	302	189	61.5
1982	576	284	292	49.3
1983	628	352	276	56.1
1984	641	345	296	53.8
1985	714	370	344	51.8
1986	953	383	570	40.2

[a] Based on two-digit industries for manufacturing and one-digit divisions for other sectors.
Source: Marfels (1988), p. 75.

instance, the data in Table 8.1 classifies a merger as horizontal if both merging firms belong to the same two-digit SIC code industry. This is a rather broad classification, which may in fact give a misleading picture of merger activity. Using separate sources of more detailed data, Eckbo constructed a sample of mergers for which information could be found at a more detailed SIC level.[6] In that sample the proportion of horizontal mergers fell to 38.2 percent for the three-digit SIC code industries and 31.2 percent for four-digit industries, when both merging firms had activities belonging to the same SIC code. Even with these fine classifications, the proportion of Canadian horizontal mergers is more than twice that of the U.S., reflecting, no doubt, the much more stringent American merger laws.

Still another major difference between Canada and the U.S. concerns the gains from the mergers for the stockholders of both firms. As Eckbo notes, most U.S. studies have found that the average merger was highly beneficial to the stockholders of the firm that did not initiate the merger (the acquired firm or target).[7] By contrast, the acquiring firms (those that initiated the merger offer) do not seem to have profited by it. In Canada, by contrast, both the acquiring and target firms' stockholders gained from the merger. This finding, developed independently and for different samples of merging firms by Eckbo (1986), and Calvet and Lefoll (1987), was based on an analysis of the pre- and post-merger stock market performance of the merging firms. The Calvet-Lefoll study also found that the pre-merger performance of the target was not significantly lower than average; this does not seem to support the inefficient managerial performance motive for mergers. The stock market studies of merging firms, though, do not allow us to distinguish between the market power and scale economies motives.

Some evidence on these motives has surfaced in recent U.S. studies, but the two approaches used to examine the question have come up with diametrically opposed results. In a number of studies summarized in his 1988 paper Eckbo examined the stock market performance of the non-merging firms that compete with the merging parties. He interprets his results as meaning that the stock market believed that the efficiency motive was predominant in most mergers. This is because rivals' performance improved significantly after both a merger announcement and after a subsequent antitrust action that reduces the likelihood of the merger. The two effects are respectively consistent with the market power and economies of scale motives, but Eckbo attributes the first to information gains to rivals that will persist even if the merger is ultimately disallowed.

By contrast, Scherer (1988) summarizes studies that examined the post-merger performance of a large population of U.S. firms during the 1960s and 1970s. These studies found that the average post-merger performance of the acquired companies declined spectacularly within a period of eight to nine years after the merger. On the other hand, these same acquired firms had a significantly higher than average performance in the years immediately preceding the merger. Hence, it seems that the merger actually created *diseconomies* of scale or scope, which the author attributed mainly to the difficulties of combining two distinct corporate cultures. Interestingly, this is the same reason for which some of the participants in a recent symposium on U.S. mergers recommended that antitrust authorities adopt a sceptical attitude towards efficiency claims by the merging parties.[8] Scherer, however, points out that his conclusions cannot be extrapolated easily to Canada, given the different structure of the much larger U.S. market.

There are as yet no Canadian studies comparable to those of Eckbo and Scherer, given the fact that Canada did not have until very recently an effective merger law. Some earlier work was carried out by the Royal Commission on Corporate Concentration (1978), but the evidence is unclear.[9] Plant-level economies of scale do not seem to have been the motive for much of Canadian merger activity during the 1960s and 1970s. Efficiency advantages accruing to merging firms have been typically in the areas of marketing, finance, R&D, etc., i.e. at the level of the firm. Surprisingly though, the most recent study of Baldwin and Gorecki (1986) seems to suggest that plant-level economies of scale may have been partly responsible for the high costs of production of Canadian firms relative to their American counterparts during that same period. In other words, the desire to rationalize inefficiently small plants was not a major merger motive, notwithstanding the existence of such plants. This is all the more surprising, given the fact that Canada had a very weak merger law during that period. As the case studies in subsequent sections show, Canadian legislation has in the past been powerless to stop mergers, even when they led to the complete monopolization of a market. For all these reasons the evidence gives us little guidance for the design and implementation of Canadian competition policy. This policy, which underwent a major revision in its merger provisions in 1986, will be reviewed in subsequent sections.

Economies of Scale and Competition

For Canada, the most serious objections to structural competition policies are the ones associated with the existence of economies of scale. These economies create a genuine conflict between the desirable level of competition and superior cost performance. This conflict has certainly been an obstacle to many of the attempts to establish an effective competition policy in Canada. Tradeoffs are involved between lower prices on the one hand, and lower costs on the other. The question is which one of these effects predominates in most cases.

As we saw in Chapter 7, a convenient method of evaluating the total impact of specific policies is by means of the change in the total (consumer plus producer) surplus (the profit rectangle plus the triangular area between the price line, the demand curve, and the vertical axis). A public policy that raises this total surplus is desirable, under the assumption that the distribution of the surplus between producers and consumers doesn't matter. Alternatively, it can be assumed (not always realistically) that it is possible to use taxation to redistribute the change in surplus in order to achieve a Pareto-superior situation.

The conflict between competition and economies of scale can be illustrated by Figure 8.2.[10] Suppose that costs are minimized at an output Q_M corresponding to the MES, which will be attained if a monopoly is established in the sector; the price that it will charge for its product is P_M. On the other hand, if such a monopoly is prevented from being established through a public intervention, the industry will consist of a number of "small" competitive firms, each one producing output Q_I and charging a "competitive" price P_c, at which the firms realize no economic profit. Total industry output is Q_M under monopoly and Q_c under the competitive alternative.

The combined surplus under monopoly is the consumer surplus, the area above the line $P_M A$ plus the area of the profit rectangle $P_M ADAC_m$. Under competition this same combined surplus is the area above the line $P_c C$. Hence, the gain or loss in total surplus in going from competition to monopoly is the difference between the two shaded areas, the triangle ABC and the rectangle $P_c BDAC_m$. These two areas depend on the following factors: the unit cost reduction from economies of scale, $P_c - AC_m$; the price increase due to monop-

FIGURE 8.2
The choice between competition and economies of scale

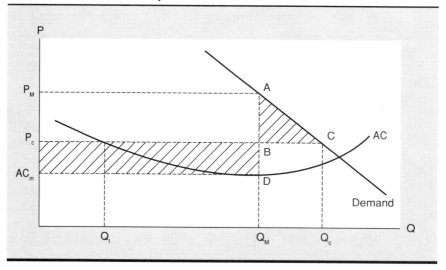

oly, $P_M - P_c$; and the slope of the industry demand curve between points A and C, which depends on the price elasticity of demand in that region.

Let ΔP and ΔQ denote respectively the lengths (AB) and (BC). The surplus test between competition and monopoly is a comparison of the quantities Q_M ($P_c - AC_m$), and $\frac{1}{2}(\Delta P)(\Delta Q)$, representing the areas of the rectangle and triangle of Figure 8.2 respectively. The test's outcome is neutral if these two areas are equal. Setting $Q_M (P_c - AC_m) = \frac{1}{2}(\Delta P)(\Delta Q)$, and re-arranging it, we get:

$$\frac{(P_c - AC_m)}{P_c} = \frac{1}{2}\frac{\Delta P}{P_c}\frac{\Delta Q}{Q_M} \qquad \textbf{Eq. (8.1)}$$

The right-hand-side (RHS) of the above relation is equal to $\frac{1}{2}\epsilon\left(\frac{\Delta P}{P_c}\right)^2$, where $\epsilon \equiv \frac{\Delta Q}{Q_M}\frac{P_c}{\Delta P}$ represents an intermediate value between the point elasticities of the demand curve at A and C, respectively equal to $\frac{\Delta Q}{Q_M}\frac{P_M}{\Delta P}$ and $\frac{\Delta Q}{Q_c}\frac{P_c}{\Delta P}$. Hence, we have:

$$\frac{P_c - AC_m}{P_c} = \frac{1}{2}\left(\frac{\Delta P}{P_c}\right)^2 \epsilon \qquad \textbf{Eq. (8.2)}$$

Table 8.2 shows the percentage cost reductions and price rises that offset each other exactly, leaving total surplus unchanged, for three selected values of the elasticity of demand as estimated from Equation (8.2). The first column gives $\frac{\Delta P}{P_c}$, while each one of the other columns shows the values $\frac{P_c - AC_m}{P_c}$ that satisfy Equation (8.2) for the corresponding ϵ. What Table 8.2 makes clear is that the benefits of scale economy gains (reflected in lowered unit costs) need not be large—relative to the price increases associated with concentrated market structures—for such structures to be preferable to a more competitive but less cost-efficient structure.

It follows, therefore, that structural antitrust policies such as those towards mergers and acquisitions should give priority and the benefit of the doubt to the realization of economies of scale. A number of qualifications, though, should be attached to such a statement. For instance, a merger may increase the industry prices but not reduce the costs for the firms that did not merge. In such a case the combined surplus test may not favour the economies of scale. Similarly, it is possible that the realization of monopoly power stemming from the merger would induce X-inefficiency by eliminating the competitive pressures. This may be especially true in industries that are protected by tariffs and/or barriers to entry. Finally, it is possible that scale economies may be achievable naturally by the growth in market demand within a short time

TABLE 8.2
Equivalent % cost reductions and price increases for selected values of the demand elasticity

% Price Increases	% Cost Reductions		
	$\epsilon = 2$	$\epsilon = 1$	$\epsilon = .5$
5	.25	.12	.06
10	1.00	.50	.25
20	4.00	2.00	1.00
30	9.00	4.50	2.25

period, without any need for a merger. Subject to these qualifications, though, the majority consensus among economists is that control of structure policies should not prevent the elimination of inefficiencies due to scale.[11]

This majority consensus is reflected in the provisions of the recently (1986) revised merger legislation. Proof of the existence of economies of scale achievable through a merger is sufficient to allow the merger to proceed, as we shall see in the next section.

Before closing this section mention should also be made of the (more realistic) mergers, in which the merging firms are multiproduct. The possible benefits from such mergers may involve economies of scope and product-specific economies of scale, as well as the more conventional economies of scale (the decline in ray-average costs). Nonetheless, the principles involved in evaluating whether a given merger is desirable or not are identical to those of the single-product firm. The probable pre- and post-merger scenarios are compared from the point of view of product prices and total cost of production. The test quantity is again the total surplus, with a consumer surplus being derived for each product. The conclusions about the dominance of the cost reduction over the price competition benefits are, if anything, more pronounced than in the case of the single-product firm.

The Merger Legislation

The first major North American legislation dealing with competition policy, the Sherman Anti-Trust Act, was established in the U.S. in 1895. A somewhat earlier law existed in Canada, but it was not implemented until many years later.[12] Overall, the U.S. legislation as defined in several subsequent acts (in particular, the Clayton Act of 1914 and the Celler-Kefauver Amendments of 1950) and as interpreted by the courts is considered the most effective body of law in the world for the promotion of competition in the economy. Its application and interpretation, though, has always been and continues to be controversial.

These controversial aspects of competition policy are, if anything, more pronounced in Canada. The contradictory welfare effects of horizontal mergers are present to a greater extent in Canada than in the U.S. The same is true of other aspects of public policy, those that deal with firms' conduct. The last major revision of the Canadian law took effect in 1986, after more than 15 years of debate. Given the disputed features of public policy related to competition, it is appropriate to summarize briefly the guiding principles of such policy, as formulated in the dominant current of economic thought. Although the extent to which policy has conformed to these principles is debatable, there is little doubt that economists have participated actively in antitrust policy, and that this participation has risen in importance over the years.[13]

Legal Principles and Problems

The structure-conduct-performance paradigm implies that the control of firms' conduct in a sector is, at least in theory, achievable through changes in the structure of the sector. Such changes can be obtained by dissolving dominant firms, by forcing such firms to divest themselves of part of their operations, or more frequently by preventing large firms from becoming even larger. In practice this last policy means some type of screening or prohibition of mergers and acquisitions by such large firms.

The economic rationale behind structural competition policies is that the "normal" market conduct of monopolized sectors results in higher prices and lower output for these sectors than if competition were to prevail. Since such conduct is undesirable on general efficiency grounds, a possible remedy would be to turn these monopolized sectors into competitive ones by breaking up the monopoly firms. Such drastic remedies have rarely been applied even in the U.S., and in almost all cases the existence of a monopoly or quasi-monopoly had to be accompanied by evidence of undesirable conduct. On the other hand, an alternative and parallel policy approach would be to prevent monopoly formation by limiting the dynamic growth of concentration in a sector, i.e. by blocking horizontal mergers involving "large" firms in the sector. A related benefit of such a policy approach is that by preventing the number of firms in a sector from decreasing one also decreases the likelihood of collusive pricing. As we saw in Chapter 4, collusive pricing is made easier when there are fewer firms in the sector.

While most economists would agree that monopolistically structured industries' performance is not always the best possible, there are some who would disagree with the necessity of applying structural remedies to the sector. They would argue that the damages caused by these remedies far outweigh their benefits. Three types of objections are raised to structural policies. The first has to do with the possible existence of economies of scale that can be realized by letting large firms become even larger, and that will be prevented by a structural policy such as, for instance, the prohibition of mergers. The second is associated with the reverse structure-performance model, and is a variant of the opinion formulated in a previous section about the role of mergers and acquisitions in the elimination of inefficient management: large firms achieve their dominant status because they are better-managed, and public policy has no business preventing the benefits of such better management from spreading to a larger part of the sector. Finally, the third objection is that the costs associated with antitrust policies may overwhelm the short-lived gains likely to accrue to monopolies. This argument hinges on the lure of profits of monopolized sectors serving to attract entry, or the imposition of curbs on pricing by monopolistic sectors as a means of deterring such entry, which we called limit-entry pricing in Chapter 5. In both instances, the negative aspects of the monopoly are going to disappear in the long run. This particular argument must be coupled with a belief that barriers to entry are either unimportant or play a socially beneficial role, as with patents.

The counterarguments to this benign view of monopolies and dominant firms tend to stress their entrenched nature, the difficulties of entry by would-be competitors, the possible erection by monopolies of costly and inefficient barriers, and the persistence of monopolies over long periods of time. Most important, according to these arguments, is the tendency of monopolies to reduce their performance standards once their dominant position has been secured. It is enough for the managers of such firms, once the pressures of competition have been removed, to achieve only sufficient profit to satisfy their stockholders while they themselves can enjoy the perks of their positions. As we saw in Chapter 7, this type of reduced performance because of the lack of competition is known as X-inefficiency.

Although no consensus exists on these opposing views, most economists would probably agree that a highly concentrated industry structure, given that all possible economies of scale have already been realized, is socially harmful because of monopolistic pricing, even in the absence of X-inefficiency. Nonetheless, the problems of public policy implementation that remain are still formidable. Suppose that in a particular merger case economies of scale are not an issue. What other kinds of problems is a structural competition policy likely to encounter in deciding whether to block the merger?

The first consideration is the objective assessment of post-merger industrial structure, which requires a good deal of judgement. Measurement and definitional ambiguities often render court actions both contentious and costly.

Typical examples of such contentious issues are the definition of the market and the product, the extent of monopoly power, and the relationship between concentration measures and market power. For instance, when defining the appropriate product and market, companies tend to use the broadest possible definitions in order to minimize the appearance of market control. The best-known (and most expensive) example is the IBM case, which was initiated in 1969 by the U.S. government. In that case the main product definition used by the government side was "general purpose electronic digital computer systems." The company, on the other hand, wanted to include special purpose computer systems (such as military, process control, and message switching), as well as programmable hand-held calculators and computer leasing and service activities. The narrow definition gave IBM a market share around 70–80 percent, while with the broad definition this share fell to 32 percent. Given such differences of opinion it is not surprising that the case dragged on for years until it was finally abandoned by the government in 1982.

For a Canadian example we turn to the two newspaper cases involving the Southam and Thompson groups, that became the focus of judicial actions in Canada in the 1970s and early 1980s as well as the object of a Royal Commission Report (1981). Here the definition of the relevant product market that was supported by the defendant companies included not only newspapers, in which uncontested monopolies existed in several cities, but also other informational media such as television and radio. With the enlarged definition the monopolies disappeared. While these cases were ultimately decided on different criteria, they also serve as examples of the ambiguities inherent to the application of the law.

The impossibility of setting clear and general legal standards for product and market definitions is matched by a similar difficulty when defining a threshold of concentration beyond which market power can be assumed to be socially harmful. Do we set a value of the concentration ratio or Herfindahl index beyond which mergers should be blocked? From what has been said until now it is clear that the uncritical application of such a threshold of concentration to all industries would result in a policy that is too permissive for some sectors and too restrictive for others. Yet judicial authorities do tend to require such clearcut standards in applying the law. If universal standards are not possible, then one should use judgment on a case-by-case basis. We should also note that in each merger case the policy choice is binary: allow or block the merger. The correct approach is (or should be) to adopt the course of action that presents the highest probable benefits from the social welfare point of view.

Canadian legislators and judges have had little success, so far, in dealing with these issues. Very few merger cases had been brought in front of the courts before 1986, and all of them had been lost by the prosecution. These cases will be reviewed in detail in the next section. They provide good illustrations of the practical problems faced by law enforcement, as well as of the long-term implications of public policy decisions for the evolution of industry structure.

The Canadian Merger Laws

Canadian competition legislation dates back to 1889, with important recent amendments in 1960, 1976, and 1986. It covers a variety of undesirable practices, of which only those related to structure will be reviewed in this section. However, the original purpose of the law was not to impose a certain structure on an industry, but to prevent exploitation of a given non-competitive structure to the detriment of consumers. Consequently, the structural impact of the competition law comes mainly through its effect on mergers and acquisitions, as well as through its prohibition of attempts to maintain a given monopoly position by tactics such as predatory pricing. The latter will be covered in the next chapter, since they refer mainly to pricing and to the prevention of entry by competitors.

Until 1986 mergers and acquisitions were dealt with under the so-called "merger and monopoly" section of the Combines Investigation Act. This act defines a merger as an acquisition of a "competitor, supplier, customer, or any other person, whereby competition . . . is or is likely to be lessened to the detriment or against the interest of the public, whether consumers, producers or others." By Section 33 of the Combines Act, the formation of a merger or monopoly is an indictable offense, punishable by a two-year imprisonment. On the other hand, a monopoly is defined as the control of a type of business throughout Canada, and the operation of that business "to the detriment or against the interests of the public." As already noted, it is the monopoly's conduct in keeping out competitors that may constitute the offense, not the existence of the monopoly.

Mergers, by contrast, would seem on the basis of the language of the law to be an easier target for prosecution if they lead to the formation of a monopoly. No conviction for merger, however, has yet been achieved. Three important judicial decisions in the 1960s and 1970s had closed the door to successful prosecution, at least till the 1986 amendments. It is still too early for a final judgment on the impact of these amendments.

A major difficulty with the merger-monopoly section, as well as with the entire pre-1986 Combines Act, was the criminal basis of that law. Criminal law has very strict rules of evidence. It also requires proof beyond reasonable doubt. As any economist would testify, such proofs are rarely if ever available on economic issues. In the absence of such proofs judges were very reluctant to convict, and tended therefore to leave a merger standing. By contrast, an economist would view the pre-1986 judicial process on mergers as a choice between two possible actions (allow or disallow the merger) in which the judge chooses one course even though the weight of the evidence points the other way, albeit not beyond a reasonable doubt.

For these reasons there is general agreement that the merger aspects of

Canadian competition policy were, at least till the 1986 amendments, the least satisfactory aspects of that policy. The law was incapable of preventing any merger or acquisition even when no social benefits could be demonstrated in its favour, unless public detriment could be shown with the stringent standards of proof required by criminal law. While there is little doubt that the small size of the Canadian market introduces a presumption in favour of economies of scale over competition in a merger case, the virtual removal of all legal barriers to mergers is hard to justify. For this reason several attempts were made to amend this particular section of the Combines Investigation Act.[14] After many abortive starts the law was finally amended in the first half of 1986. It was also renamed the Competition Act.

As already noted, it is still too early to judge the impact on mergers of the new law, given the uncertainty over its interpretation by the courts. That uncertainty is compounded by the almost simultaneous entry into effect of the Canadian Charter of Rights, which is bound to affect all court cases. Nonetheless, in the opinion of some commentators the new law represents a step in the right direction in merger cases.[15]

Briefly speaking, the new Competition Act makes merger cases now referable to a newly created special law court or tribunal, composed of laymen and judges, where they will be judged as civil rather than criminal matters. It also requires prior notification of the government of all mergers where the combined Canadian assets or revenues of the merging firms exceed $100 million and the size of the deal involves assets or sales of more than $35 million. In deciding whether to allow a given merger the tribunal is instructed to apply the test of whether it substantially lessens competition. For such a decision it must consider specific factors such as the extent of foreign competition in the market affected by the merger and whether it acted as a sufficient discipline on the market, whether the acquired party was about to fail, and the availability of substitutes and the barriers to entry into the particular market. Evidence of market share or concentration is not a sufficient basis by itself for a decision that a merger substantially lessens competition.

The new merger law also provides a defence even for mergers that are found to lessen competition "substantially." In such cases the court is to take no action if the merger is "likely to bring about gains in efficiency that will be greater than, and will offset the effects of, any preventing or lessening of competition." There are as yet no indications of what guidelines the government will use in deciding whether a particular deal lessens competition "substantially." Similarly, it is not clear how the tribunal is going to weigh efficiency gains versus competition. Nonetheless, the language of the new law is certainly consistent with the principles that most economists believe should guide structural competition policies, which were reviewed briefly in the previous section. In its first couple of years of operation the tribunal blocked one merger in its initially proposed form, involving a large dairy in western Canada. Since that case was ultimately solved by consensus, the law has not yet been tested. Its impact, however, has already been felt outside the courts, in forcing the abandonment or restructuring of deals that may run afoul of the new law.[16]

Some Earlier Case Studies

Three important merger cases, all of which were lost by the government, were *Regina v. Canadian Breweries* (1960), *R. v. B.C. Sugar Refining* (1961), and *R. v. K.C. Irving Ltd.* (1976), the last one concerning English-language newspapers in New Brunswick. The first two cases were lost at the initial stage, and the Crown chose not to appeal them. The third case, by contrast, went all the way to the Supreme Court. The government won its case in the trial court, only to see it overturned on appeal. Finally, in a far-reaching judgement, the Supreme Court of Canada sided with the appeals court in dismissing the government's case and the language of the decision made it clear that the government had no chance to secure a conviction in a merger case with the law which stood until 1986.

The *Canadian Breweries* Case

This case involved the establishment through a series of mergers of a dominant firm, Canadian Breweries, in the beer industry in much of Canada, accounting for about 50 percent of total market share by 1958. This dominant firm, though, faced significant competition from two smaller rivals, Molson's and Labatt. Further, the retail price of the product was regulated at the provincial level through Liquor Control Boards. Nonetheless, a good case can be made that in many provinces this regulation did not constitute any meaningful price restraint, since retail prices were set by a simple mark-up over the uncontrolled producers' prices.[17]

In retrospect, the judge's decision that dismissed the government case against Canadian Breweries makes good economic sense, even though the language of the decision shows that it was reached at least partially for the wrong reasons. The judge put a great deal of emphasis on the regulated nature of the beer industry, even though regulation may not protect the consumers from excessive prices, as noted above. Similarly, the judge stressed the fact that the industry did not become a monopoly, since the two smaller remaining firms provided vigorous competition. Although this fact was correct, its use as a foundation of a legal argument rebutting the accusation that the merger reduced competition is questionable. As we saw in Chapter 4, an oligopoly with a very small number of firms, in which one firm is much larger than the others and can act as a leader, is precisely the type of structure where price competition can be expected to be very small.

On the other hand, we saw in Chapter 2 that in beer brewing the minimum efficient scale at the plant level is a large percentage of the total Canadian market. The estimate in Table 2.5 shows that in 1967 one MES plant accounted for 34.5 percent of the market. Even if the much smaller Fuss-Gupta (1981) MES estimates for breweries (SIC code 1450) are accepted, they should be adjusted to account for firm level economies of scale. Scherer (1980) states that it takes 3 to 4 plants per firm to realize such economies of scale in the beer industry, principally because of marketing and investment planning advantages to multiplant firms.[18] Such advantages would justify much larger firms than those existing in Canada at the time of the decision, and they were used as an argument by the defendant in the merger case. A similar increase in concentration in the beer industry has also taken place in the U.S. As shown in a previous section, when choosing between price competition and economies of scale the presumption should most often be in favour of the latter, as happened (perhaps inadvertently) in the *Canadian Breweries* case.

The *B.C. Sugar Refining* Case

Similar optimistic conclusions, though, cannot be drawn from the other two merger cases. *B.C. Sugar Refining* in particular involved some highly questionable legal and economic arguments. In that case the government brought to court B.C. Sugar Refining for its acquisition of Manitoba Sugar, its only competitor in western Canada. The merger gave the acquiring company a 100 percent market share in B.C., Alberta, and Saskatchewan, and a 70 percent share in Manitoba, with eastern sugar refiners accounting for the remaining Manitoba sales. The firm was also protected against imports by high tariffs, which it used as a form of limit price.

In rejecting the government's action the judge cited the remaining Manitoba competition from the eastern refiners, in spite of the fact that price competition on a national basis in the sugar refining industry was constrained by a delivered price system with basing points in Vancouver, Montreal, and St. John's, Nfld.[19] He also gave weight to the fact that the western sugar refiners obtained some of their raw sugar from domestic sugar beet producers who were therefore also protected by the tariff. Although the Crown argued, in this author's opinion correctly, that the merger was detrimental to these beet producers because of the monopsony power thus created, this argument was not accepted. The most crucial aspect of the decision, however, was the judge's imposed requirement that the government must not only show monopoly power, but also that such power has been exercised to the detriment of the public.[20] In other words, the Crown must show "excessive" prices or profits, as well as the fact that such profits are detrimental to public welfare.

This ruling implied in practice that the government could not infer a detriment to public welfare from the merger's anticompetitive effects. It would also need to observe monopoly conduct in the form of "high" prices or profits, well after the merger was consummated. The public detriment had also to be proven "beyond a reasonable doubt," given the criminal nature of the law. This impossible burden of proof amounted to a virtual blank cheque for all types of mergers. Unfortunately, the government chose not to appeal the decision, with the result that its principles were accepted and subsequently used by the Supreme Court in the third major merger case brought under the pre-1986 law.

The *K.C. Irving* Case

The *K.C. Irving* case involved the successive acquisitions by one company of all English-language newspapers in New Brunswick, the last acquisition taking place in 1968. The government initiated a court case against K.C. Irving, under the merger section of the law, which went to trial in 1972. Although the Crown won its case in trial court, this decision was reversed in the New Brunswick Court of Appeal, and the reversal was upheld by a unanimous 1976 decision by the Supreme Court of Canada. This last decision was based on the government failure to show "public detriment" resulting from the merger, notwithstanding the disappearance of all competition. Thus the precedent set by the *B.C. Sugar Refining* case was firmly entrenched in the law as a result of the wording of this Supreme Court decision.

Although the legal consequences of the *K.C. Irving* case were perhaps unfortunate insofar as they rendered the government virtually powerless to act against any type of merger, the economic foundations of the final decision are considerably more defensible. As we noted in Chapter 2, the newspaper industry is one in which the relevant product market is local, rather than national or even provincial. The 1968 acquisition involved a newspaper that had no competition in its own area, while uncontested evidence was presented that earlier acquisitions had not resulted in any attempts by K.C. Irving to restrict circulation or interfere in editorial policy. Hence, the merger did not lessen competition where such existed, a fact that was noted in the Supreme Court decision. Even if a newspaper merger results in the closure of a pre-merger competitor in a given city, such a closure can probably be justified on the basis of economies of scale. This fact was used by the defence in the merger case brought against the Southam and Thompson newspaper interests following the simultaneous elimination of newspaper competition in 1980 in the cities of Ottawa, Winnipeg, and the anglophone market of Montreal. That case was hopeless from the beginning in view of the *K.C. Irving* precedent, and the charges were dismissed in 1983. For most Canadian cities there is little doubt that with current newspaper technology the newspaper industry constitutes a natural monopoly, a fact that was established by a Royal Commission in 1981.[21]

Conclusions

The structure-conduct-performance model implies that public policies trying to improve performance at the level of individual industries should aim at less concentrated industrial structures. This requires, in practice, some type of legislation blocking or screening mergers and takeovers involving large firms. The problems of interpreting and implementing such legislation are major, and the entire issue has always been and continues to be shrouded in controversy. An ideal law would be one that screens out only those mergers that result in an "unacceptable" increase in market power in a given sector, while allowing all efficiency-improving mergers to stand.

In Canada a major concern with any merger-preventing policies is that they may interfere with the realization of economies of scale at the plant or firm level. It can be shown that a strong presumption exists in favour of economies of scale when the total welfare effects of a merger are evaluated, even when there are price-increasing anticompetitive effects. For this reason merger laws have to be considerably more permissive in Canada than in, say, the U.S., given the documented existence of suboptimally-sized plants and/or firms in many sectors of Canadian industry.

Until 1986 the Canadian merger laws, far from being too restrictive, were considered completely ineffective. They were unable to prevent any one of the three merger cases that were brought in front of the courts, even when they resulted in a complete monopolization of the sector. The 1986 amendments were designed to improve that record, but their ultimate effectiveness depends on the manner of their application and interpretation by the courts.

Endnotes

1. See the detailed discussion of merger motives in Scherer (1980), pp. 118-141.

2. There are several instances in which a vertical merger may have beneficial effects from the welfare point of view, depending on the structure of the industries of the merging parties. For this reason, public policy intervention may not be warranted in such mergers. For an extended analysis see Clarke (1985), Chapter 8.

3. Examples of such policies are the extension of regulation to the entire integrated firm, or the imposition of limits on the transfer prices (the prices at which the regulated firm charges the costs of its inputs for regulatory purposes).

4. See the detailed U.S. merger data in Marfels (1988, p. 78), which can be compared with the Canadian evidence in Table 8.1.

5. See Scherer (1980), p. 124.

6. See Eckbo (1986), p. 242.

7. See Eckbo (1986), p. 238.

8. See the articles by White (1987), Fisher (1987), and Schmalensee (1987), which are also discussed more extensively in Chapter 12.

9. See Chapter 6 of the Report of the Royal Commission on Corporate Concentration (1978), and Chapter 10 of the volume of essays on that report, edited by Gorecki and Stanbury (1979).

10. The analysis follows Williamson (1968).

11. See, however, the references cited in endnote 8, which are very sceptical about the economies of scale arguments as justifications of horizontal mergers in the U.S.

12. For a more detailed account of the legislative history of Canadian competition laws see Green (1985), Chapter 8.

13. See the article by Stigler (1982), who is, however, somewhat sceptical of economists' influence on antitrust policy.

14. For a detailed account of these attempts over 1971-1975 see Stanbury (1977).

15. See the Toronto *Globe and Mail*, August 18, 1986.

16. For an example of such a case see the *Financial Post*, January 9, 1989, p. 9.

17. See Green (1985), p. 278.

18. See Scherer (1980), p. 118.

19. For a detailed account of the basing point pricing system see Scherer (1980), pp. 325-334. Basing point pricing plans are producer pricing agreements, according to which transportation costs are charged to the customer as if all producers were located at the same location (the basing point). Needless to say, this facilitates the maintenance of uniform delivered prices and reduces competitive pressures. The basing point systems are also discussed in the next chapter.

20. The language of the law (section 33 of the Combines Investigation Act) defines an illegal merger as an "acquisition . . . of a competitor, supplier, customer, or any other person, whereby competition . . . is or is likely to be lessened to the detriment or against the interest of the public . . . " From this the trial judge inferred that

public detriment must be proven in addition to the lessening of competition, which in this case amounted to the virtual monopolization of the refined sugar market in western Canada.

21. According to the principles examined in Chapter 3, this conclusion implies that the industry should be subjected to regulatory controls. Although the Royal Commission on Newspapers (1981) recommended precisely such a course of action, the controls were not imposed due to vigorous opposition from the newspaper industry.

References

Baldwin, J.R., and P.K. Gorecki. *The Role of Scale in Canada-U.S. Productivity Differences*, volume 6 of the research studies prepared for the Royal Commission on the Economic Union and Development Prospects for Canada. Toronto, Ont.: University of Toronto Press, 1986.

Baldwin, J. and P. Gorecki, with J. McVey and J. Crysdale. "Entry and Exit to the Canadian Manufacturing Sector: 1970-1979," Discussion Paper #225. Ottawa, Ont.: Economic Council of Canada, 1983.

Calvet, A.L. and J. Lefoll. "Information Asymmetry and Wealth Effect of Canadian Corporate Acquisitions," *Financial Review*, 22:4 (November 1987), pp. 415-431.

Clarke, R. *Industrial Economics*. Oxford, Eng.: Blackwell, 1985.

Eckbo, B.E. "Mergers and the Market for Corporate Control: the Canadian Evidence," *Canadian Journal of Economics*, 19:2 (May 1986), pp. 236-260.

————. "The Market for Corporate Control: Policy Issues and Capital Market Evidence," in Khemani *et al.* (1988), pp. 143-225.

Fisher, F.M. "Horizontal Mergers: Triage and Treatment," *Journal of Economic Perspectives*, 1:2 (Fall 1987), pp. 23-40.

Fuss, M. and V.K. Gupta. "A Cost Function Approach to the Estimation of Minimum Efficient Scale, Returns to Scale and Suboptimal Scale," *European Economic Review*, 15:2 (1981), pp. 123-135.

Gorecki, P.K., and W.T. Stanbury. *Perspectives on the Royal Commission on Corporate Concentration*. Scarborough, Ont.: Butterworths, 1979.

Green, C. *Canadian Industrial Organization and Policy*. Toronto, Ont.: McGraw-Hill Ryerson, 2nd Edition, 1985.

Khemani, R.S., D.M. Shapiro, and W.T. Stanbury. *Mergers, Corporate Concentration and Power in Canada*. Halifax, N.S.: Institute for Research in Public Policy, 1988.

Marfels, C. "Aggregate Concentration in International Perspective: Canada, Federal Republic of Germany, Japan and the United States," in Khemani *et al.* (1988), pp. 53-88.

Royal Commission on Corporate Concentration (RCCC). *Report*. Ottawa, Ont.: Minister of Supply and Services Canada, 1978.

Royal Commission on Newspapers. *Report*. Ottawa, Ont.: Minister of Supply and Services Canada, 1981.

Scherer, F.M. *Industrial Market Structure and Economic Performance*. Chicago, Ill.: Rand McNally, 2nd Edition, 1980.

———. "The Effects of Mergers in the United States," in Khemani *et al.* (1988), pp. 227-231.

Schmalensee, R. "Horizontal Merger Policy: Problems and Changes," *Journal of Economic Perspectives*, 1:2 (Fall 1987), pp. 41-54.

Stanbury, W.T. *Business Interests and the Reform of Canadian Competition Policy, 1971-75*. Toronto, Ont.: Methuen, 1977.

Stigler, G.J. "The Economists and the Problem of Monopoly," *American Economic Review Papers and Proceedings*, 72:2 (May 1982), pp. 1-11.

White, L.J. "Antitrust and Merger Policy: Review and Critique," *Journal of Economic Perspectives*, 1:2 (Fall 1987), pp. 13-22.

Williamson, O.E. "Economies as an Antitrust Defence: the Welfare Tradeoffs," *American Economic Review*, 58:1 (March 1968), pp. 18-36.

C H A P T E R 9

Public Policy II:

··

Policing Conduct

··

The second and perhaps most important set of public policies aimed at promoting competition across the Canadian economy is the one dealing with firm conduct in an oligopoly. As we saw in Chapters 4 and 5, there are several dimensions of firm conduct that are desirable for firms in an industry, but which nevertheless clash with the overall aims of public policy. The laws and regulations that will be examined in this chapter are designed to cope with the problems arising from this conflict between public and private objectives.

While there is some degree of controversy among economists on the overall desirability of control-of-structure policies, there is, in contrast, significant consensus about the need to prohibit certain types of firm behaviour. Nonetheless, differences of opinion do exist, especially with respect to the degree of vigour with which law enforcement should be pursued. Also, some types of conduct are recognized as being desirable in some cases and objectionable in others; however it is not always easy to tell one from the other. For this reason the debate among economists and policy-makers is just as lively as it is for the issues discussed in the previous chapter.

Most laws and regulations that will be examined here concern pricing in oligopolies or by dominant firms. As we saw in Chapter 4, firms in an oligopoly in which there is awareness of mutual interdependence tend to prefer collusive pricing, which can either be overt or tacit. The key issue is how to prove that price collusion exists in the absence of formal evidence. The body of judicial doctrine has evolved here through case studies. It was amended in 1986, with the result that there is little experience on the way the new law will be interpreted.

Price collusion is not, however, the only type of objectionable firm conduct. Another set of laws covers the so-called *vertical restraints*, of which resale price maintenance is the best-known type of illegal behaviour. These restraints may arise in the vertical relationships of a producer with its distributors, when it tries to restrict competition at the retail level of the market. In addition to resale price maintenance, the vertical restraints include tied sales and exclusive territories. They occupy an important place in competition law enforcement.

Other public policies dealing with conduct concern price discrimination and predatory pricing. The theoretical rationale for such conduct was examined in Chapters 5 and 6. These policies also present a number of difficulties in their application, principally because it is difficult to distinguish objectionable conduct from normal competitive behaviour.

There are also a number of legal issues arising in this area. Much of the legislation is criminal in nature, while part of it was transferred to civil law after 1986. There is some leeway on the part of the public authorities in prosecuting certain types of conduct which can be attacked through civil or criminal law. It would be interesting to see which road is chosen in the future (for instance, in cases of predatory conduct).

The next two sections will first examine policies, laws, and cases dealing with price collusion. Resale price maintenance, of which much has been written in recent years, is studied next. Finally, other types of vertical restraints, predatory pricing, and price discrimination will be discussed.

Price-Fixing Agreements

As we saw in Chapter 4, it is in the interests of firms in an oligopoly to collude in setting product prices. This practice runs counter to the public interest, as argued at length in earlier chapters. Accordingly, price collusion that transforms an oligopoly into a cartel is illegal. There are explicit laws forbidding formal pricing agreements between all competing firms, at least as far as the domestic market is concerned. The main areas of controversy in this section relate to two specific issues: the degree of market control that the colluding firms must possess before their anticompetitive behaviour becomes illegal, and the type of proof needed to infer collusion in the absence of a formal agreement. The second issue in particular has been a sticky point in competition law enforcement, as the case studies will show.

There is little dissent among economists on the need to prohibit price collusion.[1] At best, many convinced laissez-faire proponents would argue that collusion is difficult to achieve in practice, and likely to be ineffective in the long run because of new entry. This still does not eliminate the need for laws to prevent it from happening, since the inefficiencies that it creates may last for a long time. For this reason there have not been many objections to such laws.

On the other hand, formal collusion is not as easy in practice as it appears in theory. We saw in Chapters 4 and 5 the difficulties faced by the OPEC oil cartel to maintain its price structure in the face of changing economic conditions. Yet OPEC is a legal cartel, operating under ideal conditions from the point of view of formal coordinating mechanisms. Illegal cartels have to cope with the difficulties of infrequent meetings and the ever-present fear of discovery or denunciation.

Still, collusion does happen, and the rewards from its success can be very substantial. It is also very often treated with a certain degree of leniency by the judicial authorities, a fact that reduces its overall risk. For instance, in 1987 a number of hotels in the Ottawa-Hull area pleaded guilty to price-fixing charges in exchange for their cooperation in bringing to justice other parties to the conspiracy who had refused to cooperate.[2] The hotels had agreed to submit a common price of $62 per night for a single room for public servants on official business. The original charges involved conspiracy to lessen or prevent competition, as well as bid-rigging.

The three hotels that pleaded guilty to price-fixing received a fine of $60,000 each, and a stay of the proceedings for the bid-rigging charges. A few weeks later the remaining three defendants received an $80,000 fine each in exchange for a similar guilty plea. The maximum possible fine was $1 million. According to the public prosecutor, the excess revenue attributable to collusive pricing since the fall of 1984, when the conspiracy took place, was $98,000 for one of the hotels. In other words, the fines did not even eliminate the rewards from the illegal actions.

As with mergers, Canadian competition law in the price-fixing areas dates back to the original 1889 legislation, with important amendments in 1910, 1960, 1976, and 1986. Unlike the merger provisions of the pre-1986 law, the price-fixing sections have been significantly effective in a number of cases, although perhaps not as effective as many economists would have wanted. Several successful prosecutions had been launched, and the pace of law enforcement was picking up in recent years. Nonetheless, the two complicating factors mentioned in the beginning of this section, the extent of the conspiracy and the acceptability of circumstantial evidence, have continued to create problems for law enforcement. Unfortunately, these problems were not totally removed by the 1986 amendments.

The first factor is the least understandable from an economist's point of view. Canadian law does not prohibit price-fixing agreements between firms in the same industry. What it does prohibit are agreements that " . . . prevent, or lessen, *unduly*, competition . . . ," to adopt the exact language of the law (emphasis added). In other words, an agreement may be legal if competition is not reduced "unduly," which seems to imply that there is a permissible degree of lessening of price competition. By contrast, all price-fixing agreements are illegal in the U.S. no matter how extensive they are. In the judicial jargon the American law characterizes price-fixing as illegal per se.

It is difficult to see on purely objective economic grounds why this sensible U.S. provision has not been incorporated in the Canadian law. With the possible exception of export and specialization agreements, for which special provisions exist in the legislation, no economic case can be made that the public interest will be advanced by price-fixing. At best, it can be argued that an agreement that does not cover the entire industry will be ineffective, since the segment of the industry that is not party to the agreement would provide some price competition. Still, this does not make the agreement desirable. In fact, clauses that made price-fixing illegal per se were part of the proposals for competition law amendments for many years prior to 1986. They never made it to the final legislation, due to strong opposition from the business community.[3]

This was not the only problem with the part of the law dealing with price-fixing agreements. Prior to the 1986 amendments, the law had been interpreted as requiring the Crown to prove that the accused parties not only had entered the agreement, but also that they intended to lessen competition unduly. This so-called double intent requirement placed an impossible burden upon the prosecution. The 1986 amendments added a subsection to the existing conspiracy provisions in order to eliminate the need to prove intent. With this subsection it is now only necessary to prove that the parties did enter the conspiracy, and that this conspiracy, if carried into effect, would lessen competition unduly. It is now the agreement itself that forms the offence, and not the intentions of the colluding parties.[4]

As already noted, both the old and new forms of the competition law allow price-fixing agreements as long as there is no complete elimination of price competition, i.e. as long as there is a portion of the industry that does not subscribe to the agreement. A key question is how big this portion should be for no "undue" lessening of competition to exist. The interpretation of the intent of the law took place in a number of judicial decisions; these will be reviewed in a later section. It is sufficient to say at this point that this interpretation is quite restrictive. In practice, a price-fixing agreement has ended up with a conviction only if it resulted in an almost complete suppression of price competition, i.e. only if it covered the quasi-totality of firms in a given market.

The mitigating factor to this rather unsatisfactory state of affairs is that an agreement that leaves part of the industry outside may not last long enough to create major public detriment. The parties to the agreement will be subjected to price competition from the outsiders, or possibly from new entrants. They would then have to either abandon the agreement or face loss of market share. The OPEC experience is a case in point, and the case studies presented in a subsequent section will provide further illustration. Still, the failure to render formal price-fixing per se illegal imposes needless complications upon competition law enforcement, while providing no public benefits.

Tacit Collusion

Since formal all-encompassing price collusion is illegal, the parties that enter into it tend to leave few documentary proofs usable in a court of law. The courts have recognized this, and have at times accepted circumstantial evidence as sufficient proof of the existence of an agreement. The key issue that will be discussed in this section is what type of such evidence can be used by the prosecution to prove its case beyond a reasonable doubt.

Here we enter into a murky area of legal jurisprudence, which is complicated by economic factors. As we saw in Chapter 4, firms in an oligopoly do not always need to enter into a formal agreement in order to coordinate their prices. There are mechanisms of tacit collusion, such as price leadership, that achieve results similar to those of a price-fixing agreement without breaking the law. They are, in other words, actions that are illegal in intent, but legal in form. The question that arises, therefore, is where one should draw the line between legal and illegal observable behaviour. Is such a behaviour indirect proof of underlying illegal actions? Is it an attempt at tacit collusion and if so, should such a type of collusion be prohibited? Or are the observed coordinated responses of all firms in the oligopoly nothing more nor less than "normal" responses to common economic factors?

These questions have been at the centre of competition law enforcement on both sides of the Canada-U.S. border. The judicial term that has been coined to refer to coordinated behaviour of firms in an oligopoly that do not necessarily have a formal agreement is *conscious parallelism*.[5] This is essentially a uniformity of firm conduct stemming from an awareness of mutual interdependence and common interest, which produces results similar to those of a cartel. Since, as already noted, the similarity of firm behaviour need not imply oligopolistic coordination, but can also be a common reaction to the same economic forces, it is not surprising that conscious parallelism has not been considered illegal by itself in both Canada and the U.S. Instead, the courts have focussed on additional actions, over and above the similarity of conduct, that can be used to infer an overt or tacit intent to maintain collusive prices. Such actions are also sometimes known as *conscious parallelism plus*.

Here, though, ends the similarity between the two countries' respective policies. The list of *plus* factors that are considered sufficient to create illegal behaviour is not the same in Canada as in the U.S. The U.S. list is much longer, a fact that is not surprising given the much more vigorous pursuit of competition by our southern neighbours.

The following is a partial list of factors that have been used at times in the U.S. as indirect proof of tacit collusion:

(i) Elaborate exchanges of information between members of the same industry or trade association.

(ii) Simultaneous and substantial price increases that cannot be justified by any rise in costs.

(iii) Identical sealed bids, especially on nonstandard items.

(iv) Unnatural product standardization or false denials of interfirm quality differences.

(v) Basing-point pricing systems of partial freight absorption, to be examined in more detail below.

These factors are also often supplemented by evidence of parallel predatory behaviour by cartel members in order to keep out competitors. Such behaviour is examined in a subsequent section of this chapter.

The basing-point pricing system is a price-coordinating device that is used in bulky, standardized commodities, for which freight costs are an important component of the price paid by final consumers. Such a system guarantees that the consumers located in a given market will be faced with identical prices quoted by all oligopolistic suppliers, in spite of the fact that these suppliers' plants are not located at the same distance from the market. This implies that some suppliers will absorb freight charges by reducing their profit margins, while others will charge nonexistent freight costs (sometimes called *phantom freight*) as part of delivered price.

The best-known application of basing-point pricing is in the U.S. steel industry during the early 20th Century. That system was known as the "Pittsburgh Plus" single basing-point system, which was abandoned under pressure by the U.S. Federal Trade Commission (FTC) in 1924. Under Pittsburgh Plus, buyers were being charged freight for their steel purchases as if the producing mill were located at Pittsburgh, regardless of its true location. As a result, all producers were quoting the same steel price in any single location, although prices differed between locations depending on their distance from Pittsburgh.

Figure 9.1 illustrates the consequences of such a single basing-point pricing system. B denotes the basing point, which also happens to be the location of a mill. Point A, at a distance of x to the west of it, is the location of another mill as well as a buying centre. Point C is another important buying centre, at a distance of y east of the basing point. The production costs (including the profit markup) of a ton of steel are denoted by P, and are assumed equal in both mills. If c is the transportation cost per unit distance, then the delivered prices at A and C are $P + cx$ and $P + cy$ respectively, for both mills A and B. It follows that the customers of A located near the mill pay a phantom freight

FIGURE 9.1
Basing-point pricing

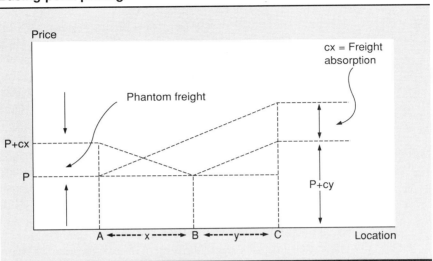

of *cx*, while the same mill's customers who are located at C are charged less than the true production and distribution cost, which is equal to $P + c(x+y)$. This nullifies all locational advantages that A and B possess at A and C respectively.

An obvious extension of this system is the multiple basing-point system, in which delivered prices are computed as if the producer were located in one of several points, depending on the location of the buyer. For instance, the Canadian sugar refining industry used during the 1950s a delivered pricing system with three basing points, Vancouver, Montreal, and St. John's, Nfld. Similarly, the FTC pressures in 1924 forced the replacement of the Pittsburgh Plus pricing by a three-point system, in which Gary and Birmingham were added to Pittsburgh. In all these cases it is the base that is closest to the buyer that is used to compute the quoted price.

Basing-point pricing is a simple and effective coordinating device in an oligopoly that facilitates price leadership enormously. It also entails a significant element of price discrimination. For these reasons it has often become the target of successful antitrust action in the U.S., where it has also been used as an indicator of the existence of restrictive agreements. In addition to steel and refined sugar, basing-point pricing has also been found in cement, corn products, and plywood.

In Canada, by contrast, the courts have taken a much more lenient view of such pricing systems. The two instances where basing-point pricing has been at the centre of a court case were sugar refining and cement. In both cases the prosecution lost, and the courts ruled that the observed coordinated behaviour was not in violation of the law.

It is only fair to note that basing-point pricing is not necessarily bad from the general welfare point of view. As with all cases of price discrimination, one can show that there exist situations in which total surplus increases if uniform delivered prices are used, rather than if each buyer pays its "fair" share of transportation costs. This, however, neglects the role of basing-point systems in maintaining price collusion, which is the main reason for their overall undesirability.[6]

The loss of the cement and sugar refining cases during the 1970s prompted widespread dissatisfaction with the state of competition law concerning price collusion. As with the merger provisions, the attempts at reform took a long time before finally becoming law in 1986. These 1986 amendments make some effort to address these concerns, but it is still too soon to tell if this effort was successful. Thus, in addition to the elimination of the double-intent requirement, a clause was inserted in the law in which it states specifically that the existence of a price-fixing agreement can be proven from circumstantial evidence. It is not indispensable for the prosecution to provide direct proof that the parties to the agreement communicated with each other. It is still necessary, though, to prove the existence of an agreement clearly enough to satisfy the requirements of criminal law, that is, beyond a reasonable doubt. This is a heavy burden of proof, given the complexity of the economic issues that have to be decided.

The new amendments do not specifically address the role of basing-point pricing in promoting price collusion, but they do contain a clause that may make its use less effective. This clause enables buyers to take delivery of the product at any chosen location where the supplier sells to other customers, and transport it to the desired location through their own arrangements. In other words, the Competition Tribunal may prohibit a seller from refusing delivery to a customer at a location where other customers are being served on the same terms. In this way the buyers' own shipping may contribute to the breakdown of the basing-point pricing. The new provision will not apply if the product in question is available from other competing sellers in the same location.

All in all, the changes in the law were far less substantive here than in the merger provisions. Consequently, it is important to examine the jurisprudence as it appears in the court cases of the late 1980s.

Some Case Studies

Unlike the merger provisions of competition legislation, where there were very few cases and all of them had been lost by the government, the record of law enforcement in price collusion and related areas is much more extensive and varied. Table 9.1 below shows the number of prosecutions undertaken as well as the success rate, in various offences related to pricing from 1890 until 1983. It is clear from the data that a large proportion of the prosecutions concluded with some sort of government victory in most areas. For the conspiracy cases in particular, the proportion reached 75 percent.

Yet these statistics are somewhat misleading. For one thing, many of these cases, such as the Ottawa-Hull hotel price-fixing case of 1987, were virtually uncontested with clearcut evidence of illegal behaviour. The truly difficult areas of tacit price collusion were tackled only recently, and with mixed success, by the anticombines authorities. It is perhaps for this reason that the success rate has been falling in the more recent years: it was only 36.4 percent in 1981-83, as compared to 100 percent in 1956-65.

A few of these cases present special interest. We shall look at five of them in some detail. Four are tacit collusion cases, in which there was indirect evidence of a price-fixing agreement. Two of the four were won and two were lost by the prosecution. Taken as a whole, therefore, the four cases can be used to illustrate the minimum amount of circumstantial evidence necessary for conviction.

In the fifth case, there was direct evidence of a formal price-fixing agreement. This occurred in the Nova Scotia fire insurance industry (*R. v. Aetna Insurance Co. et al.*, 1977), in which a large number of insurance companies in

TABLE 9.1
Combines prosecutions and successes (1889/90 - 1982/83)

Offense	1890-1940	1941-1955	1956-65	1966-75	1976-80	1981-83	1890-1983
Conspiracy	16/21	8/9	20/20	26/33	10/18	4/11	84/112
RPM/refusal to sell	—	2/2	10/10	20/22	36/47	15/26	83/108
Merger and/or monopoly	0/1	1/1	0/2	4/5	0/2	0/0	5/11
Price discrimination/ predatory pricing	—	—	0/3	1/3	0/2	2/4	3/12
Other (multiple offences)	1/1	—	—	4/6	1/2	1/3	7/12

Notes: Misleading advertising is excluded.
Successes include the granting of a prohibition order.
Time periods are defined on a fiscal year basis (ending 3/31).
Source: Gorecki and Stanbury (1984), p. 220.

the province had formed what amounted to an official cartel. This was achieved by their membership in the Nova Scotia Board of Insurance Underwriters. Member firms had to follow common rates and standardized policies, and were subject to penalties for infractions. In spite of this the firms were acquitted by the trial judge. This verdict was appealed by the prosecution, and overturned by the Nova Scotia Court of Appeals in a divided decision. The case made it all the way to the Supreme Court of Canada, which in turn reversed the decision of the Court of Appeals by a sharply divided (5-3) decision. The firms' acquittal was thus left to stand.

This case is a clear illustration of the already mentioned fact that price-fixing in Canada is not per se illegal. The existence of the formal agreement was not disputed by the defence. What apparently played a major role in the final acquittal was the coverage of the agreement, which did not include a substantial segment of the industry. That segment saw its market share increase as a result of the agreement: the share of premiums of the colluding firms fell from 83 to 71 percent between 1960 and 1970. A second and more disturbing element that contributed to the acquittal was the enunciation of the proof of the double intent requirement as a necessary condition for conviction. As we saw, the 1986 amendments (hopefully) took care of this second point, but did not go as far as establishing the per se illegality of price-fixing.

The two cases of tacit price collusion that were won by the prosecution are those already mentioned in Chapter 4, namely the electric large lamp and the Ontario metal culvert industries.[7] Both were used in that earlier chapter to illustrate the application of price leadership of the dominant firm and barometric varieties. Here our interest is in the type of indirect proof that was considered sufficient to infer the existence of a price-fixing agreement.

In both cases the evidence consisted more or less of the adoption of uniform sales policies by all firms in the industry, and an effort to enforce the application of these policies. The difficulties of enforcement ultimately caused both the failure of the parallel pricing and the conviction on price-fixing charges. This seems to be a common occurrence in colluding oligopolies: the harder it is to collude, the easier it is to detect and punish collusion. Conversely, conspiracies that are successful in avoiding violations of the cartel agreement are less likely to be reported or detected. For this reason, as George Stigler pointed out, one cannot make inferences about the frequency and effectiveness of price collusion based solely on the cases where collusion failed or was found out.[8]

In the electric large lamps case the difficulties in enforcing common sales plans stemmed from the manufacturers' lack of control over the retail side of the market. The oligopoly was very tight, with three firms controlling 95 percent of the market and Canadian General Electric Company acting as an unmistakable leader. There was therefore no difficulty in reaching an agreement on common prices at the producer level. It was, however, considerably more difficult to impose uniform prices on the retailers and distributors. There was a need for extensive consultation and communication between the three cartel members every time such uniformity was threatened. It is these contacts between the firms (for which there was documentary evidence), whose sole purpose was the maintenance of uniform prices, that were accepted as evidence of price collusion. Most economists would agree with the court that this case was well within the realm of formal price-fixing, and beyond the legally allowable conscious parallelism.

In the Ontario metal culvert industry the difficulties of price coordination arose from the relatively large number of cartel members and the ease of entry into the industry. As we saw in Chapter 4, the more members there are in the cartel the harder it is to reach an agreement, and the more probable is detection. Similarly, ease of entry will eventually undermine the cartel, given the fact that cartel profitability is bound to attract new firms to the industry.

In the metal culvert industry there was an industry association, the Canadian Steel Pipe Institute, playing a role similar to that of a central coordinating agency on behalf of the cartel. The common sales plans here consisted of the circulation to all customers and competitors of lists of prices, discounts, and credit terms, and of efforts by the industry association to establish uniformity of these lists. There was also evidence that such uniformity was achieved, since in many instances firms submitted identical bids for government contracts. A critical factor in securing conviction in this case was the improbability of achieving uniformity of prices to such an extent without an underlying agreement to avoid competition.

The metal culvert industry case has a lot of similarities with one of the two cases that were lost by the government, the *Canada Cement LaFarge Ltd.* (1973) case, insofar as much of the evidence consisted of identical bid prices in government contracts. The uniformity of prices was achieved through a basing-point system, resulting in uniform delivered prices independently of the location of the producing plants. The nature of the product is such that transportation charges are a major component of product cost. Apart from that, there was sufficient homogeneity of the product and the technology used in order to support the claim that price similarity was due to economic factors. As argued earlier, the legality of the basing-point pricing systems in Canada (in contrast to the U.S.) is the real issue here, since there was otherwise little evidence of an agreement.

The last case that will be examined here is *Atlantic Sugar Refineries Ltd.* (1980), which was lost by the prosecution, and where the decision raised the most objections from antitrust students and practitioners. This case was certainly at the centre of many of the attempts to reform the competition laws during the early 1980s, attempts that culminated in the 1986 amendments.[9] Part of the reason was that the already mentioned proof requirement of a double intent to lessen competition "unduly" was central to the eventual acquittal of the firms. This was, presumably, taken care of in the 1986 amendments. There are, however, a couple of other points that merit a closer examination of this case.

The evidence of coordinated behaviour in the sugar refining industry covered more than product pricing. There were joint efforts to prevent new entry and to deal with imports. On the pricing front, there was the ever-present basing-point system, a rule-of-thumb common pricing rule at the producing level, and a mutual awareness of price lists. One may argue either way whether this evidence was sufficient to prove the existence of an explicit agreement to avoid competition. What is more difficult to swallow is the fact that the judges at both the trial level and the Supreme Court of Canada accepted that the firms' actions indicated a tacit agreement to avoid competition, but then went ahead and acquitted the firms. Further, the language of the decisions at both levels shows that the judges were unclear about the meaning of competitive behaviour in an oligopoly. They seemed to imply that a little bit of tacit collusion is fine, provided that it does not result in a "suppression" of competition. This tacit collusion was realized by conscious attempts to maintain constant market shares of the leading firms.

To understand why an economist should object to such reasoning we must turn to the oligopoly models that we examined in Chapter 4. The three main models that we saw, the Cournot, Bertrand, and cartel models, ended up with their own industry equilibrium in which the market shares depended on industry demand and the firms' cost functions. Every time these underlying conditions changed there was a need to adjust to the new equilibrium in all three models. Yet, the adjustment process is fundamentally different. Bertrand and Cournot, being competitive models, reach the new industry equilibrium by successive competitive moves, during which the firms' market shares do not stay the same. Only in collusion do the moves from one equilibrium to another take place under constant market shares for similar-sized firms. In other words, a conscious attempt to preserve market shares is a strong indicator of cartel behaviour.

Can legal action compel firms to engage in competition when their own interests run strongly in the opposite direction, and there are structural factors allowing them to do so without overtly illegal behaviour? How strong should the *plus* factor in the conscious parallelism cases be before it results in conviction? Should it go beyond circumstantial evidence of tacit collusion, sufficient to prove it beyond a reasonable doubt? These are the questions raised by the *Atlantic Sugar* decisions. These questions would have been answered to the satisfaction of, I believe, the majority of economists if the word "unduly" were removed from the wording of the law. The per se illegality of overt or tacit agreements to lessen competition needs to be firmly established in our competition legislation, provided they are proven beyond a reasonable doubt.

As we saw earlier, this objective was not achieved by the 1986 amendments. Earlier attempts to amend the law had been much more explicit in this area than what finally emerged in the legislation. They failed because of the opposition of business groups, which caused a fifteen-year delay between the first presentation of the legislation in 1971 and the final adoption in 1986. For this reason, the new law is not expected to make much difference in the price-fixing area, as noted earlier.

One final comment needs to be made concerning the *Atlantic Sugar* case. The industry enjoys a very high degree of tariff protection, with a nominal tariff of more than 20 percent for the period covered by the indictment. Such high tariffs tend to facilitate collusion, by suppressing competition from imports and by raising the price achievable through collusion. For this reason, tariff reductions have often been proposed as substitutes for anti-combines action. They have been applied rarely, however. We shall return to this topic in Chapter 11, where the role of foreign trade in the structure-conduct-performance model is discussed.

Resale Price Maintenance

As we saw in Table 9.1, resale price maintenance (RPM) is comparable only to price-fixing as far as the caseload of anticombines authorities and their success rate are concerned. In fact, RPM occupies a special place in Canadian competition law, for it is one of the few instances where this law has gone further than the comparable U.S. statutes. The economic case against RPM has become somewhat controversial, and there have been repeated calls for the relaxation of the law. For this reason we shall pay particular attention to the economic analysis of RPM, on which much of the debate is centred. Some theoretical models examining RPM are presented in Appendix 9A.

Resale price maintenance is one of several business practices that deal with a producer's relationship with its distributors and retailers. It refers to an attempt to enforce a certain minimum retail price for the product under penalty of loss of distribution privileges. Other similar practices are territorial restrictions, tied sales, and exclusive dealing. As already noted, all these firm policies are collectively known as vertical restraints; they are covered by special provisions of the competition legislation. RPM is the most important as far as the number of cases is concerned, which is why it is examined in a special section. All other practices are dealt with in the next section.

Broadly speaking, RPM may refer to any attempt by a producer to influence the retail price of its product. This covers price ceilings as well as minimum retail prices. In practice, though, the anticompetitive effects of RPM are likely to arise from the imposition of price floors, which are the ones subject to prosecution. Currently, RPM is illegal in most countries, but the specific manner of application of the law varies widely.

The Canadian law against RPM dates from 1952. It is one of the most clear-cut pieces of competition legislation insofar as it makes the practice illegal per se. In 1960 the law was relaxed somewhat, to allow for certain exceptions known as the *loss-leader* provisions. However, as Mathewson and Winter (1985) noted, the courts have interpreted the law in a fairly stringent manner.[10] As a result, RPM is illegal except when a retailer sells below wholesale price.

In its background studies, the Royal Commission on the Economic Union and Development Prospects for Canada (also known as the MacDonald Commission on free trade with the U.S.) devoted an entire volume to vertical restraints. On the subject of RPM, that study recommended a further relaxation of the law, which in the opinion of the Commission's research coordinator would virtually eliminate all RPM prosecutions in Canada.[11] This recommendation was incorporated in the MacDonald Commission's final report, but it had not yet been adopted when this book went to print. Meanwhile a new theoretical study by Rey and Tirole appeared in 1986, in which it was shown that the anticompetitive effects of RPM may have been underestimated by the previous studies. As of this writing the issue remains unresolved on both the theoretical and legal fronts.

In fact, most reasonable observers would agree that RPM is neither always benign nor universally undesirable. Hence, there are cases where it should be prohibited and others where it should be allowed. The main problem is one of the burden of proof: should the practice be legal except when shown to be undesirable, or should evidence be presented to overturn a presumption of undesirability? The answer to this question will decide to a large extent the effectiveness of law enforcement in this area.

Whatever the merits of one or the other approach, the fact is that RPM was very popular before its legal prohibition. Thus, before 1951 it was estimated that 20 percent of goods sold through grocery stores and 60 percent of those sold through drugstores were subject to some form of RPM. The practice was also quite popular during the 1950s in the United Kingdom, but less so in the United States. It has since been outlawed in both these countries, although the legal status of RPM in the U.S. has become quite controversial during the 1980s.

The attitude that one adopts with respect to RPM depends on the underlying motivation for its use. Those who emphasize its positive aspects attribute its use to a desire on the part of the manufacturers to compete on non-price elements of the final product. Such elements are the increased availability of the product in retail outlets that would not otherwise stock it, and the enhancement of product quality through information or post-sales service. By contrast, the negative view of RPM focusses on its potential as an instrument to enforce cartel coordination: by suppressing competition at the retail level RPM makes it easier to maintain the stability of the upstream cartel. More recent objections have emphasized the effects of RPM (and, more generally, of vertical restraints) on consumer welfare when there is demand or cost uncertainty.

One possible explanation for RPM is the desire to increase the number of retail outlets carrying the product. Gallini and Winter (1983) presented a model of a monopolistic producer facing a demand curve at the retail level that is a function of both product price and number of retailers, with the latter having a positive influence on demand. The retail market is assumed monopolistically competitive, and free entry ensures that retailers earn zero economic profit. The monopolist sets the wholesale price, and may or may not decide to set a retail price by imposing a price floor on its retailers. The authors identify conditions on the demand elasticities that may render an RPM scheme profitable. In the monopolistically competitive retail market there is a market demand curve that depends on the number of retailers as well as on the product price. There are also individual demand curves for each retail firm. RPM is profitable if and only if the price elasticity of the market demand curve is less than the product of the price elasticity of an individual firm's demand curve times the elasticity of market demand with respect to the number of retailers. The authors also find conditions that make the resulting industry equilibrium socially preferable to the one resulting from a legal prohibition on RPM, on the basis of the criterion of maximization of total surplus. Last, they show that these conditions are satisfied in a simple form of the product demand function. All these results are developed in some detail in Appendix 9A.

Another popular argument of RPM defenders is the one associated with quality differentials arising at the retail level. These can be pre-sales information about product characteristics or quality, post-sales servicing, or quality certification. In all these cases it is claimed that in the absence of an RPM scheme there would be few incentives to provide these quality enhancements: consumers can get a "free ride" on them, by shopping at discount stores after informing themselves at the stores that provide the extra service. Hence, the total supply of these additional quality characteristics will be suboptimal if an adequate retail markup is not guaranteed via RPM.

Crucial to all these benign views of RPM are the assumptions about the market structure at the upstream and downstream stages of the market, the manufacturer and retailer levels. RPM is viewed as a manner of compensating the retailer for services that entail extra costs. These costs cannot be recovered in a competitive retail market. The manufacturer must therefore alter the structure of the downstream market in order to create incentives for the provision of the enhancement services. RPM is one way of such a change in structure, since it essentially transfers market power from one stage to the other. It is also claimed that alternative institutional arrangements aimed at the same objective are bound to be more costly and hence less socially efficient than RPM.

At first glance, these views appear counterintuitive. Why should a transfer of monopoly power be desirable on social grounds? Alternatively, why is it not preferable, from the consumers' point of view, to encourage more competition at the retail level by prohibiting RPM and all other types of vertical restraints? It was, however, shown that in the absence of uncertainty, and ignoring the potential benefits of improved quality or information, the consumers are generally unaffected by the presence or absence of vertical restraints. The latter affect only the distribution of the profits between the upstream and downstream producers. Further, in a wide variety of circumstances it can be shown that aggregate surplus is increased if vertical restraints are allowed.

These findings have been challenged in the most recent contribution on the subject, by Rey and Tirole (1986). These authors have examined the efficiency of various arrangements between manufacturer and retailer in the presence of demand or cost uncertainty. The cases studied include competition, RPM, and exclusive territories (ET). The authors show that in contrast to the certainty analysis, there should be a general presumption in favour of competition: in general, consumers are better off under competition than under either RPM or ET. Further, the aggregate surplus may not be enhanced by allowing vertical restraints, implying a conflict between the social and private objectives. The Rey-Tirole analysis ignores the dependence of the market demand on the number of retailers, which formed a cornerstone of the Gallini and Winter (1983) results. It also ignores the RPM effects on the supply of quality or informational enhancements by the retailer. Nonetheless, it is more general than the earlier studies in the uncertainty aspects, and hence it does tend to cast some doubts on the desirability of following the recommendations of the MacDonald Commission on the relaxation of the per se illegality of RPM.

A clear-cut case against RPM can be made when it arises in an oligopoly context, at either the manufacturer level, or more rarely the retailer level. It can be shown that when a retailers' cartel exists, RPM entails lower total surplus, as well as a transfer of surplus from the consumers and the manufacturer to the retailers. Further, the imposition of a minimum retail price and the transfer of profits may act as a shield for inefficient retailers, as with all cartels. This explanation of RPM, though, is considered to apply in only rare cases, given the fact that there seems to be more support for RPM among manufacturers than among retailers' groups. Nonetheless, some authors believe that the main economic case against RPM rests on its anticompetitive effects at the retail level.

Another reason for the adoption of RPM is the maintenance of cartel stability at the upstream level. The main Canadian example in this case is the electric large lamps price-fixing cartel, already reviewed in the previous section. As we saw, that particular cartel found it most difficult to coordinate prices at the retail level, in spite of the agreement at the manufacturer level. The existence of price competition at the retail level makes it difficult to avoid breakdowns of the cartel agreement, since retail price differences may be misunderstood for secret price concessions. In such a context, an RPM scheme would greatly facilitate price-fixing and should therefore be illegal.

What should one conclude on the basis of these arguments about the overall desirability of RPM? A pragmatic view of the net benefits of the practice would support its prohibition in the presence of a retailer or manufacturer cartel, as Mathewson and Winter (1985) recommended in their background study for the MacDonald Royal Commission.[12] It is very difficult, though, to agree with their contention that the burden of proof in showing that RPM supports a cartel at the upstream or downstream levels should rest with the government. From the point of view of cartel coordination, RPM is similar to basing-point pricing, which, as we saw in the previous section, is a powerful price-fixing tool. Its use should be illegal per se when there is market power at the producer or retailer level and the quality enhancement arguments are clearly not applicable. The retail gasoline market, where market power at the manufacturing level exists, and where several RPM cases have occurred recently,[13] is a perfect example of a market in which the practice should continue to be illegal without any further burden of proof for the prosecution.

The arguments for the beneficial effects of RPM are more convincing when it can be demonstrated that it supports quality improvements which would not be available without it because of the aforementioned free-rider problem. Such arguments were not affected by the conclusions of the Rey and Tirole (1986) study, which cast serious doubts on the overall efficiency of RPM. Thus it would seem advisable to allow RPM in such cases, with the burden of proof placed on the firm. The only disadvantage of such an approach is that it would place rather heavy analytical demands upon the trial judge.

Legally, RPM cases do not present as much interest as overt and tacit price collusion, due to the clear-cut nature of the law. Mathewson and Winter (1985) present a summary list of all Canadian RPM convictions until 1983.[14] One is struck by the small fines imposed in most cases: the maximal amount was $150,000, paid by Levi Strauss of Canada in 1979. One half of the recorded cases in 1980-83 had fines equalling $10,000 or less.

Other Types of Vertical Restraints

In addition to RPM, vertical restraints on competition at the retail level can be imposed through exclusive territories (ET), tied sales, and exclusive dealing. The legal status of most of these practices is not as clear-cut as that of RPM. They may be prohibited by the public authorities if it is established that they have anticompetitive effects. They were made part of competition law relatively recently, through the addition of a new section in the relevant legislation in 1976. The 1986 amendments leave their status unchanged, but they transfer jurisdiction to the newly-created competition tribunal. Prior to these amendments it was the Restrictive Trade Practices Commission (RTPC) that decided these cases, under civil law provisions. Relatively few cases have been brought up in Canada under these provisions.

ET or, more generally, territorial restrictions, refer to the practice by an upstream manufacturer of assigning customers on a geographical basis to different retailers. This assignment can take place through restrictions in the retailer's franchise, or through a more direct intervention of the manufacturer in the allocation of customers to the retailers. It has been a legal practice in Canada until now, given the fact that franchise contracts have not become the focus of competition policy.

The economic analysis of ET is very similar to that of RPM. Indeed, some authors have argued that ET and RPM can be substitutes, insofar as they both reduce competition at the retail level. This conclusion has been challenged in the Rey and Tirole (1986) study, where it is shown that the two practices behave quite differently under demand or cost uncertainty. They point out that from the point of view of the upstream manufacturer, ET is superior to RPM under cost uncertainty. RPM, on the other hand, dominates ET under demand uncertainty when retailers are very averse to risk, since it has better insurance properties. Consumers are likely to prefer competition to either practice when the quality enhancement dimension is ignored.

Like RPM, ET can also contribute to a cartel's market power at the manufacturer or retailer level. Nonetheless, there is little evidence that it has been used in this way in either the United States or Canada. In the U.S. the practice was initially illegal per se, but it is now subject to a rule of reason. In Canada there have been no judicial cases involving ET, but dealership assignments surfaced as an issue in one recent civil case.[15]

The practice of tying sales is defined as making the purchase of one good conditional on the purchase of another. This practice comes in two different forms: the purchaser of one unit of one product must also purchase one unit of another product, an arrangement known as *bundling*; alternatively, the purchaser of one product must also purchase all requirements for another product from the same supplier. Both types are encountered very commonly in the business world. For instance, the latter type occurs when automobile dealers link the sale of new car warranties to the customer's purchase of basic maintenance services from the dealer's own facilities. The tourist industry frequently ties the sale of discounted air tickets to the purchase of hotel and restaurant services at the destination, an example of bundling. Such practices are legal, and no one is suggesting that they be made illegal per se, even though they may reduce welfare in some cases.

Tied sales can become objectionable when they serve as an extension of monopoly power from one market to another. The market in which monopoly power exists is the *tying* market. The monopolist extends his power to the *tied* market by requiring the purchasers of its monopolized product(s) to purchase from him their requirements in that second market. This is a particularly effective measure if the two goods are complementary, as is the case of most tied sales in practice.

A classic case of such an extension of monopoly position existed in the Canadian telecommunications industry up till the mid-1970s. The sales of terminal telephone equipment were tied to the purchases of the basic telephone service, where the market was a legal monopoly. That monopoly was thus extended de facto to the supply of equipment. The practice was terminated by order of the regulatory commission, with the result that by the early 1980s the telephone equipment market had become effectively competitive.

The legal status of tied sales in Canada is covered by section 31(4) of the legislation, which gives the right to the appropriate agency to issue cease and desist orders when the practice is found to reduce competition substantially. This civil law section was added in 1976. The 1986 amendments changed the administrative part, by shifting authority from the RTPC to the newly-created Competition Tribunal. Only one case has been decided under this section as of this writing, involving the bundling of data on TV and radio audiences for sale to advertisers.[16] A company that held the monopoly in the radio market was sued by its competitor in the TV market, which alleged that the bundling practice prevented its own expansion. The RTPC agreed and issued a cease and desist order.

We close this review of vertical restraints with the practice of exclusive dealing (ED). This can take two possible forms: a requirement by a manufacturer that its retailers carry only its products to the exclusion of all competitors; alternatively, a retailer can require that a manufacturer sell its product through him or her exclusively. ED is more frequently encountered in its first form.

Legally ED is very similar to tied sales, insofar as both are covered by the aforementioned section 31(4). Only one case has been heard by the RTPC till now, involving complaints by eight dealers of equipment supplied by the Bombardier company, whose franchises were cancelled. The firm, which had the lion's share of the market in Eastern Canada, was enforcing ED contracts on its retailers. The RTPC rejected the complaint, by arguing that Bombardier's practices did not substantially lessen competition in the retail market.

The economic analysis of ED is quite complex and ambiguous in its welfare conclusions. The key element in this analysis is the modelling of the interaction between manufacturer and retailer. This interaction is in turn dependent upon the structure of the retail market. If this market is sufficiently small, so that it can support only one retailer (as it happens in many small towns), then the imposition of ED reduces the set of possible consumers' choices. This does not mean that consumers are necessarily worse off, since ED may also result in lower retail price: the retailer, in order to accept ED, may have to be offered a lower wholesale price and some of the resultant savings may be passed on to the consumers. Another effect of ED is the protection against free riders when the manufacturer offers additional information about product characteristics. In such a case ED is similar to RPM, insofar as in its absence competitors can benefit from the information without having to invest in it. Mathewson and Winter (1985) have analyzed various scenarios together with their attendant welfare effects.[17] They show that there are situations in which ED improves general welfare, and others where it does not. This means that the public policy approach to ED should be the rule of reason, as it currently is. In general, sunk investments by the manufacturer (whose benefits may be appropriated by competitors), the existence of substitute products, easy entry at the retail level, and short-lived dealership contracts are factors supporting the beneficial effects of ED.

Predatory Pricing and Other Tactics, and Price Discrimination

As we saw in Chapter 5, predatory pricing is a subset in an arsenal of tactics available to monopolies or collusive oligopolies to prevent entry by competitors. All these tactics are essentially investments by the incumbent in entry barriers, whose ultimate effect is to maintain the existing market structure. We also saw that there are many cases in which such investment may be profitable, depending on structural factors and basic conditions.

The very existence and profitability of predatory pricing has been a contentious issue in the economics literature. The classic case of predation via pricing was thought to be that of Standard Oil of New Jersey during the early part of the 20th Century. Yet, this supposed showcase came under attack from Chicago School economists,[18] who raised serious questions about the rationality of such predation under any circumstances. In fact, as we argued in Chapters 1 and 7, the infeasibility of profitable predation by any means is central to the Chicago School's view of the economic environment.

This particular part of the Chicago arguments has been decisively overturned by recent theoretical developments. The profitability of predatory tactics such as excess capacity, brand proliferation, locational preemption, and predatory pricing via reputation factors has been demonstrated in a number of theoretical and empirical case studies.[19] The key public policy issue that we'll examine in this section is the type of responses that can be made to such tactics. The dividing line between competition and predation is a very thin one, and it is not easy to derive laws and policies that are both fair and efficient.

In Canada the legal control of predatory tactics is the object of two separate sections of competition legislation. Section 33, the merger and monopoly section discussed in the previous chapter, prohibits the formation and operation of a monopoly "to the detriment or against the interest of the public . . ."; in applying the law, predatory tactics have often been included in the definition of objectionable behaviour. In section 34(1), on the other hand, there is a clause dealing specifically with predatory pricing. It prohibits, under penalty of imprisonment, pricing that is "unreasonably low, having the effect or tendency of substantially lessening competition or eliminating a competitor, or designed to have such effect."

The 1986 amendments affected, as we saw, section 33 in its merger provisions. They also brought substantial changes to the behavioural part of monopoly control. A new provision was included that deals with "abuse of dominance" by a firm or by a group of firms acting jointly. This abuse of dominance is now a civil offence under the jurisdiction of the newly-created Competition Tribunal, along with the rest of the merger provisions; it replaces the criminal offence of monopoly under the old law.

There were also substantive changes in the wording of the law. The vagueness of the "public detriment" clause has been replaced by more specific behavioural considerations. A non-exhaustive list of objectionable acts is provided, such as the squeezing of profit margins of vertically-integrated customers, the use of fighting brands, and freight equalization. The law is restricted to monopolies or near-monopolies and cartels, and the actions must prevent or lessen competition "substantially." There is also an available defence that ensures that no adverse decision will be made when the lessening of competition occurs as a result of superior competitive performance of the dominant firm or firms.

Most of the judicial cases involving predation have been brought under the more general monopoly section 33 of the old law, rather than section 34 that deals specifically with predatory pricing. Overall, there have been comparatively few such cases till now. The most famous application of the monopoly section to secure a conviction for predatory behaviour was in 1952 in the *R. v. Eddy Match Co. Ltd. et al.* case. That firm had managed to maintain a monopoly position in the market for wooden matches in Canada by absorbing its rivals or driving them out of business. A variety of tactics including but not limited to predatory pricing were used in these efforts. Section 34, on the other hand, was applied successfully in 1980, in the case of a pharmaceutical company that gave away a particular drug for free to hospitals for a year, with the purpose of eliminating a competitor.[20]

There is little doubt that the control of predatory behaviour is one of the most difficult areas of competition law enforcement. In the U.S., which pioneers in legal and economic thinking in such matters, two "frontier" cases in antitrust policy were concerned with predation.[21] These were the IBM and breakfast cereals cases, already discussed in previous chapters. Both cases were eventually abandoned by the antitrust authorities after extensive legal battles. In the IBM case the company was accused of erecting barriers to competitors' entry in the market for general-purpose electronic computer systems. This was achieved by tying sales (mostly in the form of bundling of software and servicing when leasing its computers), and by new product announcements as soon as a competitor came up with a new model. As for the breakfast cereals industry, the central issue was the erection of entry barriers by brand proliferation, as discussed extensively in Chapter 5.

The difficulties of using legal tools to prevent predatory behaviour are further illustrated by a recent case study by Lieberman (1987), in the U.S. chemical process industry. The focus in that study was on the use of excess capacity as a barrier to entry. Evidence of capacity as an entry deterrence instrument was found in only four products (aniline, sorbitol, magnesium, and neoprene rubber), representing about 10 percent of the total. However, there were also many instances where the threat of capacity expansion was used very effectively by incumbents to induce cancellation of entry plans announced by some new firm.[22] Lieberman attributes these cancellations to reputation factors. However, they are also perfectly consistent with the excess capacity argument if it is assumed (as is likely) that incumbents can expand capacity faster than a new entrant can establish itself. It is clear that such incumbent conduct is an effective predatory tactic that does not enhance public welfare. It is also very difficult to see what one can do about it. At any rate, the new Canadian law is certainly a step in the right direction, although final judgment will have to await evidence from its application.

The last public policy that will be considered in this chapter deals with price discrimination. It is covered by section 34(1) of the law in two paragraphs. One subsection prohibits discrimination by a seller between buyers of his product who all buy articles "of like quality and quantity." The second subsection is aimed at geographical price discrimination, forbidding the seller from lowering prices in one part of the country with the aim of eliminating a local competitor. In other words, the second subsection is really aimed at predatory conduct, while the first one attempts to prevent discrimination by buyer size. This last objective is not fulfilled very effectively, since large buyers clearly do not purchase similar quantities as small ones.

The price discrimination part of the law, which like most of the sections dealing with pricing is based on criminal law, has been used very rarely. Only a few investigations by the RTPC have taken place, of which only one ended up in the courts. It was lost by the prosecution.[23] Even that case was more a predatory pricing case rather than a price discrimination case. As we saw in Chapter 6, price discrimination is a tactic that is difficult to enforce; it may also be beneficial to general welfare. It can be more easily dealt with in its objectionable forms under the more general abuse of dominance provisions of the law.

Conclusions

Within the structure-conduct-performance model there are two broad categories of objectives for public policies aimed at firm conduct. The first one is applicable to those industries in which the structure is oligopolistic or monopolistic, and destined to remain so because of the existing market size and economies of scale effects. In such cases, public policies are narrowly focussed at conduct. They aim at preventing the exploitation of market power in pricing decisions. Essentially this amounts to the prohibition of overtly coordinated pricing behaviour in oligopolies.

The second category of objectives is structural in nature. Here the basic assumption is that dominant firms and/or cartels can profitably adopt behaviour that maintains the non-competitive structure of their industries even when the basic conditions indicate that it should change. This predatory behaviour can be related to pricing, investment, location, brand choice, or any other dimension of firm conduct. The aim of public policies in these instances is the discouragement of such behaviour, in a manner consistent with the basic freedom to compete against existing firms and new entrants.

Both categories of policies are fraught with difficulties and ambiguities of legal and economic nature. Policies aimed at collusive pricing must contend with the burden of proof of illegal behaviour based only on circumstantial evidence. In such cases, the legal rules must draw the dividing line between collusion and failure to compete. Also, they must decide when coordinated behaviour of firms in an oligopoly is evidence of an underlying agreement, as distinct from a common response to the same economic factors facing the industry.

The difficulties associated with the control of predatory conduct are equally formidable. Here the public authority must decide when a particular type of competitive conduct by a dominant firm or collusive oligopoly is really an attempt to avoid competition in the long run, by driving actual or potential rivals out of business. This decision has to take into account potential differences in efficiency between the target firm or firms, and the rivals that its conduct is harming. In other words, the ultimate choice of the public authority must be the course of action that will bring the greatest benefits to public welfare.

A related set of public policies is concerned with the extension of market power from an upstream to a downstream firm or industry, or vice-versa. The public welfare criterion is ambiguous here as well. As it turns out, this market power extension can be used to support quality or informational improvements that would increase welfare. It can also be used to increase the effectiveness of collusive pricing at the stage in which market power already exists. As with predatory conduct, it is not always clear which decision is best.

The existing Canadian legislation is a mixture of criminal law in the case of pricing, and civil law in most other types of conduct. The 1986 amendments were relatively less important in the conduct area than in the merger provisions. They had very little effect in the cases of price collusion, which remain under criminal law. They also did not touch the vertical restraint and price discrimination parts of the law, which continue to be a mixture of criminal and civil law; they did, however, change the administrative part of civil law enforcement, by creating the Competition Tribunal. Last, the amendments shifted part of the control of predatory behaviour to civil law. Several of these changes are considered as steps in the right direction by most economists, but the impression also exists that legislators stopped short of designing a really effective law.

Appendix 9A ECONOMIC ANALYSIS OF RESALE PRICE MAINTENANCE

In the absence of quality enhancements, RPM may be profitable for an upstream monopolist supplying a competitive retail market because it encourages an increase in the number of retail outlets offering the product. In other words, the market demand depends both on the product price and on the number of retailers stocking the product. In turn this number is a function of the retail margin. Although the competitive retail market ensures that free entry will eventually eliminate all profits, the equilibrium number of firms may be higher under RPM than in the absence of restrictions. From the upstream firm's point of view, this increase in the number of retailers may push the product demand curve sufficiently upwards in order to overcome the effects of the higher retail price.

Let W and P denote the wholesale and retail prices respectively. There are m retail firms, each one facing a demand curve depending on m, on its own price, and on all the other $m-1$ prices. Hence, the ith firm faces a demand curve $Q_i(P_1, \ldots, P_m; m)$, where P_i is the price charged by the ith firm, $i = 1, \ldots, m$. The market demand curve, on the other hand, is the sum of the m demand curves under symmetric pricing conditions, $P_1 = P_2 = \ldots = P_m$; hence, $Q(P,m) = \sum_{i=1}^{m} Q_i(P, \ldots, P; m)$. There are also the following three elasticity concepts:

$$\epsilon_D = -\frac{\partial Q}{\partial P} \times \frac{P}{Q} \qquad \epsilon_m = \frac{\partial Q}{\partial m} \times \frac{m}{Q}$$

$$\epsilon_d = -\frac{P_i}{Q_i}\left[\frac{\partial Q_i}{\partial P_i} + \sum_{j\neq i}\frac{\partial Q_i}{\partial P_j}\frac{\partial P_j}{\partial P_i}\right]$$

where ϵ_d also includes the conjectural variations, the effects of a change in price of the ith firm on all other retailers' prices. Note that $Q(P,m)$ increases in m.

We assume, for simplicity and without loss of generality, that each retailer pays a fixed cost of F, while all other variable costs (apart from the wholesale price W) are zero. There are two alternative upstream firm policies being considered.

(i) A non-integrated profit maximization at the upstream level, given that a competitive equilibrium has been established at the retail level.
(ii) An integrated profit maximization through an RPM policy, given that the retail sector stays at a zero profit level through free entry.

Under (i) the retailer profit is maximized with respect to P for a given W, while the number of firms m is given from the zero profit condition, again for a fixed W. If $\pi_i = Q_i [P_i - W]$ is the ith firm's profit, where $Q_i \equiv Q_i(P_1, \ldots, P_m; m)$, then profit maximization implies

$$Q_i + (P_i - W)\left[\frac{\partial Q_i}{\partial P_i} + \sum_{j\neq i}\frac{\partial Q_i}{\partial P_j}\frac{\partial P_j}{\partial P_i}\right] = 0$$

for which we get for $P_1 = \ldots = P_m \equiv P$,

$$\frac{P - W}{P} = \frac{1}{\epsilon_d} \qquad\qquad \textbf{Eq. (9A.1)}$$

The zero-profit condition, on the other hand, implies

$$\frac{1}{m}Q(P,m)\,[P-W] = F \qquad\qquad \textbf{Eq. (9A.2)}$$

Given (9A.1) and (9A.2) (which define implicitly m and P), the upstream producer maximizes with respect to W its profit

$$\pi(W; P,m) = WQ(P,m) - C(Q(P,m)) \qquad \textbf{Eq. (9A.3)}$$

where C is the upstream firm's cost function.

Under policy (ii), on the other hand, the upstream firm maximizes its profit given by (9A.3) with respect to both W and P, subject to only the constraint (9A.2). Let $\hat{P}$ and $\hat{W}$ denote the optimal choices resulting from this policy. The first-order conditions from the maximization of (9A.3) yield:

$$\left(\hat{W} - \frac{\partial C}{\partial Q}\right)\left(\frac{\partial Q}{\partial P} + \frac{\partial Q}{\partial m}\frac{\partial m}{\partial P}\right) = 0 \quad\text{and}\quad Q + \left(\hat{W} - \frac{\partial C}{\partial Q}\right)\left(\frac{\partial Q}{\partial m}\frac{\partial m}{\partial W}\right) = 0$$

Since the second one implies $W \neq \frac{\partial C}{\partial Q}$, the first one yields $\frac{\partial Q}{\partial P} + \frac{\partial Q}{\partial m}\frac{\partial m}{\partial P} = 0$, which becomes

$$\frac{\partial m}{\partial P} = \frac{m}{\hat{P}}\frac{\epsilon_D}{\epsilon_m} \qquad\qquad \textbf{Eq. (9A.4)}$$

On the other hand, by differentiating (9A.2) with respect to P we get $F\frac{\partial m}{\partial P} = \frac{\partial Q}{\partial P}(\hat{P} - \hat{W}) + Q + \frac{\partial Q}{\partial m}\frac{\partial m}{\partial P}(\hat{P} - \hat{W})$, which yields, after re-arranging and substituting (9A.4),

$$\frac{\hat{P} - \hat{W}}{\hat{P}} = \frac{\epsilon_m}{\epsilon_D} \qquad\qquad \textbf{Eq. (9A.5)}$$

The comparison of policies (i) and (ii) will take place under a common wholesale price equal to $\hat{W}$. Then an RPM policy is profitable if and only if $\epsilon_D < \epsilon_d\,\epsilon_m$ at the corresponding equilibrium point. This condition on the elasticities is derived from (9A.1) and (9A.5): RPM is profitable if and only if $\hat{P}$ turns out to exceed P under policy (i), which by (9A.1) and (9A.5) implies the inequality on the demand elasticities.

The evaluation of the welfare impact of RPM needs more restrictive assumptions on the shape of the demand function $Q(P,m)$. Gallini and Winter (1983) derive a condition on the elasticity ϵ_D and the consumer surplus that if satisfied guarantees that RPM is socially desirable if it is privately desirable. This condition, however, is valid only if $Q(P,m)$ is separable in P and m, i.e. if it can be written as a product of two functions $h(m)q(P)$. Last, they show that the condition is indeed satisfied if, in addition, the elasticities are constant over the relevant range.

What drives the results of the Gallini-Winter model is very clearly the dependence of the market demand $Q(P,m)$ on the number of retailers m. If this dependence is omitted, i.e. if either demand is insensitive to m or the number of retailers is fixed exogenously, then policies (i) and (ii) can be easily shown to be equivalent under certainty, and RPM is not a rational policy. The retail price P is simply a function of W, derived from the zero-profit condition (9A.2), while the market operates as if the upstream firm were a perfectly integrated monopolist. However, Rey and Tirole (1986) showed that even in such a case, RPM or exclusive territories (ET) can arise as optimal policy responses of the upstream firm under demand or cost uncertainty.

The Rey-Tirole model is a specialization of the one presented here. The cost function $C(Q(P,m))$ is assumed linear, i.e. $C(Q) = cQ$. The retailers have no fixed cost ($F = 0$), but they face a linear variable retail cost, over and above the wholesale price W, whose coefficient α may be random; they may also be charged a fixed franchise fee A. m is assumed fixed and (without loss of generality) equal to 2, while competition in retailing is ensured through the assumption of a Bertrand duopoly behaviour. Hence, the retail price P is equal to the retailers' marginal cost, i.e. $P = W + \alpha$. Last, the market demand $Q(P,m)$ is a linear function of P, with a possibly random intercept.

The authors find the wholesale price W and franchise fee A that maximize expected upstream profits under the three alternative policies of unrestrained competition (i.e. Bertrand duopoly), ET and RPM. In the latter two cases the retailers maximize profits after the uncertain demand or cost parameters have been observed, given the manufacturer's chosen W and A. The welfare implications of each policy are compared by evaluating the expected total (consumer plus wholesaler) surplus, and the wholesaler's expected profit. As noted in this text, it is no longer true that RPM would improve welfare. In fact, the study shows that when demand is linear, aggregate welfare under competition is higher than under ET or RPM, implying that anticompetitive restraints should always be prohibited.

Endnotes

1. See, however, Dewey (1979) for a spirited if not very convincing defence of collusion.

2. See the *Ottawa Citizen*, March 17, 1987.

3. See the account of the successive stages till the introduction of the final legislation in Green (1985), pp. 297-304.

4. See Canada, Consumer and Corporate Affairs (1985), pp. 26-29.

5. An extensive discussion of this concept is in Scherer (1980), pp. 513-520.

6. In fact, Thisse and Vives (1988) have argued that if a basing-point system is observed in practice, "most probably it is because it serves as a coordinating or collusive device in a situation of repeated competition" (p. 134). They reach this conclusion by showing that the system is not a rational choice for competing firms.

7. They are known as the *R. v. Canadian General Electric Co. et al.* (1976) and *R. v. Armco Canada Ltd. et al.* (1974) cases.

8. See Stigler (1964), p. 46.

9. For a hostile account of these attempts see the essay in Chapter 5 of the collection edited by Walter Block (1986).

10. Mathewson and Winter (1985), p. 11.

11. See the preface in Mathewson and Winter (1985), pp. xv-xvi. Unless referenced otherwise, most of the material in this section is based on that study.

12. ———. (1985), p. 103.

13. For instance, the 1985 conviction of Imperial Oil to a $75,000 fine, the 1986 conviction of Sunoco to a $200,000 fine, and the 1989 conviction of Shell Oil to a $100,000 fine.

14. See Mathewson and Winter (1985), pp. 103-116.

15. ———. (1985), pp. 64-65.

16. This is the case of *Bureau of Broadcast Measurement* (BBM) (1981) decided by the RTPC.

17. See Mathewson and Winter (1985), pp. 90-100.

18. In particular J.S. McGee (1958).

19. See Chapter 5.

20. This was the *R. v. Hoffman-LaRoche Ltd.* (1980) case.

21. See Caves (1987), pp. 95-96.

22. In turn, the incumbent withdrew its own expansion plans in most instances once entry was forestalled.

23. *R. v. Carnation Company of Canada Ltd.* (1969).

References

Block, W., ed. *Reaction: The New Combines Investigation Act.* Vancouver, B.C.: The Fraser Institute, 1986.

Caves, R. *American Industry: Structure, Conduct, Performance.* Englewood Cliffs, N.J.: Prentice-Hall, 1987.

Department of Consumer and Corporate Affairs. *Competition Law Amendments: A Guide.* Ottawa, Ont.: Minister of Supply and Services Canada, 1985.

Dewey, D. "Information, Entry and Welfare: The Case for Collusion," *American Economic Review,* 69:4 (September 1979), pp. 587-594.

Gallini, N. and R. Winter. "On Vertical Control in Monopolistic Competition," *International Journal of Industrial Organization,* 1 (Sept. 1983), pp. 275-286.

Gorecki, P.K. and W.T. Stanbury. *The Objectives of Canadian Competition Policy 1888-1983.* Montreal, PQ: Institute for Research in Public Policy, 1984.

Green, C. *Canadian Industrial Organization and Policy.* Toronto, Ont.: McGraw-Hill Ryerson, 2nd Edition, 1985.

Lieberman, M. "Excess Capacity as a Barrier to Entry: An Empirical Appraisal," *Journal of Industrial Economics,* 35:4 (June 1987), pp. 607-627.

Mathewson, G.F. and R.A. Winter. *Competition Policy and Vertical Exchange.* Toronto, Ont.: University of Toronto Press, 1986.

McGee, J.S. "Predatory Price Cutting: The Standard Oil (N.J.) Case," *Journal of Law and Economics,* (Oct. 1958), pp. 259-277.

Rey, P. and J. Tirole. "The Logic of Vertical Restraints," *American Economic Review,* 76:5 (Dec. 1986), pp. 921-939.

Scherer, F.M. *Industrial Market Structure and Economic Performance.* Chicago, Ill.: Rand McNally, 1980.

Stigler, G.J. "A Theory of Oligopoly," *Journal of Political Economy,* 72 (Feb. 1964), pp. 44-61.

Thisse, J.F. and X. Vives. "On the Strategic Choice of Spatial Price Policy," *American Economic Review,* 78:1 (March 1988), pp. 122-137.

CHAPTER 10

Economic

··

Regulation

··

T his chapter reviews the public policies that are collectively known under the rather misleading term of economic regulation. These policies apply to real or alleged cases of market failure in which it is decided that for some reason or other an administrative mechanism will replace all or part of the market system. As it is currently used in practice, the label of "economic regulation" covers a long list of policies and practices belonging to many different areas of economics. Some of these areas can be fitted into the structure-conduct-performance (SCP) model, while others lie outside it. The latter will be reviewed rather more briefly, in spite of the importance that some of them have assumed in recent years.

The original use of the term "regulation" was associated with the control of natural monopolies. As we saw in Chapter 3, an industry in which the minimum efficient size is close to or exceeds the size of the market must be allowed to operate as a monopoly. This also implies that public policy must impose some curbs on its pricing, as well as on other types of conduct. The economic effects of these curbs were examined in detail in that chapter. This chapter will review the basic policy issues as they have been shaped by recent regulatory decisions, and the evolving ideas about the role and impact of public policies. The discussion will draw heavily upon the theory developed earlier.

We shall, however, spend more time in this chapter on sectors subjected to direct regulation that are not natural monopolies. There are a number of such sectors within the Canadian economy. These are industries that, although oligopolistic or competitive in nature, have been subjected to a regulatory system similar to the one used for natural monopolies. For some of these industries there are sound economic reasons why the market system was not allowed to operate. In others the imposition of a regulatory regime was basically a political decision that runs counter to economic theory.

A regulatory system has been imposed on some industries that rely heavily on a production input that is a common property resource. Radio and television broadcasting and commercial fishing are typical examples of such industries. In the former, regulation comes from the necessity to allocate each broadcaster's position on the electromagnetic spectrum. In commercial fisheries, on the other hand, it is the need to prevent the depletion of the fishing stocks that mandates government intervention. In both cases the reasons for regulation are legitimate. Of interest to us, though, are the (perhaps unintended) effects upon the industry of the particular regulatory regime that was imposed, especially in relation to the professed objectives of regulation.

Little if any economic support can be found, on the other hand, for the type of regulation imposed on other industries such as some agricultural commodities (dairy products, eggs, and poultry), and parts of the transportation sector such as the taxicab business and trucking. Here, the structure of the industries would have been competitive had economic forces been allowed to operate. The regulatory regime was created for political reasons after lobbying by the producers. Some of these sectors have come under pressure to deregulate in more recent years.

Other types of regulation that will be examined in this chapter lie outside the SCP model. They refer to restrictions on firm conduct that have been imposed across the board, affecting all industries. They include environmental protection and occupational health and safety regulation, which, although they are not sector-specific in most cases, are more important in some sectors than in others. The purpose of these types of regulation is the control of the so-called *externalities*, meaning the effects that the industries' operation has upon workers and the environment. They will be covered relatively briefly in this chapter, given that they require a different methodology from the one used in the SCP model.

The next section will first examine various theories seeking to explain why regulation is introduced into a sector. Then we shall consider the regulation of natural monopolies, followed by the other sectors covered by direct regulation. The chapter closes with the study of the control of externalities.

Theories of Economic Regulation

Economic regulation, as currently practised, is a substitute for competition policy. Indeed, competition law specifically exempts from its application those industries, sectors, and professions subject to regulation. The state imposes curbs on the conduct of the regulated firm or firms according to some principle.

It also shelters these firms from competition, either among themselves or from new entrants. Questions that arise concern the rules governing the choice of sectors to which regulation should be imposed. These have produced a number of theories in which economic reasoning interacts with politics to explain the emerging pattern of regulated industries.

As noted in the previous section, there are two broad categories of regulation. Direct or old regulation is the sector-specific set of restrictions on firm conduct, initially associated with natural monopolies but eventually extended to other sectors. Indirect or new regulation is associated with environmental protection, product quality, and occupational health and safety. The theories of regulation are mostly relevant to direct regulation. Few economists would dispute the need for some type of regulation of the indirect type; the only questions concern its extent and form.

The economic rationale for regulating natural monopolies was already examined in Chapter 3. We also saw that there were a number of drawbacks to regulation from the efficiency point of view, even in these supposedly clear-cut cases. Although efforts are continuing to develop regulatory schemes that avoid these inefficiencies, it is doubtful that such schemes can succeed under all circumstances. Two obvious alternatives to the regulation of a private monopoly firm are the removal of all restrictions on conduct, and the replacement of the private monopoly with a public enterprise.

The first option was proposed by Demsetz (1968), who used the argument that a superior alternative to the regulation of a private monopoly was the auctioning of the monopoly franchise to the highest bidder. The public authority could then use the proceeds of the auction in order to correct any socially undesirable effects of the operation of the firm as an unrestricted monopolist.[1] Williamson (1976) details a case study of an attempt to apply this scheme in the allocation of a cable television licence.[2] His conclusions are that the practical problems of franchise auctioning are likely to overshadow the efficiency gains. It is, however, difficult to find these arguments totally convincing, given the limited experience and the reluctance to undertake efforts in this direction. Proposals to allocate broadcasting and cable TV licences on that same basis were also made in Canada by Perrakis and Silva-Echenique (1983, 1985). As detailed further on in this chapter, the performance of the Canadian broadcasting system has been totally unsatisfactory in relation to its public policy objectives. Hence, it is hard to see how the auctioning proposals could result in anything worse than the existing situation. At any rate, the Demsetz arguments have not found widespread acceptance to date even in the comparatively simple cable TV industry, let alone in the more difficult public utility sectors.

The public enterprise option is quite common in Canada and Europe, even though ideological considerations have prevented its widespread adoption in the U.S. This option will be examined in more detail in the next chapter. Inefficiency arguments against this option are present in an even greater degree than for private firm regulation. As we shall see, the empirical evidence shows that there is little room for choice between private and public monopolies from the efficiency point of view. The public enterprise option, though, is not applicable to regulated sectors that are not natural monopolies.

Once the two alternatives to the regulation of private firms are rejected, one must come back to the question of which industries should be regulated. The obvious economic answer is that direct regulation should be extended to cases of market failure, mainly the natural monopolies and those that use a common property resource. Yet it is equally obvious that in a substantial number of regulated industries neither one of these necessary conditions is present.

The traditional justification offered for regulation was that of "the public interest." This can be interpreted as the protection of consumers from the exploitation of monopoly power, or the correction of any other type of injustice arising out of the unfettered operation of the market.[3] Nonetheless, this kind of justification has fallen into disfavour in more recent years. The reason is the observation that regulation is considered a highly desirable state by the regulated industries. The drawbacks of the curbs on firm conduct are far outweighed by the advantages obtained from the shelter against competition.

Two lines of arguments have been put forth by Chicago-based economists to explain the role of regulation. The first one, initially proposed by Posner (1971), presents regulation as an alternative to taxation: the pattern of pricing imposed on regulated firms tends to favour one category of consumers over another. Thus, the regulatory system is being used to cross-subsidize certain groups, through what amounts essentially to a hidden tax imposed upon others. This makes these transfer taxes politically more palatable.

There is little doubt that this element has been present to some extent in the Canadian regulatory system. Examples from the regulation of airlines include the subsidization of low-density destinations by the more popular routes, and of scheduled traffic by occasional travellers. In telecommunications, the most frequently cited example is that of long-distance communications subsidizing the local telephone service, even though as we saw in Chapter 3 there are some questions about the validity of this argument. It is clear though that this theory of regulation as an adjunct to the tax system cannot account for all observed regulated industries.

The other type of argument has two variants that start from different premises but end up with the same conclusion. One formulation has been known as the *capture* theory of regulation. According to it, the initial imposition of regulation is made with the public interest in mind. Eventually, however, the regulatory system is diverted from its original purposes and ends up by becoming the servant of those that it regulates. In practice this means that the consumer protection goal of regulation is replaced by behaviour that promotes the interests of the regulated producers.

The other variant of the capture theory has been advanced by Stigler (1971). It differs from the original in its initial motivation for regulation, but not in its results. Regulation, in Stigler's view, is imposed from the outset to eliminate competition and advance the interests of the producers that are already in the sector. The power of the state is being used to generate economic profits accruing to this group. This theory fits very well with many regulated sectors such as the broadcasting system and agricultural marketing boards in Canada. In the latter case in particular, it was the producer interests that motivated regulation from the beginning.

All in all, therefore, the producer protection view of regulation in either one of its variants seems to fit the regulatory experience better than the public interest theory. It should also be noted that once established, regulation seems to acquire a certain dynamic of its own. This is particularly true in sectors in which entry is restricted by a system of transferable licences, as in broadcasting, taxicabs, and agriculture. The initial imposition of entry licensing benefits the producers that are already established; subsequent entrants do not gain, since they dissipate what would otherwise be profits by purchasing or renting the licence from an existing firm.[4] This, however, makes them strong supporters of the maintenance of the regulatory system, since they would not in its absence be able to recoup the cost of the licence.

By contrast, new regulation—the control of externalities—is almost always resisted by private firms. By forcing the producers to absorb the costs they impose on others, this type of regulation raises the cost of the final product. The firms may not always be able to pass on this cost to the buyers, especially if they are subjected to competition by foreign firms that may not be as solicitous of their workers or their environment. Hence, new regulation reduces the firms' profit margins, and finds little sympathy with business firms or their spokesmen.

The widespread concerns about the inefficiencies and inequities associated with direct regulation prompted the deregulation movement of the late 1970s and early 1980s. The impact of this movement on the Canadian economy will be surveyed in more detail on a sectoral basis; it has still not fully run its course as of this writing. Significantly, several observers have remarked that it was economic thinking that gave the initial impetus to this movement. Its crowning point came during the late 1970s when Alfred Kahn became chairman of the U.S. Civil Aeronautics Board (CAB) after a distinguished career as an economist specializing in regulatory issues. He then proceeded to deregulate the airlines in the United States,[5] a move that was followed in Canada several years later.

Given these conflicting tendencies, the picture that emerges of the regulated sectors in Canada as of the late 1980s is a confusing patchwork of differing motives and competing pressures by affected interest groups. The regulatory system is being dismantled in some industries and maintained in others, notwithstanding the fact that inefficient producer protection may have been the initial motive in both cases. Further, the confusion is exacerbated by conflicting federal and provincial jurisdictions and differences of opinion. In what follows we provide a sector by sector account of the existing situation in the most important regulated industries in Canada.

Telecommunications and Broadcasting

These two sectors are regulated at the federal level by the same agency, the Canadian Radio-Television and Telecommunications Commission (CRTC). The industry structure is rather complex in the case of telecommunications, with private and public monopolies in some services and competition in others. In broadcasting it is an oligopoly with restricted entry in radio and television, and a private monopoly in cable TV. The economic rationale is the existence of a natural monopoly in telecommunications and cable, and the allocation of a common property resource in broadcasting.

As noted in Chapter 3, the telecommunications industry is a typical case of regulated multiproduct monopolies, with exclusive franchises in some services and limited competition in others. The ownership pattern of the industry is equally confusing. The largest firm, Bell Canada, which operates in Ontario and most of Quebec, is private and regulated at the federal level; the same is true for the British Columbia Telephone Company (BC Tel). By contrast, in Alberta and the Prairie provinces the telephone service is provided by public corporations, generally provincially-owned and regulated. Private firms also operate in the Maritime provinces, but their regulation takes place at the provincial level. Long distance rates are set interprovincially by a consortium of the major telephone companies, both public and private.[6] International and overseas telecommunications are handled by Teleglobe, which was initially a public company but was sold to private investors by the Mulroney government in the mid-1980s.

For a long time, firms in the telecommunications industry operated as integrated monopolies, providing not only all services but also much of the equipment. This situation changed radically in the 1970s and 1980s, with the result that competition has now been widely introduced in many segments of the industry. The impetus for such deregulation came mainly from technological change that eroded the natural monopoly, but also from changing economic thinking along the patterns analyzed in the previous section. The regulatory changes initially took place in the U.S., and were then carried over into Canada with a five to ten year lag. Some of the U.S. changes have not yet been accepted in Canada.

The outstanding regulatory issues in the Canadian telecommunications industry as of the late 1980s are the location of the frontier of regulation, the exact form of the regulatory regime, and the relative pricing of the various services provided by the regulated firm. Most of these issues are being debated in the case of Bell Canada, which is by far the largest telecommunications firm. All of them involve disputes between the firm and the CRTC, with the occasional participation of other parties, and with the federal government acting as an arbiter of last resort.

As things stand now, the monopoly franchise of the two federally regulated companies covers the basic telephone service (both local and long distance), and nothing else. The inclusion of the long distance service within the monopoly frontier has been challenged by CN/CP Telecommunications, which is seeking to compete with Bell Canada in the provision of these services. The CRTC has rejected CN/CP's application, but this decision has been appealed to the federal government. The applicant firm is relying on the U.S. precedent, where competition in long distance telephone service was established by a landmark judicial decision in 1982.[7] That decision broke up the nationwide telecommunications monopoly of AT&T into a number of local monopoly firms handling the local service. Competitors' entry was allowed in the long distance service, where a number of firms had expressed the desire to compete prior to the 1982 decision.

While competition in long distance voice messages has not yet been allowed in Canada, there are a number of other telecommunications services that lie outside the regulated monopoly frontier. These include private lines, other types of long distance message transmission, and data transmission. These services are provided by CN/CP in competition with Bell Canada, following an important decision by the CRTC in 1979, the so-called Interconnection case. That decision forced Bell Canada to allow CN/CP's long distance network to interconnect with its own local network. This enabled CN/CP to provide point-to-point services to its customers in the non-voice telecommunications area, in competition with Bell Canada.

The Interconnection case is important both as a policy landmark and as an application of sophisticated economic theory to a real-life regulatory case. There is little doubt that without interconnection CN/CP could not compete with Bell Canada in the provision of the services that lie outside basic telephone messaging, the only service that was covered by Bell Canada's monopoly licence. Thus the result of refusing interconnection would have been the de facto extension of the regulated monopoly's frontier to encompass these services. Bell Canada basically did not dispute this assessment. It claimed, though, that the natural monopoly frontier extended beyond the telephone services, and consequently that it would be in the public interest to have all telecommunications services provided by a single monopoly firm.

The argument, therefore, boiled down to the determination of the natural monopoly frontier. Empirical evidence, under the form of competing econometric estimates of the multiproduct cost function for Bell Canada, was presented by both opposing sides. In the end the CRTC threw the burden of proof upon Bell Canada. As explained in detail in Appendix 3A of Chapter 3, this decision eventually resulted in interconnection being allowed, given the ambiguities of the statistical tests in all but the most clear-cut cases. Thus the Interconnection case was ultimately decided through a mixture of sophisticated economic reasoning and value judgments on the virtues of allowing more competition.

The other major regulatory issue in telecommunications concerns the so-called rate rebalancing, which is a long-standing objective of Bell Canada. The firm has argued that the price of the local telephone service is too low in comparison to that of long distance services. It seeks, therefore, to increase the price of the basic local service in order to reduce the long distance charges. The motivation for this request is anticipated competition in long distance service, but also, increasingly, the fear that private carriers would have an incentive to establish their own telecommunications networks if the current rate structure continues. A related but separate request of Bell Canada is the replacement of the current flat rate charges for local service by a two-part tariff that depends partly on the intensity of usage. This last item should certainly be considered desirable on efficiency grounds, and not particularly objectionable on the basis of equity. The opposition that it arouses is based more on suspicions and misunderstandings than on any legitimate reasons.

As we saw in Chapter 3, the basic arguments in rate rebalancing hinge on the share of the common costs that should be allocated to the two telephone services. The firm does not accept the fully-distributed cost concept, and it has rejected cost allocation studies that use it. On the other hand, incremental and stand-alone costs do not offer much help in this case. Similarly, the application of Ramsey prices, in which the service with the most inelastic demand (in this case the local) will carry the highest share of common costs, requires information that may not be available with the needed degree of accuracy, apart from being judged "unfair" on equity grounds.

Last, the method of regulation of private telecommunications firms continues to generate its share of controversy. While there is little opposition to the rate-of-return regulatory rule, the manner of its application is by nature controversial. Several of the general issues that arise during rate-of-return regulation were discussed in Chapter 3. Other problems may appear in specific instances. For instance, we saw in the earlier chapter that the telecommunications firms generate revenue from several products and services that lie outside the regulatory frontier. Many of these services share resources and production costs (for instance the local network) with the telephone services. They must therefore carry their share of these common costs. During the early 1980s Bell Canada reorganized its corporate structure by concentrating all regulated services into a wholly-owned subsidiary, and creating different subsidiaries for its other activities. This requires a proper costing of the resources that the regulated subsidiary provides to the other parts of the firm. It is believed that this reorganization will make it more difficult for the regulators to ensure that telephone subscribers do not pay for part of the costs of the company's other operations.[8]

The other major task of the CRTC is the regulation of broadcasting, which includes radio, television, cable TV, and pay TV. The objectives of regulatory policy in this area are qualitatively different from those in all other directly regulated sectors. Although economic issues are not unimportant in policy design and implementation, it is cultural factors that occupy centre stage. Briefly speaking, public policy makers have been concerned for a long time about the dominant role played by U.S. broadcasting signals in attracting Canadian viewers. The central objectives in the regulation of broadcasting, therefore, have been the increase in the availability and audience share of Canadian programming.

The basic regulatory method in broadcasting is a licensing system. In radio and television, the licence specifies the position in the electromagnetic spectrum that the licensee will occupy, and the power of its transmitters; this is equivalent to the specification of the audience that the licensee can reach with off-the-air broadcasting (i.e. non-cable, non-satellite TV signals). The licence becomes in this way an exclusive franchise for the use of the portion of the spectrum allocated to it. In cable TV (CATV), on the other hand, the licence specifies the geographical region that will be covered by the holder's network.

The Canadian legislation, embodied in the Broadcasting Act of 1968, states very clearly that the electromagnetic spectrum remains the property of the Canadian public. The broadcasting licences, which are renewed every three to five years, imply no legal obligation to award them to the same party. In practice, however, these licences have been transformed into de facto property rights. Not only is the licence almost always routinely awarded to the same licensee, but the CRTC also approves almost automatically its transfer through a sale to any third party that meets certain qualifications.[9] Further, all licence awards take place at a nominal price, and the public authority has no share in the price of any subsequent sale. Small wonder then that broadcasting licences have become valuable assets, generously donated to their holders courtesy of the Canadian public.

In exchange for these valuable property rights the CRTC has imposed a number of restrictions on programming content. The form of these restrictions has varied over time,[10] but their purpose has been to guarantee minimum amounts of Canadian-produced programs, and the scheduling of such programs at prime audience-viewing times. There is little doubt that these restrictions are costly for the broadcasters. As argued in a 1979 report prepared for the Economic Council of Canada,[11] it is much cheaper for them to purchase mass-produced programs from the U.S. Hence, the entire history of broadcasting regulation is full of case studies of attempts by broadcasters to comply to the letter of the regulations at as low a cost as possible. The result, documented by a series of reports that are almost unanimous in their conclusions,[12] is a failure of the professed public policy objectives of regulation.

A related aspect of television licensing is the role played by cable TV (CATV). This is a service provided to subscribers in a given geographical area under monopoly licensing. Its effects on TV broadcasting are on the one hand an extension of the potential audience for each station, but on the other hand an increase in competition between these stations. The latter effect has become particularly important in recent years, with the development of satellite transmission technology. For these reasons the regulations governing CATV are a major determinant of the market structure of TV broadcasting.

The policies of the CRTC have been geared towards increasing the revenues of the broadcasting sector, undoubtedly in the hope that they will accept more easily its cultural objectives. For this reason it has obliged CATV licensees to give priority to Canadian stations, and it has attempted at times to restrict the availability of U.S. programming. Another policy that has understandably caused a lot of controversy with U.S. broadcasters has been the discriminatory treatment of Canadian advertising by U.S. stations: a 1976 law allows the deduction of the cost of advertising directed to Canadians as a business expense only if it is placed on Canadian stations or networks. Overall, the CRTC policies amount to a regulatory definition of the market structure that a given TV station operates in.

The economic analysis of television broadcasting has been carried out in a number of studies.[13] The market structure is an oligopoly with blocked entry. Each firm draws its revenue by "producing" audience for its programs and "selling" the audience to advertisers. This is consistent with the observed practice of advertisers to pay for their messages in proportion to the station's audience. The production of audience is done by an optimal choice of the programming expenses. The exogenous factors that determine the size and quality of a given station's audience are the population it reaches, the competition it faces in its territory, and the socioeconomic characteristics (such as income) of its potential audience. These turn out to be the ultimate determinants of its profitability. Since these factors are primarily determined by the regulators, it is regulatory policy that defines how much each licensee will earn.

The analysis of the determinants of the profitability of a CATV licence is somewhat more complex. The licensee chooses the rate charged to its subscribers by maximizing profits essentially as an unregulated monopolist,[14] keeping in mind that the proportion of the population that subscribes is a decreasing function of that rate. This choice depends on the conditions of the licence award as defined by the regulators. These conditions therefore determine the size of the profits, and through them the value of the licence. After 1983 the

CATV network has also been used for the provision of pay TV, which is sold as an addition to the basic cable service.

As already noted, the achievement of the cultural objectives enunciated in the broadcasting legislation has fallen far short of expectations. Canadian programming has not increased its share of the audience despite content regulations. Nor is there any distinctive flavour to much of the programming presented in compliance with these regulations. In early 1988 the Department of Communications announced that a new broadcasting policy is being studied, after yet another critical report was issued in 1987. The principal obstacles to any such new policy are financial: audience attraction hinges on more resources being channelled into Canadian programming. The rents accruing to the private broadcasting licence holders are an obvious source of such additional funds, but neither the political will to redirect them nor the appropriate mechanisms to do so are available at this time.

As a closing remark on the regulation of the telecommunications and broadcasting sectors, we note that this task has been complicated in both instances by rapidly evolving technology. Technological change in both sectors resulted in their separation becoming somewhat blurred at the edges. For instance, communications satellites are increasingly being used by both industries. Similarly, there is competition to broadcasting in the use of the electromagnetic spectrum by some telecommunications services such as microwave radio transmission, land-mobiles, and cellular telephones. Television signals can be carried over the telecommunications networks, and broadcasting stations—using line-of-sight technology—can provide telecommunications services. Other technological changes that make the job of the regulators very difficult occur inside each sector, such as the development of low-cost antennas that capture satellite signals as an alternative to CATV, and of private telecommunications systems that allow the bypass of the common carriers' network. These technological effects have important economic implications that make the regulation of the two industries particularly difficult.

The Transportation Industries

In the transportation sector there is a wide variety of market structures and regulatory regimes. Until very recently, restrictions on new firm entry were the common denominator in all these regimes. This sector, though, is the one in which the pressures for deregulation have been strongest and most successful. Currently, most transportation industries are undergoing some sort of deregulation, with the result that the future evolution of the industries can only be the subject of conjecture. The U.S. experience, where deregulation took place a few years ago, is particularly helpful in this context.

The Canadian airline industry is regulated almost completely at the federal level. This industry is a combination of monopolies and tight oligopolies in domestic routes, and of competition in many international flights. Until recently, entry was restricted through a licensing system, while there were also controls over fares and types of service. The situation is also somewhat complicated by the presence of the publicly-owned firm Air Canada, the largest firm in the industry, which competes against private carriers on many routes.

The deregulation of airlines in the U.S. is considered to be the great success story of the deregulation movement. In its regulated state the industry was characterized by high prices and excess capacity. Entry and exit were restricted through a licensing system for every route. Price competition was almost completely absent, while most firms competed with each other through real or alleged improvements in the quality of service. Such competition dissipated part of the monopoly profits generated by maintained high prices.

The airline industry was also one in which the concept of contestable markets was initially developed and applied. As we saw in Chapter 3, a contestable market is one in which entry does not entail any irrecoverable costs. There must also be a post-entry period during which the incumbent(s) will maintain the pre-entry prices. It was claimed by the proponents of contestability that these conditions were substantially fulfilled in airlines, with capital perfectly mobile at little or no loss in and out of the market.

In their latest contribution on the subject, however, the inventors of contestability appear to have had second thoughts.[15] To begin with, although most capital is easily resaleable, the industry's customers are individual consumers, making long term sales contracts infeasible; this destroys the second requirement of contestability. In fact, it is noted in a recent study that a major U.S. airline employs approximately 150 people whose sole task is to verify (and presumably match or undercut) the fares offered by the airline's competitors, including new entrants, on its various routes.[16] Second, there have been shortages of facilities and services of air traffic control for new airlines in several airports, a fact that acts as an entry barrier: established airlines do not suffer from many of these shortages. Last, there have been shortages in the supply of efficient aircraft, with delivery lags stretching to three years in many cases. Nonetheless, the authors conclude that the industry still conforms more closely to the contestability model than to other alternative economic models, and that the deregulation experience has been on the whole positive.

There is no question that airline deregulation brought major benefits in economic efficiency. As noted in the 1981 Economic Council of Canada (ECC) report, the average cost of air travel fell dramatically in the U.S. following deregulation, because of higher utilization and increased efficiency. Average prices similarly declined, although economic profits were not entirely eliminated due to the imperfections mentioned above. Passenger travel time fell, and there were considerable improvements in efficiency through computerized routing and hub-and-spoke operations. Last, there was a reduction or elimination of cross-subsidies among various routes or classes of travellers: the relative fares of the more heavily used routes declined; peak-season travellers paid more; a premium was extracted for the security of the reservation; and so on. These last changes imply that the fare structure now approximates more closely the marginal costs of the various services.

For all these reasons the pressures for airline deregulation in Canada were very strong from the outset. The ECC report (1981) recommended a cautious and gradual liberalization of the various regulatory rules governing fares, entry, and route allocation, that stopped far short of complete deregulation. Some of its recommendations have already been implemented, while other changes are in progress. A new law, that essentially deregulates completely the domestic flights segment of the industry while maintaining service to the northern communities, came into effect in early 1988. According to this law, entry and exit for most routes would be free and subject to minimal licensing conditions. The law was passed in spite of substantial opposition from within the industry, especially from organized labour. This opposition was motivated by the consequences of the U.S. experience: deregulation resulted in a drop in the average wage in the industry, with non-unionized new entrants enjoying a cost advantage over their established competitors. There is good reason to believe that the same will happen in Canada.

Many arguments of the opponents of airline deregulation in both the United States and Canada have raised questions about two features of post-deregulation airline operations in the U.S. The first one is safety: it has been alleged that safety has declined after deregulation, even though little rigorous evidence has been offered for the allegations. The second is the increased concentration in the industry as a result of some highly publicized mergers and takeovers, which have not been challenged by antitrust authorities.

There is little doubt that the competitive pressures generated by deregulation increase the incentives for saving money by "cutting corners" on safety features. For instance, in 1987 Eastern Airlines was fined $9.5 million because of safety infractions, while in April 1988 both Eastern and its parent company, Texas Air Corp., were again facing scrutiny on suspected safety violations.[17] It is however unclear whether this decline in air travel safety, even if true, is a failure of deregulation rather than of the safety regulatory system, which should not have been affected by deregulation. It is possible that this system has not kept up with the increased traffic generated by lower deregulated fares.

The post-deregulation increase in industry concentration need not cause any concerns if the industry is contestable. If, however, the departures from contestability are important, then the increased concentration may reduce the benefits of deregulation if the market power thus generated causes higher fares. Since the degree of contestability of the airline industry is still under debate, the final outcome of the mergers on industry performance is not yet available.

The airline industry in Canada presents a number of particular factors that were not present in the U.S. Air travel is a much more essential service in Canada, as no substitutes exist for many communities. Consequently, the maintenance of air service in such communities is a necessity that requires outside financing. The largest firm in the industry is a public corporation, for which the Conservative government has recently announced plans for privatization. Perhaps more important is the fact that the supply of potential entrants to the industry is not nearly as plentiful as in the U.S.: foreign firms may not enter the industry, and there is no guarantee that a sufficient number of domestic entrepreneurs would exist were entry to become free. Hence, the contestability characteristics are considerably less pronounced than in the U.S. Nonetheless, it is highly probable that the overall benefits of deregulation in Canada will exceed its shortcomings, especially if the proper safeguards are observed. It is a safe bet that deregulation will proceed in coming years, although it is not clear whether it will endure in its current form.

Deregulation is also currently proceeding in the Canadian trucking industry, where the regulatory system is a mixture of federal and provincial jurisdictions. Most of the regulation takes place provincially, but there is also some federal regulation for interprovincial transportation. There are restrictions on cargo and price controls in some provinces, and entry restrictions almost everywhere. These last restrictions involve the acquisition of a licence, which is granted if the applicant is able to demonstrate the "public convenience and necessity" of its licensing. Needless to say, already-established trucking firms routinely oppose the granting of new licences, thus erecting effective entry barriers. In its 1981 report, the ECC cited a figure of $40 million as the annual direct costs of applying for new licences and opposing the applications of potential competitors. These direct costs of regulation are also responsible for the creation of "artificial" economies of scale due to regulation: large firms are better able to cover the costs of applying for new licences, of obtaining amendments to existing licences, and of opposing new competitors. There are also very substantial indirect costs of regulation, because of licence limits on routes and commodities and the increased collusive ability of existing firms.

The economic characteristics of the industry are particularly suited to a competitive structure. Although there are economies of scale and of scope in expanding the network of routes serviced by a trucking firm, the irrecoverable capital costs are low. The industry employs little specialized equipment that cannot be easily resold in the second-hand market. Further, most of the sales are to other producers. In the absence of regulation, such producers would be able to accept bids for long-term contracts against existing firms, something that is not possible if the customers are individual consumers. Thus the industry is very close to being contestable. As we saw in Chapters 3 and 5, this implies that competitive equilibrium would prevail even with a small number of firms.

The American trucking industry has been completely deregulated. The

ECC, in its final report, was moderate in its recommendations and stopped short of endorsing the U.S. situation. It recommended the maintenance of some entry restrictions for the industry, but the abolition of all operating restrictions on existing firms, except for health and safety requirements. Most such recommendations have been adopted at the federal level, but there is little action so far on the more important provincial front. Negotiations are currently taking place in Ontario between the industry and the provincial government on the scope and speed of the implementation of regulatory reform.

There has been little deregulation in the taxicab industry, in spite of the recommendations of the 1981 ECC report. The industry is subjected to entry licensing and price regulation, with a licence that can be sold or rented to a third party. The ECC recommendations were for a gradual deregulation of the industry, with the ultimate goal of reducing the market value of a taxicab licence to zero. The contestability properties of the taxicab industry are almost as pronounced as in trucking, implying that competitive industry equilibrium would prevail in almost every Canadian city in the absence of regulatory restrictions. Taxicabs, however, are regulated at the municipal level, with wide differences in regulatory regimes across Canada. Hence, local factors will dominate whatever reforms are adopted.

As an illustration of the type of obstacles to regulatory reform that are likely to surface at the local level, we note the example of the various municipalities in the National Capital area. In March 1988 the *Ottawa Citizen* published an investigation of the attempts to establish a unified licensing system at the regional level. These attempts were prompted by the difficulties of enforcing restrictions for fare pickup on the taxicabs licensed by different adjacent municipalities. The investigation uncovered the fact that the main obstacle to unification was the opposition of licence-holders in the City of Ottawa, who were afraid that their licences were going to lose some market value. These licence-holders were also very few in number and very wealthy. Yet, they were able to exert sufficient pressure on local politicians to derail or delay even this very modest attempt at reform. In other words, a small, well-financed group of producers, with immediate stakes in a particular regulatory issue, is most often able to impose its views to the detriment of the much larger but unorganized group of consumers of the industry product.

Trucking and the taxicab industry are classic illustrations of regulation used as an instrument of producer protection. In both instances it is the industry that wants regulation in order to restrict competition, by having entry to the sector controlled on their behalf. Once regulation is in place, the strategy is to use political power to delay reform for as long as possible.

We close this brief review of the transportation industries with the railroad sector. Here the industry structure is a duopoly on a national level, with a public and a private enterprise sharing the entire Canadian market.[18] There is, however, a substantial degree of *intermodal* competition from other transportation sectors (especially trucking) for many commodities. Further, the contestability of the industry is not an issue here: there are clearly major sunk costs of entering the sector, in the form of investment in railway track, terminals, and related facilities.

Nonetheless, there has been significant deregulation in the railroad industry in both the United States and Canada. The new Canadian legislation that deregulated airlines and interprovincial trucking also contained significant provisions concerning railroads. The intent of these provisions was to introduce more competition in the industry. Thus, railroads are now permitted to enter into confidential contracts with shippers, but may not engage in collective rate-making; this will presumably grant more bargaining power to large shippers whenever their needs can be served by overlapping track networks. There are also separate provisions that aim to protect the so-called "captive" shippers, i.e. those who have no other transportation alternatives. Last, there are provisions giving power to regulators to mandate the usage of one firm's track by the vehicles of another.

This legislation was greatly influenced by equivalent U.S. measures, adopted in the so-called Staggers Act of 1980. That act introduced rate freedom in all cases, except where the railways enjoy "market dominance." As a result of that law, industry observers have noted substantial improvements in the industry's operating efficiency, although concerns about the captive shippers segment of the industry have prompted a number of complaints.

In both countries, regulatory reform in the railroad industry has refrained from the adoption of more radical deregulation proposals.[19] Such proposals advocated the introduction of contestability elements in the industry by separating the ownership of track and vehicles. The track and related facilities, representing the sunk cost component of the industry, are the barriers to contestability. The transportation services, on the other hand, have cost characteristics that make them amenable to intramodal competition based on free entry. The separation of ownership (perhaps by nationalizing the track) would have prevented the monopolistic track owner from extending its market power to the transport services. These radical proposals encountered major opposition from the established railroads and did not make it into the legislation. Given the nature of the industry, the current legislation stops far short of removing the obstacles to competition, in spite of its professed intent.

Agricultural Marketing Boards

The term marketing board defines in general an association of all producers of a particular agricultural commodity in a given province, with powers and activities varying widely across different commodities. Marketing boards are established by a majority vote of the producers. Once the board is formed, it acquires statutory power to impose its decisions on all producers in the province.

Many marketing boards are in fact simple trade associations, with mainly promotional and educational roles. Other boards have the power to negotiate prices, on behalf of their members, with large commercial buyers and processors. In this way, small-scale farmers can increase their negotiating leverage to offset market power on the buyer side. Here, however, we are concerned with yet another category of marketing boards, the so-called *supply management* boards. These represent the ultimate in market power granted by legal means, insofar as they are compulsory producer cartels, with power to control entry into the market and to allocate quotas to individual producers.

There are currently four main categories of products subject to such supply management boards in Canada. These are dairy products, eggs, chicken, and turkeys, to which one should add the dying Ontario tobacco farming sector. It is these few products that place the marketing board system in the direct regulation category; they are also the cases where the system has been almost unanimously condemned by consumers and economists.

There is no suggestion of a monopoly structure, natural or otherwise, in any of these sectors; they would all have been competitive in the absence of regulation. The economic rationale offered for subjecting them to compulsory cartelization is the so-called *destructive competition* argument. Although this argument is not endorsed by most economists, it does nonetheless deserve to be examined carefully, given the frequency with which it is mentioned in the regulatory debate.

Allegations about the "destructiveness" of competitive behaviour imply that competition, by causing widespread business failures, ultimately destroys the competitive market structure that caused it. This presupposes that a large number of the competitive producers will act irrationally, since otherwise failures would not occur except in the case of inefficient businesses. As already noted, hardly any economist attaches credibility to such allegations. The main inconsistency in the arguments is that the destructiveness of competition is used as an argument for its suppression, while the principal adverse consequence of "destructive" competition would again be the same suppression. One is unhappily reminded of a general who destroys a city in order to save it from the enemy.

Nonetheless, a competitive market structure may be capable of improvement by outside intervention in some cases. These are situations in which market demand or supply are subject to sharp fluctuations. Producers may find it difficult to cope with such fluctuations, which are particularly acute in agricultural markets. This has led to price stabilization schemes, not all of which are economically undesirable. Their purpose is to guarantee a more or less stable level of income to the producers, based on the "average" price and quantity over an entire demand cycle. These schemes are particularly effective when the commodity is storable, as with grains.

Figure 10.1 shows the basic idea behind a price stabilization program. Product demand in this market has three possible states: expansionary, normal, and depressed, respectively D_E, D_N and D_D. Without stabilization, the corresponding price-quantity pairs would be (P_E, Q_E'), (P_N, Q_N) and (P_D, Q_D'). By contrast, a stabilization program would set the price and quantity at P_N and Q_N always. During recessions there would be an excess production of $(Q_N - Q_D)$, which would be stored in order to cover the shortage of $(Q_E - Q_N)$ that arises during the expansionary phase of the cycle. This scheme is relatively simple to administer, since it relies mainly on accurate demand-forecasting by the authority in charge of the plan. The only other requirement is the political willingness to intervene and prevent the price from rising by selling from the stored supplies. It would not involve any quotas or restrictions on supply, but

FIGURE 10.1
Price stabilization for a storable commodity

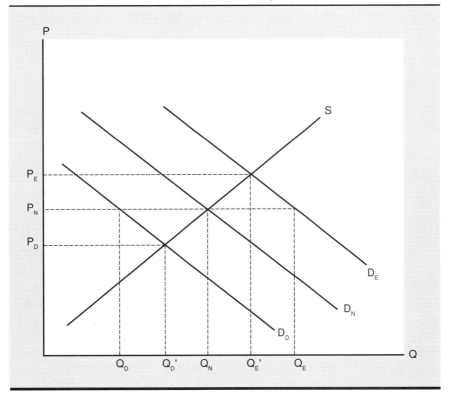

it also would not result in any higher average income for the producers.[20]

If the product price is stabilized at a higher price than P_N then there is a chronic accumulation of surpluses, as well as a drain on public money to subsidize the higher price. The agency in charge of the program can presumably recapture some of that money and get rid of surpluses by dumping them on world markets at lower prices. This situation prevails in the markets for many agricultural commodities within the European Economic Community (EEC). At the time of this writing (early 1989) the combination of price subsidies and persistent surpluses in the market for grains has created the type of general instability in the world grain markets that the stabilization programs were supposed to prevent. Such subsidies and surpluses exist in the U.S. and Canada, as well as in the EEC.

The "destructive" competition phase of the cycle is the one associated with recession, when the firms in the industry strive to maintain their market share in the face of declining demand. Some of the reduction in output that takes place during this phase occurs in the form of exit of firms from the industry, manifesting itself by business failures. It is the fact that such failures are not considered part of the normal operation of an industry that has prompted the use of the term "destructive." In addition to agriculture, for which price instability is indeed a problem, the "destructive" competition argument has been used in trucking and the airline industry. As already noted, this argument is almost universally rejected by economists.

The stabilization scheme shown in Figure 10.1 does not embody any restrictions on entry or output. The supply management schemes, on the other hand, which govern the markets for eggs, poultry, dairy products, and tobacco are quite different. As already noted, these markets have been effectively transformed into producers' cartels. They are run by producer-controlled marketing boards, with legal power to enforce their price and output decisions. Entry into the industry is completely blocked, except by displacement (purchase of the quota) of an existing producer. The economic model applicable to these markets is that of the cartel, already examined in Chapter 4.

Not surprisingly, these legal producers' cartels, the supply management schemes in force for the production of eggs, poultry, and dairy products, have been the main targets of regulatory reform. These sectors were also singled out in the ECC's regulation report of 1981. That report had recommended a partial relaxation of the regulatory regimes governing these boards, while maintaining a significant degree of protection for existing producers. Even these modest proposals, however, were vigorously opposed by the producers, with the result that no action has been forthcoming until now.

The protection accorded to producers by these legal cartels has been very significant. A number of studies have estimated the economic value of regulation in these sectors, in terms of the higher producer incomes as compared to a competitive regime. These studies have used varying methods, but they all had broadly similar results. Some of them simply analyzed the sales prices of the production quotas, which are equal to the discounted sums of the economic profits realized by the producers. Other studies have observed the prices of the products in the unregulated U.S. market, after adjusting for differences in scale and input prices. Both approaches produced consistent estimates of profits, which are basically income transfers from the final consumers to the producers. These profits are very substantial, with an aggregate value of more than $600 million in 1978 for fluid milk alone.[21]

Not surprisingly, the vested interests produced by these vast sums have created immovable obstacles in blocking any regulatory reform. These pressures have succeeded until now, notwithstanding the documented inefficiencies inherent in the cartel schemes. The agricultural cartels have responded to the pressures for reform by tightening up somewhat in their operations and eliminating some obvious sources of waste, such as the destruction of surpluses in order to keep a high product price. Better coordination and production planning, and a more rigid enforcement of the quotas, have succeeded in equating supply and demand at the cartel-determined price and output. At the same time, the producers' associations have pointed to the stability and prosperity created by the cartel system in the sectors involved. Even in the depressed agricultural markets of the mid- to late 1980s, these sectors have managed to maintain a high level of profits. These profits have come entirely at the expense of Canadian consumers, and they have accrued to the segment of the producers that were already in the industry when the system was put in place; subsequent entrants had to buy their way in.

Imports of the cartelized commodities are almost completely blocked, resulting in the large price differentials with the U.S. mentioned above. Abolition of the tariff protection would almost completely eliminate all market power of the cartels. In late 1985, a private study conducted on behalf of a major Canadian bank[22] estimated that of all agricultural commodities, the one most likely to be exempted from the free trade agreement with the United States, which was then being negotiated, was the dairy sector: both the U.S. and Canada have a tradition of protecting their domestic milk producers. By contrast, eggs and poultry would probably have to undergo significant restructuring. The exact nature of their evolution under the final form of the agreement is unclear, given that they would maintain their legal powers, although imports would be allowed to rise. Table 10.1 gives an idea of the extent of protection accorded to these two sectors; this table was drawn from this same private study.

These differentials are very substantial for both commodities, and they are similar in magnitude to the estimates of earlier studies. Borcherding and Dorosh (1981) give a figure of $.127 for the 1978 price differential of a dozen eggs between British Columbia and the adjacent state of Washington.[23] That figure is not very different in terms of 1983-85 prices from the data in Table

TABLE 10.1
Canada-U.S. price differentials, broilers and eggs

	Chicken Broilers Cdn. ¢/kg	Eggs Cdn. ¢/dozen	Exchange rate $Cdn./$U.S.
1983 March	57.76	22.42	1.2263
June	55.21	24.17	1.2323
Sept.	74.69	17.17	1.2326
Dec.	66.81	−8.77	1.2469
1984 March	41.63	2.45	1.2697
June	54.89	22.84	1.3040
Sept.	69.75	27.66	1.3145
Dec.	58.26	33.98	1.3201
1985 March	30.60	25.70	1.3840
June	32.62	26.22	1.3676
Sept.	37.08	20.05	1.3703
Average	52.66	19.44	1.2971

10.1. Part of the differential may be due to the higher costs of production in Canada, which are in turn due to the protection accorded to small producers. Nonetheless, the ECC report states that many small producers in the dairy sector have been exiting the industry, thus increasing the efficiency of the industry but also creating higher economic rents for the quota holders.

In summary, therefore, the agricultural supply management cartels are, like the trucking and taxicab industries, a classic case of political power exercised to confer economic benefits to a producer group by altering the industry structure. As such, they may also be considered as illustrations of Stigler's theory of regulation as a vehicle to suppress competition and advance producer interests. This motive was basic to the establishment of the marketing board system right from the beginning, and it continues to be responsible for its maintenance to this day.

Other Cases of Direct Regulation

We round off the discussion of direct regulation with two other sectors in which it has played an important role. These are the energy and fisheries sectors. In the former, regulation of private firms is not that important in Canada, given that electricity generation is mostly done by public enterprises; by contrast, it is precisely this sector that has provided most examples of regulation of private monopolies in the United States. In ocean fishing, on the other hand, regulation plays a major role in the operation of the sector on both the east and west coasts.

Energy-related firms are in the oil, natural gas, and electricity-producing sectors. The two most important are oil and electricity, with the former being competitive or oligopolistic in structure, and the latter dominated by public enterprises. Gas utilities, on the other hand, are private monopolies regulated at the provincial or municipal levels. There are also private monopolies in the interprovincial transmission of oil and natural gas through pipelines, with regulation taking place at the federal level via the National Energy Board (NEB).

The important regulatory issues in the energy area lie somewhat outside the boundaries of the structure-conduct-performance model. They surfaced most acutely after 1973, when the OPEC cartel's sudden increase in oil prices raised concerns in Canada about inflation, energy exports, and the long-term availability of oil. These concerns resulted in a number of policies undertaken by the federal government, culminating in the National Energy Program (NEP) of 1980. Briefly speaking, the NEP's policies included a sharp increase in the share of tax revenues accruing to the federal government, the allocation of much of these revenues to the development of new energy sources, an increase in the Canadian-owned portion of the oil industry, and the establishment of a complex oil pricing formula with different base prices for old and new oil sources.[24] These policies were very controversial right from the beginning, and were effectively abolished by the Conservative government, almost immediately after it assumed power. Some of these policies, such as the pricing formula, were objectionable on orthodox economic grounds. Others, such as the combination of taxation and development grants, were based on the assumption that the sharp rise in oil prices of the 1970s would continue into the foreseeable future. This did not turn out to be the case; the collapse of world oil prices after 1982 undermined the basis for the NEP by reducing the profitability of the new (and more expensive) oil sources such as tar sands and frontier oil. These economic reasons, as much as ideological factors, were responsible for the NEP's abandonment after 1984.

The regulation of fisheries stems from the need to prevent the exhaustion through overfishing of a renewable resource, the fishing stocks.[25] This is achieved by placing an upper limit on the amount of each fish species that may be caught in a given year. This upper limit, the Total Allowable Catch (TAC), is basically biologically determined, although economic factors also play a role. Since the TAC is a limit on the activity of all firms in the industry, the fishing season for a given species must stop once its TAC is reached. This may cause inefficiencies in the operations of the industry, since it provides an incentive for every firm to try and fish as fast as possible, lest it be overtaken by its competitors in the race to reach the TAC. Hence, firms have a tendency to overcapitalize by investing in equipment, which then stays idle for most of the fishing season.

It is interesting to note that a quota system similar to the one in the egg or dairy products sectors could eliminate the inefficiencies in this case. Each firm would be given its own individual TAC, which it may then catch throughout the season, with efficient proportions of labour and capital inputs. This is essentially the system that was proposed in the ECC's 1981 report, which has been partially implemented. Nonetheless, there are important political and jurisdictional problems, especially in the Atlantic provinces where fishing is a major activity. These have to do with intra-industry conflicts in the quota allocation between large and small producers, which have not been solved to this date.[26] Also, in some recent years the industry has not managed to reach the TAC for many important species. If this situation becomes permanent, the need for quotas and regulations may disappear and the industry can revert to its naturally competitive or oligopolistic state. This, however, does not appear to be very likely in the near future: in early 1989 many fish quotas were being sharply reduced due to overfishing.

Indirect or "New" Regulation

In the "new" regulation the regulatory controls are diffuse and affect a large number of industries.[27] The restrictions placed upon the firm pertain to the method of production and/or the type of product, and not to economic parameters such as price or investment. Also, the jurisdictional problems are much more acute than in direct regulation, given that a large portion of the relevant federal legislation depends on provincial application and enforcement.

Environmental Pollution

The regulation of environmental pollution may take place either at the level of the production process, or at the level of the quality and specification of the final product. The first approach affects virtually every industry, whose effects on the environment and methods of waste disposal must conform to accepted standards. Its impact, though, is much more severe in some industries than in others. Chemicals, pulp and paper, metal smelting and refining, and petroleum refining are obvious examples of industries in which possible environmental effects form an integral part of the production planning process. The same is true of electricity generation via coal or nuclear fuels.

The economic effects of these restrictions are multiple. In the first place, they invariably tend to raise the cost of the final product, even though their overall economic effect on society may not be negative. By forcing the polluting industries to absorb the costs that they impose upon others, the environmental restrictions end up by producing more expensive final products than would have otherwise been the case. They also tend to introduce a bias in the selection of the production processes, since some industries and/or methods of production are more affected than others. For instance, the "clean" electronics sector is much more desirable for most regions than old-style "smokestack" industries. Similarly, hydroelectric plants pollute much less than coal or nuclear-fired electricity-generating plants, in spite of their large impact on the environment. Last, conflicts tend to arise between industries because of environmental effects. Agriculture and tourism are two industries that depend crucially on a clean environment, and they both compete with polluting industries over water supply.

The second type of restrictions affects the type of final product, whose end use may by itself create environmental damage. The most obvious examples of such restrictions are automobile emission standards, which have been imposed upon the manufacturers. These also tend to increase the cost to the consumers of the final product, both directly and indirectly, through increased gas consumption.

Occupational Health and Safety

The other broad category of regulatory activities included in "new" regulation is occupational health and safety. Like the environment, this area of regulation covers virtually every industry, but it also affects some industries more than others. For this reason there are specific pieces of legislation covering "high risk" industries such as coal mining and nuclear energy, as well as general laws affecting all industries. Here the basic regulatory responsibility lies with the provinces, even though the federal government also plays an important role.

Occupational health and safety regulation is very similar to environmental protection in its economic consequences. It takes place at the levels of both production processes and product quality standards. Its immediate effect is to raise the cost of the final products. The producers are forced to pay the costs that they impose upon others, which they then attempt to pass on to the consumers. However, there are also now incentives to reduce these costs. The ultimate result may turn out to be a lower aggregate social cost. The main issues involved in both safety and the environment are the appropriate amount of prevention and the specific forms that the absorption of costs should take.

The economic analysis of the effects of "new" regulation is mostly at the level of the public policy design. At issue are the precise forms to be given to the various regulatory restrictions, so that they achieve their objectives at a minimum cost to the firms affected. Once the restrictions are in place, the firms have no choice but to comply, even though to date the enforcement has not always been strict.

As already noted, regulation in the areas of the environment and occupational health and safety is characterized by competing and overlapping jurisdictions. Provincial authorities, which have the responsibility for most of these types of regulation, have had varying attitudes towards law enforcement in this area. The impact of the regulatory restrictions upon the cost of the final product, and hence upon jobs and economic growth, has served as a powerful counterweight to concerns about health and the quality of life resulting from a clean and safe environment. Economic theory has provided some interesting ideas about an objective evaluation of such tradeoffs, even though it is not always obvious how they may be applied in concrete cases.

The economic analysis of environmental regulation is centred around the issues of the "appropriate" degree of protection to be accorded to the environment as well as the form that this protection should take. The first issue is strictly a tradeoff between economic growth and a clean environment. The second concerns the "best" design for the regulations, as well as the manner of their enforcement. In other words, the first issue is one of social objectives, while the second concerns the proper tools for enforcement.

The level of environmental quality is a function of a number of dimensions of the environment, such as air, water, and soil quality. These tend to deteriorate with industrial use and density of population, which implies a need for continuous monitoring as well as the establishment of quality standards. The maintenance of these standards requires control over the various sources that cause deterioration.

As a specific example, consider the clean air standards in a particular area. These are usually specified in terms of certain maximum contents of pollutants that form upper limits. The key question is the allocation of these pollutants to the various possible sources of emission in the area. Since the cumulative amount of pollutant emission cannot be exceeded, how is one to allocate this amount among (say) the various polluting industrial firms in the region?

There is no satisfactory solution to this problem, although there are a number of interesting proposals. One of them is the allocation of pollution *quotas* through an auction, in which firms bid for the right to pollute.[28] This is not done in practice. Instead, the policy followed most often is to restrict each firm in the area to the same emission total. This policy is the easiest to enforce, but it is also not the most efficient. Its main drawback is that it does not take into account the cost of reducing emissions, as well as the economic value of the polluting activity; both differ across industries in any given region. The best policy would be to impose the most stringent restrictions on pollutants on firms for which both the cost of emission reductions and the economic value of the polluting activity per unit emission are lowest. Even if such a scheme were politically feasible, the informational requirements for its implementation would be formidable. There would also be a strong incentive on the part of the firms to overstate the costs of pollution reduction.

The other important question is the determination of the appropriate emission standards, i.e. the maximum totals of each pollutant for the area, which were taken as granted in the above example. This is equivalent to specifying the quality of the environment to be aimed for. The price of setting too high a quality standard is a reduction in economic activity. Too low a standard, on the other hand, also involves many costs: health deterioration; reduction in other economic activities such as tourism, recreation, and agriculture; and a reduction in the general "quality of life" in the area, an intangible but no less real effect of pollution. Clearly, what is needed is a choice that balances the two effects. If a market for pollution could be established then a price system could presumably identify the optimal choice of pollution level. In the absence of a market mechanism, a tax on polluting activities could perhaps achieve the same results.

Figure 10.2 shows the idea behind a tax on polluting activities. The horizontal axis measures the level X of pollution, while the vertical axis is denominated in $. The curve SMC represents the marginal social cost of pollution, while the curve MVP is the marginal social value of the polluting activity. Their intersection determines the appropriate level of pollution. If this level, denoted by X_1, is known, then a tax equal to T_1 could achieve it, under the assumption that private and social values of economic activity were equal. Unfortunately, the exact shapes of both curves are unknown, and the level X_1 is generally determined on an ad hoc basis.

FIGURE 10.2
Optimal level of pollution

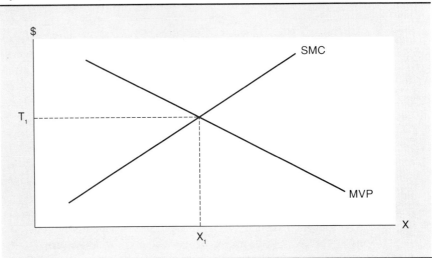

The arbitrary determination of the aimed-for pollution level is in part due to the fact that precise estimates of the costs of pollution are missing. Several of the effects of environmental deterioration are long-term, and the health hazards associated with them become apparent when it is already too late. Economic effects of pollution on other industries have sometimes been revealed in private suits brought against polluters. On the other hand, the costs of pollution reduction have been somewhat better documented. The ECC report of 1981 estimated that between $3 and $4 billion annually were spent by both the private and the public sector in capital funds for pollution control. Although these sums do not appear very large, their effect on selected industries such as pulp and paper, chemicals, and primary metals can be quite substantial. The ECC's report cites a number of submissions on the part of private firms that claim major expenditures and costs associated with pollution control. Even allowing for exaggeration in these claims, the sums involved appear quite impressive.

As noted earlier, the form of some of the environmental laws and regulations can easily transform them into barriers to entry. For instance, the Pulp and Paper Regulations under the Fisheries Act specify different standards for existing mills and for new mills, allowing about 30 percent more pollution for existing mills. To the extent that it is cheaper to pollute than not to, this differential standard gives an edge to existing producers over any possible new competitors.

The issues involved in the regulation of occupational health and safety contain many points similar to those of environmental protection. We have the same type of dual federal-provincial jurisdictions, with the provincial governments playing the major role because of their control over health. Regulation increases the costs of production, and there are incentives for shifting these costs to society in general. Nonetheless, the need for occupational health and safety regulation is better understood by the business sector, due to the significant direct costs that unsafe or unhealthy work conditions impose upon employers. Also, the regulatory mechanism is better organized, mostly under the various provincial workmen's compensation boards.

Accidents and health hazards in the workplace impose some costs to the firms because of lost production time. The costs imposed to the workers and society in general, though, are much higher, including loss of health, medical expenses, and loss of income. To some extent, workers are able to recoup some of their losses by demanding a higher wage for industries with difficult working conditions. Thus miners, loggers, and construction workers have higher incomes than the average industrial worker. It is not clear, however, how much of this premium is attributable to occupational hazards as distinct from other factors such as the seasonal nature of employment. At any rate, as long as the cost of prevention of work-related accidents and health hazards is borne solely by the employer, while their consequences are shared by other parties as well, there are incentives for inadequate prevention in the absence of regulation.

Overall, the compensation system that has been developed is similar to a public insurance scheme. Employers pay the costs of the compensation of work accident victims under the form of a payroll tax dependent on the industry. This limits their legal liability, provided they have observed the associated rules and regulations. The independently functioning workmen's compensation boards determine the relevant compensation for each accident, as well as the degree of compliance to the safety rules. These rules have been strengthened by legislation passed by many provinces during the 1970s that levies additional fines when regulations are contravened.

As this brief survey shows, for all the similarity in name new regulation has a qualitatively different economic impact on regulated industries than direct regulation. As already noted, it cannot be explained by the capture theories, given that it is almost always resisted by the affected firms. It pays comparatively little attention to economic parameters such as prices and quantities produced, and more to specific dimensions of conduct such as investment and the choice of production techniques. For this reason it is very often left outside the traditional subject matter of industrial organization. Nonetheless, it forms a large and growing aspect of government intervention in the economy that has also had some impact on the structure-conduct-performance model. This is particularly true for environmental pollution regulation which can create barriers to entry by treating the clean environment as a scarce common property resource and by imposing differential standards on existing and new firms.

Conclusions

Economic regulation of the direct type is an alternative to competition policy, even though it starts from diametrically opposed objectives. Competition policy pursues efficiency by improving the operation of the market system. Regulation, on the other hand, starts from the premise that an efficient market system is impossible. It then goes on to design an administrative mechanism that replaces the market determination of economic parameters such as prices and output quantities, while simultaneously sheltering the firms from competition.

According to economic theory, legitimate areas for the application of direct regulation are those in which there is market failure because of the existence of a natural monopoly or a common property resource. Natural monopolies exist mostly in the public utilities area, in which the market structure in

Canada is a mixture of public and private regulated monopolies. Regulation associated with a common property resource is found in broadcasting and commercial fisheries.

Direct regulation has also been extended to a number of other sectors in which market failure cannot be presumed to exist. The aim of such regulation is the protection of existing producers, most often at the expense of the consumers of the industry's product. Although economic arguments under the form of the alleged destructiveness of competition are sometimes offered in such cases, it is the political strength of the producer group that provides the main impetus to the regulatory efforts. The size of the benefits accruing to those producers already in the industry when regulation is introduced is a strong incentive to effective political action on their part.

The deregulation movement, which made its appearance in the decade of the 1970s and 1980s, was aimed especially against these cases of regulation that were not justified on economic grounds. It also encompassed certain sectors such as telecommunications in which technological developments have changed the structure of the sector. The movement had some important successes, particularly in the transportation area. Other sectors, though, have so far proved resistant to all proposals for change. Most of the current threats to the status quo of these sectors come mainly from foreign trade, which will be surveyed in more detail in the following chapter.

Finally, economic regulation traditionally encompasses restrictions on the activities of private firms, imposed to shift back to these firms the costs that their operations have imposed on others. Such restrictions exist mainly in the areas of environmental protection and occupational health and safety. Although this type of regulation lies outside the structure-conduct-performance model and belongs to a different branch of economic theory, it nonetheless represents an important area of government intervention in the economy.

Endnotes

1. In a competitive bidding environment, the value of the franchise would be equal to the capitalized stream of monopoly profits.

2. Proposals to allocate broadcasting licences in such a way were also formulated in Noll *et al.* (1973).

3. For a full statement of the public interest argument see Bonbright (1961), p. 23.

4. This, however, was not totally true in broadcasting and cable TV, in which the licence transfer prices were significantly less than the capitalized expected profits; see Perrakis and Silva-Echenique (1983, 1985).

5. See his 1979 account of that experience.

6. This is known as the TransCanada Telephone System or TCTS.

7. For an economic analysis of that decision, see the collection of essays by Evans *et al.* (1983).

8. In other words, the unregulated services must carry their share of the cost of the common resources, such as the local network and the overhead expenses.

9. A primary requirement since 1969 is that the new owner be Canadian.

10. More recently, the CRTC requires that a specific share of revenues be devoted to Canadian programming.

11. See Babe (1979), pp. 84-86.

12. The latest one is the so-called Caplan-Sauvageau report (1986).

13. For instance, Noll *et al.* (1973), Park (1975) and Perrakis and Silva-Echenique (1985).

14. See Munasinghe and Corbo (1978), and Perrakis and Silva-Echenique (1983).

15. See Baumol and Willig (1986).

16. See M. Schwartz (1986), p. 48.

17. See the *Ottawa Citizen*, April 14, 1988.

18. These are, respectively, Canadian National and Canadian Pacific (CN and CP).

19. For a review of such proposals see Cubukgil (1987).

20. An extended analysis of the welfare effects of price stabilization is in Scherer (1980), pp. 216-220.

21. See the ECC report (1981), pp. 62-63.

22. See Perrakis and Switzer (1988), Chapter 9.

23. See Borcherding and Dorosh (1981), p. 21.

24. More details on the now-defunct NEP can be found in Green (1985), pp. 357-372.

25. In addition to the 1981 ECC report, there are extended economic analyses of the regulation of commercial fishing in Scott and Neher (1981), and Lane (1988).

26. There are complaints by the small inshore fishermen that the large quotas allocated to the offshore fishing firms are reducing their own catches.

27. The material in this section is based on Chapters 8 and 9 of the ECC report (1981), as well as on Schworm (1985).

28. In other words, the right to pollute up to a given total becomes a scarce common property resource allocated through a quota system.

References

Babe, R. *Canadian Television Broadcasting Structure, Performance and Regulation*. Ottawa, Ont.: Economic Council of Canada, 1979.

Baumol. W. and R.D. Willig. "Contestability: Developments since the Book," *Oxford Economic Papers*, new series, Vol. 38, supplement (Nov. 1986).

Bonbright, J.C. *Principles of Public Utility Rates*. New York, N.Y.: Columbia University Press, 1961.

Borcherding, T. and G. Dorosh. *The Egg Marketing Board: A Case Study of Monopoly and its Social Costs*. Vancouver, B.C.: The Fraser Institute, 1981.

Caplan, G.L. and F. Sauvageau, (co-chairmen). *Report of the Task Force on Broadcasting Policy*. Ottawa, Ont.: Minister of Supply and Services, 1986.

Cubukgil, A. *Structural Change and Regulatory Reform in Rail Transport*. Discussion Paper #315. Ottawa, Ont.: Economic Council of Canada, 1987.

Demsetz, H. "Why Regulate Utilities?" *Journal of Law and Economics*, Vol. 11 (April 1968), pp. 55-66.

Economic Council of Canada. *Reforming Regulation*. Ottawa, Ont.: Minister of Supply and Services, 1981.

Evans, D.S., ed. *Breaking Up Bell*. New York, N.Y.: North-Holland, 1983.

Green, C. *Canadian Industrial Organization and Policy*. Toronto, Ont.: McGraw-Hill Ryerson, 2nd Edition, 1985.

Kahn, A. "Applications of Economics to an Imperfect World," *American Economic Review*, 69:2 (May 1979), pp. 1-13.

Lane, D. "Investment Decision-Making by Fishermen," *Canadian Journal of Fisheries and Aquatic Sciences*, 45:5 (1988), pp. 782-796.

Munasinghe, M. and V. Corbo. "The Demand for CATV Services in Canada," *Canadian Journal of Economics*, II (1978), pp. 506-520.

Noll, R.G., M.J. Peck, and J.J. McGowan. *Economic Aspects of Television Regulation*. Washington, D.C.: The Brookings Institution, 1973.

Park, R.E. "New Television Networks," *The Bell Journal of Economics*, 6: 2 (1975), pp. 607-620.

Perrakis, S. and J. Silva-Echenique. "The Profitability and Risk of CATV Operations in Canada," *Applied Economics*, 15: 6 (December 1983), pp. 745-758.

————. "The Profitability and Risk of Television Stations in Canada," *Applied Economics*, 17 (August 1985), pp. 745-759.

Perrakis, S. and L. Switzer. *Industrial and Economic Analysis*. Montreal, P.Q.: The Canadian Bankers' Institute, 1988.

Posner, R.A. "Taxation by Regulation," *The Bell Journal of Economics and Management Science*, 2:1 (Spring 1971), pp. 22-50.

Scherer, F.M. *Industrial Market Structure and Economic Performance*. Chicago, Ill.: Rand McNally, 2nd Edition, 1980.

Schwartz, M. "The Nature and Scope of Contestability Theory," *Oxford Economic Papers*, 38, Supplement (November 1986) pp. 37-57.

Schworm, W. "Public Policies for Controlling Environmental Use," *Approaches to Economic Well-Being*, D. Laidler, ed. Toronto, Ont.: University of Toronto Press, 1985.

Scott, A. and P.A. Neher, eds. *The Public Regulation of Commercial Fisheries in Canada*. Ottawa, Ont.: Economic Council of Canada, 1981.

Stigler, G.J. "Theory of Economic Regulation," *Bell Journal of Economics and Management Science*, 2:1 (Spring 1971), pp. 3-21.

Williamson, O. "Franchise Bidding for Natural Monopolies—in General and with Respect to CATV," *Bell Journal of Economics*, 7:1 (Spring 1976), pp. 73-104.

C H A P T E R 11

Other Topics of

....

Canadian Public Policy

....

This chapter examines four selected topics relevant to public policy that do not fall easily within the structure-conduct-performance (SCP) model. These topics are either macroeconomic in nature, such as the issue of protectionism and free trade and its implications for SCP, or have dynamic consequences that transcend the static nature of SCP such as patents and research and development. Last, there are also two particular issues that have attracted the attention of Canadian policy-makers several times during recent years. These are the topics of foreign investment and the public enterprise, both of which present particular interest for all students of Canadian industrial organization.

All four topics examined in this chapter have engendered major political debates on several occasions in recent years. In 1988, the Canadian House of Commons passed legislation implementing free trade between Canada and the U.S. Free trade has been and continues to be highly controversial, with two of the three major federal parties and the Province of Ontario opposed to it.

Similar controversies accompany the other three topics every time they surface for one reason or another. The issue of foreign (chiefly U.S.) investment in Canada and the alleged threat to our national sovereignty and long-term well-being has ebbed and flowed with the tides of federal politics. It also played an important part in Canada-U.S. negotiations preceding the signing of the free trade agreement. While this issue is dormant at the moment, there is no guarantee that it will not resurface in the near future.

The problem of the appropriate length of protection to be granted to patented drugs was a particularly divisive issue during 1986-87. As we shall see, this problem does not have an easy answer. The conflicts that arise between static welfare considerations and long-term growth and technological change demand a compromise that is not going to satisfy everybody. These conflicts are exacerbated by the international dimensions of the problem, given that many of the patent holders are multinational firms that perform most of their research outside Canada.

Finally, we have the case of the public enterprises in Canada, and the appropriate role that public ownership must play in our economic system. This topic has also been in the news during the 1980s, not only in Canada but in several European countries as well. Privatization of public enterprises seems to have been the fashion for some time, especially in the United Kingdom. Yet this privatization poses its own problems, especially if the market structure is a natural monopoly. The efficiency problems in the regulation of such monopolies are, as we saw in Chapter 3, not easily solvable even with the best of intentions. For this reason the Canadian economy, where public and private firms coexist sometimes within the same industry, offers an ideal environment for the study of the topic.

The next section examines the issue of foreign trade and its impact on the SCP model. A second section focusses specifically on the Canada-U.S. free trade agreement. Foreign investment comes next, followed by the patent laws, while a discussion of the public enterprise closes the chapter.

Foreign Trade and the Performance of Canadian Industry

Canadian firms have traditionally enjoyed substantial protection from competition in the international trade in goods through tariffs and quota barriers. Such barriers have not, in general, been viewed favourably by economists. Both cause pricing distortions in which prices deviate from marginal costs. In spite of this, there are some circumstances in which tariffs may be beneficial. For instance, if there are already significant distortions in the domestic economy, the tariffs can be used as a second-best measure of maximizing real income, in the spirit of the analysis that we saw briefly in Chapter 7. Similarly, tariffs are sometimes justified as a temporary measure by the "infant industry" argument, which advocates protection in the early stages of a new industry until it becomes sufficiently well established to withstand competition.[1]

More often, though, trade barriers may be explained by political arguments. Typical examples are the import restrictions that accompany government-sponsored cartels in milk, poultry, and eggs, which we saw in the previous chapter. In this case trade restrictions are an essential component of the system, which would not be able to function without them. Caves (1976) argued that tariffs in recent Canadian history reflect the politics of interest group pressure tactics. His study found that tariffs tend to be higher in industries with market power, whose profits can be used to finance lobbying efforts.

In spite of this historical reality, the fact is that the overall tendency in recent years has been towards greater trade liberalization. The origins of this process are in the General Agreement on Tariffs and Trade (GATT), established in 1948. By late 1987, over 130 countries either belonged to the GATT organization or had agreed to abide by its rules.[2] Since its inception, GATT has sponsored a number of rounds of multilateral trade barrier reductions; the Uruguay round started in late 1986. The previous Tokyo round, which ended in 1979, resulted in an overall reduction of tariffs to an average level of 5.2 percent (from 7.3 percent) in Canada, and to 4.3 percent (from 6.5 percent) in the U.S. Table 11.1 shows the tariff rates before and after the Tokyo round for most manufacturing industries in Canada and in the U.S., and in a sample of 18 industrialized nations.

The GATT has set forth a number of standards for the commercial policies of its participating nations. Examples of such standards are nondiscrimination, national treatment, and transparency of trade barriers.[3] These, however, have not always been honoured by the members, and certainly not by Canada and the United States. Examples of blatant violations of the spirit of the GATT rules are plentiful. For instance, the Canada-U.S. automotive trade agreement (or Auto Pact) was exempted from the application of the GATT rules even though it does not conform to the principle of nondiscrimination. Similarly, there are a variety of trade practices such as "voluntary" export restraints that violate the transparency of trade barriers principle. It should be noted that GATT, which is a strictly voluntary agreement, has no enforcement powers. It has itself condoned many of the violations by including among its articles an escape clause that allows increased protection against imports, to the extent that it can be shown that increased imports may cause serious injury to the domestic industry. Further, if imports are alleged to be subsidized, foreign countries are entitled to impose countervailing duties equivalent to the determined subsidy. Unfortunately, there is no general agreement on what constitutes a subsidy in most cases.

For all these reasons, GATT has not been as effective as many economists had expected. It has been estimated that over one-half of world trade is conducted under terms that defy GATT rules. For instance, these rules have never been applied to agriculture, which forms a major subject of the Uruguay round. Similarly, GATT has not liberalized trade in textiles and apparel, for which quotas have been applied on most products, largely to the detriment of less developed nations. In all these cases the GATT rules are either inapplicable or were relaxed as an exception for the affected sectors.

TABLE 11.1
Tokyo Round tariff rates by industry (Percent, weighted by own country imports, excluding petroleum)

	After			Before		
	Canada	U.S.	Sample	Canada	U.S.	Sample
Textiles	16.7	9.2	8.5	18.9	14.4	10.7
Clothing	24.2	22.7	17.5	25.4	27.8	20.7
Leather products	6.3	4.2	3.0	8.2	5.6	4.5
Footwear	21.9	8.8	12.1	24.5	8.8	12.4
Wood products	3.2	1.7	1.9	5.8	3.6	2.7
Furniture and fixtures	14.3	4.1	7.3	19.4	8.1	10.3
Paper and paper products	6.7	0.2	4.2	11.8	0.5	5.8
Printing and publishing	1.0	0.7	1.5	5.7	1.1	2.9
Chemicals	7.5	2.4	6.7	7.9	3.8	9.4
Rubber products	6.7	2.5	4.1	12.2	3.6	5.8
Nonmetallic mineral products	6.4	5.3	4.0	9.5	9.1	5.8
Glass and glass products	7.2	6.2	7.9	11.3	10.7	10.5
Iron and steel	5.4	3.6	4.4	6.7	4.7	5.8
Nonferrous metals	2.0	0.7	1.6	2.0	1.2	2.0
Metal products	8.5	4.8	6.3	14.1	7.5	9.0
Nonelectrical machinery	4.5	3.3	4.7	6.1	5.0	6.7
Electrical machinery	5.8	4.4	7.1	12.9	6.6	9.6
Transportation equipment	1.6	2.5	6.0	2.4	3.3	7.7
Miscellaneous manufacturing	5.4	4.2	4.7	8.8	7.8	7.8
All industries	5.2	4.3	5.8	7.3	6.5	7.8

Note: The countries in the sample were: Australia, Austria, Belgium, Luxembourg, Canada, Denmark, Finland, France, Germany, Ireland, Italy, Japan, Netherlands, New Zealand, Norway, Sweden, Switzerland, the UK.
Source: Deardorff and Stern (1983), p. 608.

Still, there is little doubt that GATT must receive credit for much of the liberalization in international trade that took place in the post-World War II period. This liberalization brought major benefits to participating nations. For instance, it was estimated that the Tokyo round has increased real income in the world by over $5 billion (U.S. funds). For Canada this increase was $422 million (U.S. funds), while over 25,000 new jobs were deemed to owe their existence to negotiated reductions of trade barriers.[4]

As we saw in Chapter 2, trade liberalization has had a major impact on the structure of many Canadian industries. The data in Table 2.1 showed very clearly that for most Canadian manufacturing industries both imports and exports increased dramatically over the 1966-1983 period, which includes the implementation of the Tokyo round of GATT tariff cuts. The result of this internationalization of the Canadian market is bound to make the affected industries more competitive. Much of the remainder of this section is focussed on the effects of this structural change on the conduct and performance of Canadian industries.

The implications of the trade barriers for the structure and conduct of Canadian industry were first analyzed in the pioneering study by Eastman and Stykolt (1967), which was cited extensively in Chapter 2. Figure 11.1 shows the implied analysis of firm conduct that emerges from their model. The curve DD' represents the domestic demand for the output of a Canadian industry in a totally closed economy. The line AA' is the level of product price prevailing in world markets. If tariffs and transportation costs are added to that price, then we reach the level BB', which is the highest price that domestic producers can charge; anything above that will attract massive penetration of the domestic market by imports. Hence, the effective demand curve facing the domestic firms is B*dd'*A'.

Suppose now that the structure of the Canadian industry is oligopolistic,

FIGURE 11.1
Monopoly pricing in the presence of imports and exports

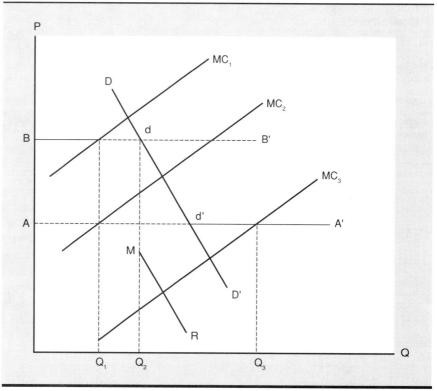

and that this oligopoly behaves collusively. Then it can be easily seen that the product price in the domestic segment of the market will depend on the location of the marginal cost curves MC of the oligopolists. The marginal revenue curve MR will coincide with BB' in the upper segment of the demand curve and will be discontinuous at d, with dM representing the size of the discontinuity gap. Beyond d', on the other hand, the cartel can effectively segment the market, by selling at a higher price at home than abroad.[5] The marginal revenue for the export market will coincide with d'A'.

For the situation depicted in Figure 11.1 the domestic price will always be equal to BB' (or a shade below it), no matter what the location of MC is. Three such possible locations, identified with the subscripts $i = 1, 2, 3$ in decreasing order of cost, are shown. The highest cost situation MC_1 has the domestic firms supplying an amount Q_1 and imports capturing $Q_2 - Q_1$. In MC_2, on the other hand, the domestic firms supply the entire home market Q_2, and do not participate in any export activity. Last, when marginal cost becomes MC_3, the cartel equates marginal revenue at home and abroad by producing a total amount of Q_3 and selling Q_2 domestically at a price BB', while exporting the rest at the world price AA'.

There are, however, conceivable situations in which the domestic sales and price need not always be equal to Q_2 and BB' respectively, no matter what the marginal cost curve is. For this to be possible, the distance between AA' and BB' must exceed the discontinuity gap dM of the marginal revenue function. If the location of the marginal cost is such that its intersection with the marginal revenue MR takes place at a level above the line AA' then the domestic sales and price would be respectively above Q_2 and below BB'. The maximum domestic sales observed in such situations occur when the marginal cost shifts down to a location similar to MC_3. They are then given by the intersection of the curve MR with the line AA'.

Several aspects of the Eastman-Stykolt analysis require further elaboration. Foremost among them is the problem of entry of new firms. The high domestic prices fostered by tariffs also create high profits for the cartel members; these profits are further bolstered by the difference between nominal and *effective* tariff rates (see below). These high profits are bound to attract entry in the domestic market by new firms or subsidiaries of foreign multinationals. Further, the high prices and profits may allow suboptimally-small firms to survive, thus encouraging high cost production. This last element of the Eastman-Stykolt analysis is the one we already encountered in Chapter 2. It is also the one that has attracted most attention and discussion over the many years since the study first appeared.

The theoretical underpinnings of the argument are rather weak.[6] Why, for instance, would an oligopolistic industry tolerate suboptimal firms when it is in everybody's interest to encourage rationalization of production? Alternatively, why would existing large firms refrain from absorbing their smaller opponents or driving them out of business? On the other hand, if no such large firms exist, would not one firm reduce its costs by growing and benefitting from economies of scale, and then use its advantages to prevail over its competitors?

There are several possible answers to these questions, none of them totally convincing. In fact, as we saw in Chapter 5, the period of the 1970s saw a progressive rationalization of production in Canadian manufacturing, perhaps associated with the on-going reduction of tariffs from the Tokyo round. Yet such a rationalization was not sufficient to eliminate the suboptimal capacity, as shown by several empirical studies. It is possible that the existence of plants below the minimum efficient size (MES) for their industry was made possible by the nature of the entry-deterring equilibrium. Alternatively, it may be product differentiation that enables small firms to prosper. This was supported by the results of the major study by Caves *et al.* (1980), cited in several previous chapters, which showed that product differentiation counteracted somewhat the negative effects of small scale on the survivability of small firms. Still another possibility is the small size and regional character of many markets, as we saw in Chapter 2: there may be sufficient demand for only one below-MES plant, which is insulated from competition by high transportation costs.

Whatever the reason may be, the fact is that there was (and most probably still is) significant suboptimal capacity in Canada and, most important for the topic of this chapter, its existence is linked to tariff protection. The key study that showed this link was by Baldwin and Gorecki (1986), which compared the performance of matched U.S. and Canadian manufacturing industries at the four-digit SIC level. A summary of their results is presented in Table 11.2. This shows the comparative Canada/U.S. total factor productivity for two benchmark years for groups of manufacturing industries. The results showed that, overall, Canadian manufacturing was lagging in performance, with productivity between 70 and 80 percent of the U.S. levels. Much of this reduced performance was directly or indirectly attributable to the existence of plant-level economies of scale that could be realized in the larger American market. Further, competition from imports was just about the only factor that showed a systematic, positive relationship with comparative productivity and performance.

The negative impact of trade barriers on performance that emerges from the Baldwin-Gorecki results may also be linked to X-inefficiency due to lack of competition. Whatever the reason, this negative effect is by itself sufficient to justify reduction of tariffs. The tariffs and other trade barriers are, however, profitable for domestic firms since they allow them to exercise market power in the spirit of the analysis in Figure 11.1. Their profits are magnified because the effective tariff rates are higher than the nominal ones for most Canadian industries.[7] These effective rates are the percentage increases in the industry's total value-added as a result of the tariff. To compute them one needs to subtract the tariffs paid for material inputs to production. Suppose, for

TABLE 11.2
**Relative Canada/U.S. productivity at the industry group level,[a]
Canada 1970 and 1979**

Number of Constituent 4-Digit Industries (1)	Industry Group (2)	1970 (3)	1979 (4)
15	Food & beverages (10)	0.7055	0.7425
1	Tobacco (15)	0.8864	1.0829
0	Rubber & plastics (16)	—	—
4	Leather (17)	0.6731	0.6661
11	Textiles (18)	0.5934	0.6902
12	Knitting mills (23)	0.5615	0.6805
5	Clothing (24)	0.6298	0.7375
6	Wood products (25)	0.5031	0.9955
2	Furniture & fixtures (26)	2.6741	2.7209
5	Paper & allied products (27)	0.5658	0.6958
1	Printing & publishing (28)	0.7307	0.9052
3	Primary metals (29)	0.8302	0.8681
7	Metal fabricating (30)	0.7438	0.8908
2	Machinery (31)	1.1952	1.2293
8	Transportation equipment (32)	0.7656	0.7794
7	Electrical products (33)	1.1299	1.1529
9	Non-metallic mineral products (35)	0.6415	0.8340
0	Petroleum & coal products (36)	—	—
6	Chemicals and chemical products (37)	0.7468	0.9459
13	Miscellaneous manufacturing (39)	0.8611	1.3057
107	Total manufacturing	0.7706 (0.5208)[b]	0.9250 (0.7238)[b]

[a] The various Canada/U.S. ratios were first estimated for the 107 4-digit industry sample. Then for each industry group, the Canada/U.S. ratio is the mean of the ratio for the 4-digit industries classified to each industry group. The number of such industries is presented in column 1.
[b] Standard deviation of the 107-industry sample.
Source: Baldwin and Gorecki (1986), p. 137

instance, that a firm imports components worth $5 000 and assembles them to make computers in Canada, where it can sell them for the world price of $10 000. If a 30 percent nominal tariff is imposed on the final product, then the domestic price rises to $13 000. If no tariffs are imposed on the components, however, then the value-added becomes $8 000, corresponding to an effective tariff of $100 \times 3\,000/5\,000 = 60$ percent. By contrast, nominal and effective tariffs are equal in this example if the 30 percent tariff is also imposed on the imported components: the firm must pay $6 500 for the components, yielding a value-added of $6 500 and an effective tariff of $100 \times 1\,500/5\,000 = 30$ percent.

In what follows, however, we shall ignore X-inefficiency and differences between nominal and effective tariff rates in order to focus on the impact on aggregate welfare of a reduction in tariffs in an industry. From Figure 11.1 we can easily see that such a reduction will eventually reduce the prices (and profits) of the domestic producers, by lowering the line BB' and displacing the kink to the right. Needless to say, this will bring benefits to Canadian consumers. Is the size of these benefits sufficient to overcome the loss in producer profits? To answer this question we shall use the combined consumer plus producer surplus tool, presented in Chapter 7 and already used several times in this text.

Figure 11.2 shows an industry in which Canada is a net importer. The domestic demand curve is DD', and the prevailing price in the world markets is P_W. A tariff is levied that raises the domestic price to P_D. For simplicity, we

FIGURE 11.2
Welfare analysis of tariff removals for a net importing sector

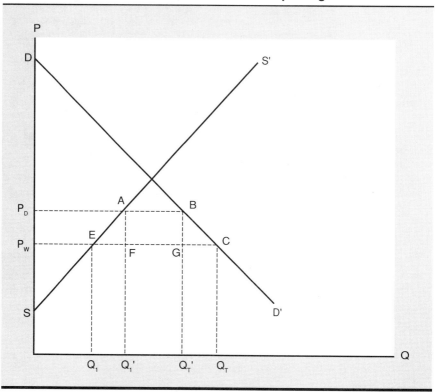

assume that transportation costs are negligible, so that $P_D - P_W$ represents only the tariff. We also assume that competitive conditions prevail domestically, so that firms equate price to marginal cost. The curve SS' is the Canadian industry's aggregate supply curve.

As the diagram shows, in the presence of tariffs the domestic firms produce an amount Q_1', while the portion $Q_T' - Q_1'$ of total domestic demand is supplied by imports. When the tariffs are removed the industry produces Q_1, while $Q_T - Q_1$ is imported. Hence, the tariff removal reduces domestic prices and expands imports, while simultaneously eliminating the tariff revenue collected by the government. The size of this revenue is equal to the area of the rectangle ABGF, i.e., the tariff rate times the imports.

To evaluate the aggregate surplus with and without the tariff we must add consumer and producer surplus with and without the tariff, and then compare the totals. With the tariff, the total surplus is equal to the areas of the triangles DBP_D and SAP_D; without the tariff it is the areas of the triangles DCP_W and SEP_W. The second total clearly exceeds the first by the size of the area ECBA. From this, however, one must subtract the tariff revenue ABGF, since it was also available to the community when the tariff was present. Hence, the net benefit of the removal of the tariff is given by the sum of the areas of the triangles AFE and BGC. This is clearly a positive quantity, implying that the removal of a tariff (and, by extension, of any other trade barrier) is beneficial even for a net importing industry.

A similar result holds also for an industry in which Canada is a net exporter. Here one must evaluate the benefits of the removal of the foreign tariff upon the Canadian public. The analysis is shown in Figure 11.3. Note that here the "world" price P_W exceeds the domestic price P_D which prevails in the presence of a foreign tariff by the size of that tariff, since otherwise exports would not be profitable. Hence, the tariff removal raises product price from P_D to P_W, expands total production from Q_T to Q_T', and reduces domestic sales from Q_1 to Q_1'. As for the total surplus comparison, it can be easily seen that the absence of a tariff will increase total surplus by the area IJKL.

These results are fairly unambiguous and non-controversial. They become considerably more complex if the assumption of perfect competition in the domestic market is removed. In such a case, the welfare effects of the tariff removal interact with the deadweight loss due to the monopoly. The final result depends on the degree of product differentiation between domestic production and imports, and the conditions of import supply. Stegeman (1984) has presented a detailed analysis of most relevant cases. A study by Ross (1988b) presents some perverse cases in which the removal of tariffs may even result in higher domestic prices and a lower aggregate welfare. In other words, under imperfect competition in the domestic market there is considerable uncertainty about the size of the benefits from free trade, which becomes very sensitive to the particular conditions prevailing in the sector.

FIGURE 11.3
Welfare analysis of tariff removals for an exporting industry

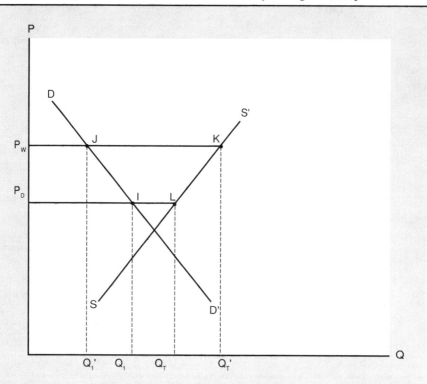

A general problem with this type of work is the piecemeal approach inherent in the total surplus method. This implies, as we recall from Chapter 7, that inter-industry effects of the removal of tariffs in a particular industry are not taken into account when we focus exclusively on the affected sector. Nonetheless, these simple demonstrations of the benefits of trade liberalizations are useful complements of more complex analyses.

Such analyses have been carried out recently in connection with the free trade agreement between Canada and the United States. The amount of discussions and level of controversy generated by this agreement warrant a more detailed discussion in the next section. As already noted, the implementation of the agreement was approved by Parliament in 1988, although there is still considerable uncertainty about the details of its application.

The Canada-U.S. Free Trade Agreement

In October 1987, Canada and the U.S. signed a bilateral agreement to establish a free trade zone, which provides for the removal of tariffs and most non-tariff trade barriers starting in 1989. As already noted, the agreement was controversial from the outset. The main bone of contention is its ultimate effectiveness in opening up the huge U.S. market to Canadian exports in the face of mounting protectionist sentiment in that country. Although it certainly provides no less access than previously available, its critics have questioned whether the possibility of increased access is worth the concessions that Canada had to make to obtain the agreement.

A different line of attack on the agreement raised questions on the necessity of bilateral trade liberalization in view of the ongoing GATT-sponsored Uruguay round of multilateral tariff cuts. Why not focus negotiation efforts on that round? The main answer is that most Canadian trade is with the U.S., especially in our export market. Thus, a bilateral arrangement may have more potential for spurring the economy than a multilateral deal. In addition, much of U.S. trade law in recent years has not been administered in the spirit of the GATT. The vulnerability of Canadian exports to adverse American actions in the area of trade barriers provides a justification of the bilateral agreement as a defensive measure, intended to insure continued access to the U.S. market.

A fair assessment of the agreement must take into account these justifications. How important is the agreement to the long-term growth prospects of the Canadian economy? How effective are its clauses in insulating Canada from protectionist U.S. actions? We shall start with the second question, which is also the most controversial.

The free trade accord eliminates all bilateral tariffs between the two countries over ten years, starting January 1, 1989. It also provides for the relaxation of many (but not all) nontariff barriers. It is not a comprehensive agreement, leaving outside several important industries while affecting others only marginally. Nonetheless, most sectors will be affected, implying that some Canadian industries will contract and lose market share to imports, while others will expand in the U.S. market at the expense of local U.S. producers. Since the latter are not expected to take their decline graciously, the ability of the agreement to prevent U.S. producers from invoking their country's trade laws in order to erect trade barriers is crucial to its evaluation.

There is no question that several U.S. actions in recent years have contravened the spirit of GATT.[8] For instance, the U.S. has imposed global quotas on carbon steel, directed at Brazil, Korea and Spain; it has spared Canada only because Canadian producers have agreed to comply with "voluntary" export restraints. As the U.S. trade balance deteriorated over the period of the mid- to late-1980s, so have protectionist decisions escalated. These decisions are taken by quasi-judicial agencies established under American trade law, which are empowered to place duties or trade restrictions on Canadian goods. They have in the past used GATT's countervail and antidumping provisions, frequently without merit.[9] Many of these provisions invoke trade sanctions when exports are being subsidized one way or another.

Unfortunately, the free trade agreement has not taken a position on what constitutes a subsidy, leaving itself open to charges that it will not stop the abuses of GATT rules. The definition of subsidies will form the subject of separate negotiations that will stretch over five or more years. As an example of the contentiousness and importance of this issue one should mention the fact that several U.S. producers have argued in the past that Canada's publicly-funded health insurance plans are a subsidy that should be countervailed. If such contentions are accepted then the only Canadian recourse is either the abandonment of the agreement, or the complete realignment of the country's socioeconomic policy to that of the U.S.

The agreement provides for the establishment of a bilateral panel to deal with trade disputes. The efficiency of this panel will be a major determinant of the success of the agreement in establishing free trade. While the panel must comply with the existing trade laws of both countries, it has jurisdiction in deciding whether these laws have been applied fairly. As for future trade laws, they are supposed to comply to the terms of the agreement. Note, however, that U.S. administration officials have argued that in the event of Canada winning an arbitration ruling against a future U.S. trade law, the U.S. can still refuse to change the law.[10] These are ominous statements that may leave precious few choices for future Canadian governments. In this author's opinion the questions about the effectiveness of the agreement in preventing arbitrary U.S. actions against Canadian exports have not been answered satisfactorily by its supporters.[11]

On the other hand, the evidence seems to indicate that the Canada-U.S. trade agreement, if allowed to function fairly, will bring significant benefits to the Canadian economy. Perhaps the most comprehensive and widely regarded sets of studies on this question are those of Harris (1984), and Cox and Harris (1986). These studies are based on an applied general equilibrium model of the Canadian economy, which avoids the pitfalls of piecemeal approaches that neglect secondary effects. The model is thus capable of showing the vulnerability of individual sectors to free trade in a consistent manner that reflects intersectoral linkages. In addition, the approach integrates for the first time SCP features that are unique to the Canadian economy, such as scale economies and imperfect competition.

For the economy as a whole, the Cox-Harris study found that bilateral free trade with the U.S. will lead to sizable gains, on the order of nine percent of GNP, over the situation prevailing in 1976. The gains, however, will not be spread uniformly among sectors. In particular, the model suggests significant labour dislocation amounting to a six to seven percent shift of employment between sectors. Table 11.3 shows the performance and vulnerability of individual sectors of Canadian manufacturing according to the Cox-Harris study.

These results appear quite impressive. In particular, all sectors are shown to gain in productivity, while most sectors gain in output. The employment picture is not as rosy, but the net effect is positive if not very large. These results, though, should be interpreted with some caution. It has been shown that the effects of free trade are quite sensitive to the existence of scale economies in individual sectors, which were assumed by the study. As we saw in Chapter 2, the balance of the evidence supports that assumption, but there is some doubt about the extent of these scale economies. Also, the data used in deriving the results of Table 11.3 does not take into account the post-1976

TABLE 11.3
The sectoral implications of free trade

	D-output	D-prod	D-emply
Textiles	1.267	0.315	0.725
Steel	0.279	0.233	0.037
Agricultural equipment	−0.101	0.232	−0.269
Urban transportation equipment	0.944	0.267	0.535
Chemicals	0.234	0.231	0.002
Food and beverages	0.246	0.269	−0.018
Tobacco	0.276	0.417	−0.099
Rubber	0.382	0.302	0.062
Leather	0.248	0.341	−0.069
Knitting	0.984	0.391	0.426
Clothing	4.789	0.601	2.616
Wood	0.150	0.309	−0.121
Furniture	−0.152	0.355	−0.374
Paper and allied products	0.599	0.214	0.317
Printing	0.359	0.198	0.135
Metal fabricating	0.147	0.229	−0.066
Non-agricultural machinery	−0.180	0.228	−0.332
Transport equipment	1.047	0.262	0.622
Electrical products	−0.005	0.269	−0.216
Non-metal mineral products	0.215	0.223	−0.006
Petroleum	0.235	0.334	−0.074
Miscellaneous manufacturing	−0.188	0.218	−0.333

Notes: Both trade liberalization experiments assume the removal of export subsidies on the appropriate trade between Canada and U.S. industries. D-output refers to the relative change in industry output over base; D-prod is the relative change in industry labour productivity over base; D-emply is the relative change in industry employment over base.
Source: D. Cox and R. Harris (1986), p. 386.

trade liberalization. For these reasons, subsequent estimates of the effects of the free trade agreement have been much more modest than the Cox-Harris results.[12]

On balance, the free trade agreement, when stripped of all posturing and political rhetoric, has the potential of being quite beneficial to Canadian welfare. It also has the potential of developing into a major political and economic nightmare. The inadequacy of its safeguards against the abuse of GATT provisions can easily be exploited by the U.S. administrative and political system under the prod of affected industries. Clearly, much of its success or failure will depend on the political will on both sides of the border to live by the spirit as well as the letter of the agreement. Unfortunately, the experience of the recent past does not leave much ground for optimism.

Foreign Investment

Foreign ownership and control of important segments of the Canadian economy have been facts of life in Canada for a very long time. In 1926, foreign-controlled firms accounted for 17 percent of the total financial capital in all Canadian industries.[13] By contrast, the share of foreign-owned capital that same year was more than twice that amount. (Foreign ownership includes minority equity holdings and debt holdings that do not control the management of the issuing firm.) While foreign ownership has had its ups and downs since that time, it is foreign control that has caused most controversy and concern in recent years. This control increased dramatically during the postwar years, reaching its peak during the late 1960s and early 1970s. It then dropped equally dramatically, perhaps as a result of a number of highly visible public policy initiatives. As a source of public concern, the issue of foreign control in Canadian industry lies dormant at present (early 1989), but it has the potential of again becoming the focus of public attention. It also played a significant role in the Canada-U.S. free trade agreement.

Apart from the control element, the large degree of foreign ownership in the Canadian economy is particularly important for its macroeconomic implications. A large degree of foreign ownership indicates that in the past the country has consumed and invested (in the aggregate) more than it has produced and saved. The difference was financed by selling claims on Canadian assets to foreigners. This implies that every year there must be a compensating outflow of dividends and interest paid to foreigners in order to service these claims. With the exception of the years 1983-85, this outflow has been large enough to eliminate any excess of exports over imports, thus leading to further accumulation of foreign claims on Canada's wealth. These macroeconomic implications need not concern us here, but they serve as a reminder that foreign ownership of Canadian assets has implications that go beyond foreign control of Canadian firms.

Foreign control has been a highly emotional issue at times, because it raises questions about national sovereignty in the face of widespread foreign (chiefly American) domination of much of Canadian industry. The high point of these concerns was in the early 1970s, following the 1972 publication of a federal government report documenting the extent of foreign control in key sectors such as manufacturing and mining. This report, also known as the Gray Report, was instrumental in the establishment of the Foreign Investment Review Agency (FIRA), the most important public policy initiative in the foreign investment area. The agency's task was to screen mergers, takeovers and new investment proposals by foreign firms, and accept only those which would provide significant net benefits to Canada.

Before reviewing FIRA's operations in detail, it is worth examining briefly the theoretical treatment of foreign investment within the context of the SCP model. Conventional economic theory interprets foreign investment as a capital flow across foreign borders, in response to actual or expected differences in profitability. Many of these differences could in theory be exploited by foreign trade, if they are due to higher product prices in the host country. Such trade may, however, be restricted by tariffs, quotas, or other barriers. In such cases the flow of capital becomes a way of overcoming the trade barriers.

This, however, does not explain why this investment results in the establishment of a foreign subsidiary, or in foreign control of a domestic corporation, rather than with a simple inclusion of some of its securities in the foreign investors' portfolio. A possible explanation is the existence of production cost advantages in the foreign country. This has undoubtedly been a major factor in the flow of international investment from industrialized to developing nations, in order to take advantage of lower labour costs. Some of the U.S. investment in the Canadian mining and natural resources industries may also have been similarly motivated. Such motivations, though, cannot explain the widespread control of much of Canadian manufacturing by American firms and their subsidiaries. For instance, in 1981, 45 percent of the total financial assets of the Canadian manufacturing sector were under foreign (chiefly U.S.) control. In some sectors such as chemicals, rubber, and tobacco, the foreign-controlled assets ranged from 75 to 100 percent.[14]

An alternative and possibly complementary justification of foreign direct investment relies mainly on market imperfections for production inputs. According to this justification, foreign direct investment is a way of transferring inputs owned by the parent firm (that are only imperfectly marketable) to the subsidiary firm. Such inputs may be related to marketing, technology, or management, for example a brand name differentiating the product, a patented method of production, or the superior skills of the parent's top management. These inputs provide certain advantages to the foreign subsidiary when it competes with domestic firms, which serve to counteract the disadvantages of operating in a foreign country. They can also themselves become sources of barriers to further entry of Canadian firms, if the advantages they confer are sufficiently pronounced.

This explanation is consistent with much of the empirical research done in Canada in the recent past, which sought to explain the incidence of foreign investment in Canadian industry. Some of these studies and their results were already reviewed in Chapter 5 in the context of entry. As we saw, the study by Caves *et al.* (1980) found that the incidence of foreign presence in Canadian manufacturing was significantly related to the advantages enjoyed by multinational firms. Hence, it is positively related to the importance in an industry of R&D spending, use of sophisticated managerial personnel, and advertising (as a proxy for product differentiation). By contrast, Canadian firms are dominant in industries where these factors are not as important. These findings were also broadly consistent with the results of a cross-sectional study on foreign ownership in Canadian manufacturing by Saunders (1982), and of a similar study on entry by Canadian and foreign firms by Gorecki (1976).

What should one conclude, from the above analysis and results, about the welfare effects of foreign investment and control in Canadian industry? First of all, it should be noted that there are some important non-economic arguments that should be taken into account before answering this question. These involve the extra-territorial application of foreign (chiefly U.S.) laws, through legal pressures on the parent corporations. Such issues were raised repeatedly in the recent past, especially since 1980.[15] They amount to attempts to impose U.S. foreign policy decisions on other countries that may not have been in agreement with them. For this reason they form arguments against complete foreign control of at least some sectors of the Canadian economy. An additional element on the issue of foreign control is the effect that such control has on innovative activity. This will be examined in detail in the next section.

Beyond these non-economic arguments, the debate about foreign investment and control has many similarities with the debate about the reverse structure-performance model. If foreign-controlled firms have efficiency advantages when they operate in Canada, then they clearly add to the welfare of Canadians. If their presence in a sector implies barriers to entry for Canadian firms, and results in market power even in the absence of any differential performance, then their net effect may be negative. It should be noted that, at least for traded goods, this market power effect cannot be exercised in the absence of barriers to foreign trade, as we saw in the previous section.[16] Hence, continuing trade liberalization is an argument for a more relaxed attitude towards foreign investment, in the absence of any concerns about innovation and the extra-territoriality of U.S. foreign policy.

In assessing public policy in the area of foreign investment, one is brought inevitably to the performance of FIRA during the 1973-1985 period of its effective existence. As already noted, FIRA was established in response to a 1972 report on foreign investment in Canada. That report had also considered a number of alternative policy options to the screening of takeovers and mergers by foreign firms (the option that was eventually adopted). An interesting option, that had also been partially embodied in earlier legislation, was the so-called *key sector* policy. This policy designates certain sectors of the economy as partially or totally closed to foreign ownership. Notable examples of such sectors are the banking and broadcasting sectors, in both of which there are sharp limits placed on foreign ownership. In particular, the designation of broadcasting as a key sector during the late 1960s ended up with massive sellouts of the assets of broadcasting and cable television firms that were foreign-controlled.[17]

The operations of FIRA were different, insofar as its mandate covered all industries. In screening the applications for a foreign takeover or investment the agency used a number of criteria, of which increases in employment and in investment seemed to be the most frequently cited in the approved proposals. Other relevant criteria were Canadian participation, additional exports, and the increased use of Canadian products, while improvements in productivity, technology, and competition were less frequently cited. The acceptance rate was very high throughout the years of FIRA's operations, never falling below 70 percent of the total number of applications.[18]

Did FIRA contribute significantly to the documented decline in foreign ownership and control in the 1970s and early 1980s? Certainly, that decline coincided with the heyday of FIRA's operations and could therefore be attributed to it, in spite of the high rate of accepted applications. For instance, it was alleged that FIRA's effectiveness is better measured by its deterrent effect. This is represented by the applications that were either withdrawn before a decision was rendered, or were never made to begin with. There is no data on the latter, while the former were on the order of 10 percent of the total disposal of applications. This is not very high, given the spectacular drop in foreign control over that same period. Undoubtedly, much of that drop must be attributed to the liberalization of foreign trade that was proceeding at a very vigorous pace throughout all those years.[19]

Whatever FIRA's role may have been, much of its effectiveness was removed at the end of 1984, in one of the first legislative actions of the newly-elected Conservative government. The size threshold of reviewable merger and takeover applications was raised from $250 000 to $5 million worth of assets of the target company, while almost all new investments were exempted. Further, the criteria for acceptance of a proposal were loosened, with all proposals providing a "net benefit" being deemed acceptable. Last, the name of the organization was changed to Investment Canada, prompting charges by opposition critics that FIRA was effectively transformed into a foreign investment promotion agency. Only in the cultural industries (for instance book publishing) did the new agency retain anything resembling its former effectiveness.

A further reduction in the barriers to American investment in Canadian firms is embodied in parts of the free trade agreement between the U.S. and Canada, discussed in the previous section. For instance, the agreement eliminates many of the restrictions to U.S. investment in Canada's banking sector, which had been designated as a key sector in previous legislation. The accord now exempts Americans from the 25 percent ceiling on foreign ownership of a Canadian chartered bank. Further, Canadian subsidiaries of U.S.-based banks will be allowed to grow, subject only to the requirement that part of their voting shares be publicly traded and widely-held within five years. The agreement also increases the access to the U.S. market for Canadian banks, and insures that U.S. and Canadian banks will be treated equally under American law. Similarly, the agreement restricts the jurisdiction of Investment Canada in the size of the projects that it may screen, with the exception of the cultural industries. The threshold of reviewable direct acquisitions of control rises immediately to $25 million (from $5 million), and will eventually reach $150 million. For indirect control the thresholds are much larger, rising to $500 million two years after the start of the agreement. In other words, all but the largest takeovers are now exempted from review and possible action.

As noted earlier, the issue of foreign control in the Canadian economy lies relatively dormant as of early 1989. Factors that contributed to this loss of interest were, in addition to the decrease in foreign control, the change in political climate with the election of a Conservative government in 1984, and the concurrent sharp increase in foreign investment and control in the U.S. economy. This last event was the result of the expansion in the U.S. foreign trade deficit, which was financed by the sale of U.S. assets to foreigners. Several Canadian firms played an important role in this financing, through a number of highly-publicized takeovers of large American firms. This helped to somewhat relieve nationalist concerns, by showing that foreign control was not a one-sided problem. Such concerns, though, are bound to resurface if the United States places any curbs on foreign investment, thereby prompting calls for retaliatory Canadian actions.

R&D and Patent Policy

There is little doubt that a large share of the credit for the growth and dynamism of modern industrial economies must be attributed to technological change. Such change comes with the introduction of new products and processes into the economy. It generally starts at the level of a given innovating firm, and eventually spreads to competitors and other related firms. It is the active commitment to research and development (R&D) spending that distinguishes the innovating firms from their passive followers. As leading students of the subject have asserted,[20] such commitment to R&D is indispensable to the long-term profitability of business firms in many important sectors. For this reason R&D has long been a major target of Canadian public policy. This policy has been embodied in grants, tax incentives, and patent laws. Only parts of these policy instruments will be reviewed here, with particular attention paid to drug patent legislation. The latter has been the subject of vigorous controversy during the mid-1980s, divided entirely along partisan and ideological lines. For this reason it is likely to resurface in the near future, following a change in the federal government.

As we saw in Chapter 5, a patent is basically a monopoly licence that grants its holder exclusive and transferable rights over the exploitation of the patented product or process. It is therefore a powerful barrier to entry that may be used to create market power. On the other hand, without patent protection the incentive to innovate will be insufficient to produce a socially optimal amount of innovation. Competitors will be quick to copy the innovation and nullify the advantage of the pioneering firm, without having to incur any of the accompanying R&D costs. For this reason it is always socially optimal to provide some patent protection to innovators, although there is less agreement on the length and degree of such protection. The best-known theoretical model for the determination of the optimal patent length is presented in Appendix 11A.

Canada's patent system, like that of the U.S., confers a 17-year exclusive right or monopoly for inventions that satisfy the criteria for novelty, usefulness, and nonobviousness. In Canada, a patent can be revoked after three years of granting if it has not been worked, although this seldom occurs. Further, exceptions to patentee powers can be imposed by Parliament; the drug patent legislation is the best-known and most controversial of such exceptions.

Before examining this legislation in detail, it is worth considering Canada's overall performance in R&D spending and technological innovation in general. For the assessment of such performance relative to that of other industrialized nations there are a number of available measures over and above R&D expenditures. An obvious such measure is the number of patents issued to Canadian firms and individuals. Table 11.4 shows the patents granted as of 1982 by seven leading industrialized nations to foreigners and to their own citizens, in absolute terms as well as relative to the size of their economy.

The table shows very clearly that Canada's patent performance has been very poor, even after adjusting for the small size of its economy. Furthermore, Canadians are by far the smallest exporters of new technologies amongst the seven nations. This relative position has stayed more or less constant over several years, as the data in Table 11.5 shows.

TABLE 11.4
Patents in seven leading industrialized nations, 1982

	GNP (U.S. $ billion)	Patents to own residents	Per billion GNP	Patents to foreign residents	Per billion GNP	Foreign patents to own residents	Per billion GNP
Canada	232.21	1 386	5.97	21 061	90.7	2 041	8.97
France	420.91	7 764	18.44	16 180	38.4	13 556	32.19
West Germany	605.01	8 279	13.68	8 009	13.2	35 142	58.08
Japan	1 102.46	42 223	41.72	8 378	8.3	24 326	24.04
Netherlands	122.27	618	5.06	6 035	49.5	6 172	50.59
United Kingdom	393.06	4 686	11.92	24 904	63.4	10 496	26.70
United States	2 650.30	33 896	12.97	23 993	9.1	56 576	21.35

Sources: International Monetary Fund (1983); World Intellectual Property Organization, (WIPO), Intellectual Property Statistics 1982 (1983).

This last table also shows that the pace of technological innovation seems to have slowed somewhat over this 10-year period. The absolute level of patents has declined, and with the important exception of Japan, the share of world patents obtained by each of these countries has either declined or remained constant. This decline was particularly pronounced for the U.S., which used to be the world leader in patents granted to one's own residents.

Canada's unsatisfactory performance in the production of new technology is explainable in large part by the low level of R&D spending relative to the size of its economy. Table 11.6 shows the level of R&D spending as a percentage of industry output for a number of selected countries. It is clear that Canada's spending is among the lowest. Moreover, this suggested underinvestment in new technology has been further supported by the high rates of return to R&D in Canada observed by a number of researchers.[21] These high rates imply that R&D investment has been kept below its equilibrium value, at which its rate of return should be equal (on a risk-adjusted basis) to that of other investment projects.

Thus, the negative image of Canadian R&D performance is consistent no matter what measure of performance is used. Each measure is by itself incomplete and at best suggestive, but the results taken as a whole are rather depressing. They acquire an added significance when one considers the sectoral distribution of technological innovation. Indeed, there are many industries for which an absence of new technology need not imply reduced performance. Examples of such traditional industries would include handicrafts, ethnic restaurants, and log homes. In most industries, however, technology does not remain stagnant. How can one distinguish those sectors for which Canada's technological lag may pose problems? How did those sectors fare in comparison to their foreign (chiefly U.S.) counterparts?

TABLE 11.5
Patents granted to own residents by seven nations and total world patents, 1972-82

Year	Total World Patents	Canada Total Patents	Per cent	France Total Patents	Per cent	Germany Total Patents	Per cent	Japan Total Patents	Per cent	Netherlands Total Patents	Per cent	United Kingdom Total Patents	Per cent	United States Total Patents	Per cent
1972	482 358	1 587	0.3	10 767	2.2	9 642	2.0	29 101	6.0	334	0.1	10 116	2.1	51 515	10.7
1973	447 919	1 486	0.3	10 817	2.4	11 191	2.5	30 937	6.9	383	0.1	9 357	2.1	51 501	11.5
1974	428 639	1 200	0.3	9 282	2.2	9 793	2.3	30 873	7.2	423	0.1	8 971	2.1	50 643	11.8
1975	412 119	1 336	0.3	4 962	1.2	9 077	2.2	36 992	9.0	429	0.1	9 120	2.2	46 603	11.3
1976	427 155	1 293	0.3	8 420	2.0	10 395	2.4	32 465	7.6	370	0.1	8 855	2.1	44 162	10.3
1977	442 430	1 260	0.3	8 361	1.9	10 815	2.4	43 047	9.7	396	0.1	7 722	1.7	41 383	9.3
1978	406 305	1 352	0.3	8 083	2.0	11 581	2.8	37 648	9.3	432	0.1	8 464	2.1	40 979	10.1
1979	386 045	1 369	0.3	6 846	1.8	10 895	2.8	34 863	9.0	455	0.1	4 182	1.1	30 605	7.9
1980	422 969	1 450	0.3	8 438	2.0	9 826	2.3	38 032	9.0	417	0.1	5 158	1.2	37 152	8.8
1981	423 348	1 526	0.4	6 855	1.6	6 537	1.5	42 080	9.9	397	0.1	6 076	1.4	39 225	9.3
1982	425 154	1 386	0.3	7 764	1.8	8 279	1.9	42 223	9.9	618	0.1	4 686	1.1	33 896	8.0

Source: World Intellectual Property Organization (WIPO), *100 Years of Protection of Industrial Property* (Geneva, Switz., 1983)

TABLE 11.6
R&D expenditures, selected countries

Country	R&D expenditures as a percentage of domestic product of industry							
	1971	1973	1975	1977	1979	1981	1982	1983
Sweden	1.4	1.5	1.6	1.9	2.0	2.3	—	2.6
Germany	1.6	1.5	1.6	1.6	2.1	2.2	2.3	2.3
United States	2.0	1.9	1.8	1.8	1.8	2.0	2.2	2.2
Japan	1.2	1.3	1.3	1.3	1.4	1.6	1.7	1.9
France	1.3	1.3	1.4	1.3	1.4	1.5	1.6	1.6
Netherlands	1.5	1.4	1.4	1.3	1.3	1.3	1.3	1.4
Canada	0.7	0.6	0.6	0.6	0.7	0.8	1.0	0.9
Norway	0.7	—	0.8	0.8	0.8	0.8	—	1.0
Denmark	—	0.6	0.6	0.7	0.7	0.8	—	1.0
Italy	0.6	0.5	0.6	0.6	0.6	0.7	0.7	0.8

Source: Statistics Canada, *Industrial Research and Development Statistics*, Catalogue #88-202, (1987).

These questions were partially answered by a 1987 study by the Economic Council of Canada (ECC). That study allocated Canadian industries into three categories: high-, mid-, and low-technology. The classification was done by constructing measures of the high-tech intensity of the industry's production process. Such measures appear frequently in studies of this type and may include comparative R&D expenditures, patents of industry participants, or judgments by expert panels. The ECC's classification is shown in Table 11.7.

The ECC study further showed that the high-tech sector has been responsible for the bulk of new jobs created in the economy in 1971-81. It has also experienced a higher rate of growth of output than the mid- or low-tech groups throughout the 1970s and early 1980s. Furthermore, it has concluded that this trend should continue as Canada's position as a supplier of natural resources to the world economy erodes through time. Canada's technological gap therefore embodies serious dangers for the future employment performance of our economy if it eventually translates into an efficiency gap with respect to our foreign competitors.

A more detailed look at the comparative technological performance between the U.S. and Canada at the sectoral level is contained in Table 11.8. The comparative data of this table includes the subset of manufacturing industries that had the highest research intensity (as measured by the ratio of R&D to sales) and the highest growth in employment in recent years. It is clear that the technological gap, although present in the overall picture, is not distributed uniformly among sectors. For some Canadian industries, such as

TABLE 11.7
Industry ranking by technological status, Canada, 1987

High-tech

Motor vehicles
Communications
Electrical products
Rubber and plastics
Metal mines
Transportation equipment
Motor vehicle parts and accessories
Machinery
Chemicals
Trade
Construction
Commercial services
Finance, insurance, and real estate
Petroleum and natural gas

Mid-tech

Agriculture
Miscellaneous manufacturing
Textiles
Nonmetal mines (excluding coal)
Coal mines
Paper
Iron and Steel

Low-tech

Nonmetallic mineral products
Printing and publishing
Fishing and trapping
Leather
Furniture and fixtures
Wood
Fabricated metals
Knitting and clothing
Tobacco
Nonferrous metals
Food and beverages
Forestry
Petroleum and coal products

Source: Economic Council of Canada, *Making Technology Work*,1987 (p. 9).

TABLE 11.8
**Comparative R&D intensities for selected high-tech industries,
U.S. and Canada**

Industry Group	SIC Code	Company R&D as percent of net sales	
		U.S. (1982)	Canada (1985)
All manufacturing industries		2.5	1.4
Drugs	283	7.1	3.9
Industrial organic chemicals	286	3.4	1.2
Office and computing machines	357	10.3	3.0
Communication equipment	366	7.2	14.3
Electronics components	367	5.5	8.3
Aircraft and parts	372	5.1	15.8
Missiles and space vehicles	376	5.1	n/a
Instruments	380	7.5	2.8

Source: P. Webre (June 1985); Statistics Canada, Cat. #88-202 (June 1987).

communication equipment and aircraft and parts, the Canadian R&D intensity clearly exceeded that of the U.S.

Although Canada's unsatisfactory innovative performance is well-documented, there is less agreement on its causes. Certainly the large degree of foreign ownership and control must be counted among them. The economies of scale and of scope involved in R&D imply that most such activities should be concentrated in a single location, which is generally the home country of a multinational firm. This has certainly been the experience in the Canadian pharmaceutical industry, which is dominated by American and European multinational corporations. The R&D conducted by the Canadian subsidiaries of these firms is mostly clinical testing for meeting the regulation requirements of the Department of Health and Welfare, as opposed to original innovations.

Surprisingly, the extensive foreign control of Canadian corporations does not seem to have helped the speed of adoption of new technology. While Canada is a major importer of new technology, as shown by the high share of patents granted to foreigners in Table 11.4, many of these patentees use their Canadian patents simply to protect their worldwide knowledge base. Several industry studies have documented the slow speed of diffusion of important innovations, such as numerically controlled machine tools and robots in manufacturing. Some recent work even suggests that multinational corporations are now less likely to transfer innovations to Canada before less developed nations.[22]

Foreign control, however, is not a sufficient explanation of the low degree of innovation in Canadian industries. The previously-cited 1987 study by the ECC showed that Canadian-controlled firms were sluggish in the adoption of microelectronics technology when compared to similar European firms. Some researchers have suggested that Canada's small, tariff-protected domestic market tends to retard both the initial adoption as well as the diffusion of new technology in Canada.[23] If this is true then one should have noticed an increase in the pace of both R&D and technological diffusion as tariffs were reduced in recent years; this does not appear to have happened.

It would seem reasonable to assume that competitive pressures would tend to at least improve the speed of diffusion of innovations, if not R&D performance. Further, an important study by Arrow (1962), presented in some detail in Appendix 11A, shows that competitive industries are generally more conducive to innovation that monopolies.[24] Note, however, that one of the most famous hypotheses in economics, originally formulated by Schumpeter (1950), asserts that exactly the opposite is true with respect to R&D: it is monopoly power that enhances R&D spending, by generating profits to finance it. That same power is eventually destroyed by new innovations, which in their turn become the foundation of the monopoly power of new firms. One can easily see the links between this train of thought and the later reverse structure-performance model.

Neither argument has generally been supported by empirical research, which has tended to yield inconclusive results on the market structure-R&D relationship. There is little doubt that financing is a major factor in the creation and adoption of new technology, but it is not the only factor. Attitudes towards risk are at least as important, given the large amount of uncertainty present in most R&D projects. One can easily argue that market power, by providing a safe operating environment free of competitive pressures, tends to promote a lower degree of risk-taking behaviour. At any rate, the empirical evidence has not uncovered a consistent relationship between market structure and innovation in the U.S.[25] For some industries such as chemicals a positive relationship was found between concentration and R&D inputs or outputs, which may be due to scale factors. For most industries, however, it is clear that firm size and industry concentration matter only up to a point. Similarly, a study by Globerman (1973) found no significant link between industry concentration and R&D inputs in a study of 15 two-digit Canadian manufacturing industries.

Whatever the reasons for the observed inadequate innovative performance in Canada, there have certainly been many public policy efforts to encourage more R&D spending. These have taken the form of direct grants, as well as numerous tax incentives. Some of the available evidence indicates that grants have been fairly effective in generating extra R&D spending in excess of the grant, especially if the recipient is a Canadian-owned firm.[26] This evidence is consistent with the experience in the United States. Mansfield and Switzer (1984) and Switzer (1984a) found that U.S. government-financed R&D generates net additional R&D spending by private firms. The situation is rather more ambiguous with respect to tax incentives. Mansfield and Switzer (1985) found that Canadian R&D tax incentives were rather ineffective: the extra R&D spending that they induced was only 30 to 40 percent of the foregone revenue. On the other hand, a recent study found that tax incentives and direct grants were more or less equivalent in their quantitative effects of generating additional R&D funds,[27] with the amount of extra R&D induced by the incentives being roughly equal to the loss in tax revenue.

It is with this background in mind that one should examine the long controversy over drug patent legislation. Its origins lay in a 1969 amendment to the Patent Act, to provide for compulsory licensing of firms to manufacture and/or import drugs for which patents were held by somebody else in Canada. The licensee had to pay a royalty rate of 4 percent to the patent holder. In fact, what the law was designed to achieve is compulsory licensing (or its threat) in order to limit the market power created by the patent.

There is wide consensus that Canada's compulsory licensing provisions injected a large degree of competition into the industry. The legislation resulted in 830 licences being granted to competitor firms from 1970 to May 1987, and served to spawn a new subsector of generic drug manufacturers.[28] In 1987 these generic firms were able to capture approximately 10 percent of the Canadian market of $2.3 billion. The competition that they provided to the multinationals, combined with substitution rules imposed by provincial drug insurance plans, led to major cost savings for consumers. For instance, it was estimated that cost savings to pharmacies and hospitals for 32 of 70 drugs that had generic competition amounted to $211 million in 1983.[29] Needless to say, these savings were almost exclusively at the expense of the major drug producers in Canada, who launched a fierce fight to repeal the 1969 amendments to the Patent Act.

In April 1984, the Eastman Royal Commission was appointed to investigate the industry and to recommend a reform of the legislation. Its 1985 report was basically a compromise position that increased the returns to the drug patent holders (mainly the industry multinationals), by extending the period of protection from compulsory licensing to four years and increasing the royalty rate above 4 percent. The new rate was intended to be variable, increasing with the patentee's R&D activities conducted in Canada. Thus the Commission was answering part of the criticisms of the compulsory licensing legislation, which asserted that the law had resulted in widespread reductions of R&D spending by the pharmaceutical industry in Canada.

The government's final legislation, passed in 1987 after a lengthy and highly divisive political debate, did not accept the basic thrust of the Eastman Commission's recommendation. Specifically, it granted a ten-year protection from compulsory licensing and did not include any incentives to increase R&D spending in Canada. Its only concession to the spirit of the compulsory licensing provisions was the establishment of a Drug Prices Review Board to monitor price trends in the industry, with powers to repeal the ten-year suspension of generic competition if a new drug's price is deemed excessive.

There is little doubt that the effective repeal of the 1969 law was not in the immediate interest of Canada. As a 1985 study by McFetridge and Corvari notes, that law had resulted in an income transfer from foreign patentees to Canadian consumers.[30] Hence, its repeal is essentially a reverse transfer, without any counterpart. About the only positive thing that one may say for the new law is that it strengthens the international system of intellectual property rights and prevents possible retaliation against Canadian patentees. In fact, there were persistent accusations during the debate in Parliament that the repeal of the 1969 law was a major objective of the U.S. delegation during the negotiations preceeding the free trade agreement. If so, it must be counted as part of the price paid to reach that agreement.

The Public Enterprise

A public enterprise is a business unit, engaged in the production and sale of a good or service, that is owned and controlled by the government or one of its agencies. This definition includes publicly-owned firms such as Ontario Hydro and the Export Development Corporation (EDC), but excludes branches of the government, such as the police and the judiciary, that provide non-marketable services. Public enterprises are obvious alternatives to private firms. For this reason there is an ongoing debate about their appropriate role and their eventual replacement by the private sector; this is known as the *privatization* issue.

There is a very large number of public enterprises in Canada, which are generally known as *Crown Corporations* (although this term may also cover government agencies that do not fit the definition of a public enterprise). Crown Corporations derive revenue from their commercial activities, relying on public money only in order to cover possible operating deficits. They can be federally or provincially chartered, depending on the range of their activities. Our purpose in this section is to examine briefly the relation of Canadian public enterprises to the structure of their particular sector, as well as the rationale and public policy objectives behind their establishment. We shall also examine the empirical evidence on their performance relative to comparable private firms.

As we saw in Chapters 3 and 10, the public enterprise is an obvious (and popular) alternative to a private regulated monopoly. This is particularly true on the European continent, where public rather than private ownership is still more prevalent in the public utilities sector. In the U.S., and very recently the United Kingdom, private monopolies are more frequent, even though public enterprises are found quite often in sectors such as municipal water supply. In Canada both types of ownership may coexist within the same sector, depending on the province and type of activity. For this reason, Canada can provide very good case studies of the comparative performance of private and public monopolies.

Not all Canadian public enterprises, however, are to be found in monopolized industries. In fact some of the most visible ones, such as Petro-Canada, the federally-owned integrated oil and gas producer, are in oligopolies with a long history of collusive behaviour. Others are found in sectors with competitive conduct, such as steel, forest products, and paper products. The historical and political factors that created such public firms must be evaluated in terms of the alternatives available when the firms were set up. Only a few representative cases will be discussed here.[31]

Broadly speaking, public enterprises in sectors that were not natural monopolies were established for a variety of seemingly "legitimate" economic reasons. Two of these reasons stand out: the desire to improve the performance of an industry that, for some reason or other, is not perceived as conforming to efficient behaviour or some other public objective; or the wish to correct a market failure, i.e. to create a desirable economic activity that the private sector is reluctant to undertake. Petro-Canada and EDC, which are discussed below, are examples of public corporations established for the above two reasons, respectively.

Other motives, though, are bound to be more controversial. For instance, several public enterprises were created in order to rescue or replace a failing private firm. Other public firms were founded for the fulfillment of regional or sectoral objectives. These may include the promotion of economic development in a depressed region, or the subsidization of economic activity in an industry segment deemed to have social importance. Examples of this last type of activity are the financing of housing and farm credit through the Central Mortgage and Housing Corporation (CMHC) and the Farm Credit Corporation. Frequently these reasons overlap, as when the federal or provincial government steps in and rescues or takes over a failing private firm because it is located in a particularly depressed area. A typical example is the Cape Breton area in Nova Scotia, in which both the federal and provincial governments took over separate parts of a failing coal and steel producing firm. Unfortunately most of these public firms end up by becoming a persistent drain on public funds. They provide most of the illustrative examples of alleged failures of public firms to be found in the literature.

A good example of a public enterprise stepping in profitably where the private sector was reluctant to enter is the case of export credit insurance through the EDC. This can be considered as an example of a successful public intervention to correct a real market failure. The reasons for this failure are unclear. They may be due to imperfect information or extreme risk aversion. Whatever the reasons, the fact is that until very recently private financial institutions stayed away from such insurance to any significant scale. Yet, as a 1982 ECC report noted, the EDC's operations had generally been profitable and quite substantial, amounting to a total of $2.7 billion of new policies issued in 1980. For exports to countries other than the U.S., the EDC had a monopoly in export credit insurance for many years. In 1980 its policies covered 9.6 percent of all exports to such countries. This is a clear-cut case of commercially worthwhile (and, one might add, quite important on social-desirability criteria) operations that would not have existed if the public sector had not stepped in.

Another potentially desirable public intervention through the creation of a public enterprise occurs when such a creation is used as a substitute for costly (and potentially ineffective) competition policies.[32] This is likely to happen when the public firm operates in a tightly oligopolistic industry. As we saw in Chapter 9, conventional legal remedies can be ineffective in such industries when the oligopoly engages in tacit collusion. A public firm that refuses to abide to the collusive price can shift the behaviour of the industry towards the competitive equilibrium. Note, however, that this implies that the public firm will refrain from maximizing its profits, since its own fortunes would rise and fall with those of the oligopoly.

Two examples of public firms that could, but did not, play such a role are Petro-Canada and the Potash Corporation of Saskatchewan (PCS). Both firms operate in oligopolistic industries in the natural resources sector. Both were also established at a time of rising prices for their industry's products. Here, however, the similarities end, for it can be argued that it is in Canada's interest to maintain collusion in the potash industry, but to inject competition in the oil industry.

The potash industry exports most of its production, and enjoys considerable market power in world markets. Since PCS is the largest firm in the industry, it can act as a leader and achieve oligopolistic coordination more effectively than a publicly-sponsored export cartel. As we saw in Chapter 4, such leadership can maintain approximately collusive prices in the oligopoly. It also avoids the political embarrassment and risks of retaliation of a formal public cartel. There are some doubts whether PCS did in fact behave as such a leader.[33] On the other hand, there were some other advantages stemming from the creation of PCS, insofar as it provided a "window on the industry." It became a source of information on industry production costs, thus allowing the government a more efficient appropriation of resource rents.[34]

The case of Petro-Canada is more complex. The company was formed in 1975, partly as a reaction to the turmoil experienced in the world oil industry during the early 1970s. Within ten years it had emerged as a large, fully integrated oil producer, operating at the exploration, development, refining, and marketing stages of the business. Hence it had achieved the power to impose competitive behaviour at the retail level of the industry. This power could have been exercised during the big drop in world oil prices of the mid-1980s, but there is little doubt that it was not. Petro-Canada's behaviour during that time was that of a loyal member of the oligopoly, with the result that Canadian retail oil prices remained at a significantly higher level than in the competitive U.S. market.

We close this section by examining the evidence concerning the efficiency of public enterprises. This is a central issue in the on-going privatization debate, as it can be argued that privatization is desirable if there are demonstrable efficiency gains. It is not so desirable if such gains are non-existent, while there are non-economic drawbacks to private ownership in a given industry.

A substantial body of economic theorizing, known as the *property rights* approach,[35] asserts that a public enterprise will always be less efficient than an otherwise identical firm under private ownership. The reasoning is a variant of an argument that we saw repeatedly in previous chapters: the stock market provides an effective mechanism for disciplining ineffective managers of a privately-owned firm; no such mechanism is available for public sector firms. Stockholders can, by selling their holdings (their property rights), depress the price of stock of an inefficiently run private firm and create conditions favourable to a hostile takeover. By contrast the general public, the owners of public firms, can exert their influence on management only through the intermediation of politicians. This is likely to be less effective than the hostile takeover mechanism of the capital markets. To begin with, there is less information about the performance of public enterprises than about private firms. Also, their ownership is by necessity very widely disseminated and essentially non-transferable, thus weakening the incentives to improve their performance. Last, intervention via the political system is likely to enter into conflict with other political objectives unrelated to efficiency.

In essence, therefore, the property rights theory is an extension of the debate about managerial objectives in the modern corporation that we saw in Chapter 7. The conclusions reached in that earlier chapter were qualified in many respects. In the presence of market power firms were pursuing identical objectives, whether managed by their owners or by professional managers, on the demand side but not on the cost side. In other words, the stock market did not always provide an effective disciplining mechanism for managerial performance, contrary to the postulates of the property rights approach. The question is whether this mechanism is still preferable to the ones provided by public ownership.

The Canadian economy is a good place to compare private and public firm performance. The two types of ownership coexist in regulated sectors such as the railroads, telecommunications, and airlines. For this reason there have been several comparative performance studies. These were reviewed in two papers by Borins and Boothman (1985) and McFetridge (1985), which reached an identical conclusion: in mature industries there is no difference in commercial efficiency between government and private enterprises. This conclusion was based on comparisons of pairs of firms in the same industry under different types of ownership. Some examples of such pairs were: the two major railroads; the two major airlines; the two large private telecommunications firms, Bell Canada and BC Tel, compared to the telephone companies of the Prairie provinces; and Petro-Canada and the rest of the Canadian oil industry. Even in cases where there seemed to be some efficiency advantage to the private firm, it could generally be explained by politically-mandated service obligations imposed to the public enterprise. Examples of such obligations are the uneconomical services to remote communities imposed upon Air Canada.

On the other hand, there is some evidence that public firms have not performed as well as corresponding private ones in more dynamic industries, in which commercially-driven technological change is expected to play a major role. This conclusion is based on several studies of the performance of Atomic Energy Canada Limited (AECL) and De Havilland Aircraft of Canada (DHC).[36] The latter firm, together with Canadair and Teleglobe Canada, was privatized by the Conservative government in 1986-87.

In summary, therefore, the conclusion that we reach from this brief survey of comparative efficiency studies is very much in line with the general discussion of efficiency in Chapter 7: the structure of the sector appears to be a much more important determinant of efficiency than the form of ownership. Regulation and the absence of competition depress both private and public performance. More surprisingly, competitive pressures stimulate public enterprises towards a more efficient performance.

What still remains an open question is whether a public firm is capable of operating efficiently in a fully-competitive commercial environment. By their nature, public firms are either located in monopolistic or oligopolistic industries, or have been established in uneconomic locations because of social objectives. This question is relevant to the on-going privatization debate for the case of Air Canada, in the event airline deregulation brings the industry to a fully-competitive structure.

Apart from this point, one cannot help but feel that, for all the heat that it generates, the privatization debate falls somewhat flat on objective grounds. The easy cases such as Canadair and DHC have already been disposed of. Privatization of Petro-Canada, Canadian National, Ontario Hydro, or the provincial telecommunications companies will not, as McFetridge (1985) noted, bring forth any great efficiency benefits.[37] Some would dearly love to privatize such voracious consumers of public subsidies as Via Rail and the Cape Breton Development Corporation, but there won't be any takers who would agree to provide the services expected from these public firms. Unless there are drastic changes in the industry structure facing a given public firm (as in the above-noted case of Air Canada), there would be few gains from any further privatizations in Canada.

On the other hand, there is a need for a better accounting of the costs and benefits of the political services provided by public enterprises, including the groups that benefit from them. These services form part of the objectives of the public firm; they should be explicitly stated and measured. In our opinion, the key issue in any further privatizations is the desirability of these often unstated political objectives, given their cost. Also, it may often turn out that there are cheaper ways to fulfill the same goals than through a public firm. Conversely, it may turn out that private ownership is not suitable for sectors in which non-commercial objectives are dominant. Perhaps the best example of such a sector is the Canadian broadcasting system, surveyed in the previous chapter.

Conclusions

The public policy issues examined in this chapter are important sources of current debate and controversy. They also lie somewhat outside the framework of the traditional SCP model. Nonetheless, they have major implications for industry structure and performance that justify the attention paid to them in policy debates.

Trade liberalization is a "milk and motherhood" issue for most economists. It leads to a more competitive structure for the affected industries and hence it also leads to improved performance, in line with the central tenets of the SCP model. The main source of debate in this chapter was the desirability of a bilateral free trade treaty with the U.S., rather than reliance on the multilateral GATT negotiations.

The conclusions seem to be that the free trade agreement has the potential to bring important benefits to Canada if allowed to function. There are, however, real possibilities that it will fall victim to protectionist U.S. pressures. Although it does contain some safeguards against abuses of the current and future retaliatory trade laws, these fall rather short of firm guarantees. The improvements that it brought in terms of Canadian access to American markets must be weighed against the loss of public policy freedom of action in the areas of foreign investment, energy pricing,[38] and patent legislation.

Foreign control of Canadian industry is no longer as important as it used to be during the late 1960s and early 1970s. Canadian industry seems to have reversed the disturbing trend that had emerged at that time, largely because of developments in the U.S. Foreign control's main drawback, apart from non-economic factors, is the negative effect on the generation and diffusion of new technology in Canada.

The inadequate Canadian performance in these areas is amply documented by several studies. It cannot be fully attributed to foreign control, although R&D at foreign-controlled firms is less responsive to public incentives such as grants and tax concessions. The effective repeal of the compulsory licensing legislation for new drugs can be interpreted as an attempt to spur increased R&D in the pharmaceutical sector. Few economists believe that this objective will be achieved, even among those who support the new law on the grounds that it will strengthen the world patent system.[39]

Last, the issue of privatization of public firms has certainly been a popular one in many countries, including Canada. As we saw, not many improvements in performance can be expected from such policies. The easy targets have already been privatized. Most of the remaining Crown Corporations are either as efficient as comparable private ones or provide political services that would not be forthcoming under private ownership.

Appendix 11A   AN ECONOMIC ANALYSIS OF PATENTS

Patents and Industry Structure

Consider an industry with constant pre- and post-invention unit costs. The patented invention is a type of process innovation that lowers the average cost curve, from C_0 to C_1 in Figure 11A.1. This innovation is sufficiently "small" in a sense that will become clear further on. The pre-innovation cost level OC_0 acts as an upper limit on the price that the inventor or patent-holder may charge under a competitive market structure. The analysis ignores all problems associated with uncertainty and the inability of the inventor to appropriate the benefits of the invention.

Under the competitive market structure shown in Figure 11A.1, price is always equal to marginal cost. Hence, in spite of the innovation the inventor continues to charge the pre-invention price OC_0, while enjoying a profit per unit output of (C_1C_0). The total profits from the invention are therefore proportional to the area of the rectangle (C_0ABC_1). By contrast, under a monopoly structure the pre- and post-invention prices are P_M and P_M' respectively, given by the intersection of the marginal revenue MR with the marginal (and average) cost curves MC_0 and MC_1.

The monopolist's corresponding profits are proportional to the areas (P_MabC_0) and $(P_M'cdC_1)$. The incentive to invent is assumed proportional to the gains from the invention, the difference $(P_M'cdC_1) - (P_MabC_0)$. It can be easily shown that this is always less than the inventor's profits under competition (C_0ABC_1), as the area (P_MabC_0) exceeds $(P_M'ceC_0)$ by definition of the

FIGURE 11A.1
Welfare comparison of competition and monopoly for a "small" innovation

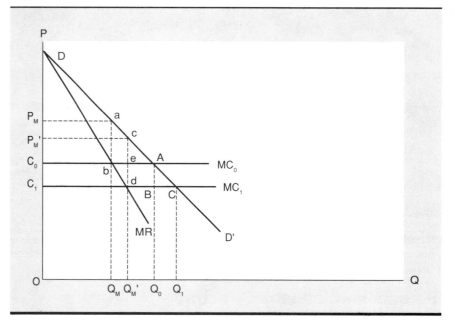

maximum monopoly profits, while $(C_0 e d C_1)$ is clearly less than $(C_0 ABC_1)$. Hence, competition provides a stronger incentive to invent than monopoly.

A similar conclusion follows for the case of a "large" innovation, shown in Figure 11A.2. Here the drop in unit cost from the invention is so drastic that the post-invention monopoly price P_M' is lower than the pre-invention unit cost (and competitive price) OC_0. The inventor would therefore be able to extract the entire monopoly profit $(P_M'ABC_1)$ no matter what the industry structure is. Nonetheless, the incentive to invent is still higher under competition: a pre-invention monopoly structure yields profits $(P_M ab C_0)$, which must be subtracted from the area $(P_M'ABC_1)$ to arrive at the incentive to invent. Hence, competition always provides better incentives for inventions.

The Optimal Patent Life[40]

Let T denote the duration of the patent. We shall assume that the patented innovation is "small", conforming to the situation depicted in Figure 11A.1. In other words, the product price is not reduced until after the patent has expired. Competitive conditions are also assumed after expiration.

FIGURE 11.A2
Welfare comparison of competition and monopoly for a "large" innovation

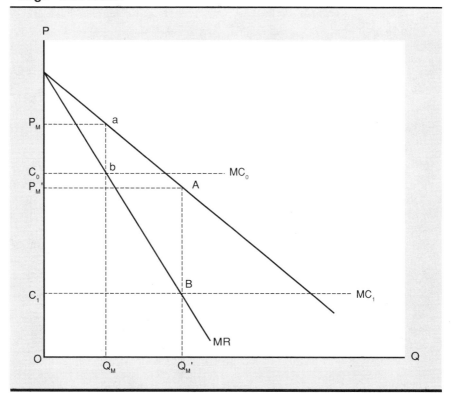

Let $H \equiv \dfrac{OC_0 - OC_1}{OC_0}$ denote the relative decrease in unit cost (and price) from the innovation. This decrease is assumed to be an increasing and concave function[41] of the R&D input per unit output, which is denoted by R. Let also s denote the price of this input, and r the rate of interest in continuous time. For a given T the inventor's net benefit is equal to the discounted profits during T minus the cost of the invention. Hence, this benefit is equal to the amount

$$(OC_0)Q_0 \left[H(R) \int_0^T e^{-rt}\, dt - sR \right] =$$

$$(OC_0)Q_0 \left[\frac{H(R)\,[1 - e^{-rT}]}{r} - sR \right] = \qquad \textbf{Eq. (11A.1)}$$

$$(OC_0)Q_0 \left[\frac{H(R)\phi}{r} - sR \right] \quad \text{where } \phi \equiv 1 - e^{-rT}$$

Maximizing (11A.1) with respect to R for a given T we get:

$$\phi \frac{dH}{dR} \equiv \phi H'(R) = sr \qquad \textbf{Eq. (11A.2)}$$

Hence, the optimal R is found at the level R*, shown in Figure 11A.3, where the slope of $H(R)$ is equal to the constant term $\frac{sr}{\phi}$. This R* is very clearly a function of T, which enters into the parameter ϕ.

The optimal T is now found by maximizing total surplus. This is equal to the inventor's profits during the patent life T, plus the increase in consumer surplus after T. It can be easily seen from Figure 11A.1 that if we ignore the issue of the distribution of the invention profits (C_0ABC_1) before and after T, this total surplus is equal to (C_0ABC_1) received in perpetuity, plus the triangle (ABC) received from T on. Hence, the net welfare gain W is given by

$$W = (C_0ABC_1) \int_0^{\infty} e^{-rt}\, dt + (ABC) \int_T^{\infty} e^{-rt}\, dt$$

$$= \frac{(C_0ABC_1)}{r} + \frac{(ABC)e^{-rT}}{r} \qquad \textbf{Eq. (11A.3)}$$

FIGURE 11A.3
Optimal choice of R + D input

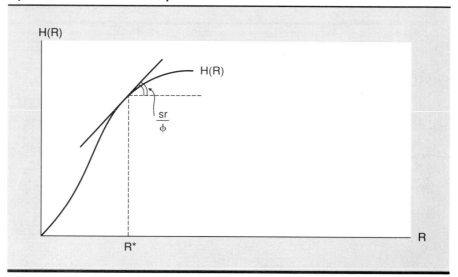

It is easy to see that $(C_0ABC_1) = (OC_0)Q_0H(R)$, while $(ABC) = \frac{1}{2}(AB)(BC) = \frac{1}{2}(OC_0)H(R)(Q_1 - Q_0)$. Setting $Q_1 - Q_0 \equiv \Delta Q$, and denoting by ϵ the price elasticity of demand, $\epsilon = \frac{\Delta Q}{\Delta P} \times \frac{(OC_0)}{Q_0}$, it is easy to see that $(ABC) = \frac{1}{2}(OC_0)Q_0 H^2 (R)\epsilon$. Ignoring, therefore, the term $(OC_0)Q_0$, we can see that W is proportional to the sum:

$$W \sim \frac{H(R)}{r} + \frac{\epsilon H^2(R)}{r} e^{-rT} \qquad \textbf{Eq. (11A.4)}$$

The optimal patent life T is now found by maximizing (11A.4) with respect to T, given that R and T satisfy (11A.2). The first-order conditions, therefore, are found from $\frac{dW}{dT} = \frac{\partial W}{\partial R}\frac{dR}{dT} + \frac{\partial W}{\partial T} = 0$, where $\frac{dR}{dT}$ is found by implicit differentiation of (11A.2). The results, after some heavy algebra, yield R and T as the solution of the system (11A.2) and (11A.5):

$$\phi = \frac{1 + \epsilon H}{1 + \epsilon H(1 + k)} \ , \ k \equiv -\frac{HH''}{2[H']^2} \qquad \textbf{Eq. (11A.5)}$$

where $H'' \equiv \frac{d^2H(R)}{dR^2}$. This system defines the patent life that maximizes total surplus.

From the analysis it appears clearly that an optimal T would always exist that is both nonzero and finite. Figure 11A.3 shows that increasing T increases ϕ, and through its effect on $\frac{sr}{\phi}$ increases the optimal R&D input R*. This raises the first term in (11A.3). On the other hand, an increase in T decreases the term accruing from the consumer surplus triangle (ABC), which is not realized until the patent has expired. Hence, the optimal T balances these two effects against each other.

Endnotes

1. For a discussion of this argument see Ethier (1983), p. 201.

2. There are currently 95 countries that are formally contracting parties in GATT. See External Affairs Canada's *Canada, GATT, and the Uruguay Round* (1987).

3. Nondiscrimination means that a reduction of tariffs granted to one country should be extended to all GATT members; exceptions are allowed for customs unions and free trade areas. National treatment implies that imports and domestic goods are treated equally once tariffs have been paid. Last, the transparency principle implies that all trade barriers should take the form of tariffs, and not quotas or discriminatory subsidies.

4. See Deardorff and Stern (1983), Table IV.

5. This may not always be possible, given that many countries have anti-dumping trade laws and regulations. Nonetheless, it has certainly taken place extensively in agriculture, including the cartelized milk, eggs, and poultry markets.

6. See the discussion in Mueller (1982) and Ross (1988a), who use arguments similar to the ones presented here. This last study has focussed mainly on the effects of trade liberalization on mergers.

7. See Wilkinson and Norrie (1975).

8. Needless to say, Canada is itself far from blameless in this respect.

9. Thus in 1985-86, allegations about dumping and export subsidization of Canadian products led to customs duties in the "shakes and shingles" and "Atlantic groundfish" cases, and to a self-imposed export tax on Canadian softwood lumber. For the merits of some of those cases see Rugman and Anderson (1987).

10. See the *Wall Street Journal*, October 6, 1987, p. B3.

11. It does provide significant protection over what existed before. That protection can be negated by new laws. Clearly, much of the agreement's effectiveness depends on the future U.S. political climate in trade matters.

12. See, for instance, Hazeldine (1987), as well as the simulations presented in the ECC's 1988 study.

13. See Green (1985), p. 35.

14. See Green (1985), p. 36.

15. Notable examples were the involvement of U.S. subsidiaries in the construction of a Soviet gas pipeline, and the U.S. embargo on trade with Nicaragua.

16. Unless, of course, there is world market power on the part of the foreign corporation.

17. See Perrakis and Silva-Echenique (1983, 1985).

18. For more details see Green (1985), pp. 457-461.

19. The massive U.S. balance of payments deficit, stimulated by their overvalued currency during much of the 1980s, may also have played a role.

20. For instance, Mansfield (1981).

21. See, for instance, Switzer (1984b) and Bernstein (1985).

22. See DeMelto *et al.* (1980), ECC (1987), McFetridge and Corvari (1985), and Mansfield (1985).

23. See McFetridge and Corvari (1985), p. 197.

24. Arrow's conclusions have been disputed by Demsetz (1969), who challenges the basis of the comparison. The Arrow conclusions, though, hold if the same industry is examined under alternative monopoly and competitive structures. By contrast, Demsetz compares two industries with the same level output under monopoly and competition.

25. See Kamien and Schwartz (1982) and Scherer (1980).

26. See Bernstein (1985). The study also suggests that foreign-owned firms are much less responsive to incentives than purely domestic firms, implying that the grant tends to displace R&D investment that was going to be spent anyway.

27. *Ibid*, pp. 35-36.

28. See the *Financial Post*, May 4, 1987, p. 44.

29. See Brogan and Roberge (1985), p. 3.

30. See McFetridge and Corvari (1985), p. 218.

31. For a full list of public enterprises in Canada as of 1980 see Green (1985), pp. 402-413.

32. See Harris and Wiens (1980).

33. See Green (1985), p. 384.

34. See McFetridge (1985), pp. 216-217.

35. For a review of the pertinent literature see Borins and Boothman (1985).

36. These were reviewed in McFetridge (1985), pp. 210-215.

37. See McFetridge (1985), p. 225.

38. The agreement removes Canada's freedom to discriminate in energy pricing between domestic consumers and exports.

39. See, for instance, McFetridge and Corvari (1985), p. 218.

40. This section is based on the classic analysis by Nordhaus (1969), and its extensions by Scherer (1972) and Nordhaus (1972).

41. Nordhaus uses the form $H(R) = hR^\alpha$, where $0 < \alpha < 1$. Scherer postulates that $H(R)$ should initially be convex.

References

Arrow, K.J. "Economic Welfare and the Allocation of Resources for Invention," *The Rate and Direction of Inventive Activity: Economic and Social Factors*. National Bureau of Economic Research. Princeton, N.J.: Princeton University Press, 1962.

Baldwin, J. and P. Gorecki, with J. McVey and J. Crysdale. "Entry and Exit to the Canadian Manufacturing Sector: 1970-1979." Discussion Paper #225. Ottawa, Ont.: Economic Council of Canada, 1983.

Baldwin, J.R. and P. Gorecki. *The Role of Scale in Canada-US Productivity Differences*. Toronto, Ont.: University of Toronto Press, 1986.

Bernstein, J. "Research and Development, Patents, and Grant and Tax Policies in Canada," *Technological Change in Canadian Industry*, D. McFetridge, ed. Toronto, Ont.: University of Toronto Press, 1985.

Borins, S.F. and B.E.C. Boothman. "Crown Corporations and Economic Efficiency," *Canadian Industrial Policy in Action*. Toronto, Ont.: University of Toronto Press, 1985, pp. 75-129.

Brogan, T. and G. Roberge. "1983 Drug Store and Hospital Drug Purchases: A Comparison of Canada and the United States," background paper for the Eastman Commission of Inquiry on the Pharmaceutical Industry in Canada. Ottawa, Ont.: Bureau of Policy Coordination, Ministry of Consumer and Corporate Affairs Canada, 1984.

Caves, R. "Economic Models of Political Choice: Canada's Tariff Structure," *Canadian Journal of Economics*, 9 (1976), pp. 278-300.

Caves, R., M. Porter, M. Spence, and W.J.T. Scott. *Competition in the Open Economy*. Cambridge, Mass.: Harvard University Press, 1980.

Cox, D., and R.G. Harris. "A Quantitative Assessment of the Economic Impact on Canada of Sectoral Free Trade with the United States," *Canadian Journal of Economics*, 19 (1986), pp. 377-394.

Deardorff, A. and R. Stern. "Economic Effects of the Tokyo Rounds," *Southern Economic Journal*, 49 (1983), pp. 605-624.

DeMelto, D., K. McMullen and R. Willis. "Innovation and Technological Change in Five Canadian Industries," Discussion Paper 176. Ottawa, Ont.: Economic Council of Canada, 1980.

Demsetz, H. "Information and Efficiency: Another Viewpoint," *Journal of Law and Economics*, 12 (1969), pp. 1-22.

Eastman, G. *Report of the Commission of Inquiry on the Pharmaceutical Industry*. Ottawa, Ont.: Minister of Supply and Services Canada, 1985.

Eastman, G. and S. Stykolt. *The Tariff and Competition in Canada*. Toronto, Ont.: Macmillan, 1967.

Economic Council of Canada. *Intervention and Efficiency*. Ottawa, Ont.: Ministry of Supply and Services Canada, 1982.

Economic Council of Canada. *Making Technology Work: Innovation and Jobs in Canada*. Ottawa, Ont.: Ministry of Supply and Services Canada, 1987.

Economic Council of Canada. *Venturing Forth: An Assessment of the Canada-U.S. Trade Agreement*. Ottawa, Ont.: Ministry of Supply and Services Canada, 1988.

Ethier, W. *Modern International Economics*. New York, N.Y.: Norton, 1983.

External Affairs Canada. *Canada, GATT and the Uruguay Round*. Ottawa, Ont.: Ministry of Supply and Services, 1987.

Globerman, S. "Market Structure and R&D in Canadian Manufacturing Industries," *Quarterly Review of Economics and Business*, 13 (1973), pp. 59-68.

Gorecki, P.K. "The Determinants of Entry by Domestic and Foreign Enterprises in Canadian Manufacturing Industries: Some Comments and Results." *Review of Economics and Statistics*, 58 (1976), pp. 485-488.

Ministry of External Affairs, Canada. *Canada, GATT and the Uruguay Round*. Ottawa, Ont.: Ministry of Supply and Services, 1987.

Privy Council, Canada, and Herb Gray. *Foreign Direct Investment in Canada*. Ottawa, Ont.: Information Canada, 1972.

Green, C. *Canadian Industrial Organization and Policy*. Toronto, Ont.: McGraw-Hill Ryerson, 2nd Edition, 1985.

Harris, R.G. "Applied and General Equilibrium Analysis of Small Open Economies with Scale Economies and Imperfect Competition," *American Economic Review*, 74 (1984), pp. 1016-1032.

Harris, R. and E. Wiens. "Government Enterprise: an Instrument for the Internal Regulation of Industry," *Canadian Journal of Economics*, 15 (1980), pp. 125-131.

Hazeldine, T. "What Do Economists Know About Free Trade?" *Canadian American Free Trade*, A.R. Riggs and T. Velk, eds. Halifax, N.S.; Institute for Research in Public Policy, 1987.

International Monetary Fund. *International Financial Statistics Yearbooks 1983*. Washington, D.C.: International Monetary Fund, 1983.

Kamien, M. and N. Schwartz. *Market Structure and Innovation*. Cambridge, Mass.: Harvard University Press, 1982.

Mansfield, E. "How Economists See R&D," *Harvard Business Review*, 59 (1981), pp. 98-106.

―――. "Technological Change and the International Diffusion of Technology: A Survey of Findings," *Technological Change in Canadian Industry*, D. McFetridge, ed. Toronto, Ont.: University of Toronto Press, 1985.

Mansfield, E. and L.N. Switzer. "Effects of Federal Support on Privately Financed R&D: the Case of Energy," *Management Science*, 30 (1984), pp. 562-571.

―――. "How Effective are Canada's Direct Tax Incentives?" *Canadian Public Policy*, 12 (1985), pp. 241-246.

McFetridge, D.G. and R.J. Corvari. "Technology Diffusion: A Survey of Canadian Evidence and Public Policy Issues," *Technological Change in Canadian Industry*, D. McFetridge, ed. Toronto, Ont.: University of Toronto Press, pp. 177-231.

McFetridge, D.G. "Commercial and Political Efficiency: a Comparison of Government, Mixed and Private Enterprises," *Canadian Industrial Policy in Action*. Toronto, Ont.: University of Toronto Press, pp. 195-230.

Mueller, R.A. "The Eastman-Stykolt Hypothesis Reconsidered," *Canadian Journal of Economics*, 15 (1982), pp. 757-765.

Nordhaus, W.D. *Invention, Growth and Welfare*. Cambridge, Mass.: Massachusetts Institute of Technology Press, 1969.

———. "The Optimum Life of a Patent: Reply," *American Economic Review*, 62 (1972), pp. 428-431.

Perrakis, S. and J. Silva-Echenique. "The Profitability and Risk of CATV Operations in Canada," *Applied Economics*, 15 (1983), pp. 745-758.

———. "The Profitability and Risk of Television Stations in Canada," *Applied Economics*, 17 (1985), pp. 745-759.

Ross, T.W. "On the Price Effects of Mergers with Freer Trade," *International Journal of Industrial Organization*, 6 (1988a), pp. 233-246.

———. "Movements Toward Free Trade and Domestic Market Performance with Imperfect Competition," *Canadian Journal of Economics*, 21 (1988b), pp. 507-524.

Rugman, A. and A. Anderson. "A Fishy Business: The Abuse of American Trade Law in the Atlantic Groundfish Case of 1985-86," *Canadian Public Policy*, 13 (1987), pp. 152-164.

Saunders, R. "The Determinants of Inter-industry Variation of Foreign Ownership in Canadian Manufacturing," *Canadian Journal of Economics*, (1982), pp. 77-84.

Scherer, F.M. "Nordhaus' Theory of Optimal Patent Life: a Geometric Reinterpretation," *American Economic Review*, 62 (1972), pp. 422-427.

———. *Industrial Market Structure and Economic Performance*. Chicago, Ill.: Rand McNally, 2nd Edition, 1980.

Schumpeter, J. *Capitalism, Socialism, and Democracy*. New York, N.Y.: Harper, 1950.

Statistics Canada, Industrial Research and Development Statistics (Catalogue 88-202). Ottawa, Ont.: Minister of Supply and Services, 1987.

Switzer, L.N. "The Determinants of Industrial R&D: a Funds Flow-Simultaneous Equations Approach," *Review of Economics and Statistics*, 66 (1984a), pp. 163-168.

———. "R&D and Total Factor Productivity Growth in Canada," paper presented to the Guelph meetings of the Canadian Economics Association (1984b).

Webre, P. *Federal Financial Support for High-Technology Industries*. Washington, D.C.: U.S. Congress, Congressional Budget Office study, June 1985.

Wilkinson, B. and K. Norrie. *Effective Protection and the Return to Capital*. Ottawa, Ont.: Economic Council of Canada, 1975.

World Intellectual Property Organization (WIPO). *100 Years of Protection of Industrial Property*. Geneva, Switz.: WIPO, 1983.

———. *Intellectual Property Statistics 1982*. Geneva, Switz.: WIPO, 1983.

CHAPTER 12

Conclusions

·····································

The four previous chapters contained a brief overview of the most important topics of current Canadian public policy, as they relate to the main industrial organization paradigm. The analytical tools needed to evaluate such policy issues were examined in the first 7 chapters. By now students should be familiar with these tools and the manner of their application. They have also acquired a significant amount of factual material about the Canadian economy. This short chapter serves as a summary and a reminder of some recurrent issues that we have encountered repeatedly throughout this text.

As noted at the beginning of this book, economists are not the only class of professionals that deal with the public policy issues examined here. The book, however, is specifically geared to their concerns. Accordingly, several important policy areas were treated in a brief and rather perfunctory fashion. These areas mainly include legal and political questions raised during policy debates. Here we present a summary of some of the relevant issues that, for the most part, lie scattered throughout the previous chapters.

Special attention is paid in this summary to lessons drawn from the recent U.S. experience. Although the legal and political system in the United States is very different from ours, this author believes that the similarities between the two systems overshadow their differences. The close relationship between the two economies, which is bound to increase when the free trade initiative surveyed in the previous chapter is fully implemented, has prompted over the years a certain convergence in their public policies towards business. This is certainly true in public attitudes towards mergers and regulation, where recent developments in Canada have brought this country closer to the U.S. situation. For this reason it is important to examine the trends in U.S. legal and economic thinking, keeping in mind that they may soon be followed in Canada.

Microeconomic Theory and Public Policy

The theoretical basis for public policy intervention was examined at length in Chapter 7. Our conclusions there were somewhat mixed: the general policy thrust towards more competition was chosen principally because of the pitfalls of most of its realistic alternatives, not because of its own merits. These merits could be proven rigorously only in the unrealistic case of perfect competition everywhere.

Pro-competitive public policies also received some support in most sectors from the piecemeal approach to public policy based on the maximization of the criterion of total surplus. This tool also provided a method for deciding when a proposed policy change was desirable. Crucial to its application was the assumption that the income redistribution consequences of such policy changes were either by themselves desirable, or could be neutralized by appropriate fiscal measures.

Two points need to be made with respect to these theoretical considerations. First of all, the available tools and models used in policy evaluation are by necessity incomplete. Every model involves a simplification of reality, in which certain (hopefully irrelevant) aspects of the real world are omitted. The conclusions drawn from such a model are accepted as valid until a subsequent researcher comes along and overturns them with a more general or accurate model. This is (or should be) the normal course of events. Unfortunately, our legal and institutional system is not sufficiently adaptable to accommodate the sometimes rapid changes in economic thinking. This creates the need for more flexible legal approaches than have been available till now.

On the other hand, the parties affected by the policies in place have the right to expect a certain degree of predictability in public actions. One cannot expect businesses to undertake long-term decisions and commitments in the face of uncertainties about the legality of some of their projects. A clear case of such a dilemma can be found in any attempt to control predatory conduct in the form of excess capacity, brand proliferation, or reputation factors. The difficulties of distinguishing such conduct from normal competitive operations demand flexibility in the law and its application. The length, irreversibility, and costliness of the decisions require predictability of public policy. As we saw in Chapter 9, this dilemma does not yet have a satisfactory solution.

The second point that needs to be made concerns the gains and losses from policy changes. These can be very substantial, and they often oppose the interests of the general public to those of a small group of producers. The latter have, therefore, a substantial stake in influencing public policy. By contrast, the gains accruing to the public at large are dissipated among a very large number of people, whose incentives for political action tend to be rather weak. For this reason there is a feeling that public policy has a tendency to favour small, well-organized and generally wealthy groups of producers, at the expense of the unorganized mass of consumers. This may help explain why several policies are currently in existence in spite of quasi-unanimous opposition from the economics profession. Notable examples include several tariffs, quotas and other non-trade barriers; the cartelized milk, eggs, and poultry sectors; and the failure to characterize price collusion as per se illegal.

The heavy impact that policy changes may have on certain isolated firms or individuals raises some interesting equity questions. Suppose, for instance, that it is decided to dismantle the milk marketing cartel, as several economists have repeatedly urged. What about a producer who entered the sector shortly before that decision was taken? Such entry involved the purchase of a quota from an existing producer, whose value would now fall to zero. Should this producer be reimbursed?

The answer given to this last question depends to a large extent on one's concept of fairness. Many economists would argue that the risk of a change in government policy is one that prudent investors should take into account before purchasing quotas; hence, no compensation is warranted when the quota becomes worthless. The opposite point of view is that a given public policy represents a public commitment to a certain course of action. Fairness requires that the economic losses created when such a course of action is reversed must be compensated. Hence, all producers must be reimbursed for the loss of their quota value, no matter how or when that quota was acquired. Between these two extremes are many intermediate positions. A "middle-of-the-road" decision would be to compensate only those who purchased quotas, with the size of the compensation declining in proportion to the time the producer has stayed in business under the marketing board system. Whatever decision is taken, the example shows clearly that the removal of an objectionable policy is bound to create its own equity problems, which are greater the longer such a policy has been in place.

Equity issues also arise when applying the total surplus tool. As we saw in earlier chapters, a policy decision based on the maximization of total surplus ignores its income redistribution consequences. This is justified if these consequences can be neutralized by appropriate fiscal actions; these actions, however, are seldom possible in the current legal setup. Suppose, for instance, that a given merger is approved on the basis of the realizable economies of scale, notwithstanding the monopoly power that it would create. Fairness would then dictate that an extra tax be imposed on the profits of the merged corporation. There is no such provision in the current Canadian law, nor is it easy to envision an appropriate change in the language of the legislation.

The above issues reflect essentially political choices, in which economic arguments have already provided the correct answers. A different set of difficulties arises when there is a lack of clarity in the economic issues themselves. These difficulties are a function of the richness and complexity of the economic models of firm behaviour under imperfect competition, which have been appearing with increasing frequency in recent years. The correct policy should be the one prescribed by the model that best fits each individual case on empirical grounds. This, however, presupposes that the law is sufficiently flexible to allow variety in policy prescriptions on a case by case basis, which seldom turns out to be the case. The pre-1986 merger provisions of the Canadian legislation are an extreme example of legal inflexibility, allowing any merger even when it would result in a complete monopolization of a sector.

Even when legal flexibility exists, it is far from certain that economic analysis will yield a clear-cut policy prescription. Many times there is sufficient ambiguity in the model's results to allow for conflicting interpretations and derived policies. Frequently the financial stakes are so large that the parties involved retain the services of the best economic talent available, in order to argue their cases in front of the appropriate authorities. Just as every defendant is entitled to a good lawyer, so every business interest is entitled to a good economist.

The result, already apparent in some areas, is an increase in the length, complexity, and cost of policy decision-making and economic litigation.[1] As it becomes clear that simplistic answers to policy questions are seldom possible or desirable, the need for sophisticated economic analysis using state of the art techniques becomes more and more pronounced. Such techniques do not come cheap, given their reliance on data collection and analysis, and economic and legal experts. Neither is it easy to communicate their results to judges, juries, and civil servants.

An example of the use of such state of the art economic thinking in a Canadian public policy decision was examined in Chapter 3, in the determination of the frontier of regulation in the telecommunications sector. Unlike what was done in most transportation industries, it was not feasible in this case to proceed to a complete deregulation of the sector. The legal and regulatory systems were, however, sufficiently flexible to accommodate many types of regimes. The economic analysis that was presented during the hearings was at the frontier of the field. Yet in the end, the results of that analysis did not yield an unambiguous policy prescription. The regulatory body had to make a final policy choice on non-economic grounds, by throwing the burden of proof on one of the two conflicting parties. That party was also the one that lost, given the impossibility of proving their case with a sufficient degree of confidence.

This course of events was not undesirable, insofar as it reflected the ambiguities of the situation. It is generally believed that most economists would not have felt uncomfortable no matter which side won. Indeed, the same regulatory body that allowed competition in the peripheral services in its Interconnection decision later decided to keep long-distance voice messages under monopoly control. When economic analysis fails to provide an answer, one must decide on the basis of a subjective evaluation of future developments. Such a decision would project the probable consequences of each course of action, and then choose the (subjectively) best course given the probabilities of their occurrence. While the subjective factor plays a major role in such a choice, the consequences of a suboptimal decision are probably not that severe.

Unfortunately, one cannot escape the thought that the behaviour of the regulatory agency in those particular instances was the exception, rather than the norm, among policy decision-makers. Far too often it is the party that challenges the status quo that must bear the burden of proof. As we noted in Chapter 7, economic analysis can seldom provide a proof with the standards expected by most judicial bodies, given the theory of the second best. Hence, there is built-in inertia in the system, especially when the decisions run counter to established economic interests. As Alfred Kahn noted (1979) in the context of his efforts to introduce marginal cost pricing in electricity generation in the state of New York:

> . . . people who think they will be injured by marginal cost pricing think they fulfill their intellectual responsibilities by a ritualistic incantation of the two magic words, "second" and "best," although some condescend further to enrich the debate by finding some economists willing to contribute some scornful allusions to neoclassical economics.[2]

In fact, one may not even need to go to such sophisticated arguments. As we saw from the example in Chapter 10, of the failed reform of the taxicab licensing system in the Ottawa area, even a tiny, very wealthy, and clearly parasitical group like the taxi licence brokers can generate sufficient political leverage to defeat any attempts for change, notwithstanding the obvious inefficiencies and inequities of the status quo.

Still, the trend towards an increasing use of economic arguments in public decision-making is unmistakable. In the next section we take a close look at public attitudes towards mergers in the U.S. They provide both a good case study of the influence of economics in legal thinking as well as an indicator of probable future developments in Canada.

Mergers and Antitrust: the U.S. Experience

Public policy towards mergers in the United States is covered by section 7 of the 1914 Clayton Antitrust Act, with its important 1950 amendments known as the Celler-Kefauver Act. It is applied by two agencies of the federal government, the Antitrust Division of the U.S. Department of Justice and the Federal Trade Commission (FTC); the latter is an independent agency created in 1914. The pattern of law enforcement has gone through various phases since the law was first enacted, following important judicial decisions. We shall limit ourselves to the situation as it appeared in late 1988.[3]

As in Canada, the purpose of the American merger legislation is the prevention of market power before it has the chance to establish itself. Accordingly, it aims to stop mergers from taking place when they may lead to the formation of a dominant firm. The problems inherent in applying this principle, however, are formidable, as we saw in earlier chapters in the Canadian context. Nonetheless, there have been some interesting developments in recent years, in which sophisticated elements of economic analysis have been used in legal decision-making. These are embodied in the 1982 Merger Guidelines, issued by the Department of Justice, which were subjected to minor amendments in 1984. Such guidelines were produced for both horizontal and vertical mergers; only the former will be reviewed here. Concurrently, the Reagan administration tried to amend the merger section of the law towards a more liberal merger policy. That attempt has so far failed in the Democratic-controlled legislative bodies.

The Merger Guidelines are important, insofar as they define the principles used in the U.S. in enforcing the merger laws. According to the law, merging firms are obliged to notify the appropriate agencies of their intentions if they exceed a certain size threshold, set at $100 million and $15 million of assets for the acquiring and target firms respectively. The merger cannot proceed until its probable impact on competition has been assessed by one of the agencies. If adverse effects are found, the merging parties can withdraw the proposal, modify it in order to comply with the law, or go to court to obtain permission. The post-1986 Canadian law follows more or less a similar procedure. The U.S. Merger Guidelines specify the types of mergers that the enforcing agency must try to stop or modify.

The Guidelines are based on many of the principles that we examined at length in this text. They start by determining the relevant market and measuring its concentration. They then proceed with an examination of the possible barriers to entry, followed by other factors that may facilitate or hinder collusion. Last, they examine the possible benefits of the merger, particularly the cost savings derived from economies of scale or scope. While this sequence of actions is fairly standard in merger law enforcement, there are important innovations in these new guidelines. These have generally met with approval from antitrust economists, even though there is substantial controversy over the manner of their application.

As we saw in Chapter 2, one innovation is the use of the more accurate Herfindahl index, rather than the concentration ratios, in measuring concentration. A more important change is the definition of the relevant market, which is now based on the concept of monopoly power.[4] Specifically, a relevant antitrust market is defined as an area and a set of products such that if a monopoly over them was established, it would be able to profitably raise prices above the current level by some minimum percentage for a significant time period. This implies that the resulting loss of sales to other producers (who are possibly making substitute products or located in other areas) must not be sufficient to eliminate all monopoly profits. The hypothetical price rise is five or ten percent, and the time period for the possible substitutions is specified as 12 months.

Conditions of entry are defined in a similar way. If the hypothetical price increase would trigger the installation of sufficient new capacity within 24 months to render the price rise unprofitable, then entry is considered easy. If entry is not easy then one must turn to concentration measures.

The Guidelines define two threshold levels of the Herfindahl index. If the post-merger value of the index is below 1000, then the merger is allowed to go through no matter what the state of entry conditions. If this value exceeds 1800 the merger would normally be blocked if it raises the index by more than 50 points. Between these values the merger would generally be blocked if it raises the index by at least 100 points.

Ease of entry is clearly the most important variable in deciding whether to intervene. Under easy entry even a merger producing a monopoly can be justified if its actions would be constrained by the likelihood of new entrants. The influence of contestability theory is clearly discernible in this set of priorities. Unfortunately, this part of the Guidelines is also the least well specified, insofar as little guidance is given on how to measure the height of entry barriers.[5]

When entry is not easy and concentration is high, there are still other factors that may make the merger allowable. Such factors are those that render price collusion difficult, as we saw in Chapter 4; they include secrecy, the presence of sophisticated buyers, the existence of long-term contracts, product heterogeneity, the exchange of information among sellers, and a past history of anti-competitive practices in the industry. These are supposed to come into play in borderline cases. No indications are given, however, on the weights to be attached to each of these factors.

Last, the issue of possible cost savings resulting from the proposed merger may be invoked when there is clear evidence that the merger will raise consumer prices. Such cost savings may come either from economies of scale or from technological improvements. The merger will not be allowed, however, if there are alternative means of achieving the same results. The Guidelines are also silent on the tradeoffs between monopoly power and efficiencies on the cost side.

This is an important difference with the post-1986 Canadian merger legislation, in which cost efficiencies are given a primary role as a justification for a proposed merger. Although the 1984 Guidelines strengthened the role of efficiencies in this respect, they still do not give them the same weight as the Canadian provisions. This, of course, reflects the fact that economies of scale and the resulting cost savings are a much less crucial issue in the U.S. than in Canada. As we saw in Chapter 2, there is generally sufficient room in the large U.S. market for individual firms to reach their minimum efficient size long before they acquire market power.

Further, the manner of application of this particular section of the Guidelines by the Reagan administration has created a significant amount of controversy. The administration has mostly ignored the distribution of the aggregate benefits from a merger between consumers and producers. The U.S. courts, however, have tended to lean more towards the consumer interests.[6] Some recent comments point out that the enforcement agencies have been too quick to believe cost efficiency claims based on rather flimsy evidence. Significantly, all three commentators in a recent symposium on the Guidelines were unanimous in their preference for the more sceptical attitude towards efficiencies of the 1982 Guidelines than for the more permissive 1984 version.[7] As they pointed out, efficiency arguments are too easily made, and even more easily believed. While all mergers are likely to provide some cost savings in overhead expenses, many of them are also likely to create diseconomies of scale due to the limits of managerial control and/or the clash in corporate cultures.

In summary, therefore, the Guidelines contain most of the relevant elements of economic analysis for the evaluation of a merger that we identified in this course. Even in the areas in which there is imprecision, as with the identification of entry barriers, one finds at least an effort to incorporate recent theoretical advances. For instance, sunk costs and scale economies are included in the list of factors to be considered in assessing ease of entry. Some commentators, however, have pointed out that more completeness and precision in this crucial aspect of merger evaluation should have been forthcoming.[8]

Ease of entry is another area in which there has been particularly sharp controversy concerning the manner of application of the Guidelines. The sector in which this controversy has been most pronounced is the by now familiar U.S. airline industry.[9] Many airline mergers were approved by the U.S. Department of Transportation in the apparent belief that the industry was close to being contestable. As we saw in earlier chapters, this does not seem to be the case. Some recent trends even point out the emergence of oligopolistic price coordination in several U.S. markets.[10] Yet there still is no agreement on how to measure the height of entry barriers or the departures from contestability.

There is also little agreement on the role of imports in defining the relevant market. The 1984 Guidelines, unlike the earlier version, allow the inclusion of foreign firms in the market definition even if they are constrained by quotas. This seems to contradict the market definition principle, based on the limits to price rises set by competition, unless it is believed that the quotas will be temporary. Economists, however, are divided on the proper treatment of imports. A "middle-of-the-road" position would be to ignore imports altogether if they are subject to quotas, and to include foreign capacity in the market definition if no quotas exist, but with less weight than domestic producers.[11] This last provision reflects the fact that increased import penetration involves some sunk costs under the form of extended distribution networks; it is also more risky than domestic output expansion, given the heavy dependence of foreign sales on the fluctuating exchange rate and the likelihood of quotas or other restrictions. For these reasons some economists would completely ignore foreign competition in assessing a merger.[12]

The 1986 Canadian law accords a star role to foreign trade (both imports and exports) in its treatment of mergers. Imports are included in the market definition, unless constrained by tariffs or quotas. Expanded foreign sales because of cost efficiencies are a major plus factor in approving a merger. Further, the presence of import competition can be used to justify exemptions from the conspiracy and exclusive dealing provisions of the law if such actions are necessary in order to rationalize production. Clearly, these differences in the legal treatment of foreign trade between the two countries reflect its much greater importance for Canada than for the U.S.

In spite of these differences, the 1984 Merger Guidelines and the 1986 Canadian law represent a convergence of public policy attitudes in the two countries. Both the stringent structural American policies of the 1960s and 1970s and the completely ineffective pre-1986 Canadian law have now been abandoned. The Canadian law remains more permissive than the latest version of the Guidelines in several respects, given the small size of the Canadian market and the Canadian dependence on foreign trade. The convergence, as well as the remaining differences, are fully in accordance with economic principles, which are becoming more and more important in public policy.

Concluding Comments

This text was geared towards using microeconomic theory in formulating public policy decisions. The tools and techniques that were presented, as well as the advice offered, were riddled with ambiguities and caveats concerning their limitations. This may cause some students to feel discouraged and deterred from using them. Such ambiguities have certainly created many doubters among the general public about the usefulness of economic reasoning in public decision-making. The late American President Harry Truman was reputed to long for the advice of a one-armed economist who would be unable to say, "On the one hand . . . but on the other hand . . . "

It would be nice to say that as time goes on the progress of economic science makes decision-making easier. Unfortunately, this is not true. To the contrary, we have been seeing an increase in the complexity and difficulty of necessary analysis, and a proliferation of exceptions to what was once accepted as perceived wisdom. There is, therefore, a strong temptation to sweep everything under the rug in favour of simplified views of the world, based on claims of "fairness" or "efficiency" put forward by well-organized groups.

This is, of course, the best justification for the use of economic analysis in evaluating such claims, its faults and ambiguities notwithstanding. The alternative to such a use in public policy is decision-making by inertia, with the public sector being dragged one way or another by the most vocal or best-financed special interests. Unlike such interests, economists do not profit from the advice that they offer.

Many of the accusations levelled against economists and their profession are well-deserved. Far too often they have been preoccupied with what they can measure, as distinct from what may really be important. Equally frequently, they have tended to lean on one side in the ever-present dilemma between efficiency and fairness. I hope that there were enough examples of such cases in this book to induce a degree of humility in future practitioners of the profession. I also hope that there is now sufficient appreciation for the potential of the subject of economics to provide an objective and unbiased view of the consequences of public action or inaction.

Endnotes

1. See the comments in Schmalensee (1982).
2. Kahn (1979), p. 12.
3. Most of the material in this section was taken from a recent symposium on horizontal mergers and antitrust, published in the Fall 1987 issue of the *Journal of Economic Perspectives*.
4. This definition is somewhat controversial. See Stigler and Sherwin (1985), who believe that it is not easy to apply. For an illustration of its application see Scheffman and Spiller (1987).
5. See White (1987), pp. 16-17.
6. See Salop (1987), pp. 8-9.
7. See White (1987), p. 18; Fisher (1987), pp. 36-39; and Schmalensee (1987), pp. 43-44.
8. See Schmalensee (1987), p. 52.
9. See the contrasting positions on a particular merger case within the U.S. airline industry by Fisher (1987) and Schmalensee (1987).
10. See *The Wall Street Journal*, August 30, 1988.
11. This emerges from the relevant comments in Salop (1987) and Schmalensee (1987).
12. See Salop (1987), p. 10.

References

Fisher, F.M. "Horizontal Mergers: Triage and Treatment," *Journal of Economic Perspectives*, 1:2 (1987), pp. 23-40.

Kahn, A.E. "Applications of Economics to an Imperfect World," *American Economic Review Papers and Proceedings*, 69:2 (1979), pp. 1-13.

Salop, S.C. "Symposium on Mergers and Antitrust," *Journal of Economic Perspectives*, 1:2 (1987), pp. 3-12.

Scheffman, D.T., and P.T. Spiller. "Geographic Market Definition Under the U.S. Department of Justice Merger Guidelines," *Journal of Law and Economics*, 30 (1987), pp. 123-147.

Schmalensee, R. "Antitrust and the New Industrial Economics," *American Economic Review Papers and Proceedings*, 69:2 (1982), pp. 24-28.

———. "Horizontal Merger Policy: Problems and Changes," *Journal of Economic Perspectives*, 1:2 (1987), pp. 41-54.

Stigler, G.J. and R.A. Sherwin. "The Extent of the Market," *Journal of Law and Economics*, 28 (1985), pp. 555-585.

White, L.J. "Antitrust and Merger Policy: Review and Critique," *Journal of Economic Perspectives*, 1:2 (1987), pp. 13-22.

Index